AF784894

Studies in Empirical Economics

Aman Ullah (Ed.)
Semiparametric and Nonparametric Econometrics
1989. ISBN 3-7908-0418-5

Walter Krämer (Ed.)
Econometrics of Structural Change
1989. ISBN 3-7908-0432-0

Wolfgang Franz (Ed.)
Hysteresis Effects in Economic Models
1990. ISBN 3-7908-0482-7

John Piggott and John Whalley (Eds.)
Applied General Equilibrium
1991. ISBN 3-7908-0530-0

Baldev Raj and Badi H. Baltagi (Eds.)
Panel Data Analysis
1992. ISBN 3-7908-0593-9

Josef Christl
The Unemployment / Vacancy Curve
1992. ISBN 3-7908-0625-0

Jürgen Kaehler and Peter Kugler (Eds.)
Econometric Analysis of Financial Markets
1994. ISBN 3-7908-0740-0

Klaus F. Zimmermann (Ed.)
Output and Employment Fluctuations
1994. ISBN 3-7908-0754-0

Jean-Marie Dufour and Baldev Raj (Eds.)
New Developments in Time Series Econometrics
1994. ISBN 3-7908-0766-4

John D. Hey (Ed.)
Experimental Economics
1994. ISBN 3-7908-0810-5

Arno Riedl, Georg Winckler and Andreas Wörgötter (Eds.)
Macroeconomic Policy Games
1995. ISBN 3-7908-0857-1

Thomas Url and Andreas Wörgötter (Eds.)
Econometrics of Short and Unreliable Time Series
1995. ISBN 3-7908-0879-2

Steven Durlauf, John F. Helliwell and Baldev Raj (Eds.)
Long-Run Economic Growth
1996. ISBN 3-7908-0959-4

Daniel J. Slottje, Baldev Raj (Eds.)
Income Inequality, Poverty, and Economic Welfare
1998. ISBN 3-7908-1136-X

Mirela Keuschnigg
Comparative Advantage in International Trade
1999. ISBN 3-7908-1156-4

Helmut Lütkepohl
Jürgen Wolters
Editors

Money Demand in Europe

With 44 Figures
and 47 Tables

Physica-Verlag
A Springer-Verlag Company

Editorial Board
Winfried Pohlmeier
University of Konstanz, Germany
Baldev Raj
Wilfrid Laurier University, Waterloo, Canada
Andreas Wörgötter
Institute for Advanced Studies, Vienna, Austria

Editors
Prof. Dr. Helmut Lütkepohl
Institut für Statistik und Ökonometrie
Wirtschaftswissenschaftliche Fakultät
Humboldt-Universität zu Berlin
Spandauer Straße 1
D-10178 Berlin, Germany
(e-mail: luetke@wiwi.hu-berlin.de)

Prof. Dr. Jürgen Wolters
Institut für Statistik und Ökonometrie
Fachbereich Wirtschaftswissenschaft
Freie Universität Berlin
Boltzmannstraße 20
D-14195 Berlin, Germany
(e-mail: jwolters@wiwiss.fu-berlin.de)

ISBN 3-7908-1182-3 Physica-Verlag Heidelberg New York

Cataloging-in-Publication Data applied for
Die Deutsche Bibliothek – CIP-Einheitsaufnahme
Money Demand in Europe: with 47 tables/Helmut Lütkepohl; Jürgen Wolters, ed. – Heidelberg: Physica-Verl., 1999
(Studies in empirical economics)
ISBN 3-7908-1182-3

This work is subject to copyright. All rights are reserved, whether the whole or part of the material is concerned, specifically the rights of translation, reprinting, reuse of illustrations, recitation, broadcasting, reproduction on microfilm or in any other way, and storage in data banks. Duplication of this publication or parts thereof is permitted only under the provisions of the German Copyright Law of September 9, 1965, in its current version, and permission for use must always be obtained from Physica-Verlag. Violations are liable for prosecution under the German Copyright Law.

© Physica-Verlag Heidelberg 1999
Printed in Germany

The use of general descriptive names, registered names, trademarks, etc. in this publication does not imply, even in the absence of a specific statement, that such names are exempt from the relevant protective laws and regulations and therefore free for general use.

Coverdesign: Erich Kirchner, Heidelberg

SPIN 10706462 88/2202-5 4 3 2 1 0 – Printed on acid-free paper

Preface

In 1999 a number of member states of the European Union will adopt a common currency. This change in the monetary system requires that a European Central Bank is set up and a common monetary policy is pursued. There is general agreement among those countries which are likely to join the common currency that price level stability has to be the ultimate objective of monetary policy. It is an open issue, however, what kind of policy is best suited for that purpose. The alternative strategies under discussion are a direct inflation targeting, an intermediate monetary targeting or a mixture of both. For these policy strategies a stable money demand relation is of central importance. Therefore a workshop on *Money Demand in Europe* was organized at the Humboldt University in Berlin on October 10/11, 1997. This research conference brought together academic and central bank economists and econometricians predominantly from Europe to discuss issues on specification, estimation and, in particular, stability of money demand relations both in a single equation and in a systems framework. In this volume revised versions of the papers presented and discussed at the workshop are collected. The volume thereby gives an overview of money demand analysis in Europe on the eve of the introduction of the Euro in some European countries. It contributes to the discussion on a suitable monetary policy for the new European Central Bank.

The articles in this volume are grouped as follows. The first two papers deal with methodological issues. Then there are eight papers discussing empirical money demand studies for individual European countries, followed by three papers with multi-country analyses. The last two of those three articles consider money demand relations at an aggregate European level. Some of the authors are working at universities and others are employed by central banks. This mix ensures a good representation of views of theorists and practitioners. Unfortunately, we have not been able to obtain studies from all European countries. In the following we shall give a brief overview of important issues dealt with in this volume.

Overview

The first paper by *David Hendry and Grayham Mizon* discusses economic policy analysis within a dynamic simultaneous equation/multiple time series framework. The authors focus on the role of exogeneity and causality properties of the variables in an analysis of transitory and permanent policy interventions. In this context, they show that cointegration and co-breaking are central properties of the variables involved. The theoretical issues are illustrated within a bivariate model for UK money and interest rates using annual data from 1871 to 1993. In contrast, *Neil Ericsson* presents a survey of the major issues related to the modeling of money demand in the by now classical Hendry-Ericsson style. Although some multiple time series tools are used in this approach, e.g., for analyzing cointegration, the main objective is to specify and investigate a conditional single equation model for money demand.

In the second part of the volume there are two studies of money demand in Scandinavian countries followed by two papers dealing with Germany, an analysis of Spanish data as well as studies for the UK, Greece and Switzerland. Using the adjustment cost augmented money-in-the-utility-function approach as a theoretical basis, *Antti Ripatti* tests the stability of the demand for M1 and harmonized M3 in Finland. It turns out that with monthly data from 1980(5) to 1995(12) a stable relation for M1 is found whereas no stable specification is obtained for M3. The paper by *Øyvind Eitrheim* derives stable empirical error correction models for quarterly broad money and consumer price inflation in Norway for the period from 1969Q1 to 1993Q4. It turns out that especially excess money has no direct effect on the development of inflation. *Michael Scharnagl* uses various estimation and testing procedures to investigate the stability of a long-run money demand function for quarterly M3 in Germany. Although the sample period from 1975Q1 to 1996Q4 includes German unification he finds a remarkably stable long-run relation. *Helmut Lütkepohl and Jürgen Wolters* construct a small macroeconomic model for the monetary sector based on quarterly German data for the period 1976Q1 to 1996Q4. Within this model they only find a weak link between money growth and inflation. In his study of quarterly Spanish data from 1979Q1 to 1993Q4, *Juan Luis Vega* detects empirical evidence of a structural break in the long-run demand for broad money in 1989. Including foreign interest rates to take care of the increasing openness of the Spanish financial system leads to a stable long-run relation for the whole estimation period. *Neil Ericsson, David Hendry and Kevin Prestwich* compare models for broad money in the UK based on annual data and data which are averaged over the phases of the business cycle for the period 1871–1993. They find that their model for annual data is clearly preferrable to a model for phase-averaged data proposed elsewhere in the literature. *Neil Ericsson and Sunil Sharma* analyze Greek money demand. They use quarterly data for the period 1976Q2–1994Q4 and find a stable relation for M3 if proper allowance is made for some major special events. The result is remarkable because Greece has gone through major political and economic changes during the observation period. The final single country study is by *Michel Peytrignet and Christof Stahel* who estimate the parameters of long-run money demand functions for Switzerland's M2 and M3 aggregates for the period from 1977Q2 to 1997Q1 and investigate their stability by extensive recursive estimations. From these stable long-run relations they derive single equation error correction models for money in the case of M2 and inflation in the case of M3.

The last set of papers deals with multi-country studies. It begins with a comparison of small monetary systems for Germany (1975Q3–1994Q4), Denmark (1975Q1–1993Q4) and Italy (1974Q1–1994Q4). *Katarina Juselius* uses these countries as representatives for large influencial, small open and large less influencial economies in the European Exchange Rate Mechanism (ERM) and detects a change in the monetary transmission mechanism in all of the countries in the mid eighties. She uses her models for analyzing the effects of joining the ERM. Three EU-wide aggregates, Currency, M1 and M3H, are analyzed by *Gabriel Fagan and Jerôme Henry* for the period

1981Q1–1994Q4. They find that all three measures of the money stock cointegrate with GDP and interest rates and conclude that the good performance of their specifications may be a result of averaging over a large area. Finally, the last paper in this volume investigates the role of wealth in an aggregate money demand relation for the European Union. *Martin Fase and Carlo Winder* estimate money demand relations for EU-wide M1, M2 and M3 for the period 1972Q1–1995Q4 and find that wealth is important in determining the broader measures M2 and M3 while it has little influence on M1. They conclude from their study that the strong increase in M2 and M3 during the last decade should not be attributed to expansionary monetary policy but rather to portfolio investment considerations.

Data

All authors were asked to make their data available for general use and further studies on issues related to their data. Most authors were able to provide their data. We have set them up in the internet at

http://wotan.wiwi.hu-berlin.de/oekonometrie/engl/data.html

Acknowledgements

In October 1997 paper presenters were asked to revise their papers in the light of the discussion during the workshop. All papers submitted were then send to referees and returned to the authors for further revision. The revised versions are included in the present volume. Not surprisingly, some papers changed quite a bit in this process and in our view most of them improved considerably in response to the referees' high quality comments and the discussion at the workshop. We are grateful to the authors for their cooperation in meeting our tight deadlines. Moreover, we would like to express our appreciation to the referees for their invaluable input to the editorial process and for enabling us to remain within the projected time frame. The referees have had a substantial impact on the successful completion of the project. Again, we have asked people from both academia and central banks to provide their comments and opinion. Furthermore, we express our appreciation for Werner A. Müller from Physica-Verlag for the smooth and pleasant cooperation in producing this volume.

A number of people helped in organizing the workshop here in Berlin. They are too numerous to be listed all. Therefore, we would just like to mention Kirstin Hubrich, SFB 373, who carried the responsibility for and most of the burden of the local organization here in Berlin. We are very grateful for her outstanding contribution to the event.

Finally, the workshop was carried out as part of the research work within Project C3 of the Sonderforschungsbereich (SFB) 373, *Simulation and Quantification of Economic Processes,* at the Humboldt University. The workshop and, hence, this volume would not have been possible without the financial support by the Deutsche Forschungsgemeinschaft, SFB 373, and by the following institutions which supported members of their staff to participate in the workshop: Deutsche Bundesbank, European Monetary Institute, De Nederlandsche Bank, Bank of Finland, Norges Bank, Swiss National Bank and the Federal Reserve Board, Washington.

Berlin, October 1998

Helmut Lütkepohl
Jürgen Wolters

Contents

Exogeneity, causality, and co-breaking in economic policy analysis of a small econometric model of money in the UK

David F. Hendry[1], **Grayham E. Mizon**[2,3]*

[1] Nuffield College, Oxford OX1 1NF, UK (e-mail: david.hendry@nuffield.oxford.ac.uk)
[2] Southampton University, S017 1BJ, UK
[3] European University Institute, I-S0016 Florence, Italy (e-mail: mizon@datacomm.iue.it)

Abstract. Since the objective of economic policy is to change target variables in the DGP, when economic policy analysis uses an econometric model, it is important that the model delivers reliable inferences about policy responses in the DGP. This requires that the model be congruent and encompassing, and hence exogeneity, causality, cointegration, co-breaking, and invariance all play major roles. We discuss these roles in linear cointegrated VARs, prior to illustrating their importance in a bivariate model of money and interest rates in the UK over the last century.

Key words: Exogeneity, causality, invariance, cointegration, co-breaking, impulse responses, money demand

JEL classifications: E41, C52

1. Introduction

A major use of empirical macro-econometric models is assessing the effects of changes in economic policy implemented by manipulating policy instruments.

---

* Financial support from the UK Economic and Social Research Council under grant L116251015, and the EUI Research Council grant *Econometric Modelling of Economic Time Series*, is gratefully acknowledged. Early research for the paper was done whilst Mizon was Visiting Fellow in the Economics Program of the RSSS at ANU, where he benefited from the excellent research environment and discussions with Adrian Pagan. We are grateful to Hans-Martin Krolzig for helpful discussions on the topic. We also thank members of the Research Department, Norges Bank, Oslo, the particpants at the *Workshop on Money Demand in Europe*, Humboldt University, October 1997, two referees, and the editors Helmut Lütkepohl and Jürgen Wolters for their valuable comments. The data may be obtained from the internet, http://wotan.wiwi.hu-berlin.de/oekonometric/engl/data.html

In this paper, attention is focused on estimating the path of the partial response of target variables $\mathbf{y}_t$ to changes in instruments $\mathbf{z}_t$. Policies may involve changes in the marginal distributions of the instruments $\mathbf{z}_t$, so issues of invariance and co-breaking must be investigated to determine whether $\mathbf{y}_t$ and $\mathbf{z}_t$ do indeed move together after a change in $\mathbf{z}_t$ (for a general analysis of co-breaking, see Hendry, 1995b).

Ericsson, Hendry and Mizon (1998a) analyze the econometric issues associated with some of the commonly-used tools of economic policy analysis, and consider many potential problems, not least that the response of interest occurs in the data generation process (DGP) rather than the model. As Banerjee, Hendry and Mizon (1996) note in their overview of research in this area, there are numerous reasons why the actual value of $\partial \mathbf{y}_{t+h}/\partial \mathbf{z}_t'$ could differ from that given by an econometric model. To investigate these further here, we distinguish between the DGP for the joint process $\{\mathbf{x}_t'\} = \{\mathbf{y}_t', \mathbf{z}_t'\}$ – of which causality, co-breaking and invariance may or may not be features – and an econometric model thereof based on a restricted information set in which the empirical counterparts of these constructs, and exogeneity, can be analyzed.

Impulse response analysis (see e.g., Lütkepohl, 1991, Runkle 1987, and Sims, 1980) is one widely-used method for evaluating the response of one set of variables to 'shocks' in another set of variables, and so is directly related to the concern of this paper. In analyzing the partial responses $\partial \mathbf{y}_{t+h}/\partial \mathbf{z}_t'$, traditional impulse-response analysis measures the response of target variables to transitory changes in the instrument innovations. However, it is also relevant to consider responses to permanent changes in the instruments (such as 'regime changes'), including changes in the mean, variance, and growth rate of $\mathbf{z}_t$. Partial responses to permanent changes in instruments will be zero unless there are co-breaking relations between the means of $y_{i,t}$ and the means of $z_{j,t}$. Further, the presence or absence of Granger causality in the econometric model has a major effect on the estimated responses independently of its occurrence in the DGP. Since there are many reasons for modelling conditional on $\mathbf{z}_t$, it is critical that the weak exogeneity of those variables for the parameters of interest (e.g., those involved in $\partial \mathbf{y}_{t+h}/\partial \mathbf{z}_t'$) can be established. Consequently, there is an important difference between economic policy analysis involving deterministic changes in parameters, and impulse-response analysis involving 'shocks' to instrument innovations. This necessitates reviewing the Lucas (1976) critique.

Section 2 presents notation and definitions concerning the DGP (§2.1), causality (§2.2), econometric models (§2.3), and exogeneity (§2.4). Section 3 then discusses economic policy analysis based on estimated partial responses between targets and instruments. The solutions to two important forms of non-stationarity (unit roots and structural breaks) are considered in §4, namely cointegration (§4.1), and co-breaking (§4.2). Section 5 analyzes target-instrument linkages, and §6 the Lucas critique. Responses in an I(0) system to permanent and transitory changes in instruments, and their relationship to Granger causality, are discussed in §7. Section 8 discusses the nature of permanent changes in instruments for implementing economic policy, and impulse response analysis, in cointegrated systems. The estimation of target-instrument linkages is illustrated in § 9 using a small model of UK money. Section 10 summarizes the major conclusions.

2. Preliminaries

2.1 The data generation process

Denote the vector of N discrete-time, real random variables by $\mathbf{w}_t$, where the joint density $\mathsf{D}_{\mathbf{w}_t}(\mathbf{w}_t|\mathbf{W}_{t-1})$ characterizes the economy under analysis, and $\mathbf{W}_{t-1} = (\mathbf{W}_0, \mathbf{w}_1, \ldots, \mathbf{w}_{t-1}) = (\mathbf{W}_0, \mathbf{W}^1_{t-1})$, when $\mathbf{W}_0$ denotes the initial conditions. $\mathsf{D}_{\mathbf{w}_t}(\mathbf{w}_t|\mathbf{W}_{t-1})$ is thus the DGP. For more details of the DGP and the other concepts discussed in this section see Hendry (1995a).

2.2 Granger causality

Causality, though a fundamental concept in interpreting and understanding what is observed, has been the subject of much controversy. One widely-used definition is Granger causality (see Granger, 1969), which, even if it does not provide the generic definition of causality, plays a major role in econometrics – see Hendry and Mizon (1997). If, in the universe of information, deleting the history of one set of variables does not alter the joint distribution of any of the remaining variables, then the omitted variables were defined by Granger (1969) not to cause the remaining variables. Formal definitions are provided in Hendry and Mizon (1997), who discuss the limitations of, and difficulties associated with, applying Granger causality empirically. For example: as the definition relates to the universe of information, it is non-operational; but Granger causality in a model does not entail its existence in the DGP, and conversely, Granger causation in the DGP need not be reflected in a model thereof; Granger causality is specific to each point in time, and could change over time, confounding empirical tests. Despite these potentially serious difficulties with the concept, Hendry and Mizon (1997) demonstrate that its role is pervasive even when Granger causality is reflecting a reduction phenomenon, i.e., the presence or absence of feedbacks in a limited data set, irrespective of whether or not they are 'genuine DGP causes', thereby affecting the estimation of policy responses from econometric models.

2.3 The econometric model

The econometric model for $n < N$ variables $\mathbf{x}_t$, a transformed subset of $\mathbf{w}_t$, is denoted by $\mathsf{f}_{\mathbf{x}}(\mathbf{x}_t|\mathbf{X}_{t-1}, \boldsymbol{\theta})$ where $\boldsymbol{\theta} \in \Theta \subseteq \mathbb{R}^q$. There also exists a 'local DGP', $\mathsf{D}_{\mathbf{x}_t}(\mathbf{x}_t|\mathbf{X}_{t-1}, \zeta)$, derived from $\mathsf{D}_{\mathbf{w}_t}(\mathbf{w}_t|\cdot)$ by reduction (see, e.g., Hendry, 1995a, and Mizon, 1995). In general, $\mathsf{f}_{\mathbf{x}}(\cdot) \neq \mathsf{D}_{\mathbf{x}_t}(\cdot)$, and this divergence may affect inferences about $\boldsymbol{\theta}$. In practice, many tests for Granger causality are based on reductions within $\mathsf{f}_{\mathbf{x}}(\mathbf{x}_t|\mathbf{X}_{t-1}, \cdot)$ (see Granger, 1969). These are tests of *empirical* Granger causality, and the absence (or presence) of feedback from one set of variables to another in the context of a model is captured in the concept of empirical Granger non-causality, denoted by its acronym EGNC. Below, we consider the implications of EGNC when estimating responses to policy changes.

2.4 Conditioning

Some variables are difficult to model, particularly policy instruments such as interest rates and tax rates. One response is to model conditionally on such variables, risking a potential loss of information. Weak exogeneity of the conditioning variables for the identified parameters of interest (denoted φ) is required for conditional inference not to result in any loss of information: see Engle, Hendry and Richard (1983). Partition $\mathbf{x}_t' = (\mathbf{y}_t', \mathbf{z}_t')$ where $\mathbf{y}_t$ is $n_1 \times 1$ and $\mathbf{z}_t$ is $n_2 \times 1$ with $n = n_1 + n_2$, and factorize $\mathsf{f}_\mathsf{x}(\mathbf{x}_t|\mathbf{X}_{t-1}, \boldsymbol{\theta})$ into $\mathsf{f}_{\mathsf{y}|\mathsf{z}}(\mathbf{y}_t|\mathbf{z}_t, \mathbf{X}_{t-1}, \phi_1)$ and $\mathsf{f}_\mathsf{z}(\mathbf{z}_t|\mathbf{X}_{t-1}, \phi_2)$. Then weak exogeneity gives the conditions under which $\mathbf{z}_t$ need not be modelled, as it ensures that φ can be learned without loss of information from ϕ_1 alone (Ericsson *et al.*, 1998a, discuss the information losses deriving from failures of these weak exogeneity conditions). Weak exogeneity therefore justifies discarding the marginal model $\mathsf{f}_\mathsf{z}(\mathbf{z}_t|\mathbf{X}_{t-1}, \phi_2)$, independently of the presence or absence of feedback between $\mathbf{y}_t$ and $\mathbf{z}_t$.

Conversely, the fact that $\mathbf{z}_t$ is weakly exogenous for φ does not imply that $\mathbf{z}_t$ causes $\mathbf{y}_t$ in any sense: for example, an irrelevant but autonomous variable will be weakly exogenous even though it does not enter the conditional density. Engle *et al.* (1983) also stressed that $\mathbf{z}_t$ may be absent from the conditional density (i.e., has zero coefficients in a model of that density), yet not be weakly exogenous.

The joint occurrence of weak exogeneity and Granger non-causality of the modelled variables for the non-modelled was defined by Engle *et al.* (1983) to be strong exogeneity, and is the requirement for 'full-sample' conditioning. This necessitates the additional condition that the econometrician's marginal model $\mathsf{f}_\mathsf{z}(\mathbf{z}_t|\mathbf{X}_{t-1}, \phi_2)$ can be expressed as $\mathsf{f}_\mathsf{z}(z_t|\mathbf{Z}_{t-1}, \phi_2)$.

3. Policy analysis

The objective of economic policy considered here is to shift to a desired value the means of some of the target variables $\mathbf{y}_t$ in their joint distribution with $\mathbf{z}_t$ in the DGP $\mathsf{D}_{\mathsf{x}_t}(\mathbf{x}_t|\mathbf{X}_{t-1}, \zeta)$ (and hence in their marginal distribution). Even for policies aimed at stabilization, such an objective must be part of the policy makers' strategy. We assume the policy maker knows $\mathsf{D}_{\mathsf{z}_t}(\mathbf{z}_t|\mathbf{X}_{t-1}, \zeta_2)$, the marginal distribution of $\mathbf{z}_t$ when $\mathsf{D}_{\mathsf{x}_t}(\mathbf{x}_t|\mathbf{X}_{t-1}, \zeta) = D_{\mathsf{y}_t|\mathsf{z}_t}(\mathbf{y}_t|\mathbf{z}_t, \mathbf{X}_{t-1}, \zeta_1) \times \mathsf{D}_{\mathsf{z}_t}(\mathbf{z}_t|\mathbf{X}_{t-1}, \zeta_2)$, which defines a policy rule for constant ζ_2. Some policies operate by changing ζ_2, so necessary conditions for these to be feasible are that ζ_2 is controlled by the policy agency and alters $\mathbf{z}_t$. An example is an interest rate, where the corresponding element of ζ_2 is the mean base rate set by a central bank. To implement the policy by changing $\mathbf{z}_t$, there must exist linkages in the DGP between $\mathbf{y}$ and $\mathbf{z}$. Partitioning $\zeta' = (\zeta_1' : \zeta_2')$, the partial response matrix $(\partial \mathbf{y}_{t+h}/\partial \mathbf{z}_t')_{|\zeta_1}$ in the DGP would be invaluable for assessing the changes in $\mathbf{z}$ required to achieve the desired mean for $\mathbf{y}$. As the DGP is unknown, this assessment is often undertaken using an econometric model, so well-specified policy links are needed to assess the responses of targets to instruments (see e.g., Granger and Deutsch, 1992).

Effective policy also relies on the estimated response in the conditional econometric model being invariant to changes in ζ_2. Hence, a necessary condition for the econometric model $\mathsf{f}_{\mathsf{y}|\mathsf{z}}(\mathbf{y}_t|\mathbf{z}_t, \mathbf{X}_{t-1}, \phi_1)$ to be useful in determining an appropriate policy is that ϕ_1 be invariant to changes in ζ_2 over the relevant range: this is the concept of super exogeneity in Engle *et al.* (1983). Since ζ_2 may change over time – and economic policy is often implemented via such changes – the marginal distributions of the instruments $\mathbf{z}_t$ may be difficult for the econometrician to model. Thus, valid conditioning is an invaluable asset in empirical modelling. This is a strong argument for conditional modelling, but puts a premium on ensuring that the conditioning variables $\mathbf{z}_t$ are indeed super exogenous for ϕ_1 if later use of the model is not to violate the assumptions supporting the conditional estimation.

In analyzing the effects on target variables of policy changes, we distinguish between regime shifts (changes in ζ_2) and structural breaks (permanent large shifts occurring intermittently). A regime shift induces a structural break when the parameters of the conditional distribution characterizing the relation of $\mathbf{y}_t$ to $\mathbf{z}_t$ change. Even when there are regime shifts in the parameters of all marginal distributions, the parameters of some conditional distributions can be constant. For example, regime shifts in ζ_2 may result in regime shifts in the marginal distribution of $\mathbf{y}_t$ (required for the policy to be effective), yet ϕ_1 need not suffer from a structural break (required for the policy response to be predictable): see §4.2, and its application to the Lucas critique in §6. Impulse-response based policy analyses are analyzed in §8.2.

4. Non-stationarities

We consider non-stationarities arising from unit roots (permanent small shifts occurring frequently, which generate $\mathsf{I}(1)$ effects) and structural breaks (see §3). These two non-stationarities are closely related (see Rappoport and Reichlin, 1989), can be hard to discriminate empirically (see Perron, 1989, and Hendry and Neale, 1991), and have similar solutions (e.g., being 'removed' by differencing: see Clements and Hendry, 1998). Since cointegration removes unit roots in $\mathsf{I}(1)$ systems by linear combinations of variables (see Engle and Granger, 1987), we introduce a similar notion, called co-breaking, for systems with structural breaks. As changes in deterministic factors seem the main source of forecast biases (see Clements and Hendry, 1998, and Hendry and Doornik, 1997), §4.2 focuses on those.

4.1 Cointegration

Consider the following n-dimensional closed, linear system as the model $\mathsf{f}_{\mathsf{X}}(\mathbf{x}_t|\mathbf{X}_{t-1},\boldsymbol{\theta})$:

$$\mathbf{x}_t = \sum_{i=1}^{s} \mathbf{A}_i \mathbf{x}_{t-i} + \boldsymbol{\delta} + \varepsilon_t \quad \text{with } \varepsilon_t \sim \mathsf{IN}_n[\mathbf{0}, \boldsymbol{\Sigma}]. \tag{1}$$

Such systems are well established for modelling $\mathsf{I}(0)$ variables, but there is an extensive literature for $\mathsf{I}(1)$ variables with cointegration amongst the elements of $\mathbf{x}_t$ (see, *inter alia*, Stock, 1987, Philips and Durlauf, 1986a, Phillips and Loretan, 1991): in particular, Baneerjee, Dolado, Galbraith and Hendry (1993) and Johansen (1995) are convenient sources. From the Granger representation theorem, when there are r $(0 \leq r \leq n)$ cointegrating relationships, (1) can be rewritten as the vector equilibrium-correction model (VEqCM):

$$\Delta \mathbf{x}_t = \sum_{i=1}^{s-1} \boldsymbol{\Gamma}_i \Delta \mathbf{x}_{t-i} + \boldsymbol{\alpha\beta}' \mathbf{x}_{t-1} + \boldsymbol{\delta} + \varepsilon_t, \tag{2}$$

where $\boldsymbol{\alpha}$ and $\boldsymbol{\beta}$ are $n \times r$ of rank r and $\boldsymbol{\Gamma}_i = \sum_{j=1}^{i} \mathbf{A}_j - \mathbf{I}_n$. When $\boldsymbol{\alpha}_\perp$ and $\boldsymbol{\beta}_\perp$ are the orthogonal complements of $\boldsymbol{\alpha}$ and $\boldsymbol{\beta}$ respectively, the necessary and sufficient condition for $\mathbf{x}_t$ not to be $\mathsf{I}(2)$ is $\text{rank}(\boldsymbol{\alpha}_\perp' \boldsymbol{\Xi} \boldsymbol{\beta}_\perp) = n - r$, where $\boldsymbol{\Xi} = \sum_{i=1}^{s-1} \boldsymbol{\Gamma}_i - \mathbf{I}_n$.

When $r = n$ there is no stochastic non-stationarity since $\mathbf{x}_t \sim \mathsf{I}(0)$, otherwise (i.e., $r < n$) $\mathbf{x}_t \sim \mathsf{I}(1)$ but this stochastic non-stationarity is removed by differencing ($\Delta \mathbf{x}_t \sim \mathsf{I}(0)$ for $0 \leq r < n$) and cointegration ($\boldsymbol{\beta}' \mathbf{x}_t \sim \mathsf{I}(0)$ for $0 < r < n$). Hence letting $\mathsf{E}[\Delta \mathbf{x}_t] = \gamma$, where $\boldsymbol{\beta}'\gamma = \mathbf{0}$, and $\mathsf{E}[\boldsymbol{\beta}' \mathbf{x}_t] = \boldsymbol{\eta}$ allows the re-definition of $\boldsymbol{\delta} = -\boldsymbol{\Xi}\gamma - \boldsymbol{\alpha\eta}$, such that (2) can be re-written in terms of variables with zero means as:

$$(\Delta \mathbf{x}_t - \gamma) = \sum_{i=1}^{s-1} \boldsymbol{\Gamma}_i (\Delta \boldsymbol{x}_{t-i} - \gamma) + \boldsymbol{\alpha}(\boldsymbol{\beta}' \mathbf{x}_{t-1} - \boldsymbol{\eta}) + \varepsilon_t. \tag{3}$$

Applying the partition $\mathbf{x}_t = (\mathbf{y}_t' : \mathbf{z}_t')'$ to (3), with the corresponding partition of the parameters, assuming constant parameters and $s = 2$ for simplicity, gives the VEqCM:

$$\begin{aligned} \begin{pmatrix} \Delta \mathbf{y}_t - \gamma_y \\ \Delta \mathbf{z}_t - \gamma_z \end{pmatrix} &= \begin{pmatrix} \boldsymbol{\Gamma}_{yy} & \boldsymbol{\Gamma}_{yz} \\ \boldsymbol{\Gamma}_{zy} & \boldsymbol{\Gamma}_{zz} \end{pmatrix} \begin{pmatrix} \Delta \mathbf{y}_{t-1} - \gamma_y \\ \Delta \mathbf{z}_{t-1} - \gamma_z \end{pmatrix} \\ &\quad + \begin{pmatrix} \boldsymbol{\alpha}_y \\ \boldsymbol{\alpha}_z \end{pmatrix} (\boldsymbol{\beta}_y' \mathbf{y}_{t-1} + \boldsymbol{\beta}_z' \mathbf{z}_{t-1} - \boldsymbol{\eta}) + \begin{pmatrix} \varepsilon_{y,t} \\ \varepsilon_{z,t} \end{pmatrix}. \end{aligned} \tag{4}$$

Another convenient representation of (4) is obtained by letting $\mathscr{I}_{t-1}$ denote the information available at time t and considering:

$$\begin{pmatrix} \Delta \mathbf{y}_t \\ \Delta \mathbf{z}_t \end{pmatrix} \Bigg| \mathscr{I}_{t-1} \sim \mathsf{N}_n \left[\begin{pmatrix} \boldsymbol{\mu}_{y,t} - \mathbf{y}_{t-1} \\ \boldsymbol{\mu}_{z,t} - \mathbf{z}_{t-1} \end{pmatrix}, \begin{pmatrix} \boldsymbol{\Sigma}_{yy} & \boldsymbol{\Sigma}_{yz} \\ \boldsymbol{\Sigma}_{yz}' & \boldsymbol{\Sigma}_{zz} \end{pmatrix} \right] \tag{5}$$

with $\mathsf{E}[\mathbf{y}_t | \mathscr{I}_{t-1}] = \boldsymbol{\mu}_{y,t}$ and $\mathsf{E}[\mathbf{z}_t | \mathscr{I}_{t-1}] = \boldsymbol{\mu}_{z,t}$ when:

$$\begin{pmatrix} \boldsymbol{\mu}_{y,t} \\ \boldsymbol{\mu}_{z,t} \end{pmatrix} = \begin{pmatrix} \boldsymbol{\rho}_{y,t} \\ \boldsymbol{\rho}_{z,t} \end{pmatrix} + \begin{pmatrix} \boldsymbol{\Gamma}_{yy} & \boldsymbol{\Gamma}_{yz} \\ \boldsymbol{\Gamma}_{zy} & \boldsymbol{\Gamma}_{zz} \end{pmatrix} \begin{pmatrix} \Delta \mathbf{y}_{t-1} \\ \Delta \mathbf{z}_{t-1} \end{pmatrix} + \begin{pmatrix} \boldsymbol{\Pi}_{yy} & \boldsymbol{\Pi}_{yz} \\ \boldsymbol{\Pi}_{zy} & \boldsymbol{\Pi}_{zz} \end{pmatrix} \begin{pmatrix} \mathbf{y}_{t-1} \\ \mathbf{z}_{t-1} \end{pmatrix}, \tag{6}$$

where we allow for potentially non-constant growth and equilibria, so:

$$\begin{pmatrix} \boldsymbol{\rho}_{y,t} \\ \boldsymbol{\rho}_{z,t} \end{pmatrix} = \begin{pmatrix} \mathbf{I}_{n_1} - \boldsymbol{\Gamma}_{yy} & -\boldsymbol{\Gamma}_{yz} \\ -\boldsymbol{\Gamma}_{zy} & \mathbf{I}_{n_2} - \boldsymbol{\Gamma}_{zz} \end{pmatrix} \begin{pmatrix} \gamma_{y,t} \\ \gamma_{z,t} \end{pmatrix} - \begin{pmatrix} \boldsymbol{\alpha}_y \\ \boldsymbol{\alpha}_z \end{pmatrix} \boldsymbol{\eta}_t \tag{7}$$

and

$$\begin{pmatrix} \boldsymbol{\Pi}_{yy} & \boldsymbol{\Pi}_{yz} \\ \boldsymbol{\Pi}_{zy} & \boldsymbol{\Pi}_{zz} \end{pmatrix} = \left[\mathbf{I}_n + \begin{pmatrix} \boldsymbol{\alpha}_y \\ \boldsymbol{\alpha}_z \end{pmatrix} (\boldsymbol{\beta}'_y : \boldsymbol{\beta}'_z) \right].$$

Note that $\mathbf{y}_t$ and $\mathbf{z}_t$ are determined from (5) via the identity $\mathbf{x}_t = \Delta\mathbf{x}_t + \mathbf{x}_{t-1}$.

4.2 Co-breaking

When $\{\mathbf{x}_t\}$ has unconditional expectation $\boldsymbol{\varrho}$ at $t = 0$, consider the equation

$$\mathsf{E}[\mathbf{x}_t - \boldsymbol{\varrho}] = \boldsymbol{\tau}_t \in \mathbb{R}^n \; \forall t > 0 \tag{8}$$

where $|\boldsymbol{\tau}_t| < \infty$. When any $\boldsymbol{\tau}_t \neq \mathbf{0}$, a deterministic structural break occurs. Co-breaking cancels such deterministic breaks across linear combinations of variables. Hendry and Doornik (1997) show that such breaks are the most pernicious for predictive failure.

Definition. *The* $n \times m$ *matrix* $\boldsymbol{\Phi}$ *of rank* m $(n > m > 0)$ *is contemporaneous mean co-breaking of order* m (CMC(m)) *for* $\{\mathbf{x}_t\}$ *in* (8) *if* $\boldsymbol{\Phi}'\boldsymbol{\tau}_t = \mathbf{0}\; \forall t \in \mathscr{T}$.

If so, then in (8), $\mathsf{E}[\boldsymbol{\Phi}'\mathbf{x}_t - \boldsymbol{\Phi}'\boldsymbol{\varrho}] = \boldsymbol{\Phi}'\boldsymbol{\tau}_t = \mathbf{0}$, so the reduced set of m linear transforms $\boldsymbol{\Phi}'\mathbf{x}_t$ is independent of the deterministic shifts. Further, CMC(m) implies CMC($m - 1$).

Mean co-breaking may seem unlikely when the $\{\boldsymbol{\tau}_t\}$ can change in any way from period to period, since a fixed matrix $\boldsymbol{\Phi}$ is required to annihilate all such changes. Nevertheless, there are many cases where co-breaking can occur even though no $\tau_{i,t}$ is constant. Let $\mathbf{M}_T^1 = (\boldsymbol{\tau}_1\; \boldsymbol{\tau}_2\; \ldots\; \boldsymbol{\tau}_T)$ where $T > n$ (otherwise CMC($n - T$) is automatic) then $\boldsymbol{\Phi}'\boldsymbol{\tau}_t = \mathbf{0}\; \forall t \in \mathscr{T}$ entails $\boldsymbol{\Phi}'\mathbf{M}_T^1 = \mathbf{0}'$, so a necessary and sufficient condition for $\boldsymbol{\Phi}'\boldsymbol{\tau}_t = \mathbf{0}\; \forall t \in \mathscr{T}$ is that $\operatorname{rank}[\mathbf{M}_T^1] \leq n - m$. This result follows immediately from the equivalence of reduced rank and linear dependence; and if $\mathbf{H}$ is any $m \times m$ non-singular matrix, then $\boldsymbol{\Phi}'\mathbf{M}_T^1 = \mathbf{0}$ implies that $\mathbf{H}\boldsymbol{\Phi}'\mathbf{M}_T^1 = \mathbf{0}$ as well. An important practical case is where breaks are related across variables: if $\boldsymbol{\tau}_t = \boldsymbol{\alpha}\mathbf{l}_t\; \forall t$ where $\boldsymbol{\alpha}$ is $n \times k$ of rank $k < n$ and $\mathbf{l}_t$ is $k \times 1$, then CMC occurs for at least order $m = n - k$. To see this, let $\mathbf{L}_T^1 = (\mathbf{l}_1\; \mathbf{l}_2\; \cdots\; \mathbf{l}_T)$ then $\operatorname{rank}(\mathbf{M}_T^1) = \operatorname{rank}(\boldsymbol{\alpha}\mathbf{l}_1\; \boldsymbol{\alpha}\mathbf{l}_2\; \ldots\; \boldsymbol{\alpha}\mathbf{l}_T) = \operatorname{rank}(\boldsymbol{\alpha}\mathbf{L}_T^1) \leq k$. Alternatively, consider the $n \times (n - k)$ matrix $\boldsymbol{\alpha}_\perp$ above, then for $\boldsymbol{\Phi} = \boldsymbol{\alpha}_\perp$, $\boldsymbol{\alpha}'_\perp\boldsymbol{\tau}_t = \boldsymbol{\alpha}'_\perp\boldsymbol{\alpha}\mathbf{l}_t = \mathbf{0}\; \forall t$. Hendry (1997) develops the implications for forecasting.

There are many examples of co-breaking: $\boldsymbol{\alpha}_\perp$ is co-breaking for shifts in $\boldsymbol{\eta}$ (see (7)), and $\boldsymbol{\beta}$ for shifts in $\boldsymbol{\gamma}$ (see §4.1); constant conditional models with changing marginals co-break for the solved form (see §6) and similar results hold for simultaneous-equations co-breaking. Not only is co-breaking possible, we show below that it is necessary for invariant policy effects when policy induces a break.

5. Target-instrument linkages

When economic policy aims to change $\mathbf{y}$ by manipulating $\mathbf{z}$, linkages must exist between these variables, both in the DGP (feasible policy) and the econometric model (relevant policy analysis). Although the DGP is unknown, we assume that the econometric model is congruent and encompassing (so that there is no evidence of the model's inadequacy currently available), and thus analyze linkages and responses in the econometric model. We draw a distinction between contemporaneous and dynamic links between $\mathbf{y}_t$ and $\mathbf{z}_t$, and so discuss the concepts of contemporaneous and Granger causality.

5.1 Contemporaneous causality

We consider two forms of contemporaneous causality; contemporaneous correlation, and a behavioural relation between $\mathsf{E}[\mathbf{y}_t|\mathscr{I}_{t-1}]$ and $\mathsf{E}[\mathbf{z}_t|\mathscr{I}_{t-1}]$.

5.1.1 Contemporaneous correlation

When $\mathbf{y}_t$ and $\mathbf{z}_t$ are contemporaneously linked via $\mathbf{\Sigma}_{yz} \neq \mathbf{0}$, letting $\mathbf{\Upsilon} = \mathbf{\Sigma}_{yz}\mathbf{\Sigma}_{zz}^{-1}$, the conditional/marginal factorization of (5) is:

$$\begin{aligned} \Delta\mathbf{y}_t|\Delta\mathbf{z}_t, \mathscr{I}_{t-1} &\sim \mathsf{N}_{n_1}[\mathsf{E}[\Delta\mathbf{y}_t|\Delta\mathbf{z}_t, \mathscr{I}_{t-1}], \mathbf{\Omega}] \\ \Delta\mathbf{z}_t|\mathscr{I}_{t-1} &\sim \mathsf{N}_{n_2}[\boldsymbol{\mu}_{z,t} - \mathbf{z}_{t-1}, \mathbf{\Sigma}_{zz}] \end{aligned} \tag{9}$$

with $\mathbf{\Omega} = \mathbf{\Sigma}_{yy} - \mathbf{\Upsilon}\mathbf{\Sigma}_{zz}\mathbf{\Upsilon}'$, which is equivalent to:

$$\begin{pmatrix} (\boldsymbol{\varepsilon}_{y,t} - \mathbf{\Upsilon}\boldsymbol{\varepsilon}_{z,t}) \\ (\mathbf{z}_t - \boldsymbol{\mu}_{z,t}) \end{pmatrix} = \begin{pmatrix} \boldsymbol{v}_t \\ \boldsymbol{\varepsilon}_{z,t} \end{pmatrix} \sim \mathsf{N}_n\left[\begin{pmatrix} \mathbf{0} \\ \mathbf{0} \end{pmatrix}, \begin{pmatrix} \mathbf{\Omega} & \mathbf{0} \\ \mathbf{0} & \mathbf{\Sigma}_{zz} \end{pmatrix}\right] \tag{10}$$

where, from (7) and (5):

$$\mathsf{E}[\mathbf{y}_t|\mathbf{z}_t, \mathscr{I}_{t-1}] = \boldsymbol{\mu}_{y,t} + \mathbf{\Upsilon}(\mathbf{z}_t - \boldsymbol{\mu}_{z,t}) = (\boldsymbol{\mu}_{y,t} - \mathbf{\Upsilon}\boldsymbol{\mu}_{z,t}) + \mathbf{\Upsilon}\mathbf{z}_t. \tag{11}$$

When (6) is static, $\boldsymbol{\mu}_{x,t} = \boldsymbol{\rho}_{x,t}$, and $\mathbf{\Upsilon}$ is co-breaking for shifts in $\boldsymbol{\rho}_{y,t}$ and $\boldsymbol{\rho}_{z,t}$ if $(\boldsymbol{\mu}_{y,t} - \mathbf{\Upsilon}\boldsymbol{\mu}_{z,t})$ is constant.

5.1.2 Behavioural relation

In addition to the contemporaneous link between $\mathbf{y}_t$ and $\mathbf{z}_t$ via $\mathbf{\Sigma}_{yz}$, we consider a schematic behavioural relation between the (historically conditioned) means of $\mathbf{y}_t$ and $\mathbf{z}_t$:

$$\mathsf{E}[\mathbf{y}_t|\mathscr{I}_{t-1}] = \boldsymbol{\mu}_y^* + \mathbf{\Psi}_t\mathsf{E}[\mathbf{z}_t|\mathscr{I}_{t-1}] \quad \text{or} \quad \boldsymbol{\mu}_{y,t} = \boldsymbol{\mu}_y^* + \mathbf{\Psi}_t\boldsymbol{\mu}_{z,t}. \tag{12}$$

Here, $\boldsymbol{\mu}_{y,t}$ denotes agents' plans about variables they control, and $\boldsymbol{\mu}_{z,t}$ the policy makers' plans, about which the agents hold (rational) expectations. Theory models of this form often occur in economics – the permanent income hypothesis is a standard example with $\boldsymbol{\mu}_{y,t}$ as permanent consumption and $\boldsymbol{\mu}_{z,t}$ as permanent income: see Friedman (1957). In general, (12) would contain observable lagged variables, but the main points of this section do not depend on that feature being made explicit.

When $\boldsymbol{\Psi}_t = \boldsymbol{\Psi}$ is constant, the plans and expectations in (12) co-break:

$$\boldsymbol{\Phi}'\boldsymbol{\mu}_{x,t} = (\mathbf{I}_{n_1} : -\boldsymbol{\Psi})\begin{pmatrix}\boldsymbol{\mu}_{y,t}\\ \boldsymbol{\mu}_{z,t}\end{pmatrix} = \boldsymbol{\mu}_y^*,$$

which is a constant vector independent of breaks. Otherwise, when $\boldsymbol{\Psi}_t$ is not constant (or $\boldsymbol{\mu}_y^*$ is non-constant, although the notation does not include this case), then $\mathbf{y}_t$ and $\mathbf{z}_t$ do not co-break.

From (11), using (12) with $\boldsymbol{\mu}_y^*$, $\boldsymbol{\Upsilon}$, $\boldsymbol{\Psi}$, and $\boldsymbol{\Omega}$ constant, we have:

$$\mathsf{E}[\mathbf{y}_t|\mathbf{z}_t, \mathscr{I}_{t-1}] = \boldsymbol{\mu}_{y,t} + \boldsymbol{\Upsilon}\boldsymbol{\varepsilon}_{z,t} = \boldsymbol{\mu}_y^* + (\boldsymbol{\Psi} - \boldsymbol{\Upsilon})\boldsymbol{\mu}_{z,t} + \boldsymbol{\Upsilon}\mathbf{z}_t. \tag{13}$$

Thus, when the parameter spaces for $\boldsymbol{\mu}_y^*$, $\boldsymbol{\Upsilon}$, $\boldsymbol{\Omega}$, and $\boldsymbol{\Psi}$ are unrestricted, $\mathbf{z}_t$ is weakly exogenous for $\boldsymbol{\Psi}$ if and only if $\boldsymbol{\Psi} = \boldsymbol{\Upsilon}\ \forall t$, in which case:

$$\mathsf{E}[\mathbf{y}_t|\mathbf{z}_t, \mathscr{I}_{t-1}] = \boldsymbol{\mu}_y^* + \boldsymbol{\Psi}\mathbf{z}_t. \tag{14}$$

Hence weak exogeneity of $\mathbf{z}_t$ for $\boldsymbol{\Psi}$ ensures that the parameters of the behavioural relation (12) can be estimated efficiently from the conditional model (13).

5.2 Granger causality

The targets and instruments can also be linked dynamically via feedback. Granger causality from instruments to targets in the DGP leads to feasible economic policy, but since the DGP is unknown we can only assess its presence by testing for EGNC in the econometric model. There are two potential sources for empirical Granger causality in (2). First, if any off-diagonal elements of any $\boldsymbol{\Gamma}_i$ are non-zero (e.g., $\boldsymbol{\Gamma}_{yz}$ and $\boldsymbol{\Gamma}_{zy}$ in (4)), then lagged differences of some variables empirically Granger cause other differences. Secondly, from (2) and $rank(\boldsymbol{\alpha}) = r$, when any columns of $\boldsymbol{\beta}$ have more than one non-zero element, some lagged levels empirically Granger cause others. Although these both operate through $\mathsf{I}(0)$ links, their consequences for estimation and inference are not necessarily the same, as demonstrated in Mosconi and Giannini (1992), Toda and Phillips (1993), and Hendry and Mizon (1997).

With the notation in (4), we can give conditions for EGNC between $\mathbf{y}_t$ and $\mathbf{z}_t$.

Lemma 1. *There will be EGNC from the target variables* $\mathbf{y}_t$ *to the instruments* $\mathbf{z}_t$ *if and only if* $\boldsymbol{\Gamma}_{zy} = \mathbf{0}$ *and* $\boldsymbol{\alpha}_z\boldsymbol{\beta}_y' = \mathbf{0}$.

These conditions are unlikely to be satisfied in practice, since the values and changes of target variables resulting from past policy are likely to influence the present choice of instrument values via $\boldsymbol{\alpha}_z\boldsymbol{\beta}_y'\mathbf{y}_{t-1}$ and $\boldsymbol{\Gamma}_{zy}\Delta\mathbf{y}_{t-1}$ respectively. For example, recent past inflation and excess demand for goods are likely to influence the tightness of monetary and fiscal policy. In turn, when the parameters of interest are those of the conditional model, $\boldsymbol{\alpha}_z \neq \mathbf{0}$ will violate weak exogeneity. The empirical example in § 9 illustrates with inverse money velocity (*mpy*) the target, and a short-term interest rate (*Rna*) the instrument.

The model estimates have $\mathbf{\Gamma}_{zy} \neq \mathbf{0}$ so that there is feedback from lagged Δmpy to Rna, even though $\boldsymbol{\alpha}_z\boldsymbol{\beta}_y' = \mathbf{0}$ as a result of $\boldsymbol{\alpha}_z = \mathbf{0}$ which implies that there is no levels feedback from mpy to Rna, and that Rna is weakly exogenous for the long run parameters $\boldsymbol{\beta}$.

Of more importance for economic policy is that changes to the instruments $\mathbf{z}_t$ affect the targets $\mathbf{y}_t$.

Lemma 2. *The policy instruments $\mathbf{z}_t$ will not empirically Granger cause the targets $\mathbf{y}_t$ if and only if $\mathbf{\Gamma}_{yz} = \mathbf{0}$ and $\boldsymbol{\alpha}_y\boldsymbol{\beta}_z' = \mathbf{0}$.*

Without causality in the DGP between the instruments and the targets, the policy will not be effective. In the econometric model, $\mathbf{\Gamma}_{yz} \neq \mathbf{0}$ ensures a predicted short-run impact; $\boldsymbol{\alpha}_y\boldsymbol{\beta}_z' \neq \mathbf{0}$ ensures a predicted permanent effect. The estimates in §9 reveal empirical Granger causality from Rna to mpy via $\boldsymbol{\alpha}_y\boldsymbol{\beta}_z' \neq \mathbf{0}$, and a short-term impact since $\mathbf{\Gamma}_{yz} \neq \mathbf{0}$. If these links indirectly reflect causation, intermediated by an omitted variable that policy influences, and which influences targets in turn, then policy will affect targets. The dynamic response of $\Delta\mathbf{y}$ to changes in the instruments can be estimated efficiently from the conditional model when $\mathbf{z}_t$ is weakly exogenous, which requires $\boldsymbol{\alpha}_z = \mathbf{0}$ (*inter alia*). However, for the outcome to be as predicted requires all the parameters involved to remain constant.

Before considering the multi-step partial response of $\mathbf{y}_{t+h}$ to permanent regime shift $\mathrm{d}\boldsymbol{\mu}_{z,t}$ and a transitory shock $\mathrm{d}\boldsymbol{\varepsilon}_{z,t}$, we examine the implications of this analysis for the Lucas (1976) critique.

6. The Lucas critique

The Lucas critique of using econometric models for economic policy analysis concerns the impossibility of constant conditional equations confronted by non-constant marginal processes in models involving expectations. Both its assertion and the converse are testable: see Hendry (1988). We now establish co-breaking and weak exogeneity conditions under which conditional models are immune to the critique.

Maintain the expectations formulation in (12) with $\mathbf{\Psi}$ constant:

$$\mathsf{E}[\mathbf{y}_t|\mathscr{I}_{t-1}] = \boldsymbol{\mu}_y^* + \mathbf{\Psi}\mathsf{E}[\mathbf{z}_t|\mathscr{I}_{t-1}], \tag{15}$$

so $\mathbf{\Psi}$ is a co-breaking vector for changes in the expectations process. From (15), letting $\mathbf{u}_t = \mathbf{y}_t - \mathsf{E}[\mathbf{y}_t|\mathscr{I}_{t-1}]$:

$$\mathbf{y}_t = \boldsymbol{\mu}_y^* + \mathbf{\Psi}\mathsf{E}[\mathbf{z}_t|\mathscr{I}_{t-1}] + \mathbf{u}_t = \boldsymbol{\mu}_y^* + \mathbf{\Psi}\mathbf{z}_t + \mathbf{u}_t - \mathbf{\Psi}\boldsymbol{\varepsilon}_{z,t}. \tag{16}$$

When $\mathbf{z}_t$ is unobserved at the time the plan is implemented, $(\mathbf{u}_t - \mathbf{\Psi}\boldsymbol{\varepsilon}_{z,t})$ is correlated with $\mathbf{z}_t$, so the conditional equation derived from (16) cannot be constant if $\boldsymbol{\rho}_{z,t} \neq \mathbf{0}$ in (6) (see e.g., Hendry, 1988), which is the Lucas critique. Nevertheless, there are conditions that sustain policy analysis in this setting.

Co-breaking in the joint distribution of $(\mathbf{y}_t : \mathbf{z}_t)$ is essential if the conditional model is to be constant, and this can occur when agents act in a contingent manner. As shown in (14) above, to obtain a constant conditional model we required (a) $\mathbf{\Psi} = \mathbf{\Upsilon}$ and (b) $\boldsymbol{\mu}_{y,t} - \mathbf{\Psi}\boldsymbol{\mu}_{z,t} = \boldsymbol{\mu}_y^*$. The first condition is for the weak exogeneity of $\mathbf{z}_t$ for $\mathbf{\Psi}$, and the second for $(\mathbf{I}_{n_1} : -\mathbf{\Psi})$ being co-breaking for $(\boldsymbol{\mu}_{y,t} : \boldsymbol{\mu}_{z,t})$. Expressed as an equation:

$$\mathbf{y}_t = \boldsymbol{\mu}_y^* + \mathbf{\Psi}\mathbf{z}_t + \boldsymbol{\upsilon}_t, \tag{17}$$

where $\mathsf{E}[\mathbf{z}_t\boldsymbol{\upsilon}_t'] = \mathbf{0}$, then (17) implies but is not implied by:

$$\mathsf{E}[\mathbf{y}_t|\mathcal{I}_{t-1}] = \boldsymbol{\mu}_y^* + \mathbf{\Psi}\mathsf{E}[\mathbf{z}_t|\mathcal{I}_{t-1}], \tag{18}$$

as $\mathbf{\Psi}$ is co-breaking for the expectations form. Thus, the conditional model has an 'expectations interpretation', but as agents act contingently on $\mathbf{z}_t$, conditioning remains valid even under regime changes.

7. Responses in an I(0) system

We now consider how changes in $\mathbf{z}_t$ might affect $\mathbf{y}_t$, and whether the econometric model will yield reliable estimates of the responses. The relation $\mathrm{d}\mathbf{z}_t = \mathrm{d}\boldsymbol{\mu}_{z,t} + \mathrm{d}\boldsymbol{\varepsilon}_{z,t}$ leads to two types of change in $\mathbf{z}_t$: one involving changes in the unconditional mean $\boldsymbol{\mu}_{z,t}$, which typically will be step changes in $\boldsymbol{\rho}_{z,t}$ – see (7); and the other involving changes in the innovations $\boldsymbol{\varepsilon}_{z,t}$, which are said to be 'shocks' in so far as they are unanticipated and transitory. Since the distribution of $\mathbf{z}_t$ also depends on $\mathbf{\Sigma}_{zz}$, another class of regime shifts arises when there are changes $\mathrm{d}\boldsymbol{\sigma}_z$ in the elements $\boldsymbol{\sigma}_z = vech(\Sigma_{zz})$ of this covariance matrix. The changes $\mathrm{d}\boldsymbol{\mu}_{z,t}$ (and possibly $\mathrm{d}\boldsymbol{\sigma}_z$) can be thought of as drawings from a distribution of infrequent but maintained changes, and thus are of a more permanent nature than the shocks $\mathrm{d}\boldsymbol{\varepsilon}_{z,t}$, which are drawings from a distribution of transitory changes $\mathrm{d}\boldsymbol{\varepsilon}_{z,t}$. There may be autonomous events (e.g., an oil price hike as in 1973) that lead to a shift in $\boldsymbol{\mu}_{z,t}$ or $\boldsymbol{\sigma}_z$, but these are different from the policy-induced regime changes $\mathrm{d}\boldsymbol{\mu}_{z,t}$ and $\mathrm{d}\boldsymbol{\sigma}_z$ considered here. The distinction between regime shifts and structural breaks in the analysis of economic policies is important because structural breaks make prediction of the response of $\mathbf{y}_t$ to regime shifts difficult, if not impossible. Indeed, when all the parameters in (5) and in (9) are non-constant prior to the policy change under analysis (perhaps because of previous structural breaks), few analytical results can be obtained.

In the 'policy-rule' case, $\mathbf{\Upsilon}$ remains constant over the change $\mathrm{d}\boldsymbol{\mu}_{z,t}$, so the change in $\mathbf{y}_t$ induced by the change in $\mathbf{z}_t$ is predictable from $\mathsf{f}_{\mathsf{y}|\mathsf{z}}(\mathbf{y}_t|\mathbf{z}_t, \cdot)$. When the policy concerns the response of $\mathbf{y}_t$ to regime changes in $\mathbf{z}_t$, the permanent changes $\mathrm{d}\boldsymbol{\mu}_{z,t}$ and $\mathrm{d}\boldsymbol{\sigma}_z$ are further categorized into those that induce structural breaks in $\mathsf{f}_{\mathsf{y}|\mathsf{z}}(\mathbf{y}_t|\mathbf{z}_t, \cdot)$, and those that leave its parameters unchanged. Since the response $\partial\mathbf{y}_t/\partial\mathbf{z}_t'$ will be reliably predicted using $\mathsf{f}_{\mathsf{y}|\mathsf{z}}(\mathbf{y}_t|\mathbf{z}_t, \cdot)$ in (9) only if there is no structural break, it is necessary for coherent inference that the parameters of (9a) be invariant to the changes $\mathrm{d}\boldsymbol{\mu}_{z,t}$ and $\mathrm{d}\boldsymbol{\sigma}_z$. However, the reverse conditioning $\mathsf{f}_{\mathsf{z}|\mathsf{y}}(\mathbf{z}_t|\mathbf{y}_t, \cdot)$ will exhibit structural changes as different policies are tried, since if $\mathsf{f}_{\mathsf{y}|\mathsf{z}}(\mathbf{y}_t|\mathbf{z}_t, \cdot)$ is invariant to the changes $\mathrm{d}\boldsymbol{\mu}_{z,t}$ and $\mathrm{d}\boldsymbol{\sigma}_z$ then $\mathsf{f}_{\mathsf{z}|\mathsf{y}}(\mathbf{z}_t|\mathbf{y}_t, \cdot)$ cannot be (see Engle and Hendry, 1993).

Having considered permanent regime shifts $\mathrm{d}\boldsymbol{\mu}_{z,t}$ and transitory shocks $\mathrm{d}\boldsymbol{\varepsilon}_{z,t}$ as means of implementing economic policy through the instruments $\mathbf{z}_t$, the systematical change in $\mathbf{y}_t$ resulting from a policy change in $\mathbf{z}_t$ is given by

$\mathbf{dy}_t = \mathrm{d}\boldsymbol{\mu}_{y,t} + \mathrm{d}\varepsilon_{y,t}$. Thus the partial response of $\mathbf{y}_{t+h}$ to a permanent change in $\mathbf{z}_t$ $(\partial \mathbf{y}_{t+h}/\partial \boldsymbol{\mu}'_{z,t})$ and to a transitory change in $\mathbf{z}_t$ $(\partial \mathbf{y}_{t+h}/\partial \varepsilon'_{z,t})$ can be evaluated.

7.1 Transitory changes

In this section we consider a first-order I(0) system, i.e. (4) with $r = n$ and $s = 1$ so that $\gamma = \mathbf{0}$, $\boldsymbol{\alpha} = \mathbf{I}_n$, and $\boldsymbol{\eta} = (\mathbf{A} - \mathbf{I}_n)\boldsymbol{\mu}_x = -\boldsymbol{\delta}$, where $\boldsymbol{\mu}_x = \mathsf{E}[\mathbf{x}_t]$. Hence (4) becomes:

$$\begin{pmatrix} \mathbf{y}_t - \boldsymbol{\mu}_y \\ \mathbf{z}_t - \boldsymbol{\mu}_z \end{pmatrix} = \begin{pmatrix} \mathbf{A}_{yy} & \mathbf{A}_{yz} \\ \mathbf{A}_{zy} & \mathbf{A}_{zz} \end{pmatrix} \begin{pmatrix} \mathbf{y}_{t-1} - \boldsymbol{\mu}_y \\ \mathbf{z}_{t-1} - \boldsymbol{\mu}_z \end{pmatrix} + \begin{pmatrix} \varepsilon_{y,t} \\ \varepsilon_{z,t} \end{pmatrix} \tag{19}$$

in which it is assumed that the autoregressive parameters $\mathbf{A}_{ij}$ are constant, at least prior to the implementation of the economic policy. Allowing for non-constant means associated with the regime shift at time t, (19) can be written in moving-average format with $h \geq 0$ as:

$$\begin{pmatrix} \mathbf{y}_{t+h} - \boldsymbol{\mu}_{y,t} \\ \mathbf{z}_{t+h} - \boldsymbol{\mu}_{z,t} \end{pmatrix} = \sum_{i=0}^{\infty} \begin{pmatrix} \mathbf{A}_{yy} & \mathbf{A}_{yz} \\ \mathbf{A}_{zy} & \mathbf{A}_{zz} \end{pmatrix}^i \begin{pmatrix} \varepsilon_{y,t+h-i} \\ \varepsilon_{z,t+h-i} \end{pmatrix}. \tag{20}$$

For policy implemented via transitory changes, these will be shocks $\mathrm{d}\varepsilon_{z,t}$ to the innovations of the marginal process of $\mathbf{z}_t$, and not shocks $\mathrm{d}\boldsymbol{\upsilon}_t$ to the innovations $\boldsymbol{\upsilon}_t$ of the conditional process. From (10), $\mathrm{d}\varepsilon_{y,t} = \boldsymbol{\Upsilon}\mathrm{d}\varepsilon_{z,t} + \mathrm{d}\boldsymbol{\upsilon}_t$, which implies $\mathrm{d}\varepsilon_{y,t} = \boldsymbol{\Upsilon}\mathrm{d}\varepsilon_{z,t}$ since the policy shocks that we consider leave $\mathrm{d}\boldsymbol{\upsilon}_t = \mathbf{0}$. Thus we distinguish two types: one in which $\mathrm{d}\varepsilon_{y,t} = \boldsymbol{\Upsilon}\mathrm{d}\varepsilon_{z,t}$ so that the shocks are being drawn to be consistent with the distribution of the innovations ε_t; and the other in which $\mathrm{d}\varepsilon_{y,t} = \mathbf{0}$. In the first case, the partial response of $\mathbf{y}_{t+h}$ to $\varepsilon_{z,t}$ using (20) and (10) is given by:

$$\begin{aligned} \left.\frac{\partial \mathbf{y}_{t+h}}{\partial \varepsilon'_{z,t}}\right|_{d\varepsilon_{y,t}=\boldsymbol{\Upsilon} d\varepsilon_{z,t}} &= (\mathbf{I}_{n_1} : \mathbf{0}) \begin{pmatrix} \mathbf{A}_{yy} & \mathbf{A}_{yz} \\ \mathbf{A}_{zy} & \mathbf{A}_{zz} \end{pmatrix}^h \begin{pmatrix} \boldsymbol{\Upsilon}_t \\ \mathbf{I}_{n_2} \end{pmatrix} \\ &= (\mathbf{I}_{n_1} : \mathbf{0}) \begin{pmatrix} \mathbf{E}_h & \mathbf{F}_h \\ \mathbf{G}_h & \mathbf{H}_h \end{pmatrix} \begin{pmatrix} \boldsymbol{\Upsilon}_t \\ \mathbf{I}_{n_2} \end{pmatrix} = \mathbf{E}_h \boldsymbol{\Upsilon}_t + \mathbf{F}_h \end{aligned} \tag{21}$$

which is equal to $\boldsymbol{\Upsilon}$ when $h = 0$ and the parameters of the conditional model are invariant to the shock. For the second type of shock, the restriction $\boldsymbol{\Upsilon} = \mathbf{0}$ is imposed, irrespective of its validity, to give the partial response of $\mathbf{y}_{t+h}$ to $\varepsilon_{z,t}$:

$$\left.\frac{\partial \mathbf{y}_{t+h}}{\partial \varepsilon'_{z,t}}\right|_{d\varepsilon_{y,t}=\mathbf{0}} = \mathbf{F}_h \text{ with } \mathbf{F}_0 = \mathbf{0} \tag{22}$$

and so reflects the dynamics of the model only. Conventional unit impulse response analysis corresponds to (22) with $\mathbf{z}_t$ a scalar ($n_2 = 1$).

The first term of the response given in (21) reflects the dynamic response to the contemporaneous causality between $\varepsilon_{y,t}$ and $\varepsilon_{z,t}$, whereas the second term is determined by the dynamics of the model. Note that if $\mathbf{z}_t$ is EGNC for $\mathbf{y}_t$ (i.e., $\mathbf{A}_{yz} = \mathbf{0}$) then $\mathbf{F}_h = \mathbf{0}$, so that empirical Granger causality is a major determinant of the response to transitory changes. Further, note that (21) gives the response $\partial \mathbf{y}_{t+h}/\partial \varepsilon'_{z,t}$ in the block-recursive reparameterization (24) of (19), in which $\mathbf{z}_t$ is determined via its marginal distribution conditional on $\mathbf{x}_{t-1}$, and $\mathbf{y}_t$ then determined conditionally on $\mathbf{z}_t$ and $\mathbf{x}_{t-1}$. The commonly-used orthogonalized impulse-response analysis with $\mathbf{z}_t$ a scalar corresponds to estimating the response $\partial \mathbf{y}_{t+h}/\partial \varepsilon'_{z,t}$ from a complete recursive reparameterization of (19) (Wold, 1949, causal ordering), which depends critically on the ordering of the variables in $\mathbf{x}_t$, whereas the block-recursive structure in (24) accords with the ordering of the policy experiment in which $\mathbf{y}_t$ are targets and $\mathbf{z}_t$ instruments. However, it will only be appropriate to estimate the response $\partial \mathbf{y}_{t+h}/\partial \varepsilon'_{z,t}$ from the conditional model alone when $\mathbf{z}_t$ is weakly exogenous for the parameters of the conditional model, and these are invariant to the shock $\mathrm{d}\varepsilon_{z,t}$. We now summarize these results in:

Theorem 3. *When an econometric model $\mathrm{f}_\mathrm{x}(\mathbf{x}_t|\mathbf{X}_{t-1}\cdot)$ is congruent and encompassing, and its parameters are invariant with respect to the policy shocks $\mathrm{d}\varepsilon_{z,t}$, then it predicts $\mathbf{y}_{t+h}$ will respond to the shocks if (a) $\boldsymbol{\Upsilon} \neq \mathbf{0}$ and $\mathrm{d}\varepsilon_{y,t} = \boldsymbol{\Upsilon}\mathrm{d}\varepsilon_{z,t}$, or (b) if $\mathbf{z}$ empirically Granger causes $\mathbf{y}$ i.e. $\mathbf{A}_{yz} \neq \mathbf{0}$.*

Whenever the shocks are drawn from a new distribution of shocks for which the parameters of the econometric model are not invariant, they will induce a structural break, and so the econometric model alone will not be able to consistently predict the effects of the policy. We note that the drawing of shocks $\mathrm{d}\varepsilon_{z,t}$ which are not accompanied by shocks $\mathrm{d}\varepsilon_{y,t} = \boldsymbol{\Upsilon}\mathrm{d}\varepsilon_{z,t}$, as is common practice in impulse-response analysis, is a particular example of drawing a shock that by construction can have no contemporaneous effect on $\mathbf{y}_t$, and so constitutes an ineffective policy in the context of a static model. If the transitory shocks $\mathrm{d}\varepsilon_{z,t}$ are stochastic, then $\mathrm{d}\varepsilon_{y,t}$ will also be stochastic, but their joint distribution will be singular whenever $\boldsymbol{\Upsilon}$ is constant (equally, $\mathrm{d}\varepsilon_{y,t}$ will have a singular distribution when $n_1 > n_2$).

7.2 Permanent changes

In this section, we first consider a static I(0) system, i.e. (1) with $s = 0$ and $r = n$ so that $\boldsymbol{\Gamma}_i = \mathbf{0} \quad \forall i$, $\boldsymbol{\alpha\beta}' = \mathbf{I}_n$, and $\boldsymbol{\delta} = -\boldsymbol{\mu}_{x,t}$, where permanent changes are allowed for by the dependence of $\mathsf{E}[\mathbf{x}_t] = \boldsymbol{\mu}_{x,t}$ on t. Permanent change denotes that $\boldsymbol{\mu}_{z,t}$ changes, and the change is maintained, so it is a regime shift in the marginal process for the instruments $\mathbf{z}_t$. In the static case, the partial response of $\mathbf{y}_{t+h}$ to $\boldsymbol{\mu}_{z,t}$ ($\partial \mathbf{y}_{t+h}/\partial \boldsymbol{\mu}'_{z,t}$) is given from (5), (6), and (12) by:

$$\frac{\partial \mathbf{y}_{t+h}}{\partial \boldsymbol{\mu}'_{z,t}} = \frac{\partial \mathbf{y}_{t+h}}{\partial \boldsymbol{\mu}'_{y,t}} \frac{\partial \boldsymbol{\mu}_{y,t}}{\partial \boldsymbol{\mu}'_{z,t}} = \mathbf{I}_{n_1} \boldsymbol{\Psi}_t = \boldsymbol{\Psi}_t \quad \forall h \geq 0. \tag{23}$$

In the absence of the behavioural relationship (12), this response will be zero. In particular, the existence of contemporaneous correlation between $\mathbf{y}_t$ and $\mathbf{z}_t$

($\boldsymbol{\Sigma}_{yz} \neq \mathbf{0}$) will not result in a non-zero permanent response in general. The discussion so far implies the following theorem.

Theorem 4. *When a static econometric model* $\mathsf{f}_{\mathsf{y}|\mathsf{z}}(\mathbf{y}_t|\mathbf{z}_t, \cdot)$ *is congruent and encompassing, and its parameters are invariant with respect to the policy regime shifts* $\mathrm{d}\boldsymbol{\mu}_{z,t}$, *then it (a) predicts the policy to be effective if* $\boldsymbol{\Psi}_t \neq \mathbf{0}$, *and (b) the conditional model yields an efficient estimate of the response* $\partial \mathbf{y}_{t+h}/\partial \boldsymbol{\mu}'_{z,t} = \boldsymbol{\Psi}$ *using* $\boldsymbol{\Psi} = \boldsymbol{\Upsilon}$ *when* $\mathbf{z}_t$ *is weakly exogenous for the unrestricted* $\boldsymbol{\Psi}$, *in which case* $\mathbf{y}_t$ *and* $\mathbf{z}_t$ *co-break.*

The responses given in (23) and by $\boldsymbol{\Upsilon}$ in Theorem 4 are different if $(\mathbf{I}_{n_1} : -\boldsymbol{\Psi})$ is not a co-breaking matrix, $\boldsymbol{\Psi}$ is non-constant, or if $\mathbf{z}_t$ is not weakly exogenous for $\boldsymbol{\Psi}$.

Corollary 5. *The only unrestricted co-breaking matrix* $\boldsymbol{\Phi}$ *satisfying the conditions of Theorem 4 is* $(\mathbf{I}_{n_1} : -\boldsymbol{\Psi})$.

Hence the super-exogeneity of $\mathbf{z}_t$ for $\boldsymbol{\mu}^*_y$, $\boldsymbol{\Psi}$, and $\boldsymbol{\Omega}$ is sufficient for the econometric model to predict that the policy $\mathrm{d}\boldsymbol{\mu}_{z,t}$ will be effective, and for its effect on $\mathbf{y}_t$ to be efficiently estimated by $\boldsymbol{\Upsilon}$. Conversely, when the policy change $\mathrm{d}\boldsymbol{\mu}_{z,t}$ induces a structural break, so that $\boldsymbol{\mu}^*_y$, $\boldsymbol{\Psi}$, (or $\boldsymbol{\Upsilon}$), and $\boldsymbol{\Omega}$ are not invariant, the policy may be effective in that $\boldsymbol{\mu}_{y,t}$ changes, but $\partial \mathbf{y}_{t+h}/\partial \boldsymbol{\mu}'_{z,t}$ is not estimable consistently from the econometric model.

Considering now the dynamic system (19) we note that the conditional/marginal factorization of (9) in this case is:

$$\begin{pmatrix} \Delta \mathbf{y}_t \\ \Delta \mathbf{z}_t \end{pmatrix} = \begin{pmatrix} (\boldsymbol{\Pi}_{yy} - \boldsymbol{\Upsilon}\boldsymbol{\Pi}_{zy}) & (\boldsymbol{\Pi}_{yz} - \boldsymbol{\Upsilon}\boldsymbol{\Pi}_{zz}) \\ \boldsymbol{\Pi}_{zy} & \boldsymbol{\Pi}_{zz} \end{pmatrix} \begin{pmatrix} \mathbf{y}_{t-1} - \boldsymbol{\mu}_y \\ \mathbf{z}_{t-1} - \boldsymbol{\mu}_z \end{pmatrix} + \begin{pmatrix} \boldsymbol{\Upsilon}\Delta \mathbf{z}_t + \boldsymbol{\upsilon}_t \\ \boldsymbol{\varepsilon}_{z,t} \end{pmatrix} \tag{24}$$

with $\boldsymbol{\Pi}_{yy} = -(\mathbf{I}_{n_1} - \mathbf{A}_{yy})$, $\boldsymbol{\Pi}_{zz} = -(\mathbf{I}_{n_2} - \mathbf{A}_{zz})$, $\boldsymbol{\Pi}_{yz} = \mathbf{A}_{yz}$ and $\boldsymbol{\Pi}_{zy} = \mathbf{A}_{zy}$. Hence:

$$\mathsf{E}[\Delta \mathbf{y}_t | \Delta \mathbf{z}_t, \mathbf{x}_{t-1}] = \boldsymbol{\Upsilon}\Delta \mathbf{z}_t + \mathbf{B}(\mathbf{y}_{t-1} - \boldsymbol{\mu}_y) + \mathbf{C}(\mathbf{z}_{t-1} - \boldsymbol{\mu}_z) \tag{25}$$

with $\mathbf{B} = (\boldsymbol{\Pi}_{yy} - \boldsymbol{\Upsilon}\boldsymbol{\Pi}_{zy})$ and $\mathbf{C} = (\boldsymbol{\Pi}_{yz} - \boldsymbol{\Upsilon}\boldsymbol{\Pi}_{zz})$.

However, maintaining the present format of (12) implies:

$$\boldsymbol{\mu}_y = \boldsymbol{\Psi}\boldsymbol{\mu}_z; \quad \boldsymbol{\Pi}_{yy} = \boldsymbol{\Psi}\boldsymbol{\Pi}_{zy}; \quad \boldsymbol{\Pi}_{yz} = \boldsymbol{\Psi}\boldsymbol{\Pi}_{zz}, \tag{26}$$

so combining (26) with (25) yields:

$$\mathsf{E}[\Delta \mathbf{y}_t | \Delta \mathbf{z}_t, \mathbf{z}_{t-1}] = \boldsymbol{\Upsilon}\Delta \mathbf{z}_t + (\boldsymbol{\Psi} - \boldsymbol{\Upsilon})[\boldsymbol{\Pi}_{zy}\mathbf{y}_{t-1} + \boldsymbol{\Pi}_{zz}\mathbf{z}_{t-1} - (\boldsymbol{\Pi}_{zy}\boldsymbol{\Psi} + \boldsymbol{\Pi}_{zz})\boldsymbol{\mu}_z]$$

Therefore, when the parameter spaces for $\mathbf{A}_{i,j}$, $\boldsymbol{\Upsilon}$ and $\boldsymbol{\Psi}$ are unrestricted, $\mathbf{z}_t$ is weakly exogenous for $\boldsymbol{\Psi}$ if and only if $\boldsymbol{\Psi} = \boldsymbol{\Upsilon}$, in which case $\mathbf{y}_t$ and $\mathbf{z}_t$ co-break and:

$$\mathsf{E}[\Delta \mathbf{y}_t | \Delta \mathbf{z}_t, \mathbf{x}_{t-1}] = \boldsymbol{\Upsilon}\Delta \mathbf{z}_t. \tag{27}$$

Generalizing (12) to include observable dynamics would introduce lags into (27). Rather than pursue this for I(0) systems, we observe that in dynamic models for many macroeconomic time series, the number of long-run equilibria is usually less than the number of modelled variables so that the VAR is of reduced rank (as in the illustration in § 9), so we now analyze the nature of policy analysis in cointegrated VARs.

8. Responses in an I(1) cointegrated system

Similar analysis to that in the previous section yields richer results for a cointegrated VAR because of the presence of cointegration. When economic policy is considered in the context of a cointegrated VAR as in (4), the natural target variables become the growth rates, $\Delta \mathbf{y}_t$, and the equilibrium relations, $\boldsymbol{\beta}'\mathbf{x}_t$, which are both I(0). Since $\mathbf{y}_t$ is I(1) it is difficult to target. Candidates for permanent shifts are changes in the equilibrium means $\boldsymbol{\eta}$ resulting (e.g.) from shifts in the attitude of policy makers to acceptable levels of disequilibria $\boldsymbol{\beta}'\mathbf{x}_t$, or shifts in the instrument variables' growth rates γ_z, whereas transitory shocks are still possible via $\varepsilon_{z,t}$. Important issues in this context include the presence or absence of structural breaks in $\boldsymbol{\beta}$ following the regime shifts in $\boldsymbol{\mu}_z$ and/or γ_z, and the predictability of the resultant changes in $\Delta \mathbf{x}_t$, and $\boldsymbol{\beta}'\mathbf{x}_t$.

8.1 Permanent changes

Since $\boldsymbol{\beta}'\mathbf{x}_t$ and $\Delta \mathbf{x}_t$ are I(0), (3) has a Wold (1938) representation:

$$\Delta \mathbf{x}_t = \mathbf{C}(L)(\varepsilon_t - \Xi\gamma - \boldsymbol{\alpha\eta}) = [\mathbf{C}(1) + \Delta\mathbf{C}^*(L)](\varepsilon_t - \Xi\gamma - \boldsymbol{\alpha\eta}) \tag{28}$$

when

$$\mathbf{C}(1) = \boldsymbol{\beta}_\perp(\boldsymbol{\alpha}'_\perp \Xi \boldsymbol{\beta}_\perp)^{-1}\boldsymbol{\alpha}'_\perp \text{ with } \Xi = \sum_{i=1}^{s-1} \boldsymbol{\Gamma}_i - \mathbf{I}_n, \tag{29}$$

so that:

$$\boldsymbol{\beta}'\mathbf{C}(1) = \mathbf{0} \text{ and } \mathbf{C}(1)\boldsymbol{\alpha} = \mathbf{0}. \tag{30}$$

Hence (28) becomes:

$$\Delta \mathbf{x}_t = \mathbf{C}(1)(\varepsilon_t - \Xi\gamma) + \mathbf{C}^*(L)\Delta(\varepsilon_t - \Xi\gamma - \boldsymbol{\alpha\eta}) \tag{31}$$

which has as solution for $\mathbf{x}_t$:

$$\mathbf{x}_t = \mathbf{K}_{\beta_\perp}\mathbf{x}_0 + \mathbf{C}(1)\sum_{i=1}^{t}(\varepsilon_i - \Xi\gamma) + \mathbf{C}^*(L)\varepsilon_t - \mathbf{C}^*(1)(\Xi\gamma + \boldsymbol{\alpha\eta}) \tag{32}$$

with $\mathbf{K}_{\beta_\perp} = \boldsymbol{\beta}_\perp(\boldsymbol{\beta}'_\perp\boldsymbol{\beta}_\perp)^{-1}\boldsymbol{\beta}'_\perp$. Premultiplying (32) by $\boldsymbol{\beta}'$ gives the corresponding moving-average representation for the cointegrating vectors:

$$\boldsymbol{\beta}'\mathbf{x}_t = \boldsymbol{\beta}'\mathbf{C}^*(L)\varepsilon_t - \boldsymbol{\beta}'\mathbf{C}^*(1)(\Xi\gamma + \boldsymbol{\alpha\eta}). \tag{33}$$

In (4), the dimensions of $\boldsymbol{\beta}_y$ and $\boldsymbol{\beta}_z$ are $n_1 \times r$ and $n_2 \times r$ respectively, and $\boldsymbol{\alpha}$ is partitioned conformably. Applying the same partition to (31) yields:

$$\begin{pmatrix} \Delta \mathbf{y}_t \\ \Delta \mathbf{z}_t \end{pmatrix} = \begin{pmatrix} \mathbf{C}_{yy}(1) & \mathbf{C}_{yz}(1) \\ \mathbf{C}_{zy}(1) & \mathbf{C}_{zz}(1) \end{pmatrix} \left[\begin{pmatrix} \varepsilon_{y,t} \\ \varepsilon_{z,t} \end{pmatrix} - \begin{pmatrix} \boldsymbol{\Xi}_{yy} & \boldsymbol{\Xi}_{yz} \\ \boldsymbol{\Xi}_{zy} & \boldsymbol{\Xi}_{zz} \end{pmatrix} \begin{pmatrix} \gamma_y \\ \gamma_z \end{pmatrix} \right] \tag{34}$$

$$+ \begin{pmatrix} \mathbf{C}^*_{yy}(L) & \mathbf{C}^*_{yz}(L) \\ \mathbf{C}^*_{zy}(L) & \mathbf{C}^*_{zz}(L) \end{pmatrix} \Delta \left(\begin{pmatrix} \varepsilon_{y,t} - \boldsymbol{\alpha}_y \boldsymbol{\eta} \\ \varepsilon_{z,t} - \boldsymbol{\alpha}_z \boldsymbol{\eta} \end{pmatrix} - \begin{pmatrix} \boldsymbol{\Xi}_{yy} & \boldsymbol{\Xi}_{yz} \\ \boldsymbol{\Xi}_{zy} & \boldsymbol{\Xi}_{zz} \end{pmatrix} \begin{pmatrix} \gamma_y \\ \gamma_z \end{pmatrix} \right)$$

so that the partial responses of $\Delta \mathbf{y}_{t+h}$ to changes at time t in $\boldsymbol{\eta}$ and γ_z are given by:

$$\frac{\partial \Delta \mathbf{y}_{t+h}}{\partial \boldsymbol{\eta}'} = -(\mathbf{C}^*_{yy,h} \boldsymbol{\alpha}_y + \mathbf{C}^*_{yz,h} \boldsymbol{\alpha}_z) = -\mathbf{C}^*_{y,h} \boldsymbol{\alpha} \tag{35}$$

and

$$\frac{\partial \Delta \mathbf{y}_{t+h}}{\partial \gamma'_z} = -((\mathbf{C}_{yy}(1) + \mathbf{C}^*_{yy,h}) \boldsymbol{\Xi}_{yz} + (\mathbf{C}_{yz}(1) + \mathbf{C}^*_{yz,h}) \boldsymbol{\Xi}_{zz}) \tag{36}$$

respectively. Noting that $\det \mathbf{C}^*(L) = \mathbf{0}$ has all its roots outside the unit circle:

$$\frac{\partial \Delta \mathbf{y}_{t+h}}{\partial \boldsymbol{\eta}'} \rightarrow \mathbf{0} \text{ as } h \rightarrow \infty$$

$$\frac{\partial \Delta \mathbf{y}_{t+h}}{\partial \gamma'_z} \rightarrow \mathbf{C}_{yy}(1) \boldsymbol{\Xi}_{yz} + \mathbf{C}_{yz}(1) \boldsymbol{\Xi}_{zz} \text{ as } h \rightarrow \infty$$

so that there are no long-run effects in the growth rate of $\mathbf{y}_t$ from shifts in the equilibrium mean $\boldsymbol{\eta}$, but shifts in the mean growth rate of $\mathbf{z}_t$ do have long run effects on $\Delta \mathbf{y}_t$. Similarly from (33) we have $\forall h \geq 0$:

$$\frac{\partial \boldsymbol{\beta}' \mathbf{x}_{t+h}}{\partial \boldsymbol{\eta}'} = -\boldsymbol{\beta}' \mathbf{C}^*(1) \boldsymbol{\alpha}$$

and

$$\frac{\partial \boldsymbol{\beta}' \mathbf{x}_{t+h}}{\partial \gamma'_z} = -[(\boldsymbol{\beta}'_y \mathbf{C}^*_{yy}(1) + \boldsymbol{\beta}'_z \mathbf{C}^*_{zy}(1)) \boldsymbol{\Xi}_{yz} + (\boldsymbol{\beta}'_y \mathbf{C}^*_{yz}(1) + \boldsymbol{\beta}'_z \mathbf{C}^*_{zz}(1)) \boldsymbol{\Xi}_{zz}].$$

8.2 Impulse changes

From the moving-average representations for $\Delta \mathbf{x}_t$ and $\mathbf{x}_t$ in (31) and (32), it is possible to derive the h-period unit impulse-response matrices:

$$\frac{\partial \Delta \mathbf{x}_{t+h}}{\partial \varepsilon'_t} = \mathbf{C}^*_h - \mathbf{C}^*_{h-1} \quad \forall h > 0 \text{ and } \frac{\partial \Delta \mathbf{x}_t}{\partial \varepsilon'_t} = \mathbf{C}(1) + \mathbf{C}^*_0 = \mathbf{I}_n \tag{37}$$

since $\mathbf{C}(L) = \mathbf{C}(1) + \mathbf{C}^*(L)\Delta$ so that $\mathbf{C}(0) = \mathbf{C}(1) + \mathbf{C}_0^* = \mathbf{I}_n$ for identification, and:

$$\frac{\partial \mathbf{x}_{t+h}}{\partial \boldsymbol{\varepsilon}_t'} = \mathbf{C}(1) + \mathbf{C}_h^* \quad \forall h \geq 0. \tag{38}$$

Using (34) yields the following policy impulse responses from (37):

$$\left.\frac{\partial \Delta \mathbf{y}_{t+h}}{\partial \boldsymbol{\varepsilon}_{z,t}'}\right|_{d\varepsilon_{y,t}=\Upsilon d\varepsilon_{z,t}} = (\mathbf{C}_{yy,h}^* - \mathbf{C}_{yy,h-1}^*)\boldsymbol{\Upsilon} + (\mathbf{C}_{yz,h}^* - \mathbf{C}_{yz,h-1}^*) \quad \forall h > 0 \tag{39}$$

and:

$$\left.\frac{\partial \Delta \mathbf{y}_{t}}{\partial \boldsymbol{\varepsilon}_{z,t}'}\right|_{d\varepsilon_{y,t}=\Upsilon d\varepsilon_{z,t}} = (\mathbf{C}_{yy}(1) + \mathbf{C}_{yy,0}^*)\boldsymbol{\Upsilon} + (\mathbf{C}_{yz}(1) + \mathbf{C}_{yz,0}^*) = \boldsymbol{\Upsilon}. \tag{40}$$

Noting that $\det \mathbf{C}^*(L) = \mathbf{0}$ has all its roots outside the unit circle:

$$\frac{\partial \Delta \mathbf{y}_{t+h}}{\partial \boldsymbol{\varepsilon}_{z,t}'} \to \mathbf{0} \quad \text{and} \quad \frac{\partial \mathbf{y}_{t+h}}{\partial \boldsymbol{\varepsilon}_{z,t}'} \to \mathbf{C}_{yz}(1) \quad \text{as } h \to \infty.$$

This follows since $\mathbf{x}_t \sim \mathsf{I}(1)$ so that there is persistence in the $\mathbf{x}_t$ process, but since $\mathbf{C}(1)$ has rank $(n-r)$ there is an attribution problem: the attribution of this persistence to $(n-r)$ particular elements of $\mathbf{x}_t$ or $(n-r)$ linear combinations of them is arbitrary. However, there are r linear combinations of $\mathbf{x}_t$ that do not exhibit persistence, the cointegrated combinations $\boldsymbol{\beta}'\mathbf{x}_t$ for which the h-period policy impulse responses are $\forall h \geq 0$:

$$\left.\frac{\partial \boldsymbol{\beta}' \mathbf{x}_{t+h}}{\partial \boldsymbol{\varepsilon}_{z,t}'}\right|_{d\varepsilon_{y,t}=\Upsilon d\varepsilon_{z,t}} = \boldsymbol{\beta}_y'(\mathbf{C}_{yy,h}^* + \mathbf{C}_{yz,h}^*)\boldsymbol{\Upsilon} + \boldsymbol{\beta}_z'(\mathbf{C}_{zy,h}^* + \mathbf{C}_{zz,h}^*) \tag{41}$$

with

$$\frac{\partial \boldsymbol{\beta}' \mathbf{x}_{t+h}}{\partial \boldsymbol{\varepsilon}_{z,t}'} \to \mathbf{0} \text{ as } h \to \infty.$$

For the special case $\mathrm{d}\varepsilon_{y,t} = \mathbf{0}$, which for $n_2 = 1$ is a commonly-used form of impulse-response analysis, the responses are obtained by setting $\boldsymbol{\Upsilon} = \mathbf{0}$ in (39), (40), and (41).

The commonly-used standard-error and orthogonalized impulses yield the following response matrices:

$$\frac{\partial \Delta \mathbf{x}_{t+h}}{\partial \boldsymbol{\varepsilon}_t^{+\prime}} = (\mathbf{C}_h^* - \mathbf{C}_{h-1}^*)\mathbf{Q} \quad \forall h > 0 \quad \text{and} \quad \frac{\partial \Delta \mathbf{x}_t}{\partial \boldsymbol{\varepsilon}_t^{+\prime}} = \mathbf{Q} \tag{42}$$

and:

$$\frac{\partial \mathbf{x}_{t+h}}{\partial \boldsymbol{\varepsilon}_t^{+\prime}} = (\mathbf{C}(1) + \mathbf{C}_h^*)\mathbf{Q} \quad \forall h \geq 0 \tag{43}$$

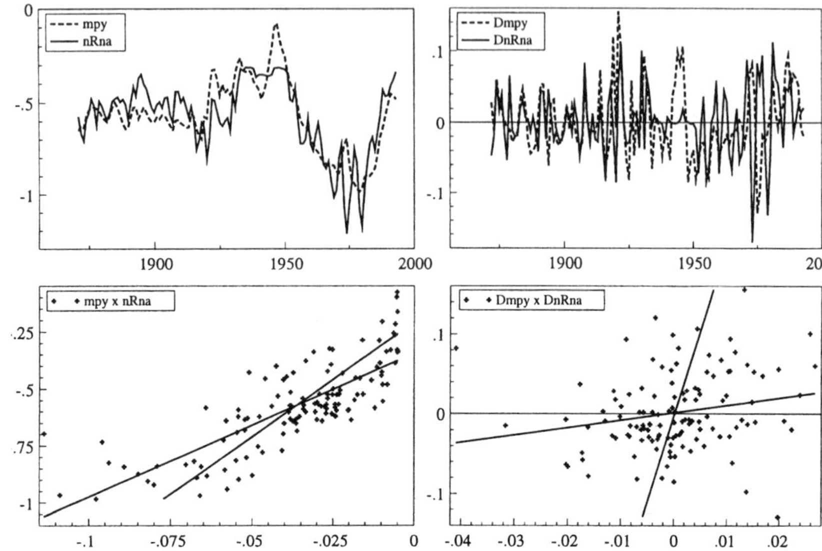

Fig. 1. Time series and cross plots of levels and differences of *mpy* and $-Rna$

with $\varepsilon_t^+ = \mathbf{Q}'\varepsilon_t$, and $\mathbf{Q} = \text{diag}(\sqrt{\sigma_{11}}, \sqrt{\sigma_{22}}, \ldots, \sqrt{\sigma_{nn}})$ for the standard-error impulses; and $\mathbf{Q} = (\mathbf{P}')^{-1}$ for the orthogonalized impulses with $\boldsymbol{\Sigma}^{-1} = \mathbf{PP}'$. Figure 5 in the next section illustrates these impulse responses for the joint modelling of inverse money velocity and a short-term nominal interest rate, and figure 6 gives similar responses in conditional models.

9. An illustration in a small model of UK money

As an illustration of the feasibility of conditional economic policy analysis, we consider a two-equation model of money and interest rates on annual data over the last century and a quarter. The basic data series are annual values of the broad money stock (M), real net national income (Y), the price level (P), and a short-term nominal interest rate (Rna), adjusted for the own rate on M, for the United Kingdom. Data from 1871 to 1975 are from Friedman and Schwartz (1982), whereas data over 1976–1993 are from Attfield, Demery and Duck (1995). Capitals denote levels and lower case the corresponding log.

Figure 1 records the time series then cross plots of $mpy = m - p - y$ and $-Rna$, then Δmpy and $-\Delta Rna$ as a 2×2 panel, ordered as $\left[\begin{smallmatrix} a & b \\ c & d \end{smallmatrix}\right]$ (negative interest rates, shown as *nRna* on the graphs, are used to highlight the correlations). The first and third figures show considerable long-run co-movement, but the second and fourth reveal substantial short-run departures and a low cross-correlation.

9.1 The empirical system

As previous evidence suggested the levels variables were I(1) (see e.g., Hendry and Ericsson, 1991), we estimated a bivariate VAR in *mpy* and *Rna* with 5 lags. Although a formulation in terms of *mpy* imposes many (possibly invalid) common factors on the dynamic specification (see Sargan, 1980), the resulting system offers a tractable illustration. Preliminary analysis showed 0–1 dummies were needed for 1919 and 1921 (boom and crash after World War I), 1926 (general strike) 1930 and1932 (the great depression), 1942–1946 (World War II), 1973 and 1975 (first oil crisis), and 1981–88 (Thatcher's 'monetary control' era); the intercept was unrestricted, but the trend was restricted to the cointegration space.

The summary results over 1876 to 1993 were as follows. First, the standard deviations of the residuals from *mpy* and *Rna* were 3.05% (expressed as a percentage of the level), and 0.77 percentage points respectively, with a cross correlation of −0.336. The correlations between actual and fitted values were 0.990 and 0.958. Other than the dummies, the F-tests on the retained regressors (distributed as $\mathsf{F}(2, 96)$ under the null; * and ** denote 5% and 1% significance) were:

Table 1. F-tests for significance of lags

variable/lag	1	2	3	4	5
mpy	177.17**	8.90**	0.72	0.82	6.76**
Rna	67.96**	11.67**	6.46**	0.66	5.02**
Trend	0.46	–	–	–	–

Thus, the longest lag is needed, but the trend is insignificant. The diagnostic tests yielded:

$$\text{System goodness of fit and evaluation}$$
$$\begin{bmatrix} \text{statistic} & mpy & Rna & \text{VAR} \\ \mathsf{F}_{\mathsf{ar}}(2,95) & 1.75 & 0.15 & - \\ \mathsf{F}_{\mathsf{arch}}(1,95) & 0.22 & 0.11 & - \\ \mathsf{F}_{\mathsf{het}}(22,74) & 0.61 & 0.67 & - \\ \chi^2_{\mathsf{nd}}(2) & 6.2^{*} & 0.11 & - \\ \mathsf{F}^{\mathsf{v}}_{\mathsf{ar}}(8,184) & & & 1.52 \\ \mathsf{F}^{\mathsf{v}}_{\mathsf{het}}(66,215) & & & 0.56 \\ \chi^{2\,\mathsf{v}}_{\mathsf{nd}}(4) & & & 6.2 \end{bmatrix}$$

The diagnostic tests are of the form $\mathsf{F}_j(k, T-l)$ which denotes an F-test against the alternative hypothesis j for both scalar and vector (or system) tests (shown as $\mathsf{F}^{\mathsf{v}}_j(k, T-l)$) of the form: 2nd-order serial correlation (F_{ar}; see Godfrey, 1978), 1st-order autoregressive conditional heteroscedasticity ($\mathsf{F}_{\mathsf{arch}}$; see Engle, 1982), heteroscedasticity ($\mathsf{F}_{\mathsf{het}}$; see White, 1980), and a chi-square test for normality ($\chi^2_{\mathsf{nd}}(2)$, see Doornik and Hansen, 1994). The only slight non-congruency is non-normality in the *mpy* equation. Figure 2 shows the fitted and actual values and the residual statistics. This system was estimated recursively, and its constancy is also acceptable as no 1-step or break-point Chow (1960) test is significant at 1% for either equation (or the system), and the 1-step residual confidence bands are reasonably constant.

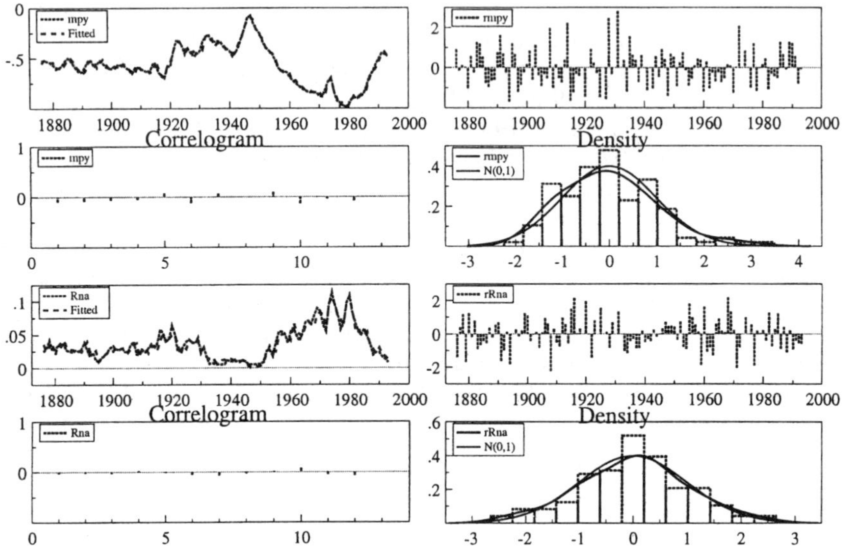

Fig. 2. System fitted and actual values, and residual statistics

9.2 Empirical cointegration

Treating this system as adequately congruent, we next tested for cointegration (and hence unit roots) using the Johansen (1988) procedure (in PcFiml: see Doornik and Hendry, 1997). This yielded:

Cointegration analysis

$$\begin{bmatrix} r & 1 & 2 \\ \ell & 1016 & 1017 \\ \lambda & 0.15 & 0.01 \\ Max & 19.0^{*} & 1.6 \\ Tr & 20.5 & 1.6 \end{bmatrix}, \begin{bmatrix} \hat{\boldsymbol{\alpha}} & 1 & 2 \\ mpy & -0.125 & 0.047 \\ Rna & 0.005 & -0.067 \end{bmatrix}$$

$$\begin{bmatrix} \hat{\boldsymbol{\beta}}' & mpy & Rna & t \\ 1 & 1 & 4.78 & -0.00002 \\ 2 & 0.064 & 1 & -0.00037 \end{bmatrix}$$

For each value of the rank r of the long-run matrix in the Johansen (1988) procedure, we report the log-likelihood values (ℓ), eigenvalues (λ) and associated maximum eigenvalue (Max) and trace (Tr) statistics, which test the hypothesis of $(r-1)$ versus r cointegrating vectors, together with the estimated cointegrating vectors ($\boldsymbol{\beta}$) and feedback coefficients ($\boldsymbol{\alpha}$).

Although the evidence is weak, previous results (see e.g., Ericsson, Hendry and Prestwich, 1998b) suggested that *mpy* and *Rna* were cointegrated, so we proceeded to impose restrictions on the $\boldsymbol{\beta}$ vector.

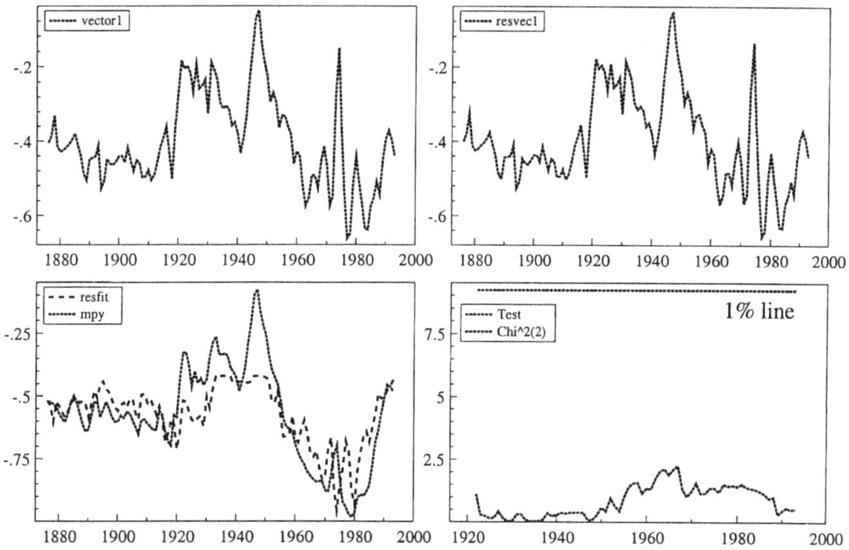

Fig. 3. Unrestricted and restricted cointegration relations

Restricted cointegration analysis

$$\begin{bmatrix} & \hat{\alpha} & SE \\ mpy & -0.120 & (0.029) \\ Rna & 0.000 & (-) \end{bmatrix}, \begin{bmatrix} & mpy & Rna & t \\ \hat{\beta}' & 1 & 4.94 & 0 \\ SE & - & (1.22) & (-) \end{bmatrix}$$

Trend deletion, and weak exogeneity of *Rna* for the long-run parameters are jointly acceptable, with $\chi^2(2) = 0.54$. The final long-run estimate is smaller than Ericsson *et al.* (1998b), but is not significantly different: fig. 3 reports both unrestricted and restricted cointegration relations, the long-run fitted values and outcomes, and the recursively-computed test of the validity of the restrictions.

9.3 Modelling the empirical system

Granting the existence of the one cointegrating relation, this allowed us to develop a simplified I(0) representation of the system in the changes Δmpy and ΔRna, together with an identity for the mean-zero equilibrium-correction relation $c = m - p - y + 0.392 + 5.0\, Rna$ (denoted EqCM on graphs). This I(0) system was simplified to a model, and the final selection (dummies not shown) was:

Model estimates

$$\begin{aligned} \Delta mpy_t &= +\underset{(0.06)}{0.54}\,\Delta mpy_{t-1} + \underset{(0.28)}{0.77}\,\Delta Rna_{t-2} - \underset{(0.02)}{0.12}\,c_{t-1} \\ \Delta Rna_t &= -\underset{(0.07)}{0.54}\,\Delta Rna_{t-2} - \underset{(0.06)}{0.15}\,\Delta Rna_{t-3} - \underset{(0.07)}{0.27}\,\Delta Rna_{t-4} \\ &\quad - \underset{(0.015)}{0.033}\,\Delta mpy_{t-1} - \underset{(0.014)}{0.074}\,\Delta mpy_{t-4} \\ c_t &\equiv c_{t-1} + \Delta mpy_t + 5.0\Delta Rna_t \end{aligned} \tag{44}$$

The likelihood-ratio test of the over-identifying restrictions was $\chi^2(20) = 24.9$. The cross correlation of the residuals remained at -0.37, and their respective standard deviations at 3.1% and 0.75 percentage points. Finally, the diagnostic statistics yielded:

Model evaluation statistic	*mpy*	*Rna*	model
$\mathsf{F}_{\mathsf{arch}}(1, 97)$	3.28	0.00	–
$\mathsf{F}_{\mathsf{het}}(28, 70)$	0.81	0.94	–
$\chi^2_{\mathsf{nd}}(2)$	4.1	0.43	–
$\mathsf{F}^{\mathsf{v}}_{\mathsf{ar}}(8, 208)$			0.66
$\mathsf{F}^{\mathsf{v}}_{\mathsf{het}}(84, 234)$			0.91
$\chi^{2\mathsf{v}}_{\mathsf{nd}}(4)$			4.61

As mentioned in discussion of lemma 1, these model estimates reveal empirical Granger causality from lagged Δmpy to ΔRna, though none from *mpy* to *Rna* since *Rna* is weakly exogenous for the parameters of the equilibrium-correction relation *c*. Equally, the discussion of lemma 2 noted that this model has empirical Granger causality from *Rna* to *mpy* since c_{t-1}, which incorporates both *mpy* and *Rna*, is included in the equation for Δmpy, but there is a positive short-term impact. Hence *Rna* is a potential instrument for changing the target *mpy*, with care given to the perverse impact.

Figure 4 shows the fitted and actual values, and the residuals, for the model. The tracking is reasonable, with correlations of actual and fitted in the I(0) system being 0.82 and 0.77, and the residuals remain near white noise, with no evidence of mis-specification.

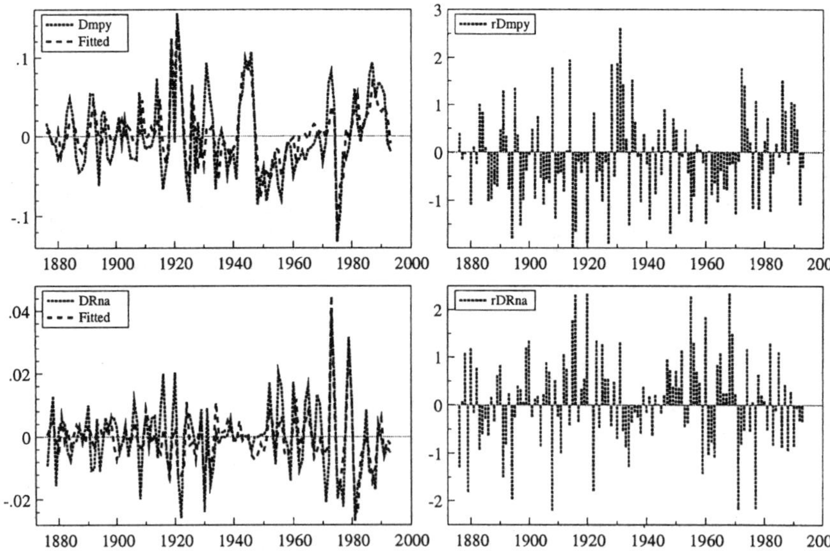

Fig. 4. Fitted and actual values, and residuals from the model

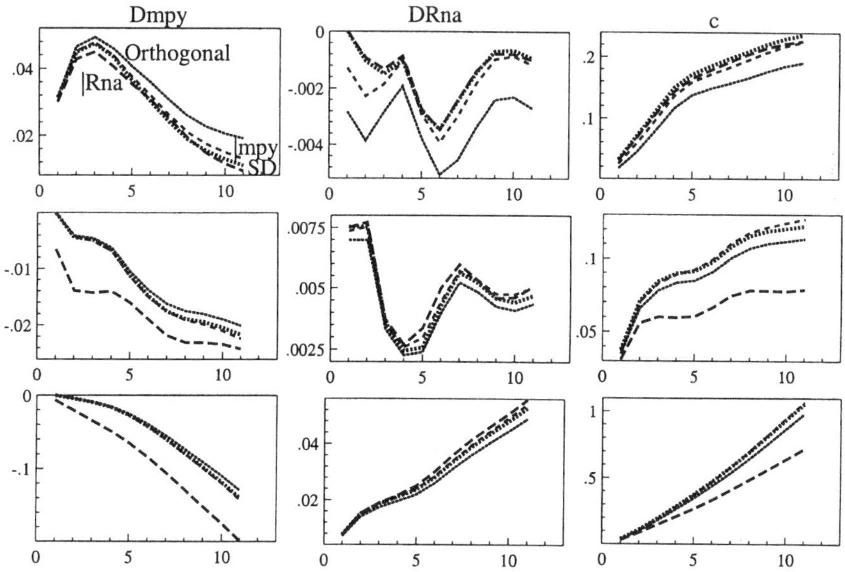

Fig. 5. Impulse responses in (i)–(iv) from the model

9.4 Empirical impulse responses

To illustrate responses to alternative forms of transitory changes we present cumulative impulse responses for shocks to the errors for five versions of this baseline model:

(i) the model just described, computing orthogonal shocks;
(ii) the model just described, computing standard-deviation shocks;
(iii) a conditional model for mpy_t given Rna_t (shown on the graph as |Rna);
(iv) a conditional model for Rna_t given mpy_t (shown as |mpy);
(v) a conditional model for mpy_t given Rna (shown on the graph as ||Rna);
(vi) a conditional model for Rna_t given mpy (shown as ||mpy).

Figure 5 records the outcomes for the first four cases; the rows correspond to shocks to *mpy*, *Rna* and *c*, and the columns to their responses. There are noticeable differences between the orthogonal and standard deviation shocks to *mpy* for all three variables, although the signs and patterns are similar.

In the last two cases, the conditioning variable is non-modelled, and hence is treated as if it were strongly exogenous. These results are shown in fig. 6, together with the baseline orthogonal shocks. Conditioning on *Rna* now has a marked effect, switching the sign of the response of *mpy* to a shock in *c*. Conversely, conditioning on *mpy* mainly affects the response of *c* to a shock to *Rna*. Since the cointegration relation treats all the variables as endogenous, whereas the conditional models do not, it is unsurprising that in those cases, shocks to *c* induce the largest changes.

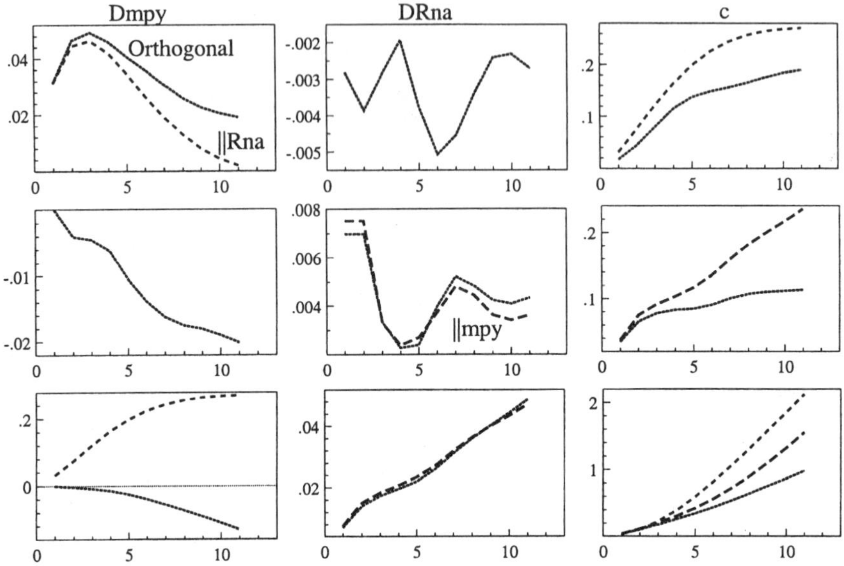

Fig. 6. Impulse responses in (v)–(vi) from the model

9.5 Empirical co-breaking

Finally, we consider co-breaking between *mpy* and *Rna*. Complete co-breaking would entail the absence of all dummies in a linear model relating them, but that is unlikely across a sample that includes two world wars, and many policy regimes: indeed, even the final model in Ericsson *et al.* (1998) requires dummies for wars and changes in Competition and Credit Control (CCC) regulations in the early 1970s and mid 1980s.

As regimes should have constant unconditional means for the policy variables, we divided the data sample into a sequence of episodes historically, shown in fig. 7, and tested for: (a) which step dummies vanished in the VAR; and (b) which of the remainder vanished in a conditional model of mpy given Rna. The first 'regime' was from 1876–1913, then 1914–18, 1919–20, 1921–33, 1934–43, **1944–51**, 1952–65, **1966–83**, and finally 1984–93 (the regimes in bold are highlighted on the graph for clarity; other regimes are shown via their corresponding dummies; the last was the omitted dummy). In addition, the earlier 0–1 dummies were retained, and the CCC dummy from Hendry and Ericsson, 1991, denoted dsc on the figure, was added.

These step dummies were added to the initial $\mathsf{I}(1)$ VAR(5), but most had negligible effects, so were eliminated; only the three shown in Table 2 remained 'significant' after reduction (ignoring their data-based selection: reduction $\mathsf{F}(12, 174) = 1.51$).[1]

[1] Results in an earlier draft were due to dropping the *trend*, inducing apparent significance of the regime step dummies. A reduction keeping *trend*, first dropping dummies, delivers the model reported, with the *trend* insignificant at the end.

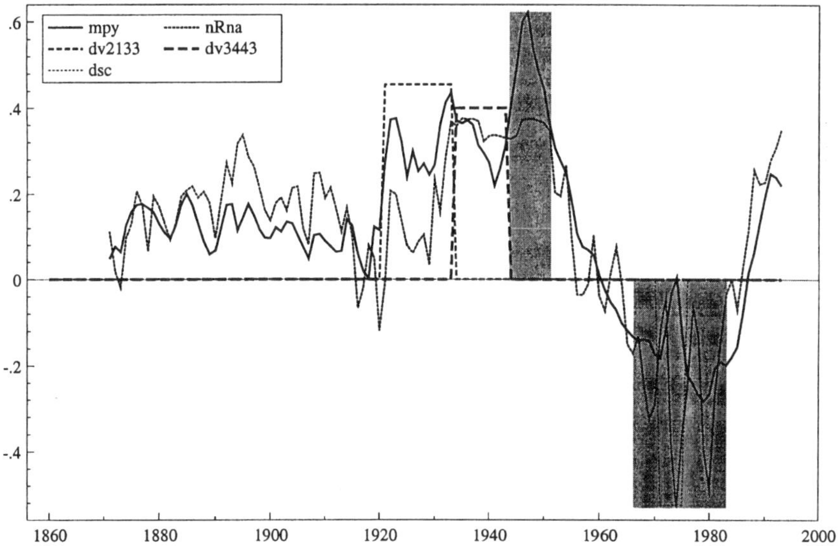

Fig. 7. Postulated regimes for money and interest rates

Table 2. F-statistic values of dummies

ds1876	4.07*	ds1934	4.15*	dsc	4.09*

The Johansen (1988) cointegration analysis still suggested neither eigenvalue was significant (at conventional levels), but as before we retained the first relation. This was restricted to eliminate the trend, and impose long-run weak exogeneity of *Rna*, with a coefficient of 5.0 as above, yielding $\chi^2(3) = 3.54$.

Cointegration analysis with regime dummies

$$\begin{bmatrix} r & 1 & 2 \\ \ell & 1025 & 1029 \\ \lambda & 0.11 & 0.05 \\ Max & 14.2 & 6.2 \\ Tr & 20.5 & 6.2 \end{bmatrix}, \begin{bmatrix} \hat{\alpha} & 1 & 2 \\ mpy & -0.102 & 0.236 \\ Rna & -0.020 & -0.065 \end{bmatrix}$$

$$\begin{bmatrix} \hat{\beta}' & mpy & Rna & t \\ 1 & 1 & 7.21 & 0.00197 \\ 2 & -0.004 & 1 & 0.00057 \end{bmatrix}$$

The system was reduced to I(0), with an over-identification test statistic of $\chi^2(22) = 21.2$ after eliminating all variables in each equation with a 't'-statistic less than 2. The only regime dummy remaining in the *mpy* equation conditional on *Rna* was *dsc* (coefficient of 0.037, 't'= 3.33), which reflected changes in credit rationing: the coefficient on ΔRna was -1, ΔRna_{t-2} became insignificant, but otherwise the equation was close to that in (44) above. Thus, there is evidence of partial, but not complete, co-breaking between *mpy* and *Rna* historically, although one cannot preclude the possibility that the incomplete co-breaking is due to the data-based construction of the dummies. If in fact they do not co-break, then regime changes in economic policy may not have their anticipated effects.

10. Conclusions

The following are the major conclusions of the paper.

(1) Since the objective of economic policy is to change target variables in the DGP, but economic policy analysis can only be done using an econometric model, it is important to have econometric models that will give reliable inferences about policy responses in the DGP. This requires that models be congruent and encompassing.
(2) It is both important and valuable to distinguish impulse-response analysis, which was designed for evaluating the effects of 'shocks' (which might include unexpected changes in economic policy) via $(\partial \mathbf{x}_{t+h}/\partial \boldsymbol{\varepsilon}'_t)$, from response analysis concerned with more permanent changes $(\partial \mathbf{y}_{t+h}/\partial \boldsymbol{\mu}'_{z,t})$. The latter is directly concerned with assessing the effects of known or foreseeable policy changes.
(3) In analyzing the effects on target variables of policy changes, it is valuable to distinguish between regime shifts and structural breaks. A regime shift is defined as any parameter change in the marginal process. A structural break occurs when the parameters of a conditional distribution, which characterizes the responses of one set of variables to changes in another, are not constant.
(4) The existence of behavioural relations between the target and instrument variables which are co-breaking matters if economic policy is to be effective when implemented via regime shifts in the instrument process. Some evidence was found of co-breaking between the interest rate and velocity of money in the UK over the last century.
(5) Given the large effect that EGNC can have on policy response analysis, both in determining the feasibility of economic policy and the form of impulse responses, it is important to evaluate its validity. The empirical illustration yielded estimates consistent with the short-term interest rate being a potential instrument to effect policy changes in the velocity of money in the UK.
(6) When using conditional econometric models, since impulse responses from conditional models are different from those from over-identified systems, it is important to ensure that the conditioning is valid. Weak exogeneity and invariance (thus super exogeneity) are critical for this. Evidence was found for the interest rate being weakly exogenous for the parameters of the equilibrium relation determining money velocity in the UK.
(7) Empirical evidence was provided of the powerful impact that conditioning assumptions in econometric models have on the computed values of impulse responses. In particular, enforcing strong exogeneity when it was invalid radically altered the impulse response to shocks in the cointegrating relationship (see fig. 6).

References

Attfield CLF, Demery D, Duck NW (1995) Estimating the UK demand for money function: A test of two approaches. Economics department, University of Bristol, Mimeo
Banerjee A, Dolado JJ, Galbraith JW, Hendry DF (1993) Co-integration, error correction and the econometric analysis of non-stationary data. Oxford University Press, Oxford
Banerjee A, Hendry DF, Mizon GE (1996) The econometric analysis of economic policy. Oxford Bulletin of Economics and Statistics 58:573–600
Chow GC (1960) Tests of equality between sets of coefficients in two linear regressions. Econometrica 28:591–605
Clements MP, Hendry DF (1998) Forecasting economic time series. Cambridge Univsersity Press Cambridge, The Marshall Lectures on Economic Forecasting: Forthcoming
Doornik JA, Hansen H (1994) A practical test for univariate and multivariate normality. Discussion paper, Nuffield College
Doornik JA, Hendry DF (1997) Modelling dynamic systems using PcFiml 9 for Windows. International Thomson Business Press, London
Engle RF (1982) Autoregressive conditional heteroscedasticity, with estimates of the variance of United Kingdom inflations. Econometrica 50:987–1007
Engle RF, Granger CWJ (1987) Cointegration and error correction: Representation, estimation and testing. Econometrica 55:251–276
Engle RF, Hendry DF (1993) Testing super exogeneity and invariance in regression models. Journal of Econometrics 56:119–139
Engle RF, Hendry DF, Richard J-F (1983) Exogeneity. Econometrica 51:277–304. Reprinted in Hendry DF (1993) Econometrics: Alchemy or Science? Blackwell Publishers, Oxford
Ericsson NR, Hendry DF, Mizon GE (1998a) Exogeneity, cointegration and economic policy analysis. Journal of Business and Economic Statistics, Forthcoming
Ericsson NR, Hendry DF, Prestwich KM (1998b) The demand for broad money in the United Kingdom, 1878–1993. Scandinavian Journal of Economics 100:289–324
Friedman M (1957) A theory of the consumption function. Princeton University Press, Princeton
Friedman M, Schwartz AJ (1982) Monetary trends in the United States and the United Kingdom: Their relation to income, prices, and interest rates, 1867–1975. University of Chicago Press, Chicago
Godfrey L (1978) Testing against general autoregressive and moving average error models when the regressors include lagged dependent variables. Econometrica 46:1293–1301
Granger CWJ (1969) Investigating causal relations by econometric models and cross-spectral methods. Econometrica 37:424–438
Granger CWJ, Deutsch M (1992) Comments on the evaluation of policy models. Journal of Policy Modeling 14:497–516
Hendry DF (1988) The encompassing implications of feedback versus feedforward mechanisms in econometrics. Oxford Economic Papers 40:132–149
Hendry DF (1995a) Dynamic econometrics. Oxford University Press, Oxford
Hendry DF (1995b) A theory of co-breaking. Nuffield College, University of Oxford, Mimeo
Hendry DF (1997) The econometrics of macro-economic forecasting. Economic Journal 107:1330–1357
Hendry DF, Doornik JA (1997) The implications for econometric modelling of forecast failure. Scottish Journal of Political Economy 44:437–461
Hendry DF, Ericsson NR (1991) An econometric analysis of UK money demand in "Monetary trends in the United States and the United Kingdom" by Milton Friedman and Anna J. Schwartz. American Economic Review 81:8–38
Hendry DF, Mizon GE (1997) On the pervasiveness of Granger causality in econometrics. European University Institute, Florence, mimeo
Hendry DF, Neale AJ (1991) A Monte Carlo study of the effects of structural breaks on tests for unit roots. In: Hackl P, Westlund AH (eds.) Economic structural change, analysis and forecasting, Berlin: Springer-Verlag, Berlin, pp. 95–119
Johansen S (1988) Statistical analysis of cointegration vectors. Journal of Economic Dynamics and Control 12:231–254
Johansen S (1995) Likelihood-based inference in cointegrated vector autoregressive models. Oxford University Press, Oxford

Lucas RE (1976) Econometric policy evaluation: A critique. In: Brunner K, Meltzer A (eds.) The Phillips Curve and Labor Markets, Vol. 1 of Carnegie-Rochester Conferences on Public Policy, pp. 19–46. North-Holland Publishing Company, Amsterdam, pp. 19–46
Lütkepohl H (1991) Introduction to multiple time series analysis. Springer-Verlag, New York
Mizon GE (1995) Progressive modelling of macroeconomic time series: The LSE methodology. In: Hoover KD (ed.) Macroeconometrics: Developments, tensions and prospects, Kluwer Academic Press, Dordrecht, pp. 107–169
Mosconi R, Giannini C (1992) Non-causality in cointegrated systems: Representation, estimation and testing. Oxford Bulletin of Economics and Statistics 54:399–417
Perron P (1989) The great crash, the oil price shock and the unit root hypothesis. Econometrica 57:1361–1401
Phillips PCB, Durlauf SN (1986) Multiple time series regression with integrated processes. Review of Economic Studies 53:473–495
Phillips PCB, Loretan M (1991) Estimating long-run economic equilibria. Review of Economic Studies 58:407–436
Rappoport P, Reichlin L (1989) Segmented trends and non-stationary time series. Economic Journal 99:168–177
Runkle DE (1987) Vector autoregressions and reality. Journal of Business and Economic Statistics 5:437–442
Sargan JD (1980) Some tests of dynamic specification for a single equation. Econometric 48:879–897. Reprinted as pp. 191–212 in Sargan JD (1988) Contributions to Econometrics, Vol. 1, Cambridge University Press, Cambridge, pp. 191–212
Sims CA (1980) Macroeconomics and reality. Econometrica 48:1–48. Reprinted in Granger CWJ (ed.) (1990) Modelling economic series. Clarendon Press, Oxford
Stock JH (1987) Asymptotic properties of least squares estimators of cointegrating vectors. Econometrica 55:1035–1056
Toda HY, Phillips PCB (1993) Vector autoregressions and causality. Econometrica 61:1367–1393
White H (1980) A heteroskedastic-consistent covariance matrix estimator and a direct test for heteroskedasticity. Econometrica 48:817–838
Wold HOA (1938) A study in the analysis of stationary time series. Almqvist and Wicksell, Stockholm
Wold HOA (1949) Statistical estimation of economic relationships. Econometrica 17:1–21

Empirical modeling of money demand

Neil R. Ericsson*

Stop 24, Division of International Finance, Federal Reserve Board, 2000 C Street, N.W., Washington, DC 20551, USA (e-mail: ericsson@frb.gov)

Abstract. This paper examines several central issues in the empirical modeling of money demand. These issues include economic theory, data measurement, parameter constancy, the opportunity cost of holding money, cointegration, model specification, exogeneity, and inferences for policy. Review of these issues at a general level is paralleled by discussion of specific empirical applications, including some new results on the demand for narrow money in the United Kingdom.

Key words: Cointegration, exogeneity, financial innovation, money demand, parameter constancy

JEL classification: E41, E52

---

* The author is a staff economist in the Division of International Finance, Board of Governors of the Federal Reserve System, Washington, DC 20551 USA, and may be reached on the Internet at ericsson@frb.gov. The views in this paper are solely the responsibility of the author and should not be interpreted as reflecting the views of the Board of Governors of the Federal Reserve System, the Reserve Bank of Australia, or any other person associated with the Federal Reserve System or the Reserve Bank of Australia. I am grateful for the generous hospitality of the Reserve Bank of Australia, where I was on secondment when this research was begun. I also wish to thank Tony Brennan, Gordon de Brouwer, Julia Campos, Ed Nelson, Jerome Fahrer, Jon Faust, Steve Grenville, David Hendry, John Irons, Katarina Juselius, Neva Kerbeshian, Helmut Lütkepohl, Dieter Nautz, Athanasios Orphanides, Kevin Prestwich, Robert Subbaraman, Timo Teräsvirta, Jenny Wilkinson, Jürgen Wolters, and two anonymous referees for helpful comments and discussions. All numerical results were obtained using PcGive Professional Version 9.0; see Doornik and Hendry (1996). This paper is a condensed version of Ericsson (1998), which provides additional empirical and analytical examples and more extensive references. The data may be obtained from the Internet at http://wotan.wiwi.hu-berlin.de/oekonometrie/engl/data.html.

1. Introduction

This paper reviews key issues that arise when empirically modeling the demand for money. For each issue, specific applications are also presented, including some new results on the demand for narrow money in the United Kingdom. Section 2 sets the stage by describing Hendry and Ericsson's (1991b) model of narrow money demand in the United Kingdom. Subsequent sections examine the underlying economic theory of the demand for money (Section 3); data measurement (Section 4); parameter constancy (Section 5); the opportunity cost of holding money, and financial innovation and deregulation (Section 6); cointegration (Section 7); model specification, including model design, dynamics, diagnostic testing, and encompassing (Section 8); exogeneity, including inversion of estimated equations, expectations, the Lucas critique, identification, and Granger non-causality (Section 9); and implications for policy (Section 10). The discussion reveals the often complicated and subtle interplay between these issues, with the sequence of their presentation reflecting those relationships: the order in which they arise in empirical practice varies considerably. The paper's structure also reflects the historical and economic importance of parameter constancy and opportunity cost, and how measurement of the latter bears on the former, with each topic occupying a full (adjacent) section. While all the issues are described in the context of estimating money demand functions, most arise in empirical modeling of economic time series generally, as discussed in Hendry (1995).

2. Empirical background

This section summarizes an empirical model of U.K. narrow money demand developed by Hendry and Ericsson (1991b). The data analyzed are nominal narrow money M_1 (M, in £ millions), real total final expenditure (TFE) at 1985 prices (I, in £ millions), the TFE deflator (P, 1985 = 1.00), the three-month local authority interest rate (R^{LA}), and the retail sight-deposit interest rate (R^{SD}). The interest rates are measured in per cent per annum, expressed as fractions. The first interest rate is the dominant short-term interest rate in the secondary market and measures the return on (some) assets outside M_1. The second interest rate is on checkable interest-bearing accounts at commercial banks and is a return on an asset within M_1. The data are quarterly and span 1963Q1–1989Q2. Money, TFE, and the deflator are seasonally adjusted. Three derived variables are also of interest: the inflation rate (Δp), the learning-adjusted retail sight-deposit interest rate (R^{SDa}), and the net interest rate $R^{LA} - R^{SDa}$ (denoted R^{net}). Hendry and Ericsson (1991b) and Ericsson, Hendry, and Tran (1994) provide further details on the data.

Hendry and Ericsson (1991b) develop a parsimonious conditional equilibrium correction model (EqCM) of money demand from this data.[1] That model is:

[1] Although Hendry and Ericsson (1991b) referred to their model as an error correction model, technically speaking it is an equilibrium correction model. See Hendry (1995, p. 213) for a discussion of the distinction between the two types of models.

$$\Delta(m-p)_t = -\underset{(0.13)}{0.69}\,\Delta p_t - \underset{(0.06)}{0.17}\,\Delta(m-p-i)_{t-1} - \underset{(0.060)}{0.630}\,R_t^{net}$$

$$- \underset{(0.009)}{0.093}(m-p-i)_{t-1} + \underset{(0.004)}{0.023} \tag{1}$$

$$T = 100[1964Q3 - 1989Q2] \quad R^2 = 0.76 \quad \hat{\sigma} = 1.313\%,$$

where t is the time subscript; T is the number of observations; R^2 is the squared multiple correlation coefficient; $\hat{\sigma}$ is the standard deviation of the residuals, expressed as a percentage of real money and adjusted for degrees of freedom; and Δ is the difference operator.[2] Capital letters denote both the generic name and the level of a variable; logarithms are in lowercase; and "levels" may mean the logarithm of the levels, with the context clarifying this. OLS standard errors are in parentheses $(\cdot)$.

3. Economic theory

In standard theories of money demand, money may be demanded for at least two reasons: as an inventory to smooth differences between income and expenditure streams, and as one among several assets in a portfolio. Both demands lead to a long-run specification of the following form:

$$M^d/P = g(I, \mathbf{R}), \tag{2}$$

where M^d is nominal money demanded, P is the price level, I is a scale variable, and $\mathbf{R}$ (in bold) is a vector of returns on various assets. The function $g(\cdot,\cdot)$ is increasing in I, decreasing in those elements of $\mathbf{R}$ associated with assets excluded from M, and increasing in those elements of $\mathbf{R}$ for assets included in M. See Goldfeld and Sichel (1990) and Laidler (1993) for extensive summaries of the literature on money demand.

Equation (2) commonly appears in log-linear form, albeit with interest rates entering in either logs or levels:

$$m^d - p = \gamma_0 + \gamma_1 i + \gamma_2 R^{out} + \gamma_3 R^{own} + \gamma_4 \Delta p, \tag{3}$$

where γ_0, γ_1, γ_2, γ_3, and γ_4 are coefficients; and, somewhat symbolically, R^{out} and R^{own} are the rates of return on assets outside of money and on money itself. Anticipated signs and magnitudes of coefficients are $\gamma_1 = 1$ (quantity theory) or $\gamma_1 = 0.5$ (Baumol-Tobin framework), $\gamma_2 \leq 0$, $\gamma_3 \geq 0$, and $\gamma_4 \leq 0$. The measure of money being modeled affects the choice of interest rates, and which are inside and outside money. Empirically, the own and outside rates of return may have coefficients of equal magnitude but opposite sign. If so, $\gamma_2 R^{out} + \gamma_3 R^{own}$ in (3) simplifies to $\gamma_2(R^{out} - R^{own})$, with the spread $R^{out} - R^{own}$ being economically interpretable as a measure of the opportunity

[2] The difference operator Δ is defined as $(1 - L)$, where the lag operator L shifts a variable one period into the past. Hence, for x_t (a variable x at time t), $Lx_t = x_{t-1}$ and so $\Delta x_t = x_t - x_{t-1}$. More generally, $\Delta_j^i x_t = (1 - L^j)^i x_t$ for positive integers i and j. If i or j is not explicit, it is taken to be unity.

cost of holding money. See Hendry and Ericsson (1991b), Baba, Hendry, and Starr (1992), and Bårdsen (1992) for examples. Finally, the inflation rate Δp measures the return to holding goods, so the coefficient γ_4 on Δp should be negative because goods are an alternative to money.

In the empirical model (1), R^{out} and R^{own} are R^{LA} and R^{SDa} respectively, so the solved long-run steady-state solution (3) for the model (1) is:

$$m - p = 0.252 + i - 6.77R^{LA} + 6.77R^{SDa} - 1.85(\Delta p \cdot 4), \tag{4}$$

where the coefficient on inflation is in units comparable to those on the interest rates. Income has a long-run unit elasticity, and coefficients on the interest rates and inflation are sensibly signed, with nonfinancial assets (goods) having a smaller long-run semi-elasticity than financial assets (narrow money and local authority deposit accounts). From (1), the short-run elasticities of money with respect to prices and income are both close to zero, contrasting with their unit long-run elasticities. Such a result is consistent with *Ss*-type models for money demand, in which short-run factors determine movements of money given desired upper and lower bands, and longer-run factors (such as the variables on the right-hand side of (4)) determine the levels of the bands themselves.

4. Data measurement

The choice and measurement of variables can influence the success of a research program. Considerations include aggregation procedures, definitional breaks, scale variables, the opportunity cost (examined in Section 6), the frequency of observation, and seasonal adjustment.

Measures of money are typically aggregates over components with different characteristics, so some researchers have developed Divisia indexes of money, aggregating over those components with weights reflecting their "liquidity", as measured through an inverse relation to the corresponding rates of return; see Barnett (1980) *inter alia*. However, Divisia indexes seem singularly unsuitable to address the ubiquitous phenomena of financial innovation and deregulation. For many samples and countries, the relevant rates of return were controlled over some subsamples and deregulated over others. A Divisia approach implies (implausibly) that liquidity suddenly changes when interest rates move upon deregulation, even when the quantities of an aggregate's components and the other characteristics of those components remain unchanged. Furthermore, standard models of agent behavior include a budget constraint, which involves simple aggregation over a portfolio of assets, yet Divisia indexes imply that agents focus on an unequally weighted aggregate.

Definitional breaks are common and often cannot be ignored. For instance, U.K. M1 and M3 have definitional breaks in 1981 of 6% and 10% respectively because the measurement of money shifts from covering the "banking sector" to covering the "monetary sector". The equation standard errors for models of M1 and M3 in Hendry and Ericsson (1991b) and Ericsson, Hendry, and Prestwich (1998) are 1.3% and 1.6%, so ignoring such breaks would (at a minimum) introduce substantial outliers and affect tests of constancy. Many other countries' series have similar breaks.

The chosen measure of money and the associated economic theory may determine the selection of the scale variable. In the portfolio theory of asset demand, wealth is a natural scale variable, while noting that flows (and hence income) may be relevant as well. Thus, wealth is often included in models of the demand for broad money. The empirical modeling of narrow money is typically based on transactions demand, in which case a flow variable such as GDP or TFE may be appropriate.

The choice of scale variable may itself affect the existence of cointegration in empirical money demand relations. For instance, GDP and TFE need not be cointegrated with each other, so picking one rather than the other as the scale variable may induce or remove cointegration in a money demand relation. Using Australian data, Juselius and Hargreaves (1992) find that the number of cointegrating vectors and their interpretation depend upon the choice of scale variable and the measure of money. More generally, in testing for cointegration across different measures of money, scale variables, and rates of return, only a few combinations might be cointegrated, even if an underlying cointegrating relationship is present.

The frequency of observation may affect both exogeneity and cointegration. If agents' decisions occur over a shorter time period than the data frequency, dynamics may be confounded and inferences about cointegration altered; see Hendry (1992).

Cointegrating vectors are invariant to a wide class of seasonal adjustment procedures; see Ericsson, Hendry, and Tran (1994). That said, the choice between seasonally adjusted and seasonally unadjusted data may affect the power of cointegration tests, the exogeneity status of variables, and dynamic specification, so this choice should be made carefully. Encompassing tests exist for comparing models with seasonally adjusted and seasonally unadjusted data, but they are more complicated than usual because the dependent variables of the two models differ, one being seasonally adjusted and the other being seasonally unadjusted. The choice between end-of-period and period-averaged data raises economic and methodological issues similar to those associated with seasonal adjustment. For additional discussion of seasonality and seasonal adjustment, see the articles reprinted in Hylleberg (1992).

5. Parameter constancy

As Judd and Scadding (1982) and Goldfeld and Sichel (1990) document, parameter constancy is a primary issue in empirical money demand studies. Thus, while strictly an aspect of model specification (Section 8), parameter constancy is considered separately. Parameter constancy is closely linked to the economic notion of parameters of interest, it is typically required for the validity of other tests performed, and constancy across policy regimes is crucial for reliable counterfactual policy simulations. A model need not be constant simply because it fits well: a model can have a high R^2, yet still be nonconstant. Nonconstancy of estimated coefficients presents both economic and statistical difficulties in conducting any inferences from the empirical model. Constancy is a particularly important issue during periods of financial liberalization and innovation, and many countries have recently experienced such developments, so this section considers implications of finding constancy or nonconstancy. Many tests of constancy are available, including some using recursive algorithms, which avoid arbitrary splitting of the sample; see Dufour (1982) for a lucid exposition.

The most satisfactory approach to explaining *nonconstancy* in existing models would be to develop a new, empirically constant model. The other (existing) models would be obtained as mis-specifications of the new model due to omitted variables, and their nonconstancies would be derivable from those mis-specifications using the formula for omitted variable bias. Such an encompassing result already exists for U.S. M1 equations. Rose (1985) develops an EqCM for U.S. M1 and finds that mis-specified dynamics in the money demand models of Goldfeld (1973, 1976) explain much of the missing money episode. Building on Rose (1985), Baba, Hendry, and Starr (1992) obtain an empirically constant EqCM for U.S. M1 over 1960–1988 and formally show how mis-specified dynamics, the measured opportunity cost, and the treatment of inflation can and did induce nonconstancy in earlier models. Relatedly, MacDonald and Taylor (1992) find a constant U.S. money demand function for annual data over 1874–1975.

While constancy is central to modeling money demand, the interpretation of empirical nonconstancy is not necessarily straightforward. For instance, models are often evaluated over a new sample by mechanistically "plugging in" new data into the existing equation. Such extensions may well be nonconstant; yet, other extensions of the same model may be constant. Specifically, changing environments may require economic adaptation of a model, as discussed in Ericsson, Hendry, and Prestwich (1998, Section IV). A model's constancy thus depends both upon how the model is formulated and upon how variables are updated for extended samples. Some of those variables may equal zero over the initial sample.

Five forms of a simple conditional linear model illustrate the potential consequences of extending a model on new data.

$$\text{\textit{Initial Model}}\ y_t = \theta' z_t + u_t \qquad t = 1, \ldots, T_1 \tag{5}$$

$$\text{\textit{Isolikelihood Model}}\ y_t = \theta' z_t + \delta' w_t + u_t \quad t = 1, \ldots, T \tag{6}$$

$$\text{\textit{Expanded Model}}\ y_t = \theta' z_t + \gamma' Q w_t + u_t \tag{7}$$

$$\text{\textit{Reparameterized Model}}\ y_t = \theta'(z_t + AQw_t) + (\gamma' - \theta' A) Q w_t + u_t \tag{8}$$

$$\text{\textit{Translated Model}}\ y_t = \theta'(z_t + A^* Q w_t) + u_t$$

$$= \theta' z_t^* + u_t \tag{9}$$

In the *initial model* (5), the variable y_t depends linearly on k variables z_t with coefficient θ, and on an error u_t. The sample period for (5) is $[1, T_1]$; in models (6)–(9), the sample period includes K $(= T - T_1)$ more observations. In the second or *isolikelihood model* (6), the initial model (5) is extended to include K linearly independent variables w_t that are zero over $[1, T_1]$ and have an arbitrary coefficient δ. Equation (6) has the same likelihood as (5). The *expanded model* (7) results if w_t enters (6) as some subset of linear combinations of w_t—Qw_t, say—with coefficient γ, where Q is some known full-rank matrix. Equation (7) can always be written as the *reparameterized model* (8), which depends upon a linear combination $(I : A)$ of $(z_t : Qw_t)$ and upon Qw_t. Finally, some linear combination of $(z_t : Qw_t)$ may exist $[(I : A^*)$, say] such that (8) depends on that linear combination alone and not on Qw_t separately. That linear combination generates the *translated model* (9), so-called because z_t has been translated into z_t^* $(= z_t + A^* Qw_t)$ over the extended sample.

Examples in Ericsson, Hendry, and Prestwich (1998, Section IV) show that constancy tests, inclusion of additional variables, and definitional changes on $\{y_t, z_t\}$ are all describable by the structure (5)–(9). One further example of particular interest involves financial innovation and interest rate spreads. Achieving the translated model (9) requires both a reduction from w_t to Qw_t to achieve the expanded model (7), and the restriction that $\gamma' = -\theta' A$ to obtain (9). One form of that restriction arises when new interest-bearing assets introduced through financial innovation transform interest rates in the initial sample into interest rate spreads in the expanded sample. The historical development of (1) illustrates just that.

Variants of the empirical model (1) were estimated initially on data through 1977 in Hendry (1979), and then on data through 1982 and 1985Q2 in Hendry (1985) and Hendry (1988) respectively, with no substantive changes in the models' empirical properties. The models in these papers have three differences with (1). Two are minor: the use of $\log(R^{LA})$ in Hendry (1979) rather than R^{LA} itself, and slightly different (and, for the most part, more general) dynamics in Hendry (1979, 1985, 1988). The third difference is major: Hendry (1979, 1985, 1988) excludes the own rate R^{SDa}, and for good reason. Retail sight deposits didn't offer any interest until 1984Q3. Estimating (1) in its "old" version over the subsample 1964Q3–1984Q2 obtains:

$$\Delta(m-p)_t = -\underset{(0.14)}{0.68}\,\Delta p_t - \underset{(0.06)}{0.18}\,\Delta(m-p-i)_{t-1} - \underset{(0.075)}{0.628}\,R_t^{LA}$$

$$\qquad - \underset{(0.010)}{0.093}(m-p-i)_{t-1} + \underset{(0.005)}{0.023} \tag{10}$$

$$T = 80[1964Q3 - 1984Q2] \quad R^2 = 0.70 \quad \hat{\sigma} = 1.344\%.$$

In the context of (5)–(9), equation (10) is the initial model (5), where T_1 is 1984Q2, y is nominal M1, z is the local authority 3-month deposit rate R^{LA}, and other variables in the relationship (other than R^{SDa}) are ignored for ease of exposition. Equation (10) is empirically constant in sample, as discussed below.

When the sample is extended through 1989Q2, the initial model (10) is highly nonconstant. It fails miserably on Chow's statistic: $F(20, 75) = 5.18$ [0.0000], where "$F(\cdot,\cdot)$" specifies the asymptotic distribution under the null hypothesis, "5.18" is the observed value of the statistic, and the asymptotic p-value appears in square brackets. That is, $\delta = 0$ in (6) is strongly rejected. Recursive estimates and related statistics also show the model's nonconstancy. Panel A in Figure 1 plots the recursively estimated coefficients (first five graphs), the 1-step residuals and $0 \pm 2\hat{\sigma}_t$, the 1-step Chow statistics normalized by their one-off 5% critical values, and two sets of break-point Chow statistics likewise normalized. Towards the end of the sample, coefficient estimates (particularly on Δp_t, $\Delta(m-p-i)_{t-1}$, and R_t^{LA}) and the equation standard error $\hat{\sigma}_t$ alter markedly, both numerically and statistically. The 1-step Chow statistics and the first graph of break-point Chow statistics high-

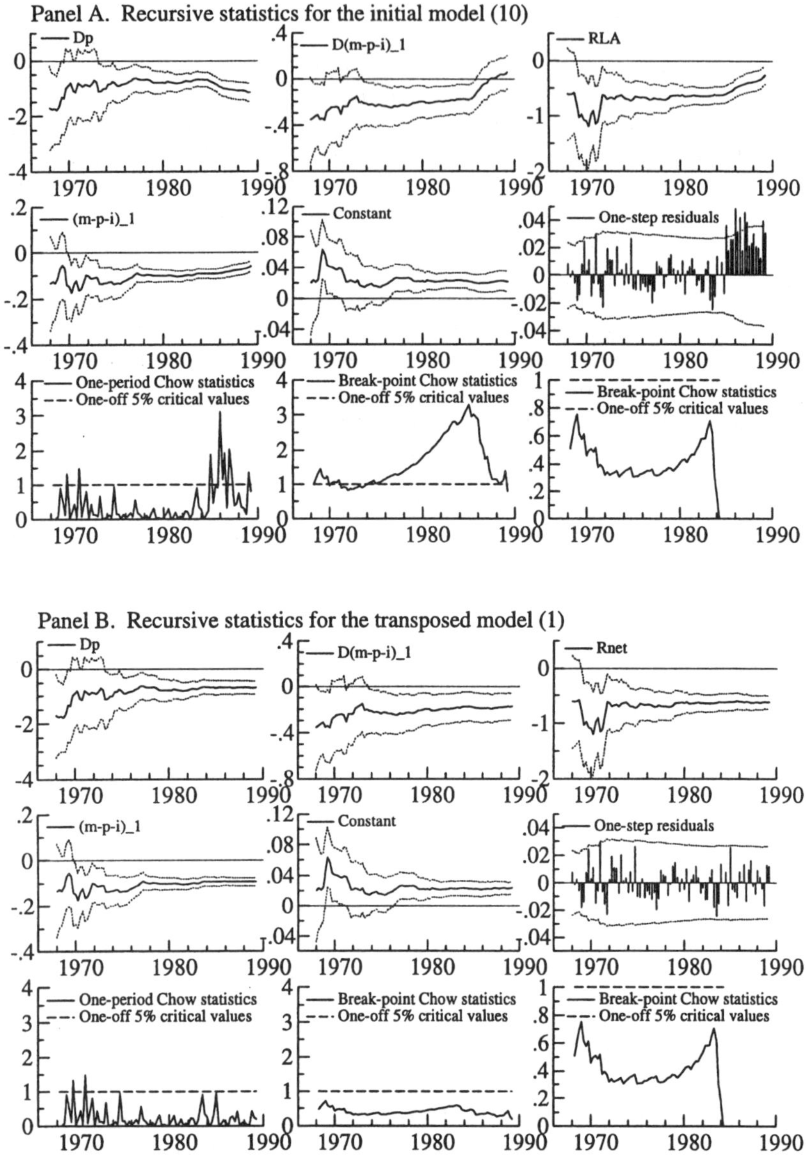

Fig. 1. Recursive estimates, 1-step ahead residuals, 1-step Chow statistics, and two sets of break-point Chow statistics for the initial model (10) with R^{LA} (panel A) and for the translated model (1) with R^{net} (panel B), both over $[1, T]$

light the magnitude and timing of that nonconstancy. However, prior to 1985, coefficient estimates move little relative to their estimated uncertainty. And, aside from two minor outliers around 1970, the 1-step residuals and the second sequence of Chow statistics (which extends through only 1984$Q2$) also point to the in-sample constancy of (10).

Trivially, the original parameters in (10) are constant over the extended sample if a dummy is added for each observation in the forecast period, giving the isolikelihood model (6). More interestingly, an empirically acceptable expanded model (7) exists, with Qw_t being the learning-adjusted interest rate on sight deposits (R_t^{SDa}). The F-statistic for testing the reduction from (6) to (7) is just $F(19, 75) = 0.82$ [0.68]. Finally, $\gamma = -\theta$ (and so $A^* = -1$) is a statistically acceptable restriction, with $F(1, 94) = 0.13$ [0.72]. The spread $R^{LA} - R^{SDa}$ is thus a suitable translation of the original variable R^{LA}, resulting in (9) algebraically and (1) empirically. Panel B in Figure 1 plots the same statistics as in Panel A, but for the translated model (1). That model's coefficients are very constant over the full sample, and they are close to the coefficients of the initial model (10) estimated over the (initial) subsample. Only the measurement of the data changes, and that, only for the extended portion of the sample. Constancy is an operational concept for the expanded and translated models, with each being testably constant over the whole sample period, i.e., relative to the isolikelihood model.

Economically, the introduction of interest-bearing sight deposits requires a more general measure of the opportunity cost of holding money. Initially, the opportunity cost is the outside interest rate R^{LA}. Once sight deposits begin earning interest, the opportunity cost becomes the differential relative to the own rate, i.e., $R^{LA} - R^{SDa}$. From a slightly different perspective, the opportunity cost for the entire sample is the differential $R^{LA} - R^{SDa}$, which is observationally equivalent to the outside rate R^{LA} over the initial subsample. Similar situations arise for measuring the opportunity cost of holding M1 in the United States, M3 in Greece, and broad money in the United Kingdom: see Baba, Hendry, and Starr (1992), Ericsson and Sharma (1998), and Ericsson, Hendry, and Prestwich (1998).

Before turning to opportunity cost *per se*, two observations are germane. First, researchers sometimes examine the stability of velocity in order to assess the stability of money demand functions. This is inadvisable because velocity may be nonconstant due to financial innovation, even while a money demand function on the same data has empirically constant parameters. Second (and conversely), a money demand function might be nonconstant and dectectably so, yet constancy tests on velocity could have low power because velocity imposes short-run as well as long-run unit homogeneity of money with respect to prices and incomes, a restriction that is frequently rejected empirically.

6. The opportunity cost of holding money

Standard economic theory posits that the demand for an asset depends upon its opportunity cost—the cost of holding that asset rather than some other asset. This section examines the measurement of the rates of return that enter the opportunity cost of holding money, the construction of the opportunity cost from those rates, and the implications of financial innovation and deregulation for the measurement of the opportunity cost. The discussion focuses on the opportunity cost of holding narrow money. For broad money, the same issues apply, but with a different allocation of assets within and outside of money, and hence with different empirical rates of return to money and to assets outside of money; see (e.g.) Wolters, Teräsvirta, and Lütkepohl (1998).

While the opportunity cost is arguably an aspect of data measurement (Section 4), its central role in money demand merits separate treatment.

6.1 Rates of return and the construction of the opportunity cost

Rates of return may be conveniently categorized as own rates and outside rates. Section 5 illustrated with U.K. M1 how important accounting for the own rate can be. In the United States, M1 includes NOW and SuperNOW accounts, and M2 includes CDs and passbook accounts, all earning interest. One measure of the opportunity cost is the differential between the T-bill rate and some function of these own rates. Empirically, the choice of measure matters. T-bill rates in the late 1980s were 5%–10%, whereas the differential between the T-bill rate and the NOW rate was only a few percent. The differential between the T-bill rate and the SuperNOW rate was only a few tenths of a percent, implying virtually no opportunity cost for SuperNOW accounts. Baba, Hendry, and Starr (1992) found that proper measurement of the opportunity cost is crucial for obtaining sensible results. Nonconstancy and lack of cointegration could easily arise if the own rate were ignored: introduction of the financial instrument would create a structural break in the mis-specified model, which would also likely induce an apparent unit root. More generally, a lack of cointegration could arise from mis-measurement of the own rate, e.g., if the average return on an asset is used in modeling but the marginal return actually matters, if the composition of the asset is heterogeneous, or if the relative sizes of the asset's components vary over time. These situations may characterize the demand for aggregates like M1 and broad money, both of which have interest-bearing and non-interest-bearing components; cf. Moore, Porter, and Small (1990).

Choice of the rates of return on alternatives to money is also important. In the United Kingdom, the short-term market is dominated by 3-month local authority deposits. Long rates appear statistically unimportant in the demand for M1, provided that that short-term rate is included; see Hendry and Ericsson (1991b). In the United States, the situation appears more complicated. Baba, Hendry, and Starr (1992) require interest rates on non-M1 M2, T-bills, and (risk-adjusted) long-term bonds. In general, accounting for risk may be important if assets differ in their riskiness. The inflation rate can also affect the opportunity cost of holding money, as the former measures the cost of buying a good tomorrow rather than today. Studies of money demand and currency substitution often find that inflation is important: see Ahumada (1992) and Kamin and Ericsson (1993) for examples on Argentine data.

The differential between two rates of return is a natural transformation for characterizing the opportunity cost. The differential may be between two interest rates, or between an interest rate and inflation, where the latter is also interpretable as a real interest rate. While the opportunity cost is often characterized as the differential between the rates of return on two assets (money and an asset outside money), *several* assets may be important in fact, due to the heterogeneity of asset markets and the sometime nonzero transactions cost of moving between assets. Money demand thus may depend upon the rates of return of the various components of money and upon the rates of return of the various alternatives to money. Even so, differentials may still be helpful in transforming this information, as in Baba, Hendry, and Starr (1992), Bårdsen (1992), and Ericsson and Sharma (1998).

6.2 *Financial innovation and deregulation*

The example in Section 5 above showed how financial innovation and deregulation could affect the measurement of the opportunity cost of holding money. For European countries, "1992" resulted in considerable changes in the banking sector, particularly in terms of the range of financial assets available to residents in a given country. A single European central bank could entail yet further changes.

Financial innovation and deregulation may entail effects additional to changes in the opportunity cost, as when capital controls or other quantity constraints are removed; and their presence is detectable in part with tests of parameter constancy: see Ericsson and Sharma (1998). Relatedly, economic agents may take time to adjust to financial innovation and deregulation, with empirical models needing to reflect that adjustment process. For instance, (1) incorporates learning about the own rate through an ogive weighting function B_t, where:

$$B_t = (1 + \exp[a_0 - a_1(t - T_1 + 2)])^{-1} \quad t > T_1, \tag{11}$$

and zero otherwise. The learning-adjusted own rate R_t^{SDa}—which enters (1) through R_t^{net} — equals $B_t R_t^{SD}$, where $a_0 = 5$ and $a_1 = 1.2$ were chosen, based on earlier evidence for the United States. The implied learning is rapid, with $B_t = 0.50$ after one year and $B_t = 0.99$ after two years. Even while this transition involves relatively few observations, the empirical need for a learning function is apparent from estimating (1) *without* B_t, i.e., with $R^{LA} - R^{SD}$ in place of R^{net}. The standard set of recursive statistics indicates nonconstancy around 1985 in that modified version of (1).

The formulation in (1) has a slight drawback: it treats the learning coefficients (a_0, a_1) as known. While an early version of Hendry and Ericsson (1991b) estimated those coefficients by nonlinear least squares, current software now permits estimation by *recursive* nonlinear least squares, allowing both estimation of (a_0, a_1) and evaluation of the resulting model's constancy. Estimation over the full sample obtains:

$$\Delta(m-p)_t = -\underset{(0.13)}{0.69}\,\Delta p_t - \underset{(0.06)}{0.17}\,\Delta(m-p-i)_{t-1} - \underset{(0.062)}{0.643}(R_t^{LA} - B_t R_t^{SD})$$

$$- \underset{(0.009)}{0.094}(m-p-i)_{t-1} + \underset{(0.004)}{0.024} \tag{12}$$

$$\text{with } B_t = \left[1 + \exp\left(\underset{(1.5)}{3.2} - \underset{(0.32)}{0.75}(t - T_1 + 2)\right)\right]^{-1} \tag{13}$$

$$T = 100[1964Q3 - 1989Q2] \quad R^2 = 0.76 \quad \hat{\sigma} = 1.319\%.$$

The coefficient estimates and estimated standard errors in the linear formulation (1) are virtually identical to comparable coefficients and estimated standard errors in (12). Each coefficient in B_t is significant at the 95% level, even though those coefficients are estimated on effectively under a dozen observations. The residual standard error actually falls slightly from (12) to (1), so the imposed values of a_0 and a_1 in the latter are statistically acceptable.

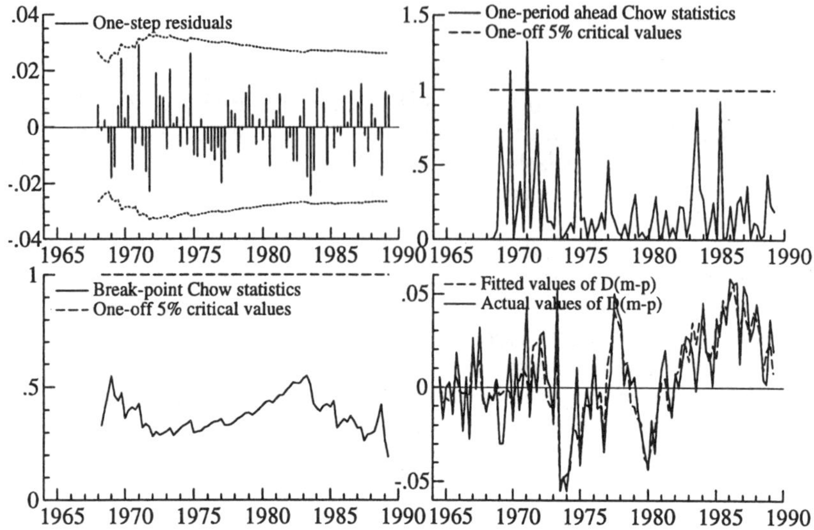

Fig. 2. One-step residuals, 1-step Chow statistics, break-point Chow statistics, and actual and fitted values of $\Delta(m-p)_t$ for the nonlinear translated model (12)–(13) over $[1, T]$

Figure 2 graphs the 1-step residuals, recursive 1-step and break-point Chow statistics, and the fitted and actual values for the nonlinear model (12). That model appears constant. Thus, the learning by economic agents about financial innovation can be empirically important in modeling money demand, above and beyond the effects of financial innovation itself; and that learning process can play a role in the constancy or nonconstancy of empirical models.

7. Cointegration

Cointegration provides an analytical and statistical framework for ascertaining the long-run relationship between nonstationary economic variables, such as money, prices, and income, and rates of return. Proper choice of variables (discussed in Section 4) and of estimation technique (this section) are both central to obtaining sensible results. While cointegration may have policy implications, it need not (Section 10). See Engle and Granger (1991), Banerjee and Hendry (1992), Ericsson (1992b), Banerjee, Dolado, Galbraith, and Hendry (1993), Johansen (1995), and Hoffman and Rasche (1996) for recent surveys on and applications of cointegration.

Engle and Granger (1987) proposed a (subsequently) very popular procedure for testing for cointegration, in which residuals from a static regression of integrated variables are tested for having a unit root. The static regression is interpreted as a cointegrating relation if the hypothesis of a unit root in the residuals is rejected, where tests for a unit root are typically based on the augmented Dickey-Fuller (1981) statistic. If the variables are cointegrated, the residuals can be treated as the equilibrium correction term in subsequent specification of a dynamic model for the variables involved. While intuitive and easy to implement, the Engle-Granger procedure often has little power to detect cointegration, and the long-run coefficient estimates from the static regression can be badly biased in finite samples; see Banerjee, Dolado, Hendry, and Smith (1986) and Kremers, Ericsson, and Dolado (1992).

Johansen (1988) provides an alternative. The Johansen procedure is an asymptotically fully efficient, maximum likelihood-based systems technique for determining the number of cointegrating vectors (not possible via the Engle-Granger procedure) and for estimating and conducting inference about the cointegrating vectors. Asymptotic critical values for testing the number of cointegrating vectors appear in Osterwald-Lenum (1992) *inter alia*. The estimation procedure in Phillips (1991) is also FIML, but it is not designed to detect how many cointegrating vectors exist. The number of cointegrating vectors may be at issue in money demand studies, as there could be several: money demand (between $m-p$, i, Δp, $\mathbf{R}$), term structure (between the interest rates), real interest rates (between Δp and a nominal interest rate), and aggregate demand (between i, Δp, a trend, and possibly $\mathbf{R}$). Economically, identifying these cointegrating vectors is of considerable interest. Statistically, estimating the cointegrating vectors and testing which equations they enter is necessary for evaluating the common (and often implicit) assertion of weak exogeneity. The order of integration of money and prices also may be at issue; see Johansen (1992). For the data analyzed above, the Johansen procedure provides clear evidence of one cointegrating vector involving $m-p$, i, Δp, and R^{net}; see Ericsson, Campos, and Tran (1990), Hendry and Mizon (1993), Ericsson, Hendry, and Tran (1994), and Hendry and Doornik (1994). That cointegrating vector is interpretable as a money demand function with coefficients similar to those in (4), which were solved from the conditional EqCM (1).

Some studies test for cointegration between money and income by using an augmented Dickey-Fuller test on the velocity of money. This procedure imposes unit homogeneity of income. If that condition is violated but money and income are still cointegrated (as in a Baumol-Tobin framework), testing the stationarity of velocity is an inconsistent procedure for testing cointegration between money and income. Even if long-run unit homogeneity holds, such a test imposes short-run as well as long-run unit homogeneity and may thereby lose power by the implicit common factor restriction; see Kremers, Ericsson, and Dolado (1992).

For integrated data, cointegration implies (and is implied by) an equilibrium correction representation of the data. EqCMs provide a framework for analyzing long-run relations and short-run dynamics jointly, and they represent a dynamic generalization of partial adjustment models: see Phillips (1954) and Hendry, Pagan, and Sargan (1984). Also, EqCMs nest both models in differences alone and models in levels alone, permitting easy comparison of such models. Conditional EqCMs have been empirically successful in many instances. However, their discussion requires the concepts of weak and super exogeneity (Section 9).

8. Model specification

This section examines three issues in model specification: model design, dynamics, and diagnostic testing (including encompassing).

8.1 Model design

Model design is anything but routine. While "failed" tests may indicate the sorts of mis-specification present, most tests have power against a wide range of alternatives, including those other than the one for which the test was designed. Thus, "rejection of the null does not imply the alternative". Even so, test rejections are informative by demonstrating that the model can be improved. At issue is the reason for model failure and hence the direction for an operational improvement of the model.

That suggests modeling "specific to general". However, the contrasting approach of "general to specific" has several advantages. Simplifications in going general to specific are reductions themselves, paralleling the reductions in moving from a data generation process to a model. Tests of simplifications check whether or not the corresponding reductions are valid. By construction, simplified models are nested in the initial general model, aiding control of Type I errors. While the simple-to-general approach cannot be excluded a priori as a route for finding a better model, it generally uses data information in an inefficient and inconsistent manner. See Hendry and Richard (1982), Ericsson, Campos, and Tran (1990), and Hendry (1995) for further details. Even so, the development of empirical models over time is often specific-to-general in nature, with researchers discovering shortcomings of existing models and proposing new solutions. While this aspect of modeling is at odds with the general-to-specific approach, encompassing (Section 8.3) provides a partial resolution.

Equation (1) has been designed using a general-to-specific approach, with one possible sequence of simplifications given in Ericsson, Campos, and Tran (1990); see also Ericsson, Hendry, and Tran (1994). The simplifications are of several types common in modeling money demand: from I(1) to I(0) variables (cointegration), from a system of equations to a conditional model (weak exogeneity), from two interest rates to a spread (aggregation), from many to few lags (lag length), and from several right-hand side untransformed variables to a small subset of transformed variables (dynamic specification and economic restrictions).

8.2 Dynamics

At its heart, dynamic specification involves the parameterization of lag coefficients and the choice of lag length. The former involves the choice between partial adjustment and equilibrium correction models, the inclusion of autoregressive errors, and the inclusion of inflation. See Hendry, Pagan, and Sargan (1984) for a comprehensive discussion of dynamic specification.

The partial adjustment model is a special case of the EqCM and is testable as such. On U.S. data, Rose (1985) tests the partial adjustment model in Goldfeld (1973, 1976) against an EqCM and rejects the corresponding restrictions. Hendry and Ericsson (1991b) find such restrictions for models on U.K. data also rejected.

Likewise, autoregressive errors can be rewritten as a restricted specification in the dynamics of the economic variables. This common factor (or comfac) restriction is easy to test with a Wald statistic based upon the unrestricted estimates of the parameters in an autoregressive distributed lag model; cf. Hendry and Mizon (1978).

In models of real money demand, the inclusion or exclusion of inflation is an issue of dynamic specification. Exclusion imposes equality of the short- and long-run elasticities of nominal money with respect to prices. Often, that restriction is resoundingly rejected: see Ahumada (1992), Bårdsen (1992), Hendry and Ericsson (1991a, 1991b), and Wolters, Teräsvirta, and Lütkepohl (1998) *inter alia.*

Dynamic specification arises naturally in general-to-specific modeling. Analysis of money demand might begin with determination of lag length and testing for cointegration in a vector autoregression. That system also permits testing for weak exogeneity (thereby permitting sub-system or single-equation modeling), for feedback (which might occur from agents' decisions and from policy rules), and for constancy.

The specification of the equilibrium correction term itself can involve dynamics through the dating of the variables involved. Equation (1) is invariant to whether $(m - p - i)$ appears at $t - 1$ or $t - 2$ because (1) includes $\Delta(m - p - i)_{t-1}$. However, in general, such a choice may entail a more (or a less) parsimonious representation for the EqCM. Mixed dating is permissible, as in $[(m - p)_{t-1} - i_t]$, and it is common in the partial adjustment literature; see Goldfeld (1973, 1976). Mixed dating may achieve some parsimony in dynamic specification, as in (for instance) $-0.4[(m - p)_{t-1} - i_t]$ rather than $-0.4[(m - p)_{t-1} - i_{t-1}] + 0.4\Delta i_t$. Economically, mixed dating may reflect the information set relevant or available to economic agents when they are making their decisions on how much money to hold.

8.3 Diagnostic testing and encompassing

In order to sustain inference, it is necessary for an empirical model to satisfy a range of hypotheses relating to goodness-of-fit, absence of residual autocorrelation and heteroscedasticity, correct functional form, valid exogeneity, predictive ability, parameter constancy, the statistical and economic interpretation of estimated coefficients, and the validity of a priori restrictions. Standard tests now exist for these hypotheses, and they are often formulated in a Lagrange multiplier framework as tests for omitted variables. See Hendry and Richard (1982), Hendry (1995, p. 366, Table 9.1), and Doornik and Hendry (1996) for detailed discussions, references, and computational details.

For (1), no standard diagnostic statistics are significant at their 5% critical values. Equation (1) is empirically constant (Panel B in Figure 1); and it is a statistically acceptable reduction of a fifth-order autoregressive distributed lag in money, prices, income, and the interest rates, with the corresponding F-statistic being $F(25, 70) = 0.97$ [0.51]. These statistics bear the caveat that they are interpretable in part as design criteria rather than evaluation criteria, thereby affecting the tests' power. That said, the statistics indicate that (1) is well-designed, with statistical properties that mimic those of the data generation process, if it were known. Also, the statistics play an important evaluative role, as a model essentially equivalent to (1) was designed on data through only 1977, yet the statistics for (1) use data through 1989.

Because a model may be *designed* to satisfy the usual hypotheses regarding mis-specification, additional criteria are required to evaluate it more fully.

One such criterion is encompassing, under which an empirical model accounts for the properties of rival models; cf. Mizon and Richard (1986) and Hendry (1995, Chapters 9 and 14). An encompassing approach helps avoid duplication and redundancy in research relative to existing results. For example, Rose (1985) obtains an EqCM for U.S. narrow money demand with constant parameters over the 1970s, thereby showing how Goldfeld's "missing money" of the mid-1970s turned on dynamic mis-specification. However, Rose's model breaks down in the 1980s. Using an empirical model similar to Rose's but which accounts for financial innovations and the riskiness of alternative assets, Baba, Hendry, and Starr (1992) find a money demand equation with a constant parameterization for 1960–1988. Each new model accounts for the results of the previous models and so encompasses them. A similar chronology of (mostly) encompassing models also exists for money demand in the United Kingdom. Relevant papers include Hacche (1974), Hendry and Mizon (1978), Coghlan (1978), Hendry (1979), Friedman and Schwartz (1982), Hendry (1985), Davidson (1987), Cuthbertson (1988), Hendry (1988), Ericsson, Campos, and Tran (1990), Hendry and Ericsson (1991a, 1991b), Hendry and Mizon (1993), Ericsson, Hendry, and Tran (1994), Hendry and Doornik (1994), and Ericsson, Hendry, and Prestwich (1998). Goodhart (1989) provides a comprehensive historical and policy perspective.

Two implications follow from obtaining an empirically less-than-successful model. First, economic inferences drawn from that model may or may not be affected by its empirical inadequacies, but it is impossible to determine whether those inferences are affected in fact until a superior model is designed. Second, weaknesses in existing models imply opportunities for further development, thereby defining a progressive research strategy in which new findings encompass previous ones and also offer value added. Once a model encompasses all pre-existing models, the newly established (encompassing) model serves as a sufficient statistic for those previously existing models. Thus, any further development need only encompass that one model, thereby simplifying and streamlining modeling efforts. Ericsson (1992a) and Hendry (1993) document several such research programs.

9. Exogeneity

Whether a variable is exogenous depends upon whether that variable can be taken as given without losing information for the purpose at hand. The distinct purposes of statistical inference, forecasting, and policy analysis define the three concepts of weak, strong, and super exogeneity. Engle, Hendry, and Richard (1983) clarify these concepts, and Ericsson (1992b) provides examples from a simple bivariate normal distribution. This section briefly discusses implications for inversion of estimated equations, expectations and the Lucas critique, identification, and Granger causality.

Under super exogeneity, inverting a conditional model is invalid. That said, it is precisely what occurs when estimated money-demand functions are inverted to obtain prices as a function of money (common among macroeconomists) or to obtain the interest rate as a function of money (common among macro-modelers). For instance, the P^* model proposed by Hallman, Porter, and Small (1991) is interpretable either as an inverted money demand equation or as an assumed lack of weak exogeneity of prices for the money-demand cointegrating vector. Coefficient estimates from inverted models may differ greatly from the inverses of the money demand coefficients because inversion in regression is not inversion of a non-stochastic equation. Also, if prices are super exogenous in an empirically constant money demand model and if the price process alters, the inverted model will be nonconstant, as demonstrated empirically in Hendry (1985) and Hendry and Ericsson (1991a, 1991b).

One appeal of rational expectations models is their aim to isolate "deep structural parameters", which are invariant to policy changes and to other changes in the agents' environment. Tests of parameter constancy are thus needed to substantiate that the isolated parameters are actually invariant to the changes that occurred in sample. Tests of parameter constancy also provide a mechanism for assessing the applicability of the Lucas (1976) critique. For example, Cuthbertson (1988) interprets a conditional empirical money demand model similar to (1) as being solved from an expectations-based framework, but Hendry (1988) refutes that interpretation by demonstrating the constancy of that model. Relatedly, the empirical presence of super exogeneity immunizes a conditional model from the Lucas critique; see Hendry (1995, Chapter 14). Even under super exogeneity, the decisions of policy makers can influence agents' behavior, but they do so through the outcomes of the policy makers' decisions, rather than through the policy makers' rules themselves.

The empirical evidence for the Lucas critique is surprisingly scant. Ericsson and Irons (1995) examine the nearly 600 articles published during 1976–1990 citing Lucas (1976) and find virtually no empirical evidence for it. Much of the supposed evidence is just evidence that particular models are empirically nonconstant—a *non sequitur*. In a similar bibliographic search for articles citing Engle, Hendry, and Richard (1983), Hendry (1988), and Engle and Hendry (1993), Ericsson and Irons (1995) find a notable and growing literature that substantiates super exogeneity empirically, with many of those cites being articles on money demand.

The estimated relation in a constant conditional model may be interpreted as a money demand function for at least three reasons. First, being a conditional model, its parameterization is unique. Second, from institutional knowledge, the supply equations for many countries are interest rate policy functions, which shifted as economic policy regimes changed. Consequently, combinations of the supply and demand equations would be nonconstant, yet many estimated demand functions are constant. In effect, the shifts in the supply function identify or over-identify the demand function, in the sense of the Cowles Commission. Third, the estimated coefficients may have sensible interpretations as demand responses but be problematic in a policy reaction function.

Granger (1969) is quite clear that Granger causality and economic causality are not the same. Granger causality is defined with respect to the parameters of a reduced form (typically, a vector autoregression), so it has no immediate implications for the structural parameters. Also, Granger causality is not invariant to the addition of new variables to the system, a phenomenon frequently noted in the empirical literature on causality between money and prices. Granger causality *is* an important issue in forecasting, as both Granger (1969) and Engle, Hendry, and Richard (1983) discuss, but it is neither necessary nor sufficient for policy analysis. Specifically, Granger causality has no implications for the direct controllability of inflation through affecting money growth: inflation might be super exogenous in a conditional money-demand equation, yet money growth might Granger-cause inflation.

10. Inferences for policy

Cointegration, exogeneity, and parameter constancy may have implications for policy analysis, although often in conjunction with each other rather than separately. Cointegration between money and other variables has no implications *per se* for predicting inflation or for monetary targeting. Rather, the role of excess money in the determination of inflation turns on the weak exogeneity of prices or the lack thereof.

Changes in policy-makers' rules or reaction functions may change the cointegration and/or exogeneity properties of the system. For instance, if a policy maker reacts to the money-demand cointegrating vector that appears in the economic agents' conditional model for money, weak exogeneity for that cointegrating vector is lost. Alternatively, if a cointegrating vector appears in only the reaction function and the policy maker then decides to ignore that disequilibrium information, that cointegrating vector disappears from the system.

While parameter constancy is a central issue in modeling money demand, the efficacy of monetary targeting does not follow from a stable money demand function, which can even imply that monetary targeting would be problematic. To illustrate, Baba, Hendry, and Starr (1992) obtain a money demand equation in which the volatility of the long-term interest rate risk-adjusts the long rate itself. According to their model, monetary targeting (as under the Fed's New Operating Procedure) increased the volatility of the long rate. That induced agents to move out of bonds into money, increasing the demand for money and counteracting attempts to control money growth. Establishing an empirically constant, well-specified money demand function may thus shed light on what sorts of monetary policy are advisable and what sorts are not.

11. Concluding remarks

This paper has reviewed several key issues in the empirical modeling of money demand, with a model for U.K. narrow money demand illustrating each issue. Interactions between issues can be subtle, as exemplified by the constancy of translated models when financial innovation has occurred. More generally, this paper provides a practical "check-list" for empirical studies of money demand, both those existing and those being undertaken.

References

Ahumada H (1992) A dynamic model of the demand for currency: Argentina 1977–1988. Journal of Policy Modeling 14, 3:335–361

Baba Y, Hendry DF, Starr RM (1992) The demand for M1 in the U.S.A., 1960–1988. Review of Economic Studies 59, 1:25–61

Banerjee A, Dolado JJ, Galbraith JW, Hendry DF (1993) Co-integration, error correction, and the econometric analysis of non-stationary data. Oxford University Press, Oxford

Banerjee A, Dolado JJ, Hendry DF, Smith GW (1986) Exploring equilibrium relationships in econometrics through static models: Some Monte Carlo evidence. Oxford Bulletin of Economics and Statistics 48, 3:253–277

Banerjee A, Hendry DF (eds.) (1992) Testing integration and cointegration. Special Issue, Oxford Bulletin of Economics and Statistics 54, 3: August

Bårdsen G (1992) Dynamic modeling of the demand for narrow money in Norway. Journal of Policy Modeling 14, 3:363–393

Barnett WA (1980) Economic monetary aggregates: An application of index number and aggregation theory. Journal of Econometrics 14, 1:11–48

Coghlan RT (1978) A transactions demand for money. Bank of England Quarterly Bulletin 18, 1:48–60

Cuthbertson K (1988) The demand for M1: A forward looking buffer stock model. Oxford Economic Papers 40, 1:110–131

Davidson JEH (1987) Disequilibrium money: Some further results with a monetary model of the UK. Chapter 6 in: Goodhart CAE, Currie D, Llewellyn DT (eds.) The operation and regulation of financial markets, Macmillan, London, pp. 125–149

Dickey DA, Fuller WA (1981) Likelihood ratio statistics for autoregressive time series with a unit root. Econometrica 49, 4:1057–1072

Doornik JA, Hendry DF (1996) PcGive professional 9.0 for Windows. International Thomson Business Press, London

Dufour J-M (1982) Recursive stability analysis of linear regression relationships: An exploratory methodology. Journal of Econometrics 19, 1:31–76

Engle RF, Granger CWJ (1987) Co-integration and error correction: Representation, estimation, and testing. Econometrica 55, 2:251–276

Engle RF, Granger CWJ (eds.) (1991) Long-run economic relationships: Readings in cointegration, Oxford University Press, Oxford

Engle RF, Hendry DF (1993) Testing super exogeneity and invariance in regression models. Journal of Econometrics 56, 1/2:119–139

Engle RF, Hendry DF, Richard J-F (1983) Exogeneity. Econometrica 51, 2:277–304

Ericsson NR (ed.) (1992a) Cointegration, exogeneity, and policy analysis. Special Issues, Journal of Policy Modeling 14, 3 and 4: June and August

Ericsson NR (1992b) Cointegration, exogeneity, and policy analysis: An overview. Journal of Policy Modeling 14, 3:251–280

Ericsson NR (1998) Empirical modeling of money demand. International Finance Discussion Paper, Board of Governors of the Federal Reserve System, Washington, D.C., available on the WorldWide Web at www.bog.frb.fed.us/pubs/ifdp/1998/

Ericsson NR, Campos J, Tran H-A (1990) PC-GIVE and David Hendry's econometric methodology. Revista de Econometria 10, 1:7–117

Ericsson NR, Hendry DF, Prestwich KM (1998) The demand for broad money in the United Kingdom, 1878–1993. Scandinavian Journal of Economics 100, 1:289–324

Ericsson NR, Hendry DF, Tran H-A (1994) Cointegration, seasonality, encompassing, and the demand for money in the United Kingdom. Chapter 7 in Hargreaves CP (ed.) Nonstationary time series analysis and cointegration, Oxford University Press, Oxford, pp. 179–224

Ericsson NR, Irons JS (1995) The Lucas critique in practice: Theory without measurement. Chapter 8 in Hoover KD (ed.) Macroeconometrics: Developments, tensions and prospects, Kluwer Academic Publishers, Boston, Massachusetts, pp. 263–312 (with discussion)

Ericsson NR, Sharma S (1998) Broad money demand and financial liberalization in Greece. Empirical Economics 23:417–436

Friedman M, Schwartz AJ (1982) Monetary trends in the United States and the United Kingdom: Their relation to income, prices, and interest rates, 1867–1975. University of Chicago Press, Chicago

Goldfeld SM (1973) The demand for money revisited. Brookings Papers on Ecomomic Activity 1973, 3:577–638 (with discussion)

Goldfeld SM (1976) The case of the missing money. Brookings Papers on Economic Activity 1976, 3:683–730 (with discussion)
Goldfeld SM, Sichel DE (1990) The demand for money. Chapter 8 in Friedman BM, Hahn FH (eds.) Handbook of monetary economics, Volume 1, North-Holland, Amsterdam, pp. 299–356
Goodhart CAE (1989) The conduct of monetary policy. Economic Journal 99, 396:293–346
Granger CWJ (1969) Investigating causal relations by econometric models and cross-spectral methods. Econometrica 37, 3:424–438
Hacche G (1974) The demand for money in the United Kingdom: Experience since 1971. Bank of England Quarterly Bulletin 14, 3:284–305
Hallman JJ, Porter RD, Small DH (1991) Is the price level tied to the M2 monetary aggregate in the long run? American Economic Review 81, 4:841–858
Hendry DF (1979) Predictive failure and econometric modelling in macroeconomics: The transactions demand for money. Chapter 9 in Ormerod P (ed.) Economic modelling: Current issues and problems in macroeconomic modelling in the UK and the US, Heinemann Education Books, London, pp. 217–242
Hendry DF (1985) Monetary economic myth and econometric reality. Oxford Review of Economic Policy 1, 1:72–84
Hendry DF (1988) The encompassing implications of feedback versus feedforward mechanisms in econometrics. Oxford Economic Papers 40, 1:132–149
Hendry DF (1992) An econometric analysis of TV advertising expenditure in the United Kingdom. Journal of Policy Modeling 14, 3:281–311
Hendry DF (1993) Econometrics: Alchemy or science? Blackwell Publishers, Oxford
Hendry DF (1995) Dynamic econometrics. Oxford University Press, Oxford
Hendry DF, Doornik JA (1994) Modelling linear dynamic econometric systems. Scottish Journal of Political Economy 41, 1:1–33
Hendry DF, Ericsson NR (1991a) An econometric analysis of U.K. money demand in 'Monetary trends in the United States and the United Kingdom' by Milton Friedman and Anna J Schwartz. American Economic Review 81, 1:8–38
Hendry DF, Ericsson NR (1991b) Modeling the demand for narrow money in the United Kingdom and the United States. European Economic Review 35, 4:833–881 (with discussion)
Hendry DF, Mizon GE (1978) Serial correlation as a convenient simplification, not a nuisance: A comment on a study of the demand for money by the Bank of England. Economic Journal 88, 351:549–563
Hendry DF, Mizon GE (1993) Evaluating dynamic econometric models by encompassing the VAR. Chapter 18 in Phillips PCB (ed.) Models, methods, and applications of econometrics: Essays in honor of A. R. Bergstrom, Blackwell Publishers, Cambridge, Massachusetts, pp. 272–300
Hendry DF, Pagan AR, Sargan JD (1984) Dynamic specification. Chapter 18 in Griliches Z, Intriligator MD (eds.) Handbook of econometrics, Volume 2, North-Holland, Amsterdam, pp. 1023–1100
Hendry DF, Richard J-F (1982) On the formulation of empirical models in dynamic econometrics. Journal of Econometrics 20, 1:3–33
Hoffman DL, Rasche RH (1996) Aggregate money demand functions: Empirical applications in cointegrated systems. Kluwer Academic Publishers, Boston, Massachusetts
Hylleberg S (ed.) (1992) Modelling seasonality. Oxford University Press, Oxford
Johansen S (1988) Statistical analysis of cointegration vectors. Journal of Economic Dynamics and Control 12, 2/3:231–254
Johansen S (1992) Testing weak exogeneity and the order of cointegration in UK money demand data. Journal of Policy Modeling 14, 3:313–334
Johansen S (1995) Likelihood-based inference in cointegrated vector autoregressive models. Oxford University Press, Oxford
Judd JP, Scadding JL (1982) The search for a stable money demand function: A survey of the post-1973 literature. Journal of Economic Literature 20, 3:993–1023
Juselius K, Hargreaves CP (1992) Long-run relations in Australian monetary data. Chapter 10 in Hargreaves CP (ed.) Macroeconomic modelling in the long run, Edward Elgar, Aldershot, Hants., England, 249–285
Kamin SB, Ericsson NR (1993) Dollarization in Argentina. International Finance Discussion

Paper No. 460, Board of Governors of the Federal Reserve System, Washington, D.C., November
Kremers JJM, Ericsson NR, Dolado JJ (1992) The power of cointegration tests. Oxford Bulletin of Economics and Statistics 54, 3:325–348
Laidler DEW (1993) The demand for money: Theories, evidence, and problems. Fourth Edition, HarperCollins College Publishers, New York
Lucas Jr RE (1976) Econometric policy evaluation: A critique. In Brunner K, Meltzer AH (eds.) The Phillips curve and labor markets, North-Holland, Amsterdam, Carnegie-Rechester Conference Series on Public Policy, Volume 1, Journal of Monetary Economics, Supplement, 19–46 (with discussion)
MacDonald R, Taylor MP (1992) A stable US money demand function, 1874–1975. Economics Letters 39, 2:191–198
Mizon GE, Richard J-F (1986) The encompassing principle and its application to testing non-nested hypotheses. Econometrica 54, 3:657–678
Moore GR, Porter RD, Small DH (1990) Modeling the disaggregated demands for M2 and M1: The U.S. experience in the 1980s. In Hooper P, Johnson KH, Kohn DL, Lindsey DE, Porter RD, Tryon R (eds.) Financial sectors in open economies: Empirical analysis and policy issues, Board of Governors of the Federal Reserve System, Washington, D.C., pp. 21–105 (with discussion)
Osterwald-Lenum M (1992) A note with quantiles of the asymptotic distribution of the maximum likelihood cointegration rank test statistics. Oxford Bulletin of Economics and Statistics 54, 3:461–472
Phillips AW (1954) Stabilisation policy in a closed economy. Economic Journal 64, 254:290–323
Phillips PCB (1991) Optimal inference in cointegrated systems. Econometrica 59, 2:283–306
Rose AK (1985) An alternative approach to the American demand for money. Journal of Money, Credit, and Banking 17, 4, Part 1:439–455
Wolters J, Teräsvirta T, Lütkepohl H (1998) Modelling the demand for M3 in the unified Germany. Review of Economics and Statistics, 80: 399–409

Stability of the demand for M1 and harmonized M3 in Finland

Antti Ripatti*

Bank of Finland, Box 160, FIN-00101 Helsinki, Finland (e-mail: antti.ripatti@bof.fi)

Abstract. We derive a theoretical model for the demand for money using the adjustment cost augmented money-in-the-utility-function approach. The steady-state – utility function – parameters of the model of narrow money (M1) estimated with cointegration techniques are stable over the foreign exchange rate regime shift; whereas in the model of harmonized M3 (M3H) they are *not* stable. The theoretical model fits the M1 data. The adjustment cost parameters of the M1 model describing the dynamics of the demand for money might indicate technological improvements in banking and payments during the sample period. These results suggest that from the Finnish point of view M1 would be a more appropriate intermediate target for monetary policy than harmonized M3.

Key words: Money-in-the-utility-function model, structural breaks, demand for money, narrow money, harmonized M3

JEL classification: C22, C52, E41

1. Introduction

One possible choice for the monetary policy strategy of the future European System of Central Banks (ESCB) is to use money as an intermediate target

---

* The views expressed are those of the author and not necessarily the views of the Bank of Finland. I thank Juha Tarkka, Jouko Vilmunen, Pekka Ilmakunnas, Erkki Koskela, Paolo Paruolo, Anders Rahbek, Pentti Saikkonen, Juha Seppälä, Matti Virén and the participants of ESEM96 meeting and 'Money Demand in Europe' conference (October 1997, Berlin) for useful comments and discussions and two anonymous referees and the editors for profound and constructive comments. The usual disclaimer applies. The data may be obtained from the internet, http://wotan.wiwi.hu-berlin.de/oekonometrie/engl/data.html

(see, eg EMI (1997)). This requires a stable demand for money relationship. The stability of different money measures could vary across European countries. The main candidates under investigation are narrow liquid money (M1) and harmonized broad money (M3H)[1]. From the perspective of the economic and monetary union (EMU), it is important to find a money measure whose demand is *stable* in all the participating countries and for which the national money demand parameters are as close as possible to average union values.

The aim of this study is to analyse the stability of the demand for these two money measures in Finland. We build on the recent European tradition of empirical research[2] on the demand for money by linking the time series econometrics of nonstationary variables to the theoretical model. We estimate and test the stability of the preference and techonology parameters of the theoretical model. In contrast to the pure time series approach, we have the possibility of relating possible structural changes to the preference or technology part of the model.

In section 2, we derive the demand for money from the money-in-the-utility-function approach. To estimate the parameters in the presence of integrated variables, we log-linearize the first-order condition. The first-order condition is then linear in the levels of the variables but nonlinear in the parameters. The steady-state part, ie the preference parameters, of the first-order condition can be estimated with cointegration techniques and the other, techonology parameters with the generalized method of moments estimator for given estimates of steady-state. The econometrics is overviewed in section 3 and the estimates[3] are reported and the stability evaluated in section 4. The final section concludes and discusses the policy implications of the empirical results.

2. Theoretical background: Money-in-the-utility-function model

Although Lucas (1988) prefers to base the "money demand model", or rather the relationship between money, consumption and interest rates, on the cash-in-advance constraint, we have chosen to include real balances directly to the utility function. Feenstra (1986) demonstrates the functional equivalence between using real balances as an argument in the utility function and liquidity cost models while Croushore (1993) demostrates the equivalence between shopping time and money-in-the-utility-function (MIUF) models. We are also interested in the dynamics of this relationship. The strong persistence of nominal balances – and the growth rate thereof – might implicate that changes in nominal balances involve transactions costs. One may argue for the existence of adjustment costs by the fact that the transformation of bonds

---

[1] The European Monetary Institute (EMI) is still working on harmonization rules for various money measures. The present measure of M3H will probably not be the final measure.

[2] Examples are Cuthbertson and Taylor (1990), Hendry and Ericsson (1991), Baba, Hendry and Starr (1992), Juselius (1996), Fase (1994), Wolters, Teräsvirta and Lütkepohl (1998).

[3] The cointegration estimation is done with CATS in RATS by Hansen and Juselius (1995) except for the small sample simulations, which are performed with Gauss utilizing the CIA code by Paolo Paruolo. The GMM estimation is done with Gauss, part of the code is based on the Hansen/Heaton/Ogaki GMM package by Ogaki (1993). I thank Paolo Paruolo and Masao Ogaki letting me use their code.

to money balances is not without costs. Furthermore, since most of the money measures contain bank accounts, there are certainly costs involved in adjusting money balances. Alternatively, adjustment costs can be viewed as an analytically convenient modelling device. To be able to study the dynamics of money demand we incorporate adjustment costs into our model. In the case of adjustment costs, the MIUF approach is also analytically simpler for our purposes.

There are not many empirical money demand studies in which the estimated parameters are based on an explicit theoretical model. The following studies are quite close to ours: Poterba and Rotemberg (1987) base their empirical investigation on the liquidity cost approch; Lucas (1988) and Sill (1995) rely on the 'cash-in-advance' constraint.

We start with an MIUF model in which the *household* optimizes the discounted sum of expected utility from consumption and money:

$$\max E_0 \sum_{t=0}^{\infty} \delta^t \left(u(C_t) + \mathfrak{Z}_t v\left(\frac{M_t}{P_t}\right)\right). \tag{1}$$

The household allocates its real income y and other earnings among consumption goods (C_t: real value of consumption), bonds (B_t: real value of bonds denominated in units of time t consumption) which pay a gross real return $1+r_t$ (from time t to time $t+1$), and real money balances M_t/P_t which pay a gross return P_t/P_{t+1}; for some definitions of money, money also pays a nominal return (own-yield of money) $O_t \equiv 1 + o_t$. Whenever it adjusts its money balances between period $t-1$ and period t, the household suffers losses (in real terms) $a(M_t, M_{t-1}, M_{t-2})/P_t$. $\mathfrak{Z}_t$ is a stochastic weight on the real money balances in the utility function. It allows shocks to the liquidity services of money, ie velocity or money demand shocks. The household's budget constraint is

$$C_t + B_t + \frac{M_t}{P_t} + \frac{a(M_t, M_{t-1}, M_{t-2})}{P_t} \leq y + \frac{O_{t-1}M_{t-1}}{P_t} + (1+r_{t-1})B_{t-1}. \tag{2}$$

The first-order conditions of the household's optimization problem (1) subject to (2) are

$$\delta E_t\{(1+r_t)u'(C_{t+1})\} = u'(C_t) \tag{3}$$

$$\begin{aligned} \mathfrak{Z}_t v'\left(\frac{M_t}{P_t}\right) &= u'(C_t)[1 + a'_{M_t}(M_t, M_{t-1}, M_{t-2})] \\ &\quad - \delta E_t\left\{\frac{u'(C_{t+1})P_t}{P_{t+1}}[O_t - a'_{M_t}(M_{t+1}, M_t, M_{t-1})]\right\} \\ &\quad + \delta^2 E_t\left[\frac{u'(C_{t+2})P_t}{P_{t+2}} a'_{M_t}(M_{t+2}, M_{t+1}, M_t)\right]. \end{aligned} \tag{4}$$

We assume that a nominal bond exists in our generic economy. The condition (3) for the nominal bond is given by

$$(1+i_t)\delta E_t\left\{\frac{1}{P_{t+1}}u'(C_{t+1})\right\}=\frac{1}{P_t}u'(C_t), \tag{5}$$

where $I_t \equiv 1 + i_t$ is a gross return of the nominal bond. If we combine the additional assumptions that

$$\operatorname{cov}_t\left(\frac{P_t}{P_{t+1}}\frac{u'(C_{t+1})}{u'(C_t)}, [O_t - a'_{M_t}(M_{t+1}, M_t, M_{t-1})]\right) = 0 \text{ and}$$

$$\operatorname{cov}_t\left(\frac{P_t}{P_{t+2}}\frac{u'(C_{t+2})}{u'(C_t)}, a'_{M_t}(M_{t+2}, M_{t+1}, M_t)\right) = 0$$

with the equation (5), the condition (4) for nominal money can be written as

$$\begin{aligned}\mathfrak{Z}_t\frac{v'\left(\frac{M_t}{P_t}\right)}{u'(C_t)} &= a'_{M_t}(M_t, M_{t-1}, M_{t-2}) + 1 - \frac{O_t}{I_t}\\ &\quad + \frac{1}{I_t}E_t a'_{M_t}(M_{t+1}, M_t, M_{t-1})\\ &\quad + E_t\frac{1}{I_t I_{t+1}}a'_{M_t}(M_{t+2}, M_{t+1}, M_t).\end{aligned} \tag{6}$$

The covariance conditions hold for example if consumers are risk neutral and inflation is deterministic or if the net own-yield of money, $O_t - a'_{M_t}(M_{t+1}, M_t, M_{t-1})$ and the expected marginal adjustment costs are deterministic. The left-hand side of equation (6) is the marginal rate of substitution of consumption for real balances. The right hand side is the rental cost, in terms of consumption good, of holding an extra unit of real balances for one period. Due to the adjustment costs the rental cost differs from the usual one $1 - O_t/I_t$.

Next we parametrize the utility function to the constant relative risk aversion (CRRA) form as follows

$$u(C_t) = \begin{cases}\frac{1}{1-\rho}C_t^{1-\rho} & \text{if } \rho \neq 1\\ \log C_t & \text{if } \rho = 1\end{cases}, \quad v\left(\frac{M_t}{P_t}\right) = \begin{cases}\frac{1}{1-\omega}\left(\frac{M_t}{P_t}\right)^{1-\omega} & \text{if } \omega \neq 1\\ \log\left(\frac{M_t}{P_t}\right) & \text{if } \omega = 1\end{cases}$$

and the adjustment cost function $a(\cdot)$ as follows:

$$a(M_t, M_{t-1}, M_{t-2}) = \frac{\kappa}{2}[(M_t - M_{t-1}) - \nu(M_{t-1} - M_{t-2})]^2, \tag{7}$$

where κ and ν are adjustment cost parameters. The adjustment cost function expresses the notion that it is differences in the growth rate of money that affect costs, not the growth rate itself, as is typical (Cuthbertson and Taylor 1987, Cuthbertson and Taylor 1990, among others). However, if the parameter ν is zero, the adjustment cost function is the typical one. The chosen functional form allows for persistence not only in the level of money balances but also in the growth rate of money. Hence it tracks autocorrelation in the money growth. Tinsley (1993) argues that use of the simple quadratic form of adjustment costs in levels is the reason why the cross-equation restrictions implied by the rational expectations hypothesis are usually rejected in empirical excercises. He suggests that one should use a temporally richer specification of the adjustment cost function. A drawback of our parameterization is that there might exist offsetting changes in money balances, which would imply zero adjustment costs[4]. This is also true in the case of positive ν with the adjustment cost specification which is quadratic in changes. However, our formulation is slightly more general but contains the above-mentioned drawback.

It is standard practice to estimate such first-order conditions with generalized method of moments (GMM) estimators. However, what is sometimes overlooked – typically in the studies of the early 1980s – is the problem of non-stationarity in mean. Stationarity of stochastic processes is the key assumption of GMM. If that is rejected, as is often the case for macroeconomic time series, one should use other estimators, which unfortunately exist for linear models only. Thus, it is necessary to linearize the first-order conditions. We use the first-order Taylor approximation around the steady-state. In the steady-state, the stochastic processes should have finite variance, which is not the case if any of the variables in the model are $I(1)$. It is, however, possible that a linear combination of $I(1)$ variables is stationary. If so, the variables are cointegrated. We think that the linearized version of the steady-state solution of the model should represent the stationary linear combination of the variables. This would make it possible to linearize this model also.

In order to log-linearize equation (6), we first seek the stationary equilibrium for equation (6) and then use the first-order Taylor approximation around the stationary equilibrium. For the stationary equilibrium, the adjustment costs are zero and $C_t = C$, $I_t = I$, $M_t = M$, $O_t = O$, $P_t = P$, $\mathfrak{Z}_t = \mathfrak{Z}$ $(\forall t \geq 0)$. We denote logarithmic variables in the lower case (eg $\log C \equiv c$), $\zeta_t = \log \mathfrak{Z}_t$ and $I \equiv 1 + i$ and $O \equiv 1 + o$. In the stationary equilibrium, equation (6) reduces to

$$1 - \frac{O}{I} = \mathfrak{Z} C^{\rho} \left(\frac{M}{P} \right)^{-\omega}, \tag{8}$$

which is like the usual, static demand for money function. From the first-order Taylor approximation around the (log of) stationary equilibrium, we obtain the following log-linear Euler equation:

$$\begin{aligned} \Delta m_t = [I + \nu(1+\nu)]^{-1} \Bigg\{ & \frac{(i-o)\omega}{\kappa M} \left(m - p - \frac{\rho}{\omega} c \right) + \frac{O}{\kappa M} (i - o) \\ & - I^{-1} \nu E_t \Delta m_{t+2} + [1 + \nu(1 + I^{-1})] E_t \Delta m_{t+1} + I \nu \Delta m_{t-1} \\ & - \frac{(i-o)\omega}{\kappa M} \left(m_t - p_t - \frac{\rho}{\omega} c_t \right) - \frac{O}{\kappa M} (i_t - o_t) + (1 - O/I)(\zeta_t - \zeta) \Bigg\}, \end{aligned} \tag{9}$$

[4] This was pointed out by a referee.

where the last term, $(1 - O/I)(\zeta_t - \zeta)$, is the deviation of the log-linearized velocity shock from its steady state value. In the case of integrated (of order one) variables, the left hand side of equation (9) is stationary. In order to have a stationary right hand side, the levels of the variables in the right hand side, $z_t = [m_t, p_t, c_t, i_t, o_t]'$, should be cointegrated. This particular parameterization (9) suggests two cointegration vectors. The first is the net opportunity cost of money[5], $i_t - o_t$, and the second is the 'adjusted' velocity, $m_t - p_t - (\rho/\omega)c_t$. However, other parameterizations with different numbers of cointegration vectors are also possible. When we have five integrated (of order one) variables, there can be at most four cointegrating vectors. Consequently, one should test for the cointegration rank and then use the restrictions implied by the theoretical model to identify the cointegration vectors.

One can, for example, combine the two levels terms in the right hand side of (9). Such parameterization corresponds to the single cointegrating vector case. If we also assume that the own-yield is zero, ie $o = 0$ or equivalently $O = 1$, we obtain the following version of equation (9):

$$\Delta m_t = [I + v(1+v)]^{-1}\left\{\frac{i\omega}{\kappa M}\left(m - p - \frac{\rho}{\omega}c + \frac{1}{i\omega}i\right) - I^{-1}vE_t\Delta m_{t+2}\right.$$
$$+ [1 + v(1 + I^{-1})]E_t\Delta m_{t+1} + Iv\Delta m_{t-1}$$
$$\left. - \frac{i\omega}{\kappa M}\left(m_t - p_t - \frac{\rho}{\omega}c_t + \frac{1}{i\omega}i_t\right) + (1 - I^{-1})(\zeta_t - \zeta)\right\}. \tag{10}$$

This is the form we will use in the analysis of M1 data.

3. Econometric setup

The econometric methods are briefly described in the following sections. The principal tools used in the following statistical analysis of the demand for money are the Euler equation estimation by GMM and cointegration analysis in the ML framework of Johansen (1991). Under the assumption of non-stationary variables, the theoretical model yields restrictions on the co-integration vectors. Given the estimated cointegration vectors, the estimation of the rest of the parameters of the Euler equation (9) relies on the GMM approach of Hansen (1982).

To illustrate how the estimation can be performed in two steps, we write equation (9) in the following form

$$\Delta m_t = [I + v(1+v)]^{-1}\left\{m^\star - I^{-1}vE_t\Delta m_{t+2} + [1 + v(1 + I^{-1})]E_t\Delta m_{t+1}\right.$$
$$\left. + Iv\Delta m_{t-1} - \gamma\beta' z_t + (1 - O/I)\zeta_t\right\} \tag{11}$$

[5] If the opportunity cost and own-yield of money are cointegrated then bank's interest rate margin is stationary.

where $m^\star \equiv ((i-o)\omega/\kappa M)(m-p-(\rho/\omega)c)+(O/\kappa M)(i-o)-(1-O/I)\zeta$, $\gamma' \equiv [(O/\kappa M) \quad (\omega(i-o)/\kappa M)]$ and

$$\beta = \begin{bmatrix} 0 & -1 \\ 0 & 1 \\ 0 & \frac{\rho}{\omega} \\ 1 & 0 \\ -1 & 0 \end{bmatrix} \quad \text{and} \quad z_t = \begin{bmatrix} m_t \\ p_t \\ c_t \\ i_t \\ o_t \end{bmatrix}.$$

If the variables in z_t are integrated order one, $I(1)$, the model can be interpreted as a sort of forward-looking error correction model, where β represents the cointegration vectors and the rest of the parameters come from the short-run dynamics. Due to the non-stationarity one cannot estimate the parameters of the system by GMM, which assumes stationarity of the stochastic processes. According to Dolado, Galbraith and Banerjee (1991), if the forcing variables are integrated of order d ($\sim I(d)$) the endogenous variable m_t is also integrated of the same order. In the case of quadratic adjustment costs, they propose a two-step estimation procedure:

1. The parameters in β can be estimated using the ML of Johansen (1991), which will be described in the following section. Since the parameters of the cointegration vectors β are superconsistent one can treat the estimates of $\hat{\beta}$ as fixed in the second stage[6].
2. In the second step all the variables of the model are stationary. In this case, one can estimate the rest of the parameters by GMM.

The next section summarizes ML estimation of the cointegration vectors and the following section discusses the GMM estimation of the model with special emphasis on the stability of the parameters.

3.1 Johansen's VAR model

We present the FIML estimation within the VAR of the cointegration relations and methods for testing the long-run structural hypothesis. The following presentation is based on Johansen (1988, 1991, 1995) and Johansen and Juselius (1990). The p-dimensional VAR process in levels, $A(L)z_t = \mu + \Psi D_t + \varepsilon_t$ ($\varepsilon_t \sim \text{NID}(0, \Sigma)$), can be written in the difference form

$$\Delta z_t = \Pi z_{t-1} + \Gamma_1 \Delta z_{t-1} + \cdots + \Gamma_{k-1} \Delta z_{t-k+1} + \mu + \Psi D_t + \varepsilon_t, \qquad t = 1, \ldots, T, \quad (12)$$

[6] Superconsistency means that the estimated parameters of the cointegration vectors converge much faster to the true values than do the parameters of, for example, ordinary least squares regression of stationary variables. Due to this fact, one is able to treat the parameters of the cointegration vectors as (asymptotically) fixed in the subsequent analysis of stationary variables.

where $\Pi = -I_1 + \sum_{i=1}^{k} A_i$, $\Gamma_i = -(\sum_{j=i+1}^{k-1} A_j)$, μ is constant and D_t is the vector of deterministic variables. The Π matrix has a reduced rank in the case of cointegration (rank(Π) $< p$). Any reduced rank matrix can be presented as a product of two full-rank matrices $\Pi = \alpha\beta'$.

Johansen (1988) and Johansen (1991) show that the ML estimator of the space spanned by β is the space spanned by r canonical variates reflecting the r largest squared canonical correlations between residuals of the least squares regressions of contemporaneous differences on lagged differences and levels on lagged differences. It is important to note that one can estimate only the space spanned by β, not the individual cointegration vectors.

Johansen (1988) derives a likelihood ratio test for testing the number of cointegration vectors, ie the rank of Π. Osterwald-Lenum (1992) has simulated the critical values of these test statistics for $p = 12$. It has been shown in some simulation studies (Eitrheim 1991, Toda 1995, Haug 1996), that using the asymptotical tables might be misleading in small samples. For this study, we have simulated the model, under the null, in order to obtain empirical critical values for the trace tests.

3.2 GMM estimation of the Euler equation and tests of parameter stability

Since the parameters $\hat{\beta}$, estimated by cointegration methods, are super-consistent, one can estimate the rest of the model parameters $\Theta = \{m^*, I, O, \nu, \omega, \kappa M\}$ using the GMM of Hansen (1982) taking $\hat{\beta}$ as given. We define the 5-dimensional vector of variables $w_t = [\Delta m_{t+2}, \Delta m_{t+1}, \Delta m_t, \Delta m_{t-1}, \hat{\beta}' z_t]'$. The total number of parameters is $j \equiv \dim(\Theta)$.

Given the instrument[7] set $\mathbf{x}_t$ (l-dimensional vector; see table 3) we define the orthogonality conditions – implied by the Euler equation (9) – as

$$h(\Theta, w_t) = \{-[I + \nu(1+\nu)]\Delta m_t + m^\star - I^{-1}\nu\Delta m_{t+2} + [1 + \nu(1 + I^{-1})]\Delta m_{t+1} + I\nu\Delta m_{t-1} - \gamma\hat{\beta}' z_t\}\mathbf{x}_t, \tag{13}$$

where $h(\Theta, w_t)$ is a $l \times 1$ vector-valued function. Note that we estimate the constant term, $m^\star$, as a separate, unrestricted parameter. This takes into account the growth component of the variables, which is only implicitly accounted for in the linearization of the model. Let Θ^* denote the true value of Θ such that $E(h(\Theta^*, w_t)) = 0$, $\mathcal{W}_T \equiv [w_1, \ldots, w_T]$ and $g(\Theta, \mathcal{W}_T) \equiv 1/T \sum_{t=1}^{T} h(\Theta, w_t)$. The idea behind GMM is to choose Θ so as to make the sample moment $g(\Theta, \mathcal{W}_T)$ as close as possible to the population moments. Thus, the GMM estimate $\hat{\Theta}$ is the value of Θ that minimizes

$$Q(\Theta, \mathcal{W}_T) = [g(\Theta, \mathcal{W}_T)]' \hat{S}_T^{-1} [g(\Theta, \mathcal{W}_T)]. \tag{14}$$

Due to the two period forecast and velocity shock, the error term[8] $I^{-1}\nu\varepsilon_{t+2} - [1 + \nu(1 + I^{-1})]\varepsilon_{t+1} + (1 - I^{-1})\zeta_t$ is an MA(2) process. This is the

[7] Instruments should be chosen so as to correlate as much as possible with Δm_{t+2} and Δm_{t+1} but not with the forecast error. The lagged error correction terms, for example, typically contain much information on the endogenous variables involved.

[8] We denote $\Delta m_{t+j} = E_t \Delta m_{t+j} + \varepsilon_{t+j}$.

fact that has to be taken into account in the estimation of the asymptotic covariance matrix S. We use the VARHAC estimator by den Haan and Levin (1996) and quadratic spectral kernel estimator by Newey and West (1994).

Due to the financial deregulation, we test for the stability[9] of the parameters. The financial deregulation culminated at the end of 1986 when the major part of the restrictions on the deposit and lending rates were abolished. At the beginning of 1987 the Bank of Finland started its open market operations. We test for a structural change at that time.

The total full sample size is T. Let T_0 denote the possible break point, $\mathscr{W}_{T_0} \equiv [w_1, \ldots, w_{T_0}]$, $\mathscr{W}_{T-T_0} \equiv [w_{T_0+1}, \ldots, w_T]$, $g(\Theta_0, \mathscr{W}_{T_0}) \equiv 1/T_0 \sum_{t=1}^{T_0} h(\Theta_0, w_t)$, $g(\Theta_1, \mathscr{W}_{T-T_0}) \equiv 1/(T - T_0) \sum_{t=T_0+1}^{T} h(\Theta_1, w_t)$ and Θ_0 and Θ_1 the first and second subsample parameters. One can consider, for example, January 1987 ($= T_0$) as a possible break point. According to Hamilton (1994), one approach is to use the first subsample to estimate $\hat{\Theta}_0$ by minimizing

$$Q(\Theta_0, \mathscr{W}_{T_0}) = [g(\Theta_0, \mathscr{W}_{T_0})]' \hat{S}_0^{-1} [g(\Theta_0, \mathscr{W}_{T_0})],$$

where $\hat{S}_0$ is the (first subsample) estimate of the covariance matrix. Hansen (1982) shows that

$$\sqrt{T_0}(\hat{\Theta}_0 - \Theta_0^*) \xrightarrow{d} N(0, V_0).$$

$\hat{V}_0$ can be estimated from

$$\hat{V}_0 = (\hat{D}_0 \hat{S}_0^{-1} \hat{D}_0')^{-1}, \quad \text{where } \hat{D}_0 \equiv \frac{\partial g(\hat{\Theta}_0, \mathscr{W}_{T_0})}{\partial \Theta_0'}.$$

One also computes the analogous measures for the second subsample $T - T_0$. We denote $\pi \equiv T_0/(T - T_0)$. Andrews and Fair (1988) suggest the test statistic

$$\text{AF} = T(\hat{\Theta}_0 - \hat{\Theta}_1)' \{\pi^{-1} \hat{V}_0 + (1 - \pi)^{-1} \hat{V}_1\}^{-1} (\hat{\Theta}_0 - \hat{\Theta}_1) \tag{15}$$

to test the null hypothesis $\Theta_0 = \Theta_1$. The test statistic AF $\xrightarrow{d} \chi^2(j)$. If one does not know the date of the possible structural break, one can repeat the test for different choices of T_0 and choose the largest value of the test statistic. Andrews (1993) derives the asymptotic distribution of such a test. The test setup entails the limitation that each of the subsample sizes should approach infinity. This is also a drawback of the Ghysels and Hall (1990b) setup.

Ghysels and Hall (1990b) propose a test whereby they estimate the model using the first subsample and then examine whether the orthogonality conditions of the model are satisfied over the second subsample using the parameter estimates obtained from the first subsample. The null and alternative hypotheses for the test are

---

[9] Hamilton (1994) and Oliner, Rudebusch and Sichel (1996) survey structural stability tests using the GMM approach. See also Hoffman and Pagan (1989), Ghysels and Hall (1990a) and Dufour, Ghysels and Hall (1994).

$$H_0 : E(h(\Theta_0, w_t)) = 0,\ t = 1, \ldots, T_0 \quad \text{and}$$

$$E(h(\Theta_0, w_t)) = 0,\ t = T_0 + 1, \ldots, T$$

$$H_1 : E(h(\Theta_0, w_t)) = 0,\ t = 1, \ldots, T_0 \quad \text{and}$$

$$E(h(\Theta_0, w_t)) \neq 0,\ t = T_0 + 1, \ldots, T.$$

The test statistic is defined as

$$\text{GH} = (T - T_0)[g(\hat{\Theta}_0, \mathscr{W}_{T-T_0})]' \hat{V}_1^{-1} [g(\hat{\Theta}_0, \mathscr{W}_{T-T_0})],$$

where

$$\hat{V}_1 = \hat{S}_1 + (\pi)^{-1} \tilde{D}_1 (\hat{D}_0' \hat{S}_0^{-1} \hat{D}_0)^{-1} \tilde{D}_1'$$

$$\hat{D}_0 = \frac{\partial g(\hat{\Theta}_0, \mathscr{W}_{T_0})}{\partial \Theta'} \quad \tilde{D}_1 = \frac{\partial g(\hat{\Theta}_0, \mathscr{W}_{T-T_0})}{\partial \Theta'}.$$

The test statistic GH $\xrightarrow{d} \chi^2(l)$. Oliner et al. (1996) study different choices of weighting matrix V_1. Matrices S_i $(i = 0, 1)$ can be consistently estimated for each subsample using covariance matrix estimators by, eg, Newey and West (1994) or den Haan and Levin (1996). In addition to the subsample estimates, one candidate is the full sample estimate.

4. Estimation results

In the following two subsections, we present the results for estimation of the parameters of the theoretical model. First we estimate the steady-state part of the theoretical model. Parameters in the steady-state part of the model reflect the parameters of the utility function[10]. That is, we test for cointegration and estimate the restricted[11] cointegration space β implied by the theoretical model. In order to evaluate the stability of the utility function parameters, we test recursively whether the estimated, restricted full-sample cointegration space lies within the space estimated recursively for the period 1985–1995.

We proceed with the given cointegration vectors (estimated from the full sample) and estimate the rest of the parameters of the Euler equation (9). The rest of the parameters in the Euler equation are related to the adjustment cost function. We also test for the stability of these parameters.

4.1 Data

The data is Finnish monthly data[12] covering January 1980–December 1995. Narrow money (M1) contains cash held by the public and transactions ac-

[10] The scale elasticity is ρ/ω. In the M1 model, the opportunity cost semi-elasticity is $1/(\omega i)$.
[11] We test for the restrictions implied by the theoretical model.
[12] The data is from the Bank of Finland database. The M3H data is unofficial estimate.

counts at the banks. Harmonized broad money (M3H) contains M1 plus all other accounts (including foreign currency) at the banks and money market deposits and repos at the banks. Prices are measured by consumer price index (1990 = 100). Consumption is replaced by the monthly GDP volume indicator, which is a combined index of various indicators such as industrial production, retail sales, consumption of electricity, etc. The opportunity cost of money is the covered 1-month Eurodollar rate for the markka for the pre-1987 period and 1-month HELIBOR (money market rate) since that.

We do not have a measure for the own-yield of M1. Some part of it (cash and checkable accounts) has zero yield. The yield for the rest is impossible to evaluate since the interest is usually paid on the minimum balance for the month and we do not have data on intramonth deposits. We believe that zero (or constant) own yield is a fairly good approximation for the period at hand. In the theoretical model, this means that we have the restriction $O = 1$ ($o = 0$). The own-yield of M3H is a weighted average of the after-tax deposit rates. We use current weights.

The drawback of using monthly data is that they contain many exogenous shocks which are usually smoothed out in the annual or quarterly data. We try to model the most important ones: the seasonal pattern of the GDP volume indicator is changed by the construction cycle (`JULY`). The same variable was influenced by the harbour workers strike in June 1991 (`TRAF`). Money balances were influenced by the following exogenous factors. The timing of tax rebates was changed in 1991–1995 (`REBATE`). Devaluation speculations (`DSPEC`) are visible in the money market rate. That variable is also a measurement of currency substitution. Capital gains taxation was changed in 1988/89 (`CGAINT`). Bank office workers went on strike in February 1990 (`BSTRIKE1` and `BSTRIKE2`). The witholding tax was introduced in January 1991 (`WTAX`). The dummies are impulse dummies, ie they take the value unity in the indicated period and zero otherwise. They are used in the difference parts of the error correction models.

The set of deterministic dummy variables differs between the M1 and M3H models (see table 3). The M3H system is augmented with the dummy `MFREST`, which is unity for the pre-1987 period, during which the Ministry of Finance restricted banks' certificates of deposit (CD) issues and the Bank of Finland did not use CDs in its open market operations, and zero otherwise. That dummy enters into the cointegration space and is restricted to enter only into the cointegration relations between own-yield and opportunity cost of money.

4.2 *Estimates of steady-state parameters*

We impose the price homogeneity restriction[13] on the model by analyzing real money in the steady-state. The adjustment cost function in the theoretical model is parametrized to allow lag length three; $k = 3$ in equation (12). This lag length is long enough to yield zero residual autocorrelations. The vector error correction model is augmented with the centred seasonal dummies and with the set of intervention dummies. These are listed in table 3.

[13] Note, however, that we introduce this price homogeneity also into the short-run dynamics. Ripatti (1994) cannot reject long-run price homogeneity.

Table 1. Trace tests of cointegration rank

M1[a]					M3H[b]			
λ	Trace test	95% fractile[c]	95% asymptotic fractile[d]	H_0	λ	Trace test	95% fractile	95% asymptotic fractile
0.186	42.16	31.22	29.38	$r = 0$	0.173	53.81	51.55	47.21
0.013	3.19	15.51	15.34	$r \leq 1$	0.072	17.93	31.63	29.38
0.003	0.64	4.41	3.84	$r \leq 2$	0.016	3.73	17.53	15.34
				$r \leq 3$	0.004	0.73	5.14	3.84

[a] Since we have no measure of the ow-yield of money, the dimension of the M1 model is three instead of four.
[b] The dummy MFREST has been included in the deterministic part of the M3H model in the estimation and the simulation of the test statistic.
[c] See footnote 14.
[d] See footnote 15.

Table 2. Residual diagnostics

M1[a]					M3H			
ARCH(3)	Autoc.	Norm.	R^2	Equation	ARCH(3)	Autoc.	Norm.	R^2
0.03	0.17	3.12	0.77	$\Delta(m-p)_t$	2.16	0.13	2.09	0.34
9.81	0.09	0.04	0.95	Δc_t	10.60	0.04	6.45	0.95
1.11	0.21	47.54	0.36	Δi_t	6.88	0.90	80.27	0.56
				Δo_t	0.59	0.59	87.45	0.31

[a] The test statistics ARCH(3) for no ARCH of the third degree is $\chi^2(3)$ distributed; Autoc. is the p-value of the LM test for up to 12th order autocorrelation of residuals; Jarque-Bera normality (as null) test statistic is $\chi^2(2)$ distributed.

Table 1 reports the trace tests for cointegration rank. According to the trace test and reported 95 per cent *empirical*[14] fractiles, there exists one cointegration vector in the M1 system, as is predicted by the theory. The empirical significance level for the null of no cointegration is less than 0.01.

The determination of the cointegration rank of the M3H system is more problematic. The difference between empirical and asymptotic critical values is quite small[15]. Comparison of the trace tests with the empirical critical values indicates that the cointegration rank is one. If we include the dummy variable MFREST in the cointegration space, the trace test value for $r = 0$ is 57.91 while the *asymptotic* 95 per cent fractile is 55.67. For the null hypothesis $r \leq 1$ the trace test value is 21.22 and the the *asymptotic* 95 per cent fractile is 35.71 (the significance level is approximately 0.5). This leads to the conclusion that the cointegration rank is one.

The normality of residuals is violated in the interest rate equations (table 2). This is due to the excess kurtosis. The autocorrelation figures show only slight

[14] The empirical fractiles of the trace test are based on 10 000 replications under the null.
[15] The asymptotical critical values are obtained from Johansen (1995), table 15.3. One should note that the asymptotic critical values are not the correct ones since we have a set of noncentred dummies in the model. However, they are the ones that are given by econometric software packages such as PC-FIML or CATS in RATS.

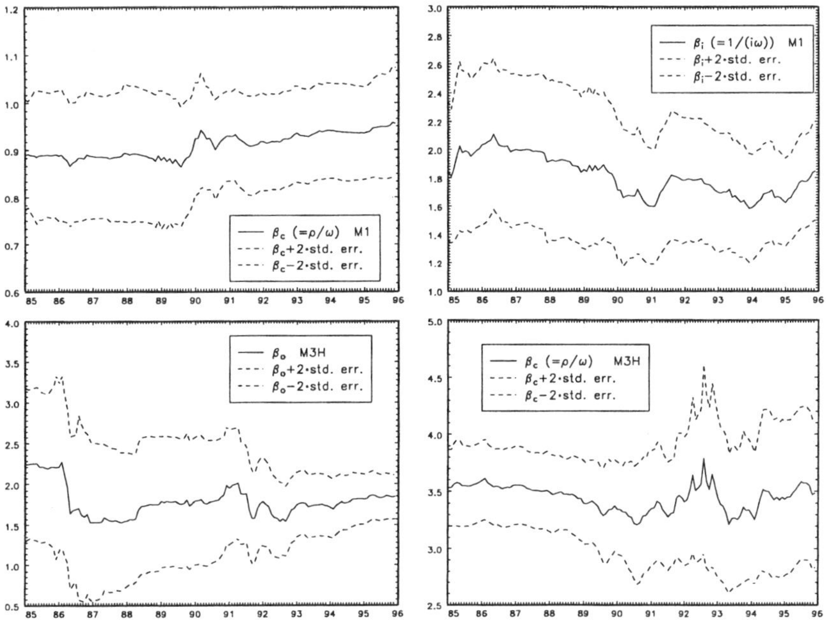

Fig. 1. Recursive estimates of the scale elasticity (β_c) and the opportunity cost semi-elasticity (β_i) of M1 and the own-yield semi-elasticity (β_o) and the scale elasticity (β_c) of M3H

residual autocorrelation in the 12th lag in the equation for Δc_t in the M3H system.

Next we test for the restrictions on the β-space implied by the Euler equations (9) and (10). For the M1 model, there are no restrictions in the cointegration space. However, we test for the unit scale elasticity since the free estimate is very close to one (0.95). The restriction is not rejected (p-value $= 0.49$). The restricted cointegration vector is

$$\hat{\beta}'_{M1} z_t = [(m-p)_t - c_t + 1.807 i_t]. \tag{16}$$

The results contradict the results of Ripatti (1994), where the estimated scale elasticity was significantly below one and the interest rate semi-elasticity only sightly above one. The unit scale elasticity implies that the risk aversion parameters in the utility function are equal, ie $\hat{\rho} = \hat{\omega}$. The recursive estimates of the scale elasticity and opportunity cost semi-elasticity are in figure 1. The graphs indicate that the parameters have been fairly stable during the past ten years. However, the scale elasticity has slightly increased during the 1990s which explains the differences in Ripatti (1994) and this study. The left panel of figure 2 clearly supports the conclusion that the parameter estimates of the steady-state are stable[16].

[16] Hansen and Juselius (1995) provides an attractive way to test the stability of the parameters of the cointegration vector. We estimate the cointegration space using the full sample and test recursively whether the estimated sub-sample cointegration space (β_τ, $\tau = T_f + 1, \ldots, T$, where T_f is the starting point of recursive testing) contains the full-sample cointegration space $\hat{\beta}_{T_0}$, ie $\mathscr{H}_{\beta_\tau} : \hat{\beta}_{T_0} \in \mathrm{sp}(\beta_\tau)$, $\tau = T_f, \ldots, T$.

In the estimation of the M3H model with no restrictions, the first cointegration vector might be interpreted as the spread between the opportunity cost and the own-yield of money and the second cointegration vector (possibly non-stationary) as the velocity equation with scale elasticity greater than unity. The dummy variable MFREST is restricted to the first cointegration vector. The coefficients of real money and GDP do not differ significantly from zero in the first cointegration vector. According to the theoretical model, one should include the second cointegration vector in the analysis. The trace test does not indicate stationarity, even though it is assumed so in the following procedures.

I restrict the cointegration space in the following way (as implied by the theoretical model):

$$\hat{\beta}'_{\mathrm{M3H}} z_t = \begin{bmatrix} 0 & +0 & +i_t & -o_t & -0.029\,\mathtt{MFREST} \\ (m-p)_t & -3.26c_t & +0 & +0 & +0 \end{bmatrix},$$

where the coefficients of MFREST in the first vector and c_t in the second vector are estimated freely. These restrictions are not supported by the data (p-value < 0.001). If we estimate the own-yield semi-elasticity freely (1.8 times the opportunity cost semi-elasticity[17]), the restrictions are not rejected (p-value $= 0.2$). If we assume (as the trace test indicates) that there is only one cointegration vector in the M3H model, the test results concerning the first cointegration vector are almost identical. The recursive test statistic for the hypothesis that the estimated full sample cointegration space lies within the cointegration space for the sub-samples ending in 1985 onwards (figure 2) indicates serious instabilities during the 1990s of the recursive period.

The coefficient of the dummy MFREST indicates that the banks' interest rate marginal was on the average three percentage points higher during the period of regulation of CD issues, before 1987. The deregulation significantly reduced the banks' margin by boosting the average cost of liabilities. The scale elasticity in the second cointegration vector is much too high to be reliable. It implies that the risk aversion measure of real money is three times as large as for consumption.

The recursive estimates of the M3H model further illustrate the problem. The own-yield elasticity varies between 1.5 and 2.3 during the recursive period (lower left panel of figure 1); the scale elasticity varies between 3.2 and 3.9 and the confidence interval actually *widens* during the recursive period.

Finally, we augment the M3H model with the variable that is the logarithmic difference between M3H and M1. If the coefficient of the variable in such a modification of the M3H model is unity, the model is a genuine M1 model and the aggregation from M1 to M3H is not valid. The estimated cointegration space with the own-yield of money restricted to zero is as follows (standard errors in parentheses below the coefficients):

---

[17] We use the after-tax own-yield of money and the ordinary opportunity cost of money. The results do not differ when using the after-tax opportunity cost of money – the coefficient is 1.6. We have chosen to use the ordinary opportunity cost of money instead of the after-tax opportunity cost since firms have the possibility of subtracting interest expenditures from taxes and they can also use foreign subsidiaries in order to avoid paying taxes on interest income.

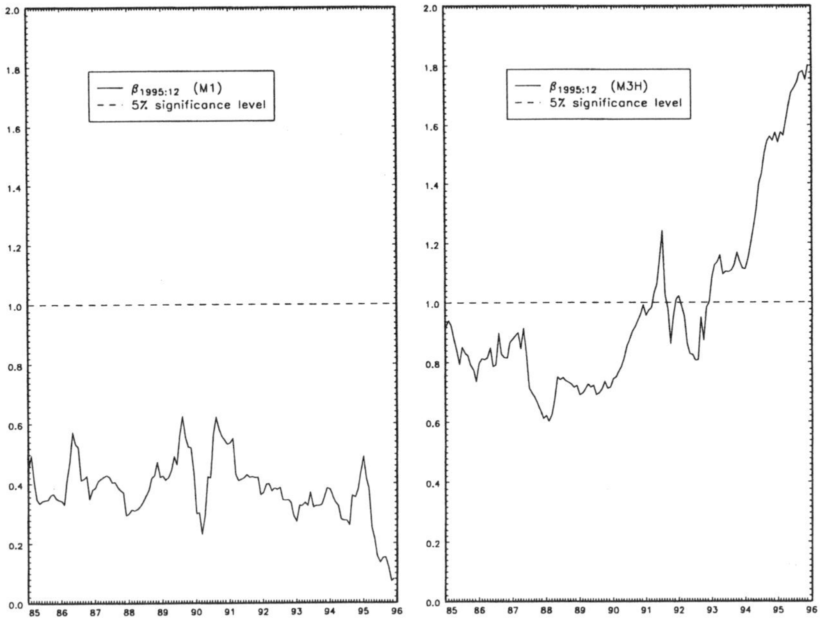

The 5% significance level of a single test scaled to unity. The coefficients of the pre-determined variables (dummies etc) and short-run dynamics are the full sample estimates computed before the recursive test. Note that the null hypothesis in M1 case also contains unit scale elasticity.

Fig. 2. Recursive tests for restricted $\hat{\beta}_{1995:12} \in \text{sp}(\hat{\beta}_\tau)$, $\tau = 1985:1, \ldots, 1995:12$

$$\hat{\beta}'[z_t' \quad (m3h_t - m1_t)]'$$

$$= \begin{bmatrix} (m3h-p)_t & -0.94c_t & +1.75i_t & +0 & -0.98(m3h_t - m1_t) \\ & (0.13) & (0.19) & & (0.05) \end{bmatrix}.$$

It is clear that the estimated model is the same as the M1 model. Evidently, this suggests that the theoretical model which is consistent with the M1 model is not consistent with the M3H model[18].

We summarize this section by the fact that the steady-state parameters, ie the utility function parameters of the M1 model, are stable. We can continue on to the estimation of the adjustment cost parameters of the M1 model, ie the

[18] We have tried several other specifications of the M3H system. The deterministic trend in the cointegration space – restricted to the second cointegration vector – yields plausible parameters estimates for fixed exchange rate period (1980–1992). According to the test results, the velocity seems to be trend stationary. However, the forecasting performance of such a model is very unpleasant. The trend does not fit to the cointegration space at all during the floating exchange rate regime. We have also augmented the original variable set with some other variables which might capture the financial deregulation of 1980's and the broken trend in the decline of the velocity in 1990's. An example of this kind of variable is the stock of CDs issued by the banks and the Bank of Finland. The parameter estimates of such models are not plausible and those kinds of variables are not consistent with the theoretical model.

Table 3. Deterministic variables and instruments

	M1	M3H
Δm_t and cointegration relations adjusted[a] for	CGAINT, BSTRIKE1, BSTRIKE2, TRAF, DSPEC, REBATE, JULY, WTAX and 11 centred seasonals	CGAINT, BSTRIKE1, BSTRIKE2, TRAF, DSPEC, REBATE, JULY and 11 centred seasonals
Instruments	Constant, Δm_{t-j}, Δp_{t-j}, Δc_{t-j}, Δi_{t-j} $(j = 2, 3)$ and $(m_{t-j} - p_{t-j} - \hat{\beta}_1 c_{t-j} + \hat{\beta}_2 i_{t-j})$ $(j = 1, 2, 3)$	No GMM estimation.

[a] These are the variables that are used in the separate regressions in order to condition on the seasonality and various tax and strike effects.

dynamics of the M1 system. The parameters of the M3H model are neither stable nor of plausible size.

4.3 Estimates of adjustment cost parameters

We proceed with the GMM estimation of the first-order condition (10). The M3H model does not fulfil the key assumptions of GMM: stationarity is violated by the error correction terms. Consequently, there is no point in estimating the Euler equation of the M3H.

We do not estimate the deterministic variables, such as seasonal, strike and other dummies, with the GMM; that would be computationally burdensome and would increase the number of instruments needed. However, before the GMM estimation we run extra OLS regressions in which we condition on the variables listed in table 3. The instrument sets used in the GMM estimation are also listed in table 3. The test of overidentification restrictions (J-test) yields very low p-values when the instrument set is augmented with the zero and one-lag variables. This is obvious since the household makes current consumption decision at the same time as the money holding decision. The same is possibly true with the price and interest rate decisions. Hence, with that instrument set, the moment conditions are violated. In the iteration of the GMM objective (14), we follow the guidance of Hansen, Heaton and Yaron (1996). Since the weighting matrix in the objective function is also a function of the parameters, we iterate that as well. This of course increases the computational burden.

In the GMM estimation of the M1 model we faced numerical problems in estimating the linearization point of the opportunity cost of money, I. Therefore we decided to fix it into the level of 1.05. This influences the estimate of the preference parameters, ρ and ω, since they are derived from the long-run elasticities and from the linearization point of the opportunity cost of money[19]. By fixing I we also fix the risk aversion parameters to the fairly high

[19] That is also the reason why the standard error of the estimates of ρ and ω are not computed.

level[20]. The risk aversion 11.1 is fairly high according to the estimates that have been obtained, for example, by Braun et al. (1993) and Roy (1995).

The full sample estimate of the level of adjustment costs, κM, differs significantly from zero. The lagged adjustment cost, ν, is also significant. Given the present level of M1 and the average monthly growth rate during past years, the full sample estimates of the adjustment cost parameters imply monthly adjustment costs of FIM 50 million[21]. This is roughly 0.025 per cent of M1, which is fairly low, but since money is the asset that is the cheapest to adjust, we consider these numbers fairly realistic. The data support our specification of the adjustment cost function since both of the adjustment cost parameters differ significantly from zero. The usual quadratic-in-levels specification of adjustment cost function is too restrictive. The test for overidentification restrictions (J-test) does not reject the validity of instruments for the full sample. The residuals show second order autocorrelation, which is taken into account in the design of the weighting matrix and in the standard errors.

In the estimation, we test for a structural break at the end of 1986, the end of the period of financial deregulation. The Bank of Finland started open market operations in March 1987, at which time the bank quotas for CD issues were abolished. The parameter estimates and the test statistic for the structural stability tests are presented in table 4. The parameter stability tests, described in section 3.2, give conflicting results. The Andrews and Fair test statistic indicates structural change while the Ghysels and Hall test statistic does not.

The last two columns of table 4 give parameter estimates from the financial deregulation period and the free capital markets period respectively. The estimates of the adjustment cost parameters clearly vary. In the first subsample the estimate of the level parameter, κM, is essentially lower while the estimate of the lagged change parameter, ν, is much higher. For the first subsample, the moment conditions are rejected by the J-test. Consequently the estimation results concerning the first subsample are unreliable. The parameter estimates of the second subsample are closer to their full sample counterparts. The lower estimates of the adjustment cost parameters might reflect the advances[22] in payment technology for transactions accounts and in banking in general that have occurred since the latter part of the 1980s.

---

[20] The risk aversion parameters of the capital asset pricing models are typically in the range 0.5–4. For example, the multicountry (Germany, Japan, USA) estimates of Roy (1995) are typically close to the lower bound of the range in the models in which the bond is the only asset. When the set of assets is augmented with stocks, the risk aversion parameter tends to get estimates between 2 and 6. Braun, Constantinides and Ferson (1993) extend the approach, relaxing the time separability of the utility function, ie to allow for habit persistence. Their point estimates for the risk aversion parameter for six large industrial countries vary between 0.35 (Japan) and 12 (Canada). Unfortunately, such studies have not been implemented with Finnish data.

[21] Assuming that there are approximately 5 million bank accounts in Finland and that the monthly service fee is FIM 10 per account per month, we end up with the estimated level of adjustment costs.

[22] In Finland, the number of automatic teller machines (ATM) per capita is among highest in the world. Also other electronic payment systems are very highly developed in Finland. The share of debit card payments and electronic funds transfers at point of sale (EFT-POS) is very high. Giro payments are the most important form of funds transfer. On the other hand, the shares of cheque and currency payments are very low. Cheques are presently used mainly in large-value payments.

Table 4. Parameter estimates of the Euler equations for M1

Parameter[a]	1980:5–1995:12	1980:5–1986:12[b]	1987:1–1995:12[c]
$I = (1 + i)$	1.05	1.05	1.05
v	−0.45 (0.09)	−1.76 (0.34)	−0.30 (0.05)
κM	9.36 (4.59)	0.47 (0.15)	7.72 (3.79)
ω	11.07	11.07	11.07
ρ^d	11.07	11.07	11.07
Δm_{t+2}	0.54 (0.24)	0.70 (0.12)	0.34 (0.07)
Δm_{t+1}	−0.33 (0.23)	0.61 (0.09)	−1.77 (0.11)
Δm_{t-1}	1.37 (0.13)	0.45 (0.13)	1.31 (0.08)
Coefficient of the error correction[e] term	−0.07 (0.04)	−0.49 (0.22)	−0.08 (0.04)
p-value of the J-test	0.29	0.003	0.12
p-value of the parameter stability tests		AF[f] :< 0.001; GH[g] :> 0.99	

[a] Standard errors are in parentheses below the parameter value. The standard error of the "derived" parameters, ie parameters that are computed from the original free parameters, are based on delta method. However, they do not account for the uncertainty of the cointegration parameters.
[b] Period of the financial deregulation.
[c] Period of free capital markets.
[d] In M1 system $\rho = \omega$ due to the unit scale elasticity.
[e] For M1, this is the loading of the single cointegration vector, ie $m_t - p_t - (\rho/\omega)c_t + (1/\omega i)i_t$.
[f] Andrews and Fair (1988) test statistics.
[g] Ghysels and Hall (1990b) test statistics, based on the weighting matrices of each sub-sample.

The recursive estimates of κM, v and constant term are not very convincing[23]. The lagged adjustment cost parameter, v, varies considerably. The p-values of the J-test show that the last years of the sample period are influential with respect to the moment condition.

5. Discussion

Starting from the dynamic money-in-the-utility-function model and assuming adjustment costs of changing money holdings, we derived the first-order condition describing the demand for money. For integrated (of order one) variables, the log-linearized version of the first-order condition leads to the hypothesis of two cointegration vectors and to the restrictions on those cointegration vectors. The theoretical model is designed for the analysis of the harmonized

[23] Due to the computational burden we cutted the iteration in recursive estimation on quite "early" stage of the iteration. Due to that reason the standard errors and estimates do not correspond to those reported in table 4.

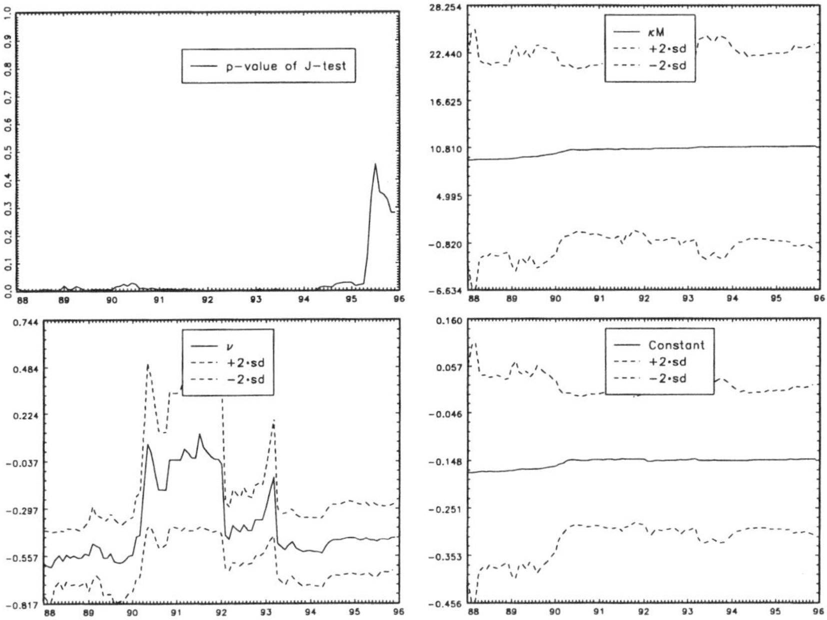

Fig. 3. Recursive estimates of some parameters of the Euler equation for M1

monetary aggregate, M3H, but it can also be used to the analysis of narrow money, M1.

The estimates of the steady-state parameters of the first-order conditions of the M1 model are stable. The test for cointegration rank supports the single cointegration vector. The unit scale elasticity implies that the risk aversion parameters of consumption and money are identical. The interest rate semi-elasticity is reasonable, 1.8. The recursive estimation of these parameters and the recursive test of the constancy of the full sample cointegration space displays no instability. The GMM estimation of the Euler equation of M1 produces parameters of reasonable size and sign when the linearization point of the opportunity cost of money is fixed. The system might indicate instabilities in the adjustment cost parameters, which may reflect advances in the banking, payment and transfer technologies during the sample period or the impact of financial deregulation.

The test statistics for the M3H system do not support the restrictions on the utility function parameters implied by the model: First, the empirical and asymptotic critical values imply a single cointegration vector. Second, this cointegration vector relates the opportunity cost of money and the own-yield of money, but not their difference as the theoretical model predicts. Third, when assuming that there exist two cointegration vectors, the second cointegration vector implies scale elasticity of about three, which is very large compared with typical international estimates of values between one and two. Finally, the recursive estimation of the scale elasticity betrays significant un-

[24] See van Riet (1993) and Browne, Fagan and Henry (1997) for a survey of the demand for money in Europe and Papi and Monticelli (1995) for some recent results.

steadiness. The hope for a proper aggregation from M1 to M3H is ruined by the fact that adding the difference between M3H and M1 to the cointegration space of the M3H model leads exactly to the model of M1. Since the M3H model does not satisfy the presumption of GMM estimation there is no use to apply GMM method for the Euler equation of M3H.

The non-existence of cointegration between price level and M3H implies that the levels of M3H and consumer prices might not be related. The long-run income elasticity of M3H is approximately twice the magnitude of the European aggregates[24]. Hence, the inclusion of the Finnish M3H would increase aggregation bias in the demand for Europe-wide M3H. The steady-state parameters in the demand for M1 in Finland are much closer to their EU-wide counterparts. Consequently, the aggregation of Finnish M1 to the EU-wide M1 is on much more solid ground. The results suggest that from the Finnish point of view M1 would be a more appropriate intermediate target for monetary policy than harmonized M3.

References

Andrews DWK (1993) Test for parameter instability and structural change with unknown change point. Econometrica 61:821–856

Andrews DWK, Fair RC (1988) Inference in nonlinear econometric models with structural change. Review of Economic Studies 55:615–640

Baba Y, Hendry DF, Starr RM (1992) The demand for M1 in the U.S.A., 1960–1988. Review of Economic Studies 59:25–61

Braun PA, Constantinides GM, Ferson WE (1993) Time nonseparability in aggregate consumption: International evidence. European Economic Review 37:897–920

Browne FX, Fagan G, Henry J (1997) Money demand in EU countries; a survey. Staff paper 7/1997, European Monetary Institute

Croushore D (1993) Money in the utility function: Functional equivalence to a shopping time model. Journal of Macroeconomics 15:175–182

Cuthbertson K, Taylor MP (1987) The demand for money: A dynamic rational expectations model. Economic Journal 97(Supplement):65–76

Cuthbertson K, Taylor MP (1990) Money demand, expectations, and the forward-looking model. Journal of Policy Modeling 12(2):289–315

den Haan WJ, Levin A (1996) A practioner's guide to robust covariance matrix estimation. Discussion Paper 96-17, University of California, San Diego to be appear in Handbook of Statistics 15 (Chapter 12, 291–341)

Dolado J, Galbraith JW, Banerjee A (1991) Estimating intertemporal quadratic adjustment cost models with integrated series. International Economic Review 32(4):919–936

Dufour J-M, Ghysels E, Hall A (1994) Generalized predictive testst and structural change analysis in econometrics. International Economic Review 35:199–229

Eitrheim Ø (1991) Inference in small cointegrated systems, some Monte Carlo results. Working Paper 1991/9, Bank of Norway

EMI (1997) The single monetary policy in stage three: Elements of the monetary policy strategy of the ESCB. Report, European Monetary Institute, February

Fase MMG (1994) In search for stability; an empirical appraisal of the demand for money in the G7 and EC countries. De Economist 142(4):421–454

Feenstra RC (1986) Functional equivalence between liquidity constraints and the utility of money. Journal of Monetary Economics 17:271–291

Ghysels E, Hall A (1990a) Are consumption-based intertemporal capital asset pricing models structural. Journal of Econometrics 45:121–139

——— (1990b) A test for structural stability of Euler parameters estimated via the generalized method of moments estimator. International Economic Review 31:355–364

Hamilton JD (1994) Time series analysis. Princeton University Press, Princeton, NJ

Hansen H, Juselius K (1995) CATS in RATS. Estima, Evanston, Illinois

Hansen LP (1982) Large sample properties of generalized method of moments estimator. Econometrica 50(4):1029–1054
Hansen LP, Heaton J, Yaron A (1996) Finite-sample properties of some alternative GMM estimators. Journal of Business and Economic Statistics 14(3):262–280
Haug AA (1996) Tests for cointegration: A Monte Carlo comparison. Journal of Econometrics 71(1&2):89–117
Hendry DF, Ericsson NR (1991) Modelling the demand for narrow money in the United Kingdom and the United States. European Economic Review 35:833–886
Hoffman D, Pagan A (1989) Post-sample prediction tests for generalized method of moments estimators. Oxford Bulletin of Economics and Statistics 51:331–343
Johansen S (1988) Statistical analysis of cointegrating vectors. Journal of Economic Dynamics and Control 12:231–254
——— (1991) Estimation and hypothesis testing of cointegration vectors in Gaussian vector autoregressive models. Econometrica 59:1551–80
——— (1995) Likelihood-based inference in cointegrated vector autoregressive models Oxford University Press, Oxford
Johansen S, Juselius K (1990) Maximum likelihood estimation and inference on cointegration – with application to the demand for money. Oxford Bulletin of Economics and Statistics 52(2):169–210
Juselius K (1996) An empirical analysis of the changing role of the german bundesbank after 1983. Oxford Bulletin of Economics and Statistics 58(4):791–819
Lucas Jr RE (1988) Money demand in the United States: A quantitative review. Carnegie-Rochester Conference Series on Public Policy 29:137–168
Newey WK, West K (1994) Automatic lag selection in covariance matrix estimation. Review of Economic Studies 61:631–653
Ogaki M (1993) GMM: A user guide. Working Paper 348, University of Rochester
Oliner SD, Rudebusch GD, Sichel D (1996) The Lucas critique revisited: Assessing the stability of empirical Euler equations for investment. Journal of Econometrics 70:291–316
Osterwald-Lenum M (1992) A note with quantiles of the asymptotic distribution of the maximum likelihood cointegration rank test statistics: four cases. Oxford Bulletin of Economics and Statistics 54(3):461–472
Papi L, Monticelli C (1995) EU-wide money demand; an assessment of competing approaches. Quaderni di ricerca 63, Università degli Studi di Ancona; Dipartimento di economia
Poterba JM, Rotemberg JJ (1987) Money in the utility function: an empirical implementation. In: Barnett WA, Singleton KJ (eds.) New approaches to monetary economics, Cambridge University Press
Ripatti A (1994) Econometric modelling of the demand for money in Finland. D:79, Bank of Finland, Helsinki
Roy A (1995) Multicountry comparison of the consumption based capital asset pricing model: Germany, Japan and USA. Discussion Paper 209, LSE Financial Markets Group, An ESERC Research Centre
Sill K (1995) Some empirical evidence on money demand from a cash-in-advance model. Working Paper 95-20, Federal Reserve Bank of Philadelphia
Tinsely PA (1993) Fitting both data and theories: Polynomial adjustment costs and error-correction decision rules. Finance and Economics Discussion Series 93-21, Federal Reserve Board
Toda HY (1995) Finite sample performance of likelihood ratio tests for cointegrating ranks in vector autoregressions. Econometric Theory 11(5):1015–1033
van Riet AG (1993) Studies of EC money demand: survey and assesment. Quarterly Bulletin, De Nederlansche Bank, pp. 63–77
Wolters J, Teräsvirta T, Lütkepohl H (1998) Modelling the demand for M3 in the unified Germany. Review of Economics and Statistics, 80:399–409

The demand for broad money in Norway, 1969–1993

Øyvind Eitrheim*

Research Department, C-51, Norges Bank (The Central Bank of Norway), Box 1179 Sentrum, N-0107 Oslo, Norway (e-mail: oyvind.eitrheim@norges-bank.no)

Abstract. Cointegration analysis is applied to investigate the long run relationships between money, prices, and wages in Norway. Broad money is determined endogenously, and monetary balances were exposed to large shocks during the period of financial deregulation in the midst of the 1980s. In the long run these shocks are absorbed, and a long run demand for money relationship is identified in which real money is determined by real income, the relative price on financial assets (the yield spread) and the relative price on goods (the own real interest rate). Money adjusts dynamically to changes in the exchange rate and private wealth. Domestic price inflation is affected by imported inflation including currency depreciation (a pass through effect), domestic cost pressure (unit labour costs), and excess demand in the product market (output gap effect).

Key words: Money demand, price/wage formation, cointegration, dynamic specification, conditional models, error correction

JEL Classifications: C22, C32, E31, E41

1. Introduction

The purpose of this paper is two-fold. First we set out to model the empirical relationship between broad money and prices, real output and interest rates in the Norwegian economy over the period from 1969 to 1993. The deregulation

* This paper was presented at the workshop "Money Demand in Europe", at the Humboldt University in Berlin, October 10–11, 1997. Thanks to Erik Biørn, Neil R. Ericsson and Grayham Mizon for their comments on previous versions of the paper and to two anonymous referees and the editors for helpful suggestions.

of the financial markets in Norway was a gradual process during the 1980s and comprised the abolition of credit ceilings, interest rate controls, and was ended with the complete removal of capital controls in 1990. In the midst of the 1980s the deregulation of the banking sector was followed by a massive credit expansion which contributed to a rapid downturn in the velocity of money. The empirical model should account for the observed characteristics of money balances through this period.

Secondly we want to model broad money in a multivariate cointegration framework, taking properly account of the nonstationary nature which seems to be inherent in many macroeconomic time series. On the one hand we want to explore the cointegration between money, prices, real output and interest rates, but since modern types of empirical price/wage models typically predict that prices, wages, productivity and unemployment are cointegrated, we will present a framework in which we can simultaneously identify the equilibria for money, prices and wages. We then derive empirical error correction models for broad money and consumer price inflation which are consistent with the equilibria derived from the cointegration analysis. Finally we test the robustness of the maintained hypothesis embedded in the inflation model that there are no direct effects from monetary variables against some of the alternatives suggested in Juselius (1992), who has incorporated disequilibrium measures from other markets in a model of Danish consumer price inflation.

2. Economic theory

Money demand

Milbourne, Bucholtz, and Wasan (1983) and Smith (1986) derive dynamic equations for aggregate money holdings from "target-threshold" models of the type introduced by Miller and Orr (1966) and Akerlof (1979). The resulting partial adjustment equations define a long run target for money, m_t^*, towards which actual money holdings is gradually adjusted. The partial adjustment model has been criticized for its unreasonably long adjustment time (before reaching the target m_t^*), possibly due to the simple dynamic representation of the model which allows for only one lag. It thus seems reasonable to allow for a more flexible dynamic specification to capture the short run changes in m_t, and Nickell (1985) has showed that partial adjustment models will in many cases be observationally equivalent to an error correction model. The "target" m_t^* is defined as a linear function of $z_t = (p_t, y_t, \mathbf{R}_t)'$, i.e. $m_t^* = \beta' z_t$, assuming that the forcing variables are the price level p_t, real income y_t and a vector with interest rates $\mathbf{R}_t$[1]. In contrast to the partial adjustment model, the error correction model allows for more flexible dynamic responses in money balances to shocks in the explanatory variables. In the empirical models in this paper we have used $\mathbf{R}_t = (RB_t - RT_t, RT_t - \Delta_4 p_t)'$. RB_t is the yield on assets outside money (government bonds with six years maturity), RT_t is the own interest rate on money (the time deposits rate) and $\Delta_4 p_t$ is the annual rate of inflation. Hence, $(RB_t - RT_t)$ (the "yield spread") represents the nominal opportunity cost of holding money relative to other financial assets, while the

[1] Variables in lower case denote logarithms.

"own real interest rate" $(RT_t - \Delta_4 p_t)$ can be interpreted as a measure of the return on money relative to consumer goods. Assuming homogeneity of degree one in the price level, the long run (cointegrating) relationship for money balances m_t can be formulated as (omitting the intercept):

$$m_t - p_t = \beta_{m,y} y_t + \beta_{m,rbt}(RB_t - RT_t) + \beta_{m,rtd4p}(RT_t - \Delta_4 p_t) \tag{2.1}$$

Eitrheim (1996) provides empirical evidence which supports the interest rate restrictions incorporated in (2.1). The potential links between money and the price/wage determination are investigated using a model for the "price/wage" formation where the aggregate price and wage level, (p_t, w_t), is determined simultaneously and are affected by traditional explanatory variables like productivity, zy_t, import prices, pb_t (imported inflation), and the rate of unemployment, u_t (the Phillips-curve effect).

Price and wage determination

As background for the discussion of the empirical price model, I will set out a simple model of wage and price formation presented in Bårdsen, Fisher, and Nymoen (1995). Bargained nominal wages depend on a combination of firm-side variables (e.g. productivity, producer prices and the payroll tax rate) and variables which affect the take-home pay (e.g. consumer prices and the income tax rate) as well as variables which capture the effect on wage/price formation from labour market pressure (unemployment). We follow Bårdsen et al. (1995) and postulate the following equations for the equilibrium wage level, w_t^{**}, and the producer price level, pp_t^{**}.

$$w_t^{**} = \alpha_1 pp_t + (1 - \alpha_1)p_t + \theta zy_t - \beta_1 t1_t + \beta_2 t2_t - \kappa_1 u_t$$

$$pp_t^{**} = m_{pp} + w_t - zy_t + t1_t$$

where pp_t and zy_t denote producer prices and productivity respectively, p_t the consumer price level, u_t unemployment, $t1_t$ the payroll tax rate and $t2_t$ the income tax rate. To simplify the exposition we follow Bårdsen et al. (1995) and set $\theta = 1$ and $\beta_2 = 0$. The equilibrium producer price level is a constant mark-up m_{pp} on normal unit labour costs and the equilibrium wage "share" depend negatively on the payroll tax rate and the rate of unemployment, i.e.

$$w_t^{**} - zy_t - \alpha_1 pp_t - (1 - \alpha_1)p_t = -\beta_1 t1_t - \kappa_1 u_t$$

The consumer price level, p_t, is homogeneous of degree one in domestic producer prices, pp_t, and import prices in domestic currency, pb_t, and also includes net indirect taxes $t3_t$:

$$p_t = \eta pp_t + (1 - \eta)pb_t + t3_t$$

3. The cointegration of money, prices and wages

Complete and partial VAR models

A "complete" VAR model with $k = 5$ lags forms the starting point for the cointegration analysis of n variables stacked in the vector X_t, where we assume that X_t is a nonstationary I(1) process. We transform the model to I(0)-space using the interim multiplier representation, and apply the following vector error correction model (VECM):

$$\Delta X_t = \sum_{i=1}^{k-1} \Gamma_i \Delta X_{t-i} + \alpha\beta' X_{t-k} + \sum_{i=0}^{k-1} \Psi_i \Delta W_{t-i} + \mu_0 + \Phi S_t + \varepsilon_t \tag{3.1}$$

ΔW_t contain variables that are not modelled explicitly in the VECM, and we refer to them as "unmodelled variables" (Hendry (1995)). The differencing indicates that the levels of W_t are nonstationary I(1), and they will not enter into the long run system of cointegrating relationships. The role of ΔW_t is to allow for shocks in the unmodelled variables to be transmitted into the system. S_t contains three seasonal dummies, but will also frequently include intervention dummy variables and variables which enter the model at a particular lag only. Finally, we assume that $\varepsilon_t \sim Niid(0, \Lambda)$. The "long run" part of the model, allows for "linear" feedback of the stationary error correction terms in $\alpha\beta' X_{t-k}$, where β is a $n \times r$ matrix with r cointegration vectors and α is a $n \times r$ matrix with feedback coefficients (loading factors).

To arrive at the "partial" VAR model we factorize the simultaneous density function for the partitioned vector $X_t = (Y_t' | Z_t')'$ into a conditional density function for m variables Y_t given the $(n - m)$ variables Z_t, and a marginal density function for Z_t. Provided Z_t is weakly exogenous with respect to the parameters in the conditional distribution of Y_t given Z_t, we may then focus on the conditional model for Y_t given Z_t without loss of information. Conditioning will be useful below because X_t in our case will involve a large number of variables. Later in this section we present results on the cointegration properties in a "joint" dataset where we have merged together a "money demand" and a "price/wage" dataset, each of which has been typically chosen to derive long run money demand and price/wage relationships respectively, of the type described in section 2 above.

The merging of "money demand" and "price/wage" data

The "money demand" data

The "money demand" dataset is represented by the vector $X_{m,t}$ (lower case letters denote variables in logarithms):

$$X_{m,t} = (m_t, p_t, y_t, RB_t, RT_t)'$$

$$\Delta W_{m,t} = (\Delta nok_t, \Delta lw_t)'$$

$$D_{m,t} = (M2D914_t, S4 * \Delta_4 RT_t, D701_t, PDUM_t)'$$

$$S_{m,t} = D_{m,t}$$

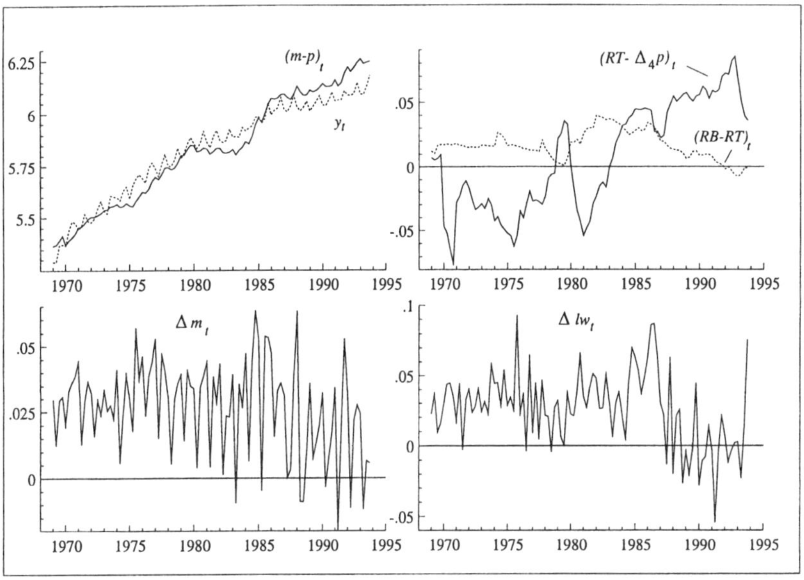

Fig. 3.1. Some variables in the "money demand" dataset. Data are updated through 1993q4

m_t is measured as the quarterly average of end-of-month money holdings, corrected for measurement problems in the deregulation period from 1984(1)–1988(4) as discussed in Klovland (1990), p_t is the consumer price index, y_t is real GDP, RB_t is the yield on government bonds (with 6–10 years maturity), and RT_t is the interest rate on time deposits. The unmodelled (stationary) variables in the "money demand" analysis are changes in the nominal effective exchange rate Δnok_t and the change in nominal household wealth Δlw_t. The vector with dummy variables, $D_{m,t}$, include a dummy variable for the release of tax-exempted savings deposits ($M2D914_t = 1$ in 1991(4) else 0) and the variable $S4 * \Delta_4 RT_t$ which is intended to pick up the effect from accrued interest earnings, which are capitalized at the end of each year. This representation allows for a simple but flexible seasonal response in m_t in years when there have been large changes in the interest rate level during the preceeding 4 quarters. Some of the main series are graphed in figure 3.1.

The "price/wage" data

The second set of variables is the "price/wage" dataset which was used in Bårdsen et al. (1995) to model aggregate prices and wages as a function of aggregate labour productivity zy_t, the unemployment rate u_t, import prices pb_t, the aggregate payroll tax rate $t1_t$, the indirect tax rate $t3_t$[2] and the length

[2] The tax-rates are measured in logarithms, i.e. as $t1_t = \ln(1 + T1_t)$, where $T1_t$ is the payroll tax rate, and $t3_t = \ln(1 + T3_t)$, where $T3_t$ is the indirect tax rate.

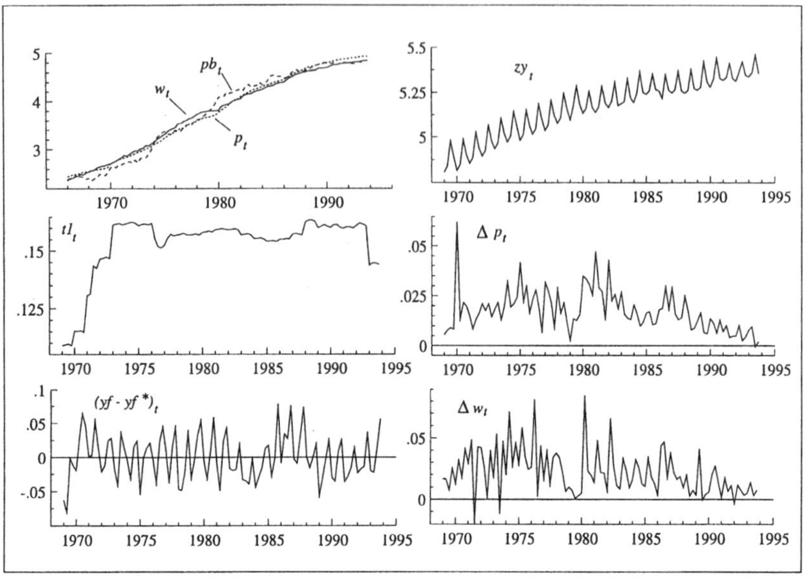

Fig. 3.2. Some variables in the "price/wage" dataset. Data are updated through 1993q4

of the working day h_t. To account for potential effects from excess demand in product markets, they also include a measure of the output gap, $(yf - yf^*)_t$[3].

$$X_{pw,t} = (p_t, w_t, zy_t, pb_t, t1_t, t3_t, u_t)'$$

$$\Delta W_{pw,t} = \Delta h_t$$

$$D_{pw,t} = (D701_t, PDUM_t, D802_t, WDUM_t)'$$

$$S_{pw,t} = (D'_{pw,t}, (yf - yf^*)_{t-1})'$$

In addition to the variables in $X_{pw,t}$, the authors introduce dummy variables, $D_{pw,t}$ to account for one-off effects from the introduction of VAT in 1970(1), $D701$ and the periods with price-freeze in the 1970's, $PDUM_t$, and wage freeze in the 1970's and 1980's, $WDUM_t$ and $D802$ (cf. the data definitions in the appendix and Bårdsen et al. (1995) for more details). The rate of change in the length of the working day, Δh_t, is included as an unmodelled (stationary) variable. Some of the main series are graphed in figure 3.2.

Inference on cointegration in a partial system

The cointegration analysis is performed on a "joint" dataset where we merge the "money demand" and the "price/wage" data described above. Eitrheim

[3] The output gap, $(yf - yf^*)_t$, is calculated using the Mellin and Teräsvirta (1992) filter with parameters $(m = 2, \lambda = 1600)$, which corresponds to the Hodrick-Prescott filter with $(\lambda = 1600)$.

(1996) (essay 4) analysed the cointegration properties in a complete system for the 11 variables in $X_t = (m_t, p_t, w_t, y_t, RB_t, RT_t, zy_t, pb_t, t1_t, t3_t, u_t)')$, applying the multivariate VAR-approach to cointegration analysis described in Johansen (1991) using a VAR model with five lags. The results, based on a sequence of repeated cointegration *Trace* test statistics to updated samples (providing "recursive" evidence on cointegration), indicates that there may be as much as seven cointegrating relationships between the eleven variables. For many reasons, such a large system is cumbersome to work with and calls for some simplifications in order to obtain a more manageable system. In this section we present empirical evidence on the cointegration properties in a partial system for

$$Y_t = (m_t, p_t, w_t)', \quad (m = 3 \text{ endogenous variables})$$

given

$$Z_t = (y_t, RB_t, RT_t, zy_t, pb_t, t1_t, t3_t, u_t)', \quad ((n-m) = 8 \text{ exogenous variables})$$

The vector of unmodelled variables is

$$\Delta W_t = (\Delta nok_{t-1}, \ldots, \Delta nok_{t-4}, \Delta lw_{t-2}, \Delta h_t)'$$

where the lags are determined from previous analysis of the "money demand" and "price/wage" datasets separately, and we have finally included the lagged output gap $(yf - yf^*)_{t-1}$ in S_t along with the following dummy variables, hence

$$D_{mpw,t} = (M2D914_t, S4 * \Delta_4 RT_t, D701_t, PDUM_t, D802_t, WDUM_t)'$$

$$S_t = (D'_{mpw,t}, (yf - yf^*)_{t-1}, Seasonals)'$$

The cointegrating rank is then tested in the partial system using the *Trace*-test described in Johansen (1992) and further discussed by Dengsøe, Johansen, Nielsen, and Rahbek (1994), using critical values which applies for the case with $(n-m) = 8$ exogenous nonstationary variables (cf. the extended and recalculated tables of critical values reported in Eitrheim (1996) (essay 1, appendix E)) and where we also report a *Trace*-test where we apply the small sample correction advocated by Reimers (1992)[4]. Although the small sample corrected test statistics reported in table 3.1 provide somewhat mixed evidence, with support for either one or three cointegrating relationships, it seems that this procedure may tend to overcorrect and if we also consider the recursive evidence provided in Eitrheim (1996) (essay 4), the results support that there are $r = 3$ cointegrating relationships in this partial system.

[4] The numerical results in this section were obtained by using a collection of Gauss procedures labelled M3, cf. Eitrheim (1996) (software appendix) for a brief presentation.

Table 3.1. Cointegration analysis of a partial VAR(5) model for $\Delta Y_t = (\Delta m_t, \Delta p_t, \Delta w_t)'$, using the joint "money demand" and "price/wage" dataset. *Trace* tests with and without small sample corrections using data from 1969(1) to 1993(4).

Endogenous variables : $(m_t, p_t, w_t)'$
Exogenous variables : $(y_t, RT - \Delta_4 p_t, pb_t, zy_t, (RB - RT)_t, u_t, t3_t, t1_t)'$,
Predetermined variables : $(\Delta nok_{t-1}, \ldots, \Delta nok_{t-4}, \Delta lw_{t-2}, \Delta h_t)'$
Dummy variables : $(M2D914_t, D701_t, D802_t WDUM_t, PDUM_t, S4 * \Delta_4 RT_t, (yf - yf^*)_{t-1})'$
Deterministic variables $(Const, S1_t, S2_t, S3_t)'$

Eigenvalues	*Trace* tests for cointegration				
λ_i	H_0	H_1	$\lambda_{trace,57}$	λ_{trace}	95%
0.6024	$r = 0$	$r \geq 1$	82.3715	191.5617	–
0.4146	$r \leq 1$	$r \geq 2$	42.7109	99.3278	45.0150
0.3673	$r \leq 2$	$r \geq 3$	19.6869	45.7834	16.869

95% fractiles for the case with $(n - m) = 8$ exogenous nonstationary variables are from Eitrheim (1996), essay 1 (appendix E).

Long run relationships for money, prices and wages

The cointegration vectors have been estimated subject to the overidentifying restrictions presented above, using the "switching algorithm" discussed in Johansen (1995) and we obtained the following results:

$$m_t = p_t + \underset{(0.11)}{0.76}\, y_t - \underset{(0.59)}{3.73}(RB_t - RT_t) + \underset{(0.44)}{1.67}(RT_t - \Delta_4 p_t) + constant$$

$$p_t = \underset{(0.06)}{0.45}\, pb_t + \underset{(0.09)}{0.55}(w_t + t1_t - zy_t) + t3_t + constant \qquad (3.2)$$

$$w_t = p_t + zy_t - \underset{(0.01)}{0.07}\, u_t + constant$$

The long run income elasticity in the money demand relationship is 0.76 with an estimated standard error of 0.11, hence unity lies marginally outside a 95% confidence interval. The own real interest rate effect and the yield spread effect both have their expected signs, and they are significantly different from zero when evaluated by standard errors which are calculated by the method proposed in Johansen (1995). Eitrheim (1995) provides empirical evidence on the stability of the parameters in (3.2), applying the methods proposed in Hansen and Johansen (1993) (repeatedly using the "switching algorithm" to an updated sample, while keeping the short run parameters at their full sample estimated values). The price/wage equations correspond fairly well to the estimated long run model reported in Bårdsen et al. (1995), although we find a higher import price elasticity in (3.2) (0.45 compared to 0.35).

4. Empirical models for money and prices

The money demand equation

We derive a conditional error correction model for broad money, Δm_t, where we have performed a general-to-specific simplification of an autoregressive distributed lag model with five lags[5]. The information set used in the general model is:

$$\mathcal{I}_{m,t} = (y_{t-i}, p_{t-i}, RB_{t-i}, RN_{t-i}, RT_{t-i}, lw_{t-i}, nok_{t-i}, m_{t-1-i};\ i \geq 0)$$

During the reduction process we have excluded insignificant variables/lags and made transformations where the coefficients showed significant effects of comparable magnitude. The money market interest rate, RN_t, was excluded from the model, while we have retained the other variables. The final results are reported in equation (4.1). Ordinary equation standard errors appear in parentheses (.), and we report the Hansen (1992) tests for stability of each of the individual coefficients in curly braces {.}.

$$\begin{aligned}
\Delta m_t = &- \underset{\substack{(0.0436)\\ \{0.2971\}}}{0.0967}(\Delta\Delta nok_{t-1} + \Delta\Delta nok_{t-3}) + \underset{\substack{(0.0455)\\ \{0.1200\}}}{0.1895}\,\Delta lw_{t-2} \\
&+ \underset{\substack{(0.0621)\\ \{0.0596\}}}{0.1331}(\Delta m_{t-1} + \Delta m_{t-3}) - \underset{\substack{(0.0372)\\ \{0.4003\}}}{0.2650}(\Delta m_{t-2} - \Delta m_{t-4}) \\
&- \underset{\substack{(0.0260)\\ \{0.0594\}}}{0.1461}(m_{t-1} - p_{t-1}) + \underset{\substack{(0.0221)\\ \{0.0593\}}}{0.1199}\,y_{t-1} \\
&+ \underset{\substack{(0.0486)\\ \{0.1835\}}}{0.1363}(RT_{t-1} - \Delta_4 p_{t-1}) - \underset{\substack{(0.1146)\\ \{0.0614\}}}{0.3307}(RB_{t-1} - RT_{t-1}) \\
&+ \underset{\substack{(0.0097)\\ \{0.1068\}}}{0.0274}\,M2D914_t + \underset{\substack{(0.1620)\\ \{0.0976\}}}{0.3024}\,S4 * \Delta_4 RT_t \\
&+ \underset{\substack{(0.0025)\\ \{0.0945\}}}{0.0181}(S1_t + S3_t) - \underset{\substack{(0.1182)\\ \{0.0584\}}}{0.5514} + \hat{\varepsilon}_t
\end{aligned} \tag{4.1}$$

$T = 100[1969(1) - 1993(4)]$	$R^2 = 0.76 \quad \hat{\sigma} = 0.0093$	$DW = 2.18$
$k = 12$	$AIC = -9.2522 \quad SC = -8.9395$	$HQ = -9.1256$
$F_{AR,1-4}(4,84) = \underset{(0.2487)}{1.3776}$	$F_{ARCH,1-4}(4,84) = \underset{(0.1116)}{1.9380}$	$\chi^2_N(2) = \underset{(0.0000)}{7.8669^{**}}$
$F_{ENC}(38,50) = \underset{(0.4860)}{1.0065}$	$F_{RESET}(2,86) = \underset{(0.0867)}{2.5159}$	
Stability:	$S_{BH,SIG}(1) = 0.1177$	$S_{BH,JNT}(13) = 2.0902$
Non-linearity:	$F_{STRNL,L,d=1}(30,58) = \underset{(0.4359)}{1.0416}$	$F_{STRNL,4,d=1}(10,58) = \underset{(0.4011)}{1.0682}$
	$F_{STRNL,3\mid 4,d=1}(10,68) = \underset{(0.5280)}{0.9114}$	$F_{STRNL,2\mid 34,d=1}(10,78) = \underset{(0.3459)}{1.1376}$
	$F_{STRNL,3\mid 24,d=1}(10,78) = \underset{(0.1856)}{1.4238}$	
STR Structural break	$F_{STRSB,3}(33,55) = \underset{(0.0977)}{1.4800}$	$F_{STRSB,2}(22,66) = \underset{(0.0194)}{1.9534^{*}}$
	$F_{STRSB,1}(11,77) = \underset{(0.0578)}{1.8619}$	

[5] The numerical results presented in this section were obtained using PcGive Professional version 9.00; cf. Hendry and Doornik (1996) and a collection of Gauss procedures labelled M3, cf. Eitrheim (1996) (software appendix) for a brief presentation.

The diagnostic tests in the reported regressions include test statistics (with p-values below in parenthesis) against various alternative hypotheses[6]. The growth in money is negatively affected by a currency depreciation and positively affected by a change in (lagged) household wealth (which is heavily influenced by changes in housing prices). The implicit restrictions in (4.1) are accepted against the unrestricted general model using the parsimonious encompassing test $F_{ENC}(38, 50) = 1.01$. There is no indication of serial correlation nor heteroscedasticity in the residuals, but the normality test fails due to some large errors e.g. in 1984(4) and 1988(1). This fact and also the fairly large standard error of 0.93% per quarter reflects the fact that we have used a minimum of dummy variables to account for episodes with unexplained shocks in the money holdings, not picked up by the model. Such large errors could easily be a source of parameter instability. The Hansen (1992) tests for stability in the individual coefficients show no significant sign of a break, although the test is close to significance for $(\Delta m_{t-2} - \Delta m_{t-4})$. The variance stability test and the joint stability test are not significant, although the test statistic $F_{STRSB,2}(22, 66) = 1.9534$ is significant at the 5% level and suggests that there has been a structural break in the model. Further tests for parameter nonconstancy and also for particular forms of nonlinearity in the functional form were further investigated in Eitrheim (1996), (essay 4), and the results strongly supported a linear dynamic specification although with some indications of parameter instability, in particular for the lagged dynamic effects from transformations involving Δm_{t-i}, $i > 0$ (as noted above) as well as for changes in exchange rates $(\Delta\Delta nok_{t-1} + \Delta\Delta nok_{t-3})$ and household wealth Δlw_{t-2}. This is also picked up by the plot of recursive coefficients shown in figure 4.1 although the overall picture is that the estimated parameters seem to be reasonably constant across the sample, notwithstanding these indications of parameter non-constancy. The recursive 1-step CHOW-tests in figure 4.1 are significant in some of the periods with large errors, in particular 1984(4) and 1988(1), and this is also picked up by the "break point" (Ndown) CHOW tests and "forecast" (Nup) CHOW tests.

The implicit long run relationship for money, m_t^* in (4.1) is given by (omitting the intercept)

$$m_t^* = p_t + \underset{(0.0371)}{0.8207}\, y_t - \underset{(0.7456)}{2.2635}(RB_t - RT_t) + \underset{(0.2549)}{0.9329}(RT_t - \Delta_4 p_t) \qquad (4.2)$$

where we have calculated the standard errors using the procedure suggested in Bårdsen (1989). The long run income elasticity is of a comparable magnitude to what was reported in (3.2) above, 0.82 vs 0.76. We note however, that the "yield spread" and the "own real interest rate" effects seems to be smaller

[6] In the first three lines we report measures of goodness of fit, model selection criteria and tests for residual autocorrelation, ARCH and normality, cf. Hendry and Doornik (1996) for references and details. $F_{ENC}(q, T-k-q)$ tests the validity of q simplifying restrictions in a more general model (parsimonious encompassing), $S_{BH,SIG}(1)$ is the variance stability test described in (Hansen (1992)) (with 5% critical value 0.47) and $S_{BH,JNT}(q)$ is the joint stability test of the variance and all coefficients simultaneously (Hansen (1992)) ($q = 13$ implies a 5% critical value of 3.15), $F_{STRNL,L,d=1}$, $F_{STRNL,4,d=1}$, $F_{STRNL,3|4,d=1}$, $F_{STRNL,2|34,d=1}$ and $F_{STRNL,3|24,d=1}$ form a sequence of LM-type linearity tests against nonlinear smooth transition regression alternatives (Luukkonen, Saikkonen, and Teräsvirta (1988)) and $F_{STRSB,i}$, $i = 3, 2, 1$ form a sequence of LM-type tests of parameter constancy against alternatives with continuously changing parameters (Lin and Teräsvirta (1994)).

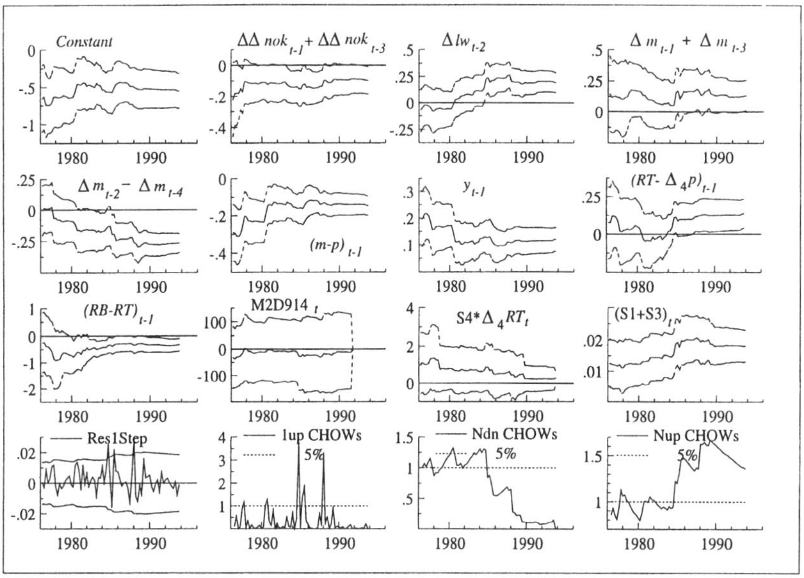

Fig. 4.1. Recursive coefficients in the Δm_t equation (plus/minus two standard errors)

than the corresponding estimates in (3.2), i.e. −2.26 vs −3.73 and 0.93 vs 1.67 respectively.

The price equation

The empirical model of consumer price inflation is derived from a generalized version of the theoretical model for price/wage inflation presented in section 2. The information set is similar to the one used by Bårdsen et al. (1995), but we have allowed for a slightly more general dynamic specification, starting out with five lags in a general unrestricted autoregressive distributed lag model using the information set:

$$\mathcal{I}_{pw,t} = (p_{t-i}, w_{t-i-1}, pb_{t-i}, zy_{t-i}, t1_{t-i}, t3_{t-i}, u_{t-i}, h_{t-i}, (yf - yf^*)_{t-1};\ i \geq 0)$$

The empirical cointegration results in (3.2) using the joint "money demand" and "price/wage" dataset are consistent with the key properties of the long run wage/price model in section 2 as well as the empirical results in Bårdsen et al. (1995). We have applied this result in the following, assuming that the (long run) price level relationship $p_t^* = 0.45pb_t + 0.55(w_t + t1_t - zy_t) + t3_t$ enters the error correction term $(p_{t-1} - p_{t-1}^*)$ at the first lag in the price equation. In contrast to the simultaneous determination of prices and wages in Bårdsen et al. (1995) we have focused on modelling prices alone, and we have removed the contemporaneous change in the wage level Δw_t from the right hand side of the price equation to avoid a simultaneity problem, while retaining all the other variables in both the price and wage equations. In addition we have allowed for more lags in the dynamic specification of the model, and include five lags in the "unrestricted reduced form" price model. In light of this "reduced form" interpretation we would expect to find significant effects from the variables Δh_{t-i} and $\Delta t1_{t-i}$, $i = 0, \ldots, q$, as well as from $(w - w^*)_{t-1}$, which only enters in the wage equation in Bårdsen et al. (1995). Since their empirical results indicate that the link from wages to prices is rather weak, we should perhaps not be too surprised to find that these variables are not significant in our final model which is derived by following a similar strategy to the one used above for the Δm_t-equation. The final results are reported in (4.3).

$$\begin{aligned}
\Delta p_t = {} & \underset{\substack{(0.0145)\\ [0.0832]}}{0.0373}\,\Delta pb_t - \underset{\substack{(0.0183)\\ \{0.0848\}}}{0.0609}\,\Delta_4 zy_t - \underset{\substack{(0.1114)\\ \{0.4655\}}}{0.2067}\,\Delta tl_{t-2} \\
& + \underset{\substack{(0.0170)\\ \{0.0901\}}}{0.0410}\,\Delta\Delta w_{t-3} - \underset{\substack{(0.0449)\\ \{0.2066\}}}{0.0889}\,\Delta h_{t-4} + \underset{\substack{(0.1371)\\ \{0.1032\}}}{0.5365}\,\Delta tl_{t-4} \\
& + \underset{\substack{(0.0273)\\ \{0.0554\}}}{0.1627}(\Delta p_{t-2} + \Delta p_{t-4}) + \underset{\substack{(0.0117)\\ \{0.6169^*\}}}{0.0644}(yf_{t-1} - yf^*_{t-1}) \\
& - \underset{\substack{(0.0074)\\ \{0.0956\}}}{0.0808}(p_{t-1} - t3_{t-1} - 0.45pb_{t-1} - 0.55(w_{t-1} + tl_{t-1} - zy_{t-1})) \\
& + \underset{\substack{(0.0037)\\ \{0.0950\}}}{0.0491}\,D701_t - \underset{\substack{(0.0019)\\ \{0.2739\}}}{0.0053}\,WDUM_t - \underset{\substack{(0.0014)\\ \{0.0971\}}}{0.0133}\,PDUM_t \\
& - \underset{\substack{(0.0009)\\ \{0.1290\}}}{0.0042}(S1_t + S3_t) + \underset{\substack{(0.0010)\\ \{0.0513\}}}{0.0091} + \hat{\varepsilon}_t
\end{aligned} \tag{4.3}$$

$T = 100[1969(1)\text{–}1993(4)]$	$R^2 = 0.90$ $\quad \hat{\sigma} = 0.0035$	$DW = 1.84$
$k = 14$	$AIC = -11.1708$ $\quad SC = -10.8061$	$HQ = -11.0232$
$F_{AR,1-4}(4, 82) = \underset{(0.2660)}{1.3295}$	$F_{ARCH,1-4}(4, 82) = \underset{(0.9187)}{0.2335}$	$\chi^2_N(2) = \underset{(0.6871)}{0.4028}$
$F_{ENC}(43, 43) = \underset{(0.3751)}{1.1026}$	$F_{RESET}(2, 84) = \underset{(0.4840)}{0.7320}$	
Stability:	$S_{BH,SIG}(1) = 0.1429$	$S_{BH,JNT}(15) = 2.9587$
Non-linearity:	$F_{STRNL,L,d=1}(30, 56) = \underset{(0.5313)}{0.9649}$	$F_{STRNL,4,d=1}(10, 56) = \underset{(0.8269)}{0.5755}$
	$F_{STRNL,3\|4,d=1}(10, 66) = \underset{(0.2083)}{1.3818}$	$F_{STRNL,2\|34,d=1}(10, 76) = \underset{(0.4156)}{1.0443}$
	$F_{STRNL,3\|24,d=1}(10, 76) = \underset{(0.2798)}{1.2403}$	
STR Structural break	$F_{STRSB,3}(33, 53) = \underset{(0.4711)}{1.0153}$	$F_{STRSB,2}(22, 64) = \underset{(0.2395)}{1.2522}$
	$F_{STRSB,1}(11, 75) = \underset{(0.4714)}{0.9807}$	

The diagnostic tests indicate that the price equation is reasonably well specified according to these criteria, with a standard error of $\hat{\sigma} = 0.35\%$ per quarter. The implicit restrictions are accepted against the unrestricted general model using the parsimonious encompassing test $F_{ENC}(43, 43) = 1.10$. The one-step residuals are reported in figure 4.2 along with the one-step and the

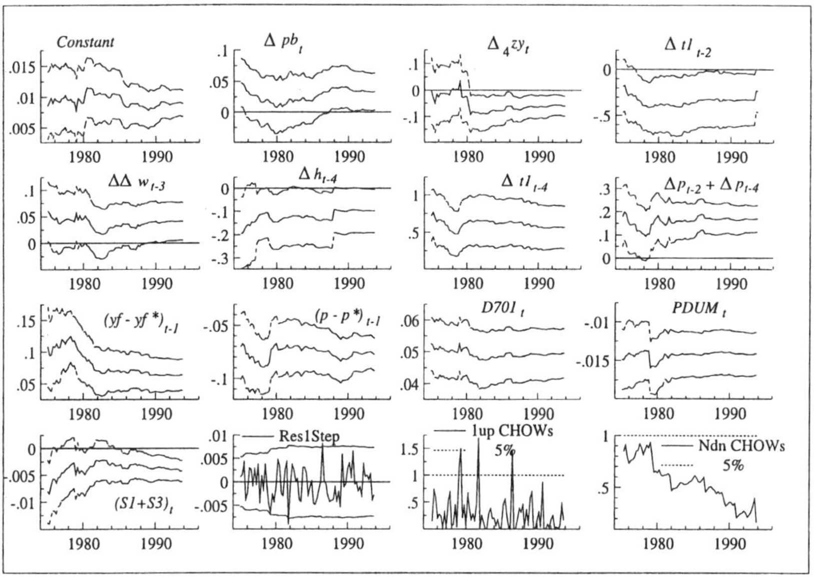

Fig. 4.2. Recursive coefficients in the Δp_t equation (plus/minus two standard errors)

break-point CHOW tests and the recursive estimates of the coefficients. Despite some outliers, the model seems to perform reasonably well, although we note that the Hansen (1992) stability test for the output gap coefficient is significant.

We distinguish between three different sources of inflation impulses in (4.3), i.e. from "imported inflation" (including currency depreciation) through increasing import prices, pb_t, "domestic cost pressure" reflected in unit labour costs, $w_t + tl_t - zy_t$, and finally, from "excess demand" measured by the output gap, $(yf_t - yf_t^*)$. Monetary shocks or financial market shocks may of course contribute to generate inflation impulses through these channels whenever such shocks affect one or more of the variables associated with them. In this section we will investigate another possibility, namely that shocks in monetary or financial variables have "direct effects" on inflation which have been "neglected" in the modelling of Δp_t in equation (4.3). Results for Denmark in Juselius (1992) indicate that "monetary variables" are important explanatory variables in an empirical model for Danish inflation and that they have clearly significant "direct" effects. If similar effects can be traced on Norwegian data, this would cast some serious doubt on the specification of the price equation reported in Bårdsen et al. (1995) and also on the price equation in (4.3).

Tests for neglected monetary effects on inflation

We have tested the robustness of the price equation (4.3) with respect to "neglected" monetary effects on inflation by subjecting this equation to a sequence of tests for omitted variables. First, we tested for the additional influence of the own real interest rate, $(RT_{t-1} - \Delta_4 p_{t-1})$, the yield spread, $(RB_{t-1} - RT_{t-1})$, and disequilibrium indicators for the monetary sector (excess money, $m_{t-1} - m^*_{t-1}$), the labour market (excess wages, $w_{t-1} - w^*_{t-1}$) and the product market (excess consumption, $c_{t-1} - c^*_{t-1}$), which are constructed from the relevant long run cointegrating relationships[7]. The results showed that the additional variables are insignificant, whether examined individually or jointly. The lagged error correction term for broad money, $m_{t-1} - m^*_{t-1}$, seems to be clearly non-significant when it is added to the price equation (4.3). This is an important result, since it provides corroborative evidence that prices are weakly exogenous for the parameters in the long run money demand relationship. We also find the weak exogenity of prices acceptable from a theoretical point of view, interpreting this evidence in light of the "target/threshold" theory or "buffer stock" theory of the demand for money (cf. section 2), and it is also a frequently reported result in the empirical money demand literature (cf. Hoover (1991), Bårdsen (1992), Hendry and Ericsson (1991), Engle and Hendry (1993) and Hendry and Mizon (1993) for examples). We have also tested the price equation (4.3) for the potential influence from variables which turned out to excert significant effects on Danish inflation in Juselius (1992). Since lagged deviations from purchasing power parity, $ecm_{ppp,t-1} = (p_{t-1} - pf_{t-1} - nok_{t-1})$ and lagged deviations from uncovered interest rate parity, $ecm_{uip,t-1} = (RN_{t-1} - RF_{t-1} - \Delta_4 nok_{t+3})$ seems to transmit significant inflation impulses into the Danish inflation process (Juselius (1992)), it is interesting to see whether similar results applies for Norway[8]. It seems however to be no empirical support for similar effects from variables like $ecm_{ppp,t-1}$ and $ecm_{uip,t-1}$ on Norwegian inflation, as were reported in the model of Danish inflation in Juselius (1992), cf. Eitrheim (1995) for further details.

5. Concluding remarks

A long run demand for money relationship is identified in which real money is determined by real income, the relative price on financial assets (the yield spread) and the relative price on goods (the own real interest rate). In the short run broad money adjusts dynamically to deviations from its long run target level, and also reacts to shocks in the exchange rate or private wealth. An equation for consumer price inflation was derived under the maintained hypothesis that there are no direct effects from monetary variables like e.g. excess money holdings, and the results indicate that we can distinguish between three key sources of inflation impulses to a small open economy like Norway, i.e. from imported inflation including currency depreciation (a pass through effect), from domestic cost pressure (unit labour costs) and from excess demand in the product market (output gap effect) respectively.

---

[7] For details on the long run cointegrating relationship for real private consumer expenditures, see Brodin and Nymoen (1992).

[8] pf_t denotes the foreign price level, RF_t denotes the foreign short interest rate, nok_t is the exchange rate, and RN_t denotes the short run (3 months) Euro-NOK interest rate.

Appendix: Variable symbols and definitions

Symbol	Definition
m_t	Nominal stock of money, $m_t = \ln M2K_t$, (quarterly average of end-of-month observations), corrected for measurement problems during the period 1984(1)–1988(4) as described in Klovland (1990)
p_t	Consumer price index, 1 in 1991 (logs)
w_t	Wage per hour, mainland economy (logs)
y_t	GDP, volumes in fixed 1991-prices (logs)
RB_t	Rate of return on central government bonds (annualized)
RT_t	Interest rate on time deposits (annualized)
zy_t	Productivity in the mainland economy (logs), excluding oil and shipping industries (value added per man hour at factor costs)
pb_t	Import price index, 1 in 1991 (logs)
$t1_t$	$t1_t = \ln(1 + T1_t)$, where $T1_t$ is the payroll tax rate
$t3_t$	$t3_t = \ln(1 + T3_t)$, where $T3_t$ is the indirect tax rate
u_t	Log of total unemployment rate, registered unemployed + persons on labour market programmes in per cent of the "labour force" (number of employed wage earners + unemployment).
nok_t	Effective exchange rate index (logs), using competition weights
lw_t	Nominal household wealth (logs), which includes net financial wealth + housing capital evaluated at market prices
h_t	Normal working hours per week (logs)
$M2D914$	Dummy variable for the release of tax-exempted savings, 1 in 1991(4), zero otherwise
$D701$	VAT dummy. 1 in 1970(1), zero otherwise.
$PDUM$	Composite dummy for introduction and lift of direct price regulations. 1 in 1971(1), 1971(2), 1976(4) and 1979(1), −1 in 1975(1), 1980(1), 1981(1) and 1982(1), zero otherwise.
$D802$	Dummy for lift of wage-freeze, 1 in 1980(2), zero otherwise.
$WDUM$	Composite dummy for wage freeze: 1 in 1979(1), 1979(2), 1988(2) and 1988(3).
yf_t	GDP excl. oil & shipping (mainland economy), volumes in fixed 1991-prices (logs)
$(yf_t - yf_t^*)$	Output gap, calculated with the smoothing filter algorithm proposed in Mellin and Teräsvirta (1992) ($m = 2, \lambda = 1600$)
pf_t	Foreign consumer prices, 1 in 1991 (logs)
RF_t	Foreign money market interest rates (3 months, annualized)
RN_t	Interest rate on 3 month Eurokrone deposits (annualized)

The data may be obtained from the internet, http://wotan.wiwi.hu-berlin.de/oekonometrie/engl/data.html

References

Akerlof GA (1979) Irving Fisher on his head: The consequences of constant target-threshold monitoring of money holdings. Quarterly Journal of Economics 93:169–188

Bårdsen G (1989) Estimation of long run coefficients in error correction models. Oxford Bulletin of Economics and Statistics 51:345–350

Bårdsen G (1992) Dynamic modelling of the demand for narrow money in Norway. Journal of Policy Modelling 14:363–393

Bårdsen G, Fisher PG, Nymoen R (1995) Business cycles: Real facts or fallacies. Working paper 1995/1, Norges Bank, Oslo

Brodin PA, Nymoen R (1992) Wealth effects and exogeneity: The Norwegian consumption function 1966(1)–1989(4). Oxford Bulletin of Economics and Statistics 54:431–454

Dengsøe I, Johansen S, Nielsen B, Rahbek A (1994) Test for cointegration rank in partial systems. Unpublished paper, Institute of Mathematical Statistics, University of Copenhagen

Eitrheim Ø (1995) The demand for broad money and tests for neglected monetary effects on inflation. Empirical evidence for Norway 1969–1993. Working paper 1995/8, Norges Bank, Oslo

Eitrheim Ø (1996) Four essays on the multivariate modelling of nonstationary economic time series. Ph.D. thesis, Department of Economics, University of Oslo

Engle RF, Hendry DF (1993) Testing super exogeneity and invariance in regression models. Journal of Econometrics 56:119–139

Hansen BE (1992) Testing for parameter instability in linear models. Journal of Policy Modelling 14:517–533

Hansen H, Johansen S (1993) Recursive estimation in cointegrated VAR-models. Preprint 1993/1, Institute of Mathematical Statistics, University of Copenhagen

Hendry DF (1995) Dynamic econometrics. Oxford University Press, Oxford

Hendry DF, Doornik JA (1996) Empirical econometric modelling using PcGive 9.0: for Windows. International Thomson Business Press, London

Hendry DF, Ericsson NR (1991) Modeling the demand for narrow money in the United Kingdom and the United States. European Economic Review 35:833–886

Hendry DF, Mizon GE (1993) Evaluating dynamic econometric models by encompassing the VAR. In: Phillips PCB (Ed.) Models, methods and applications of econometrics, Basil Blackwell, Oxford, pp. 272–300

Hoover KD (1991) The causal directions between money and prices. Journal of Monetary Economics 27:381–423

Johansen S (1991) Estimation and hypothesis testing of cointegration vectors in Gaussian vector autoregressive models. Econometrica 59:1551–1580

Johansen S (1992) Cointegration in partial systems and the efficiency of single equation analysis. Journal of Econometrics 52:389–402

Johansen S (1995) Identifying restrictions of linear equations. Journal of Econometrics 69:111–132

Juselius K (1992) Domestic and foreign effects on prices in an open economy: The case of Denmark. Journal of Policy Modeling 14:401–428

Klovland J (1990) Wealth and the demand for money in Norway, 1968–1989. Discussion paper 01/1990, Bergen: Department of Economics, Norwegian School of Economics and Business Administration

Lin C-FJ, Teräsvirta T (1994) Testing the constancy of regression parameters against continuous structural change. Journal of Econometrics 62:211–228

Luukkonen R, Saikkonen P, Teräsvirta T (1988) Testing linearity against smooth transition autoregressive models. Biometrika 75:491–499

Mellin I, Teräsvirta T (1992) Estimating the smoothing parameter in piece-wise linear regression. In: Griffiths WE, Lütkepohl H, Bock ME (Eds.) Readings in Econometric Theory and Practice. Contributions to Economic Analysis. A volume in honour of George Judge, Elsevier Science Publishers B.V., Amsterdam , pp. 215–241

Milbourne R, Bucholtz P, Wasan MT (1983) A theoretical derivation of the functional form of short run money holdings. Review of Economic Studies 50:531–541

Miller MH, Orr D (1966) A model of the demand for money by firms. Quarterly Journal of Economics 80:413–434

Nickell S (1985) Error correction, partial adjustment and all that: An expository note. Oxford Bulletin of Economics and Statistics 47:119–129

Reimers HE (1992) Comparisons of tests for multivariate cointegration. Statistical Papers 33:335–359

Smith G (1986) A dynamic Baumol-Tobin model of money demand. Review of Economic Studies 53:465–469.

The stability of German money demand: Not just a myth*

Michael Scharnagl

Deutsche Bundesbank, Wilhelm-Epstein-Str. 14, D-60431 Frankfurt/Main, Germany (e-mail: michael.schamagl@bundesbank.de)

Abstract. The stability of German money demand has been analyzed in a series of papers in recent years, especially since unification. In this paper the critical question of stability is reviewed, using various estimation techniques and testing procedures for long-run stability. To take financial innovations into account, the opportunity cost measure is calculated by differentiating between traditional savings deposits and special savings facilities, which are a major form of financial innovation in Germany. Overall, there are strong indications of a stable long-run money-demand relationship.

Key words: Money demand, stability tests, financial innovations

JEL classifications: C22, C51, C52

1. Introduction

Owing to its importance for targeting monetary aggregates, money demand in Germany has always been a focus of interest. The stability of German money demand has been analyzed in a series of papers in recent years. Before reunification, the main focus was on the importance and implications of financial innovations. Since then, the focus has shifted to the question of whether there were structural breaks owing to reunification.

Using single-equation error-correction models or the Johansen procedure,

---

* I am indebted to G. Coenen, D. Gerdesmeier, B. Landau and A. Worms of the Deutsche Bundesbank, H.-E. Reimers, J. Wolters, two anonymous referees, as well as the participants in the workshop on "Money demand in Europe" for valuable comments. The data may be obtained from the internet, http://wotan.wiwi.hu-berlin.de/oekonometrie/engl/data.html

the studies mainly test whether there is a cointegrating relationship for the full sample or various subsamples that can be identified as a money-demand function. However, they do not explicitly take the nonstationary aspect of the variables into account when testing for the stability of the long-run relationship or the whole dynamic system.

Some studies use a (financial) wealth variable in addition to real GDP as the transactions variable to take account of an income elasticity that is greater than one (Gerdesmeier (1996), Möller and Jarchow (1996)), although there is no theory of the demand for money that postulates this parameter restriction. Other studies get coefficient estimates of unity by including the rate of inflation as an I(1) variable in the long-run relationship (Wolters and Lütkepohl (1997)).

This paper deals with the role of financial innovations and German reunification in German money demand. It is shown that the stability of the money demand function is not adversely affected by these factors. The analysis is restricted to the traditional approach of using real GDP and an opportunity cost measure as determinants of real money demand. The calculation of the M3 rate takes into account the differentiation between traditional forms of savings deposits and the relatively recent so-called special savings facilities. The return of the latter is much more market-oriented.

The paper is organized as follows. In section 2 several reasons for possible instabilities are discussed. A brief overview of the various approaches to estimating German money demand and their results is given in section 3. In section 4 the econometric methodology used is described. The empirical results are presented in section 5. Section 6 provides a summary.

2. Historical perspective

2.1 Financial innovations

A closer look at international evidence reveals that the development of the German financial markets was rather smooth, primarily owing to early measures of deregulation and liberalization, as well as a high degree of adaptability of the universal banking system to new needs. Nevertheless, Germany experienced innovations concerning financial assets with a potential influence on monetary policy. This applies particularly to euro deposits, commercial papers, money-market funds, and special savings facilities. From the viewpoint of monetary policy, on the one hand, these innovations bear market-related interest rates; on the other, they enjoy a high degree of liquidity. Therefore, it has become more difficult to differentiate between money and monetary capital.

Recently, savings deposits have increased rather strongly. The underlying time trend is strongly dominated by so-called special savings facilities. Investment in these facilities at three months' notice, which are part of M3, expanded especially in 1992/93 and owing to the revision of savings-transaction regulations in mid-1993. At the moment the expansion is continuing without slowing down. An incentive for credit institutions to promote such savings deposits was lower minimum reserve requirements than those on time deposits. Another reason could have been that investors focused more attention on returns. Despite their formal short-term notice, these savings facilities have a fairly long-term character, as only long-term non-terminability can ensure attractive yields, whereas savings deposits at "factual" three months' notice have a liquid character.

Money-market funds have been admitted in Germany since August 1994. At the beginning, a strong demand for these assets was discernible, reaching its peak for tax-law reasons in December 1994. Since April 1995, however, the demand has been leveling off, most probably because of low interest rates. These financial assets are highly liquid, as balances can be drawn on at one day's notice.

Financial innovations in general may affect both the stability of money demand and the adequate definition of money. They may also affect the appropriate kind of aggregation of financial assets. Whether or not instabilities resulting from financial innovations exist also depends on the definition of stability. Adequately respecified equations may still give time-invariant coefficients.[1] The rise in interest rates of M3 components more or less raises M3's own interest rate, thereby leading to effects on the interest-rate elasticity and possibly on the degree of control by the monetary authority.

The Bundesbank observes other measures of money, like M3 extended, which incorporates euro deposits and money market funds. In terms of the stability of the demand function, controlability, weak separability or the money-price relationship, Scharnagl (1996) shows that M3 has the most favorable results.

In this analysis, M3 is considered in its simple sum version. As already mentioned, financial innovations may change the optimal definition of money. This may create a need for a change in the definition of money used for monetary policy, especially by adding new components. Other types of aggregation are more robust to such phenomena. Divisia aggregates, for instance, incorporate "product innovations," but are not able to cope with "process innovations" (Ford et al. (1992)). There are some empirical studies for Germany indicating that, in practice, there are no relevant differences between simple sum and Divisia aggregates (Herrmann et al. (1994), Gaab (1996)), but it may be a matter of time before significant differences arise, and it may be due to the insufficient accuracy of the data available.

2.2 German unification

The monetary union between western and eastern Germany took place in July 1990. This caused a sharp increase in M3 (by 15%) and in GDP (by 8%). This 15% jump seemed to be an overly wide margin, but may have been necessary owing to the need for rapid economic restructuring in eastern Germany. Not only the sharp jump in the level of M3 but also a different behavior on the part of West and East German investors could have led to a change in the interest elasticity of M3. Because of the relatively low weight of eastern Germany, however, the impact on total money demand might have been quite moderate.

[1] See, e.g., the analysis by Ericsson et al. (1997) of the UK long-run money demand function.

3. Overview of recent studies

The vast literature on money demand in Germany differs in several respects.

Variables
Most of the studies on German money demand rely on M3, as M3 is the official target of the German central bank (Hansen and Kim (1995), Wolters et al. (1996), Wolters and Lütkepohl (1997)). Money-demand functions are in most cases specified in real terms. Exceptions to this are the Deutsche Bundesbank (1995a) and Gerdesmeier (1996). The scale variable is mostly represented by an income variable. Nevertheless, some of the studies additionally use a wealth variable (Gerdesmeier (1996), Möller and Jarchow (1996), Kole and Meade (1995)). Opportunity costs are usually defined by a long-term interest rate, sometimes its own rate of interest is also taken into account, as M3 contains interest-bearing components (Herrmann et al. (1994), Issing and Tödter (1995), Wolters et al. (1998), Wolters and Lütkepohl (1997)). Only a few studies include measures for currency substitution like the expected change in exchange rates (Deutsche Bundesbank (1995b), Tullio et al. (1996), Seitz and Reimers (1997)). In this context, perfect foresight, a random walk or some form of adaptive expectations is usually assumed.

Econometric methodology
A major result of many studies is the existence of a long-run equilibrium relationship. The Engle-Granger regression applied by Issing and Tödter (1995) gives stationary residuals. Hansen and Kim (1995) and Wolters et al. (1998) get loading coefficients of error-correction terms in respective models that are significantly different from zero. Likelihood ratio tests for significant eigenvalues in vector error-correction models indicate the existence of cointegration relationships. This is already an important fact pointing to the stability of the money-demand equation.

In addition to that, the analysis by Wolters et al. (1998) shows that the demand for M3 can be adequately characterized by a linear model. Nonlinearities might, for instance, be caused by financial innovations. They test for nonlinearities in the context of STR (smooth transition regression) models.

Stability tests
In earlier years the majority of studies concentrated on the existence of a cointegrating relationship, while in the last few years explicit tests for stability have been widely used. In light of the discussion on the exogeneity of break points by Perron (1989) and Rappoport and Reichlin (1989), even in the case of unification, recursive methods have to be applied because, owing to expectational effects, the timing is not known any more.

Gaab and Liedtke (1992) get variations in the long-run parameters for M3 using the Johansen procedure recursively. This study does not contain explicit tests on the significance of parameter variations. Hansen and Kim (1995) apply several tests for constancy of the long-run parameters. Their results are not unequivocal. Preliminary tests that assume no cointegration under the null hypothesis point to the existence of a long-run relationship. Then, applying stability tests for this relationship implies that there was a structural break owing to unification. Relying on the opposite version of the null hypothesis (cointegration), the LM test of Quintos and Phillips (1993) and the L_c test of Hansen (1992), however, provide evidence of stability.

On the basis of money-demand equations for West Germany, Gerlach (1994) performs static out-of-sample forecasts for unified Germany for the period from 90Q1 to 92Q4. Forecast errors turn out to be within confidence bands. The fact that forecast errors are positive in mean could be interpreted as a minor level shift in the demand for money. It does not provide enough evidence of an unstable money demand, because there are no changes in long-run elasticities.

Wolters and Lütkepohl (1997) obtain a stable relation if they take short-term variations of interest elasticity into account, which reflect different reactions of monetary capital to interest-rate variations in the period 1994/95. The Stock specification that underlies their specification differs slightly from the usual form, as it allows for a different type of adjustment process.

4. Econometric methodology

4.1 Estimating long-run relationships

In the present paper, different procedures for the estimation of long-run relationships are applied. This may help to give an impression of the sensitivity of the empirical results.

Until recently, the two-step Engle-Granger (1987) procedure was the dominating approach in estimating long-run coefficients. In the first step, these are estimated separately from the short-run dynamics. In spite of the theoretical super-consistency of the estimators of the long-run coefficients, there may still exist a substantial bias in small samples, resulting from neglecting the short-run dynamics in the static regression. This disadvantage is avoided in the Stock (1987) procedure, where the short-run dynamics and the long-run coefficients are estimated simultaneously. Another alternative is the dynamic OLS procedure suggested by Stock and Watson (1993). There, the potential simultaneity bias in the static long-run regression is accounted for by augmenting the regression by leads and lags of first differences of the right-hand side variables.

By applying the maximum likelihood approach developed by Johansen (1988, 1995) (trace test), we analyze whether there is cointegration between individually integrated variables and whether the variables explaining the demand for money are weakly exogenous, i.e., whether the equation can be interpreted as a money-demand function or not. Testing for exogeneity conditional models can possibly be derived. Another useful approach is the fully modified regression of Phillips and Hansen (1990), which assumes an à priori strict exogeneity of the explanatory variables. The simultaneity bias is corrected for by nonparametric modifications. To improve the finite sample properties, Gregory et al. (1996) suggest a correction of the endogenous variable for serial correlation before running the FMOLS regression ("corrected FMOLS").

4.2 Testing for stability

Cointegration implies the existence of a long-run relationship. Otherwise, the estimated linear combination would not be stationary. Stability of the money-demand function also implies that the parameters are stable. In order to find possible instabilities, estimation procedures are applied recursively. There is instability if the coefficients vary significantly when new observations are added. Nevertheless, it has to be kept in mind that there is a tendency for the path of coefficients to become flatter with an increasing number of observations. This might obscure instabilities. Another point to keep in mind is that OLS is very sensitive to new observations in small samples.

Test procedures that take the nonstationary aspect into account are proposed both by Hansen and Johansen (1993) and by Hansen (1992). Hansen and Johansen suggest the recursive estimation of a vector error-correction model. Non-constancy of cointegrating vectors and loading coefficients is reflected in time-varying eigenvalues. In a series of likelihood ratio tests, we can test whether the recursively estimated cointegration vectors are consistent with a specific cointegration space. The latter constitutes the space spanned by the cointegration vectors of the full sample. The recursive cointegrating vectors are estimated under the restriction that the coefficients of the short-run dynamics equal their full sample estimates. The test statistic, which is χ^2-distributed, compares the eigenvalues of the recursive version with the eigenvalues of the full sample version.

The starting points of Hansen's tests (supF, meanF, L_c) are the residuals of a fully modified OLS regression. These residuals are mixed normally distributed; therefore, F tests are applicable. The supF test is similar to a recursive Chow breakpoint test, which compares the parameters of different subsamples. Monte Carlo simulations indicate that the supF test reacts slowly to structural breaks in the long-run relationship (Kim (1994)). Sufficient data are needed after the break, relative to the sample length before the break. Otherwise, the test results are dominated by the stable part of the sample. The analysis by Gregory et al. (1996) shows that Hansen's test has good size properties when there are no structural breaks. The size deteriorates as the number of regressors increases. The meanF test and the L_c test treat the coefficients as martingale processes.

5. Empirical analysis

5.1 Data

The monetary aggregate (m) considered is M3, as it is the official target of the Bundesbank. Real money is calculated by using the GDP deflator (p). The transactions variable (yr) is specified by real GDP. For reasons of consistency, money and the transactions variable are deflated by the same index. From a theoretical point of view, the opportunity costs should be measured by the difference between a long-term interest rate and M3's own interest rate since M3 contains components that yield market-oriented returns. For the long-term rate, the yield of German government bonds seems to be the appropriate choice.

However, calculating M3's own interest rate poses problems. Unlike traditional forms of savings deposits, special savings facilities yield interest rates that are closely connected to money-market rates, while traditional forms yield interest rates that are relatively low and vary very little over time. Special

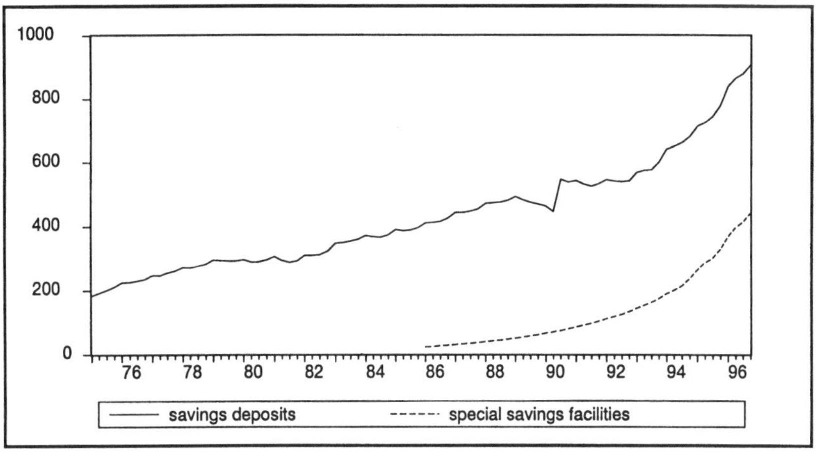

Fig. 1. Savings deposits versus special savings facilities

savings facilities cannot be differentiated according to their periods of notice before December 1993.

As can be seen from Fig. 1, special savings facilities show a strong increase in relation to all savings deposits. Because of a lack of data, special savings facilities at three months' notice are calculated – as a rather crude approximation – by assuming constant annual growth rates for the period 1986 to 1994.

The relevant interest rates are not available before November 1996. If the interest rate for savings deposits is used for all savings deposits up to that point, M3's own rate of return is underestimated. If one uses proxies for the rate of special savings facilities, e.g., the rate of "small" time deposits, one cannot allow for substitution effects. This is because decreasing rates of time deposits – relative to the rates of special savings facilities – cause a shift from time to savings deposits. If it is only caused by reallocation, the sum of both components will not change. If the M3's own rate is calculated by using the rate of time deposits, then M3's own rate will decrease. By using the appropriate rates, the overall effect may not be a decrease – at least, not to that extent.

For calculation of M3's own rate of return, lagged and variable weights are used. The weights are the relative portions of the components in M3. An alternative way might be the use of constant weights [mean of the full sample or of various sub-samples (e.g., Wolters et al. (1998))]. In the latter case, factors like the increasing importance of special savings facilities may not be adequately reflected.

In the following, two different measures of opportunity costs are used: a long-term rate of interest (rl) and the differential between the long-term rate and M3's own rate (rdsosp). M3's own rate is calculated by differentiating between traditional savings deposits and special savings facilities. In spite of the problems mentioned, for special savings facilities the rate of "small" time deposits is used to take into account the higher returns relative to those of traditional savings deposits. Figure 2 shows the time series of these measures. The time series of the interest differential is relatively similar to when there is

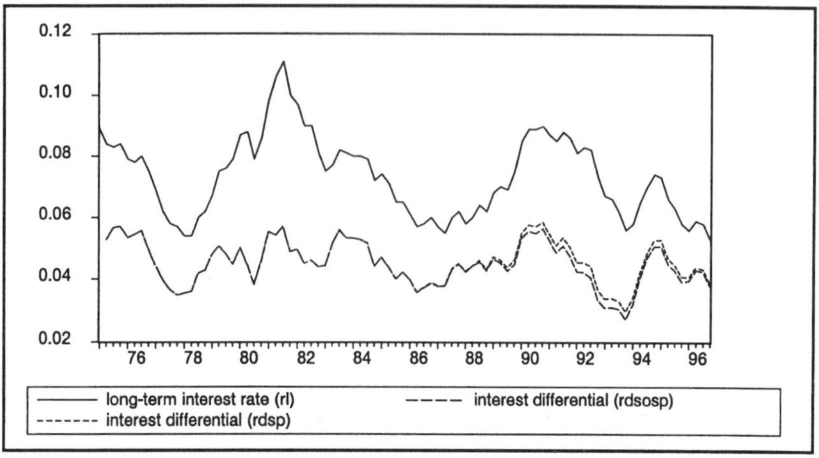

Fig. 2. Long-term interest rate versus interest differentials

no differentiation between traditional forms of savings deposits and special savings facilities (rdsp). Another possibility would be to use the rate of time deposits as the marginal rate of M3. That approach is not followed here.

The time series are not seasonally adjusted, because Ericsson et al. (1994) have shown that seasonal adjustment may imply adverse effects on the loadings. Seasonality is therefore modelled by deterministic seasonal dummies. The data are for the period from the first quarter of 1975 to the fourth quarter of 1996. The money stock variable and the opportunity cost measures are quarterly averages. All variables except interest rates are in logs.

For analyses in the Johansen framework CATS in RATS was used. The FMOLS and SupF results are calculated by the COINT 2.0 procedure in GAUSS. The other procedures were programmed in GAUSS 386.

5.2 Testing for unit roots

The nonstationarity of the various time series is tested by means of the augmented Dickey-Fuller test (ADF) and the Kwiatkowski et al. test (KPSS). The first test assumes a unit root under the null hypothesis, while the KPSS test assumes stationarity instead. These different formulations of the null hypothesis might have some influence on the results. In classical tests the null hypothesis is rejected only if there is strong evidence against it.

The ADF test of the variables in levels accounts for possible structural breaks in the various series owing to unification. Although the breakpoint seems to be known, a sequential approach is used (Banerjee et al. (1992)). Because of expectational effects, the break might have occurred earlier by at least the fourth quarter of 1989. The opening of the border might have caused an exceptional increase in West German GDP. The lag length is determined by deleting insignificant lag orders by means of the t-test, starting at a maximum order of eight. For the KPSS test the quadratic spectral kernel with a bandwidth of 8 is used, as Monte Carlo experiments by Lee (1996) show

Table 1. Testing for unit roots[2]

variable	specification	ADF	KPSS
m – p	T, C C	–3.26 –8.43*	
yr	T, C C	–2.86 –11.56*	
Δp	C C	–2.80 –4.86*	0.26
rl	C C	–2.99 –3.86*	0.13
rdsosp	C C	–4.69 –5.54*	0.22

better size and power properties if the bandwidth is determined exogenously, instead of using the plug-in method proposed by Andrews (1991).

In each panel, the first line contains the results for the test in levels, the second line the results for the tests in first differences. Typically, the tests indicate a unit root in the time series, i.e., they are integrated of order one. Exceptions might be interest rates and the inflation rate. For the long-term rate and the interest differential, the results are not unique. This is connected with the relatively low power of the ADF test. In the case of the ADF test, the null hypothesis of a unit root in levels cannot be rejected, whereas in the case of the KPSS test, the null hypothesis of stationarity cannot be rejected.

However, the autocorrelation function of interest rates shows a relatively slow decay. It is much slower than is normally characteristic of stationary variables. Therefore, it may be better to assume interest rates to be non-stationary. Estimating a fractional integrated model applying the Geweke-Porter-Hudak (1983) procedure yields a parameter value of 0.61.

The results are also of interest for the question as to whether the inflation rate, in addition, should be included in the long-run relationship as a measure of opportunity costs. In some studies, e.g., Wolters and Lütkepohl (1997), this is done to account for the decreasing trend of the velocity of money in the sample period. This approach is not followed here, since the unit root tests give indications of the stationarity of the inflation rate.

5.3 Testing for cointegration and weak exogeneity

In the following, a three-dimensional vector error-correction system for real money, real GDP and an interest rate variable is analyzed. The lag order k is chosen – starting from a lower lag order – in order to get white noise residuals. The models estimated contain an unrestricted constant, centred seasonal

[2] T represents a time trend, C a constant in the regressions. Critical values for ADF are from MacKinnon (1991), for the ADF test allowing for structural breaks from Banerjee et al. (1992) and for KPSS test statistics from Kwiatkowski et al. (1992).* means significance at the 5% level.

dummies and four lags. In the short-run dynamics the inflation rate is included to relax the assumption of price homogeneity. Also included are three impulse dummy variables: D903 = 1 in 90Q3, D934 = 1 in 93Q4 and 94Q1 and D944 = 1 in 94Q4, 0 otherwise. D903 accounts for the increase in money owing to unification. D934 and D944 allow for extreme variations in the demand for money that can be explained by changes in tax regulations for investment funds. Since the beginning of 1994, following the distributing funds, the tax withheld on interest income has been payable on interest income from growth funds as well. This led to massive sales of such papers by domestic nonbanks at the end of 1993, thus driving M3 up. At the beginning of 1995, property tax for household wealth was increased from 0.5% to 1.0%, although, among other things, investment in money market funds was exempted. At the end of 1994, therefore, noticeable shifts from M3 components to money-market certificates occurred.

The values of the trace statistics are presented in Table 2. Owing to the modifications (inclusion of dummy variables and of the inflation rate in the short-run dynamics), the tabulated critical values in Hansen and Juselius (1995) are not valid any more. However, the test statistics for $r = 0$ are clearly above the relevant critical value; hence the trace test indicates the existence of one long-run relationship. LM(1) and LM(4) are multivariate versions of Lagrange Multiplier test statistics for autocorrelation of orders one and four. NV is the multivariate version of the test for normality. Marginal significance levels are given in parentheses.

Variables are weakly exogenous with respect to cointegrating vectors if the corresponding long-run relationship is not significant in the respective equations for the short-run dynamics. Since the results in Table 3 indicate that real

Table 2. Testing for cointegration

null hypothesis	rl	rdsosp	critical value (5%)
$r = 0$	40.82	37.58	29.38
$r = 1$	9.01	13.55	15.34
$r = 2$	0.04	0.82	3.84
LM(1)	6.76 (0.66)	4.15 (0.90)	
LM(4)	10.73 (0.29)	16.28 (0.06)	
NV	10.52 (0.10)	8.88 (0.18)	

Table 3. Testing for weak exogeneity

	rl	rdsosp
$\hat{\alpha}_1$	−0.13 (6.03)	−0.11 (5.05)
$\alpha_2 = \alpha_3 = 0$	0.70 (0.71)	1.37 (0.51)

GDP and the measure of opportunity costs are weakly exogenous for the long-run parameters and there is just one long-run relationship, the equation estimated can be interpreted as a demand for money function. The adjustments to disequilibria occur via changes in real money.

$\hat{\alpha}_1$ are the loading coefficients of the equilibrium error in the dynamic equation for real money (t-values are included in parentheses) for the two versions of opportunity costs. In all cases the ECM terms have signifcant influence on the development of money. The cells corresponding to $\alpha_2 = \alpha_3 = 0$ give the values of the test statistics of the joint hypothesis that the transactions variable and the opportunity cost variable are weakly exogenous (marginal significance levels are given in parentheses).

5.4 Estimation of long-run parameters

Table 4 shows the income elasticities $\hat{\beta}_1$ and interest semi-elasticities $\hat{\beta}_2$ for the various models and procedures for the period from 1975 to 1996 (t-values in parentheses). The t-values for the coefficients of the Stock regression are calculated by the respective Bewley-transformed equation. The results of the Johansen procedure are those of the partial model, where one cointegrating relationship and weak exogeneity of real GDP and the interest rate variable are imposed. The short-run dynamics include the inflation rate Δp_t. In the framework of the FMOLS methodology, the long-run variance is calculated by means of the quadratic spectral (qs) kernel. Simulation analyses have shown that the specific form of weighting (Bartlett, Parzen, qs) is of little relevance. Much more important is the choice of the lag truncation parameter. Here, the bandwidth is determined by the automatic procedure suggested by Andrews (1991), using pre-whitened residuals, because of good small-sample properties.

Without exception, Table 4 contains income elasticities ($\hat{\beta}_1$) that are greater than one. The χ^2 test statistic in the Johansen framework corresponding to the null hypothesis $\beta_1 = 1$ gives 13.70 (marginal significance $=$ 0.00) for the rl case. This implies a decreasing trend in the velocity of money (see Fig. 3).

Table 4. Results for long-run coefficients

	rl		rdsosp	
	$\hat{\beta}_1$	$\hat{\beta}_2$	$\hat{\beta}_1$	$\hat{\beta}_2$
DOLS	1.31 (62.94)	−0.85 (2.67)	1.30 (60.86)	−0.86 (1.12)
Stock (Bewley)	1.30 (31.52)	−0.70 (1.16)	1.27 (2.40)	−2.40 (2.09)
FMOLS	1.33 (23.17)	−0.79 (1.01)	1.33 (26.47)	−1.13 (0.89)
corrected FMOLS	1.32 (16.80)	−1.34 (1.27)	1.32 (15.75)	−2.01 (0.95)
Johansen	1.23 (45.56)	−1.01 (2.48)	1.20 (34.23)	−2.44 (1.99)

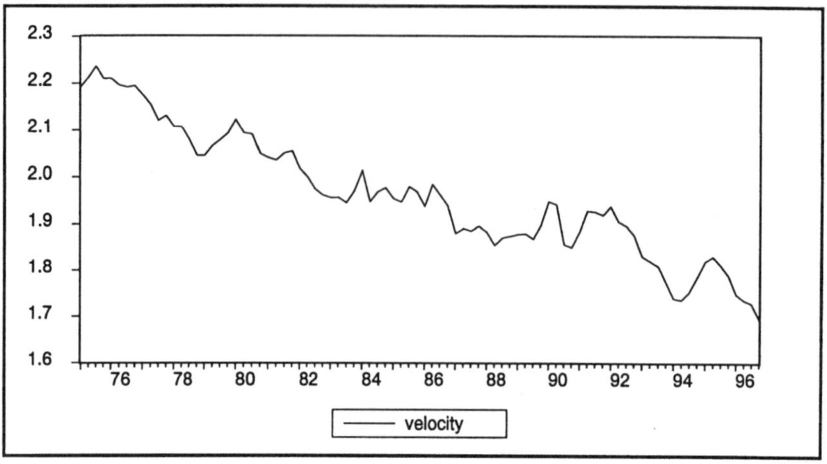

Fig. 3. Income velocity of M3

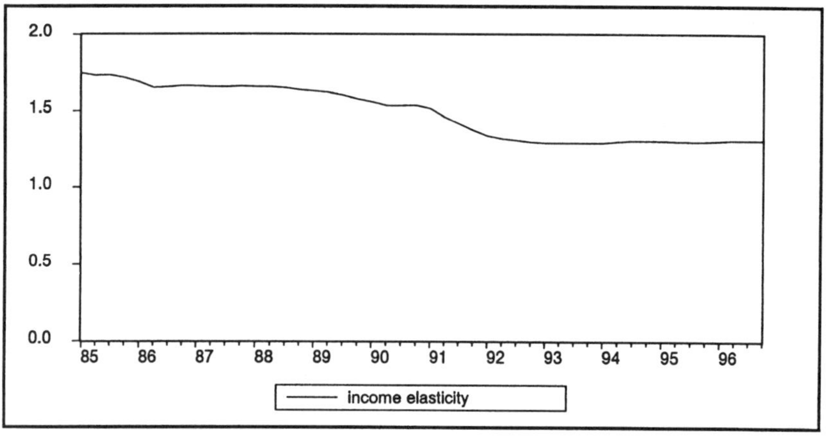

Fig. 4. Recursive long-run income elasticities

As Gerdesmeier (1996) shows, one reason for this could be the wealth accumulation motive for holding money. Möller and Jarchow (1996) and Kole and Meade (1995) get the same results. These studies also show that consideration of a wealth variable is not necessary to obtain a stable demand for money equation. The transactions variable also accounts for wealth effects if the latter variable is omitted, especially if wealth is approximated by financial wealth, as financial wealth and real GDP seem to be cointegrated.

5.5 Tests for long-run stability

Figure 4 shows the development of the long-run income elasticity estimated by recursive DOLS. There is not much variation over time.

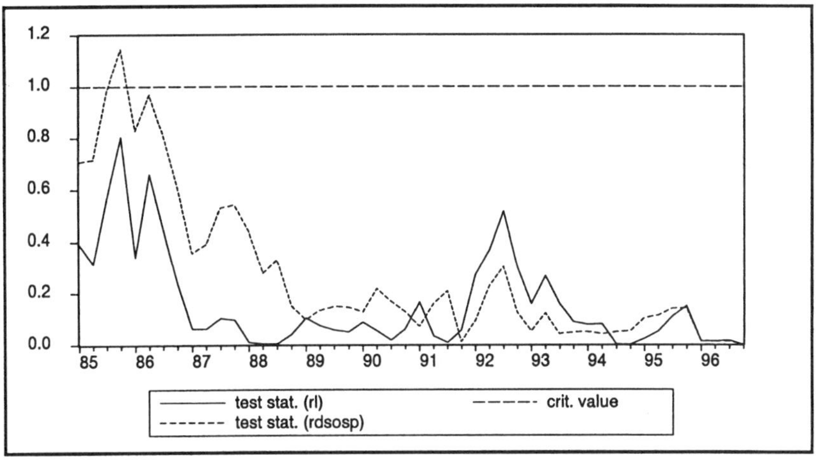

Fig. 5. Recursive test by Hansen and Johansen

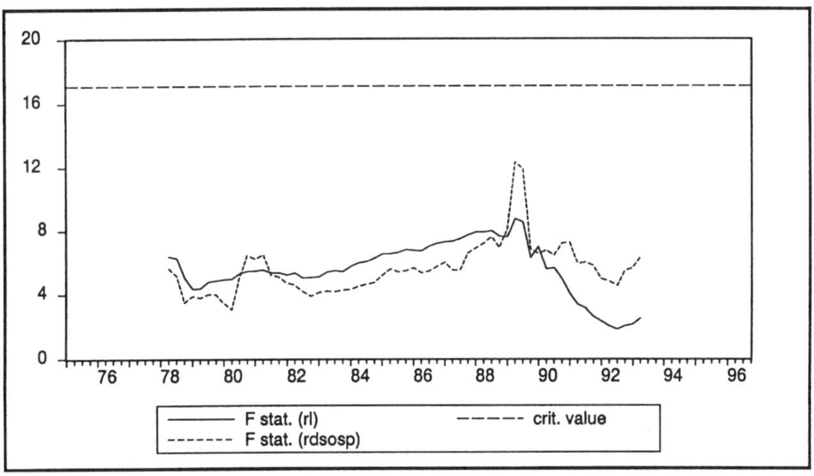

Fig. 6. Recursive F-statistics

The recursive analysis starts in 1985, so as to get enough observations for the estimation of the first subsample. Figure 5 shows the path of the recursive likelihood ratio test statistics by Hansen and Johansen (1993). For the various subsamples, it is always below the critical value (5% level), with one exception in the rdsosp model. The cointegrating vectors (coefficients) for the different subsamples – conditional on the same short-run dynamics – are not significantly different from that of the full sample.

The test procedure in the fully modified framework by Hansen (1992) gives the same result (Table 5). Figure 6 shows the recursively estimated F-statistics that are the basis of the supF and the meanF statistics. The relevant critical value is 17.30 (5% level).

A problem in the application of the supF test or the meanF test is the

Table 5. Testing for long-run stability

	rl	rdsosp	critical value (5%)
supF	8.73	12.33	17.30
meanF	5.58	5.61	7.69
L_c	0.63	0.52	0.78

"trimming," i.e., the first and the last observations have to be truncated in order to stabilize the test statistics. Otherwise these statistics would tend towards infinity with a high probability. According to Andrews (1991), the test is restricted to an interval given by $t \in (0.15, 0.85)$.

The advantage of the L_c statistics is that there is no necessity for trimming, i.e., testing for stability is possible over the whole range of observations. The results show that the null hypothesis of stability cannot be rejected for the full sample.

6. Conclusions

The demand for money in Germany is remarkably stable. The present paper confirms this by making use of different alternative estimation procedures. This leads to the conclusion that the preconditions for monetary targeting in Germany still apply, as there is also a long-run relationship between money and prices (Deutsche Bundesbank (1997)). This stable relationship may be a contribution to a stable European demand for money.

References

Andrews DWK (1991) Heteroskedasticity and autocorrelation consistent covariance matrix estimation. Econometrica 59:817–858

Banerjee A, Lumsdaine RL, Stock JH (1992) Recursive and sequential tests of the unit root and trend-break hypothesis: Theory and international evidence. Journal of Business and Economic Statistics 10:271–288

Deutsche Bundesbank (1995a) Review of the monetary target and restructuring of the minimum reserve regulations. Monthly Report 47, July:19–37

Deutsche Bundesbank (1995b) Demand for money and currency substitution in Europe. Monthly Report 47, January:33–49

Deutsche Bundesbank (1997) Review of the monetary target, Monthly Report 49, August:17–32

Engle RF, Granger CWJ (1987) Cointegration and error correction: Representation, estimation, and testing. Econometrica 55:251–275

Engle RF, Hendry DF, Richard J-F (1983) Exogeneity. Econometrica 51:277–304

Ericsson NR, Hendry DF, Tran H-A (1994) Cointegration, seasonality, encompassing, and the demand for money in the UK. In: Hargreaves CP (ed.) Nonstationary time series analysis and cointegration, Oxford University Press, Oxford, pp. 179–224

Ericsson NR, Hendry DF, Prestwich KM (1997) The UK demand for broad money over the long run. Nuffield College, Oxford

Ford JL, Peng W, Mullineux AW (1992) Financial innovation and divisia monetary aggregates. Oxford Bulletin of Economics and Statistics. 54:87–102

Gaab W (1996) On the demand for divisia and simple-sum M3 in Germany. In Mullineux A (ed.) Financial innovation, banking and monetary aggregates, Edward Elgar, pp. 160–186

Gaab W, Liedtke O (1992) On the long-run relationship between money, output and interest rates: A cointegration analysis for West Germany. Recherches Economiques de Louvain 58:455–471

Gerdesmeier D (1996) The role of wealth in money demand. Discussion Paper, Deutsche Bundesbank

Gerlach S (1994) German unification and the demand for German M3. Working Paper, No. 21, Bank for International Settlements, Basle

Geweke J, Porter-Hudak S (1983) The estimation and application of long memory time series models. Journal of Time Series Analysis 4:221–238

Gregory AW, Nason JM, Watt DG (1996) Testing for structural breaks in cointegrated relationships. Journal of Econometrics 71:321–341

Hansen BE (1992) Tests for parameter instability in regression with I(1) processes. Journal of Business and Economic Statistics 10:321–335

Hansen G, Kim R-J (1995) The stability of German money demand. Tests of the cointegration relation. Weltwirtschaftliches Archiv 131:286–301

Hansen H, Johansen S (1993) Recursive estimation in cointegrated VAR-models. Preprint 1993, No. 1, Institute of Mathematical Statistics, University of Copenhagen

Hansen H, Juselius K (1995) CATS in RATS: Cointegration analysis of time series. Evanston

Herrmann H, Reimers H-E, Tödter K-H (1994) Weighted monetary aggregates for Germany. Discussion Paper, Deutsche Bundesbank

Issing O, Tödter K-H (1995) Geldmenge und Preise im vereinigten Deutschland. In: Duwendag D (ed.) Neuere Entwicklungen in der Geldtheorie und Währungspolitik, Duncker & Humbolt, Berlin, pp. 97–123

Johansen S (1988) Statistical analysis of cointegration vectors. Journal of Economic Dynamics and Control 12:231–254

Johansen S (1995) Likelihood-based inference in cointegrated vector autoregressive models. Oxford University Press, Oxford

Kim R-J (1994) Analyse kointegrierter Modelle. Haag und Herchen, Frankfurt

Kole LS, Meade EE (1995) German monetary targeting: A retrospective view. Federal Reserve Bulletin 81:917–931

Kwiatkowski D, Phillips PCB, Schmidt P, Shin Y (1992) Testing the null hypothesis of stationarity against the alternative of a unit root. Journal of Econometrics 54:159–178

Lee J (1996) On the power of stationarity tests using optimal bandwidth estimates. Economics Letters 51:131–137

MacKinnon J (1991) Critical values for cointegration tests. In: Engle RF, Granger CWJ (eds.) Long-run economic relationships, Oxford University Press, Oxford, pp. 276–276

Möller H, Jarchow H-J (1996) Zur Umlaufsgeschwindigkeit von M3. Jahrbücher für Nationalökonomie und Statistik. 215:308–327

Perron P (1989) The great crash, the oil price shock and the unit root hypothesis. Econometrica 57:1361–1401

Phillips PCB, Hansen BE (1990) Statistical inference in instrumental variables regression with I(1) processes. Review of Economic Studies 57:99–125

Quintos CE, Phillips PCB (1993) Parameter constancy in cointegrating regressions. Empirical Economics 18:675–706

Rappoport P, Reichlin L (1989) Segmented trends and non-stationary time series. Economic Journal 98:449–475

Scharnagl M (1996) Monetary aggregates with special reference to structural changes in the financial markets. Discussion Paper, Deutsche Bundesbank

Seitz F, Reimers H-E (1997) Currency substitution: A theoretical and empirical analysis for Germany and Europe. Manchester School, forthcoming

Stock JH (1987) Asymptotic properties of least squares estimators of cointegrating vectors. Econometrica 55:1035–1056

Stock JH, Watson MW (1993) A simple estimator of cointegrating vectors in higher order integrated systems. Econometrica 61:783–820

Tullio G, de Souza E, Giucca P (1996) The demand for money functions in Europe and in Germany before and after the fall of the Berlin Wall. In: De Grauwe P, Micossi S, Tullio G (eds.) Inflation and wage behaviour in Europe, Clarendon Press, Oxford, pp. 310–338

Wolters J, Lütkepohl H (1997) Die Geldnachfrage für M3: neue Ergebnisse für das vereinigte Deutschland. Ifo Studien 43:35–55

Wolters J, Teräsvirta T, Lütkepohl H (1998) Modelling the demand for M3 in the Unified Germany. Review of Economics and Statistics, 80: 399–409

A money demand system for German M3*

Helmut Lütkepohl[1], **Jürgen Wolters**[2]

[1] Institut für Statistik und Ökonometrie, Wirtschaftswissenschaftliche Fakultät, Humboldt-Universität, Spandauer Str. 1, 10178 Berlin, Germany (e-mail: /luetke@wiwi.hu-berlin.de)
[2] Institut für Statistik und Ökonometrie, Fachbereich Wirtschaftswissenschaft, Freie Universität, Boltzmannstr. 20, 14195 Berlin, Germany (e-mail: /jwolters@wiwiss.fu-berlin.de)

Abstract. A small macroeconomic model is constructed starting from a German money demand relation for M3 based on quarterly, seasonally unadjusted data for the period from 1976 to 1996. In contrast to previous studies we build a vector error correction model for M3, GNP, an inflation rate and an interest rate spread variable to represent opportunity costs of holding money. Furthermore, import price inflation is added as an exogenous variable. The model is used to analyze the relation between money growth and inflation by means of an impulse response analysis.

Key words: Cointegration analysis, impulse response analysis, monetary policy, money demand, structural vector autoregressive model

JEL classifications: C32, E52, E41

1. Introduction

For more than 20 years the Deutsche Bundesbank has used a money growth target to control inflation in Germany. A detailed account of this policy is given by Issing (1997). A stable money demand relation is an important prerequisite for such a policy strategy. Since the late eighties this policy is based on the money stock variable M3. Therefore a number of studies have analyzed the stability of money demand relations for M3 for the unified Germany (e.g., Tullio, de Souza & Giucca (1996), Hansen & Kim (1995), Issing & Tödter

* We thank Gerd Hansen for soliciting two anonymous referee reports on an earlier version of this article and thereby helping in the editorial process for this volume. We are grateful to him, Timo Teräsvirta, Kirstin Hubrich and the two referees for comments that helped us to improve our paper. Financial support was provided by the DFG, Sonderforschungsbereich 373.

(1995), Deutsche Bundesbank (1995), Scharnagl (1998) and Kole & Meade (1995)). All these studies focus on a single equation analysis. Stability of a money demand relation can be viewed as a necessary condition for using a money growth target for controlling the price level because without such a relation the current monetary policy has little theoretical basis. On the other hand, a stable money demand relation is not a sufficient requirement for this policy strategy. In this study we will therefore construct a small macro model for the money stock, income, inflation and an opportunity cost variable for holding money based on an interest rate spread. This system enables us to get a more complete picture of the effects of monetary policy.

Systems analyses for German M3 with a similar objective have also been conducted by Hansen & Kim (1996), Juselius (1996, 1998), Hubrich (1998) and Deutsche Bundesbank (1997). All these studies differ in important respects from our present analysis. Hansen & Kim (1996) use seasonally adjusted data and analyze the preunification period only. Obviously, an event like the German unification is expected to result in major shifts and adjustment processes in the economic system. Since the Bundesbank has continued its policy of monetary targeting after the German monetary unification (GMU) on July 1, 1990, it is of importance to check whether the conditions in the underlying economic system are still suitable. Moreover, Hansen & Kim (1996) include the beginning of the seventies in their sample period when the Bundesbank did not pursue a policy of monetary targeting. Including two different policy regimes in the sampling period may distort the results and estimators. It may in fact require appropriate modifications of the model.

Juselius (1996) uses quarterly data from 1975 to 1994 and finds a break in her model in 1983. She focusses on analyzing the possible differences in the monetary mechanisms in the two regimes. The analysis starts from a full vector autoregressive model and centers on the long-run relations. Hubrich (1998) uses quarterly data from 1979 to 1994 and also analyzes the long-run relations in a small money demand system for German M3. She finds some evidence for stable long-run relations for the period before and after the GMU. This obviously contrasts with the results of Juselius (1996). Based on a full vector error correction system the Deutsche Bundesbank (1997) computes impulse responses which show significant effects of shocks in M3 on the price level but not vice versa. This result supports the view that M3 is a useful indicator for controlling inflation. Details of other interactions between the variables of the model are not provided.

For a more complete picture of the channels of monetary policy it is necessary, however, to consider the dynamics of the system in more detail. Therefore we will attempt to specify a small model with a more complete specification of the dynamic structure. We use seasonally unadjusted data for the period 1976(1) to 1996(4). The money demand relation is the central function of interest here. Therefore the ingredients of such a function are the core variables of our system, namely money, income, prices and interest rates. Since M3 is the intermediate target of the Bundesbank we use this variable here as our measure of the money stock. Clearly a model which fully explains all the variables of interest in the money demand relation would require modelling the whole economy. Since this is an infeasible task we focus on the variable of main interest, namely M3, and specify the other variables only partially.

In the next section we will briefly review the theoretical background of our model and the general modelling framework. In Section 3 the empirical model is specified and estimated. An analysis of the dynamic interrelationships between the variables of the model is presented in Section 4 and conclusions are given in Section 5.

2. The theoretical model

For a period covering German unification, Wolters, Teräsvirta & Lütkepohl (1998) (henceforth WTL) and Wolters & Lütkepohl (1997) (henceforth WL) find a stable long-run money demand relation for M3 of the following form

$$(m-p)_t = \beta_1 y_t + \beta_2 \Delta p_t + \beta_3 (R-r)_t + v, \tag{2.1}$$

where m_t is the logarithm of M3, y_t is the logarithm of real GNP, p_t is the logarithm of the GNP deflator, hence, $(m-p)_t$ is the logarithm of real M3 and $\Delta p_t := p_t - p_{t-1}$ is the quarterly inflation rate. Moreover, R_t is a long-term interest rate ('Umlaufsrendite') and r_t is the own rate of M3 so that $(R-r)_t$ represents the opportunity costs of holding M3 rather than longer term bonds.[1] The models in WTL and WL are based on quarterly seasonally unadjusted data for the periods 1976(1) to 1994(2) and 1976(1) to 1996(1), respectively. The series are plotted in Fig. 1 for 1976(1) to 1996(4) which is the observation period we will use in the following. Looking at the graphs of the time series $(m-p)_t$ and y_t a remarkable level shift due to the GMU in 1990(3) becomes apparent. It turns out that this feature can be captured by a shift in the intercept term v in the relation (2.1). On the other hand, Δp_t and $(R-r)_t$ do not show apparent breaks due to the GMU.

Obviously, in (2.1) money demand depends on income y_t which represents the transactions volume and on variables representing opportunity costs for holding money. This is obvious for the interest rate differential $(R-r)_t$. There is some ambiguity in the interpretation of the role of the inflation rate Δp_t (see also Goldfeld & Sichel (1987)). Normally it is seen as a measure of opportunity costs for holding real assets. However, it may also represent the kind of adjustment process used by agents. More precisely, it may capture whether agents actively adjust their nominal portfolios only or also passively adjust their assets induced by changes in the price level. WL show within a cost minimization framework based on the approaches by Hendry & von Ungern-Sternberg (1981) and Hwang (1985) that therefore the inflation rate enters the long-run relation even if it does not appear in the desired long-run money demand relation.

WTL found $(m-p)_t$, y_t and Δp_t to be $I(1)$ variables, that is, variables which are stationary after differencing once, whereas $(R-r)_t$ is stationary. WTL also found that there is just one cointegrating relation for $(m-p)_t$, y_t and Δp_t which may be interpreted as a long-run money demand function.[2] Thus, we proceed under the assumption that a relation $(m-p)_t - \beta_1 y_t - \beta_2 \Delta p_t$ is stationary if a level shift for the post-GMU period is properly accounted for. Because further stationary variables may influence a cointegration relation

[1] For the precise definitions of the variables and the data sources see the Appendix.

[2] See Table 1 of WTL for a cointegration analysis for the period 1976(1)–1994(2).

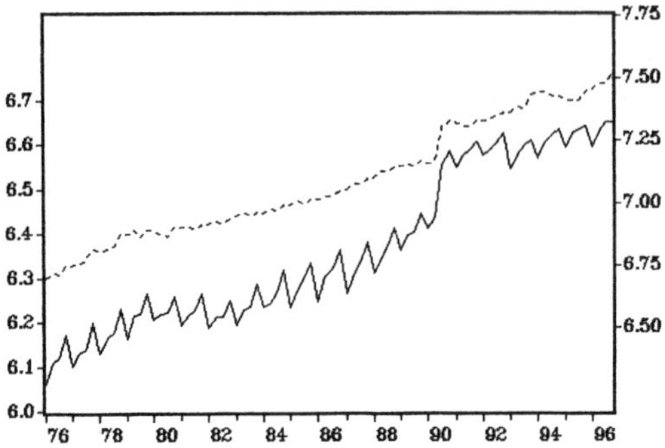

logarithms of real GNP y_t (—) and M3 $(m-p)_t$ (---)

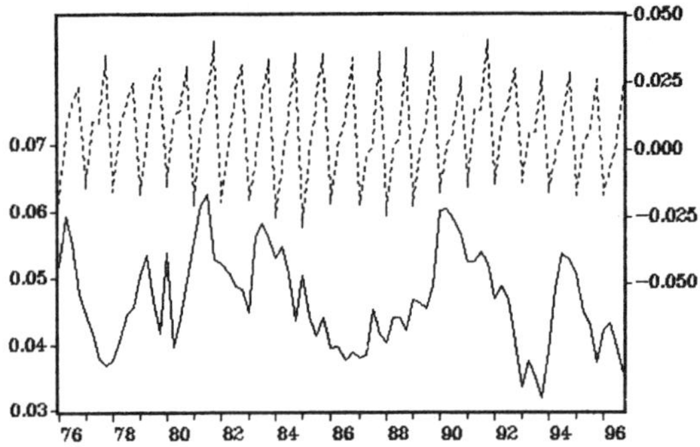

interest rate spread $(R-r)_t$ (—) and quarterly inflation rate Δp_t (---)

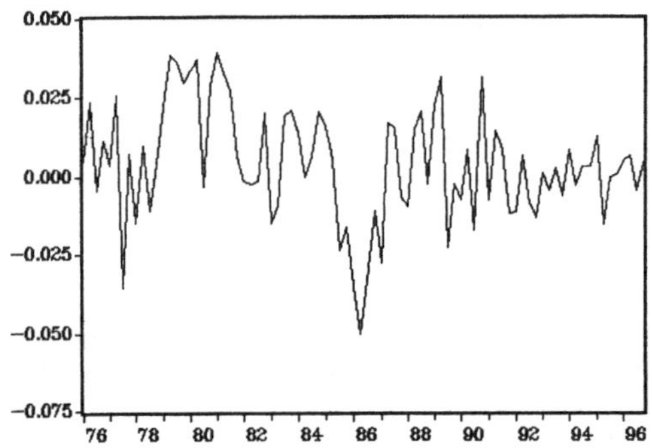

quarterly import price inflation rate Δpm_t

Fig. 1. Time series used

and because the interest rate differential turned out to be an important opportunity cost variable in the fully specified equation, it was included in the long-run relation. Given this relation the central variables in the transmission mechanism for monetary policy are $(m-p)_t$, y_t, Δp_t and $(R-r)_t$. Hence, in the following we will construct a four equation model for these variables.

We will do so in the general context of a multivariate error correction model (ECM) of the form

$$\Gamma_0 \Delta z_t = \alpha\beta' z_{t-1} + \Gamma_1 \Delta z_{t-1} + \cdots + \Gamma_p \Delta z_{t-p} + \Phi x_t + \Xi D_t + u_t, \tag{2.2}$$

where $z_t = [(m-p)_t, y_t, \Delta p_t, (R-r)_t]'$, x_t is a vector of exogenous or unmodelled variables, D_t includes all deterministic terms and u_t is the error vector which is assumed to be serially uncorrelated with zero mean and constant nonsingular covariance matrix. The Γ_i are structural coefficient matrices which is emphasized by the fact that Γ_0 is not a priori assumed to be an identity matrix. The first term on the right-hand side of the system (2.2) is the error correction term with $\beta' z_{t-1}$ representing the cointegration relations and α being the loading matrix containing the weights of the cointegration relations in the equations of the system. In our case we have basically just one cointegration relation, namely the long-run money demand function. In addition the interest rate spread $(R-r)_t$ is stationary and, hence, may be regarded as a cointegration relation in a set-up like (2.2). However, alternatively one may just reparameterize a model such as (2.2) by eliminating all differences of stationary variables. Such a reparameterization complicates the notation when the full model is of interest in EC form. It is quite natural when the individual equations are considered, however. Therefore we will use such a form in the empirical analysis of the next section where we focus on the individual equations of the system. Thereby we just have to consider one cointegration relation in all the equations.

Because Germany is an open economy we use the logarithm of an import price index pm_t as an exogenous variable which captures the effects of the exchange rate and therefore is an important variable for influencing the monetary transmission mechanism in Germany (see also Issing & Tödter (1995), Hansen & Kim (1996) and Deutsche Bundesbank (1997)). Since pm_t is also $I(1)$[3] and we have taken care of the nonstationarities of the endogenous variables with a cointegration relation already, we include Δpm_t, the inflation rate of import prices, which is a stationary variable. A period of unusually slow and even negative growth of the money stock due to an enormous substitution into short-term interest bearing assets not included in M3 has occurred in 1994 and 1995. WL found that this phenomenon could be well explained by allowing for a higher interest rate elasticity in this period. This effect can be captured by a variable $d_t(R-r)_t$, where $d_t = 1$ for 1994(3)–1995(4) and zero elsewhere. The variable $d_t(R-r)_t$ is therefore active for just a period of six quarters. It may also be thought of as a component of the vector of exogenous variables for notational convenience although it is, of course, part of the endogenous variable $(R-r)_t$.

The vector of deterministic terms D_t includes an intercept term, seasonal dummies and other dummies representing special events. For instance, the shift in the long-run relation due to the GMU has to be matched by a shift dummy and its first differences which results in an impulse dummy for 1990(3) in the short-term part of the model. Since the deterministic terms appearing in the individual equations differ, we will discuss them in more detail when we present the individual equations in the empirical analysis of the next section.

---

[3] An augmented Dickey-Fuller test for Δpm_t with a constant and four lags shows a t-value of -3.53, thus rejecting nonstationarity of Δpm_t at the 1% level.

3. The empirical model

3.1 The money demand equation

We do not simply use the relation from WL here because our data set has been extended. Instead we reestimated the money demand relation.[4] In WL the maximum lag length of the stationary variables was two. Given the strong seasonal pattern of the inflation rate (see Fig. 1), a lag length of two is clearly insufficient for the full system. Therefore we allow for up to four lags in the multivariate model. Hence, for consistency, we also use four lags of the stationary variables initially in setting up the money demand relation. More precisely, we use the simple Stock (1987) estimation approach, regressing in our case $\Delta(m-p)_t$ on $(m-p)_{t-1}$, y_{t-1}, Δp_{t-1}, all differences of these variables up to lag order four, the interest rate differential up to lag order four, $d_t(R-r)_t$, an intercept term, seasonal dummy variables (denoted by d_{jt}), a step dummy $S90q3_t$ and impulse dummies $I90q3_t$, $I92q4_t$ and $I93q3_t$.[5] The following equation results by going through a model reduction procedure as in WTL and WL where successively the least significant variables are eliminated:[6]

$$\begin{aligned}
\Delta(m-p)_t = & -\underset{(-5.0)}{0.104}(m-p-y)_{t-1} - \underset{(-6.9)}{1.399}\,\Delta p_{t-1} - \underset{(-4.8)}{0.205}\,\Delta y_{t-1} \\
& - \underset{(-7.7)}{1.093}\,\Delta^2 p_t - \underset{(-2.3)}{0.230}\,\Delta^2 p_{t-4} - \underset{(-4.4)}{0.582}(R-r)_{t-1} \\
& + \underset{(2.2)}{0.390}(R-r)_{t-3} - \underset{(-2.1)}{0.363}(R-r)_{t-4} \\
& - \underset{(-5.9)}{0.407}\,d_t(R-r)_t + \underset{(8.8)}{0.176} - \underset{(-10.4)}{0.101}\,d_{1t} - \underset{(-9.4)}{0.072}\,d_{2t} \\
& - \underset{(-14.9)}{0.055}\,d_{3t} + \underset{(5.4)}{0.014}\,S90q3_t + \underset{(17.7)}{0.131}\,I90q3_t \\
& - \underset{(-3.3)}{0.022}\,I92q4_t - \underset{(-2.7)}{0.018}\,I93q3_t + \hat{u}_{mt}
\end{aligned} \tag{3.1}$$

$T = 84$ [1976(1)–1996(4)]

$\bar{R}^2 = 0.93$	SE $= 0.0062$	JB $= 1.00$ (0.61)
LM(1) $= 0.73$ (0.40)	LM(4) $= 0.64$ (0.64)	LM(8) $= 0.56$ (0.80)
ARCH(1) $= 0.12$ (0.73)	ARCH(2) $= 0.24$ (0.79)	ARCH(4) $= 0.51$ (0.73)

The numbers in parentheses behind the values of the test statistics are the corresponding p-values. JB is the Jarque-Bera test for normality, LM(k), $k = 1, 4, 8$, are Lagrange-multiplier (LM) tests for autocorrelation based on 1,

[4] The computations reported in this section were done by EVIEWS 2.0.

[5] The precise definition of the dummy variables is as follows: $S90q3_t$ is 1 from the third quarter of 1990 onwards and zero before that quarter. $I90q3_t$, $I92q4_t$ and $I93q3_t$ are 1 in 1990(3), 1992(4) and 1993(3), respectively, and zero elsewhere. Possible reasons for $I92q4_t$ to be important are the September 1992 crisis in the European exchange rate mechanism (ERM) and the reintroduction of a withholding tax on interest income in Germany, effective January 1, 1993, whereas $I93q3_t$ captures a further ERM crisis in July 1993 (see also Kole & Meade (1995) and WL).

[6] t-ratios in parentheses underneath the estimated coefficients.

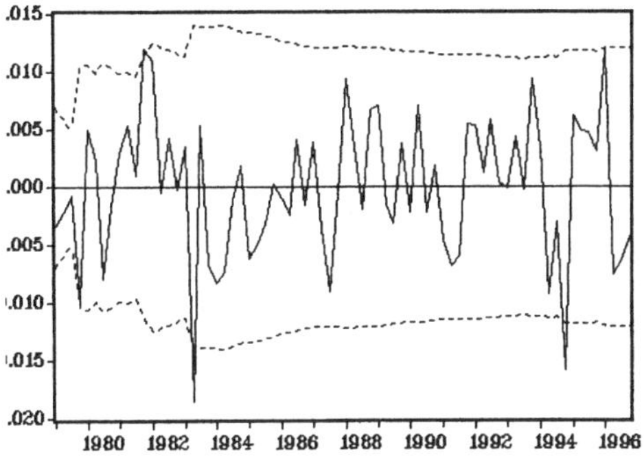

recursive residuals (—) and ±2 standard errors (---)

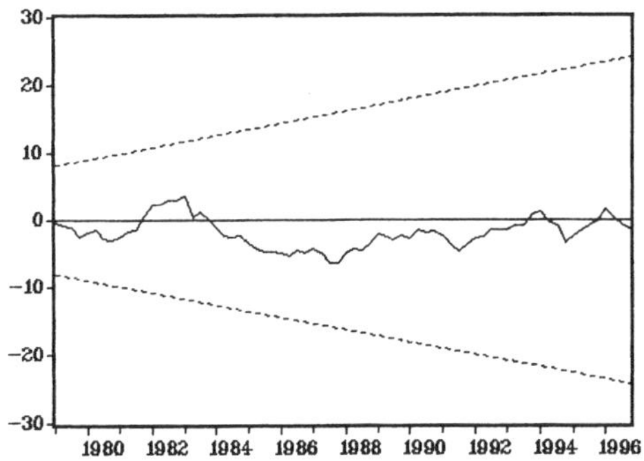

CUSUMs (—) and 5% significance bounds (---)

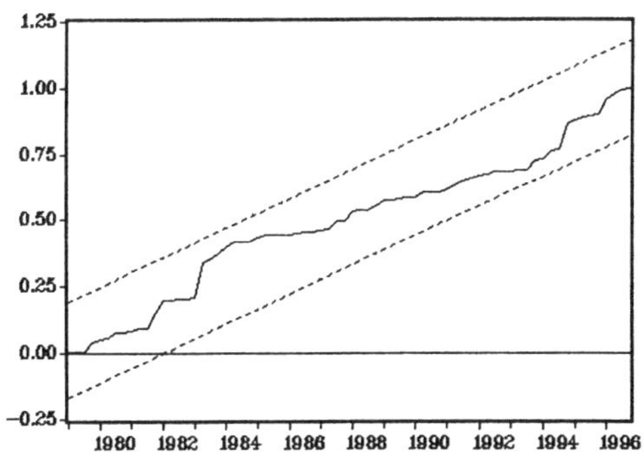

CUSUM-of-squares (—) and 5% significance bounds (---)

Fig. 2. Recursive residuals and CUSUM tests of model (3.1)

4 and 8 lags, respectively, and ARCH(k) is an LM test for autoregressive conditional heteroscedasticity of order k, $k = 1, 2, 4$ (see, e.g., Hendry (1995) for more details on these tests). Obviously, in the present case all p-values exceed usual significance levels substantially and, hence, none of the test statistics is significant at conventional levels. In other words, we conclude that the residuals do not show signs of autocorrelation, conditional heteroscedasticity or nonnormality. Moreover, in Fig. 2 recursive residuals, CUSUM and

CUSUM-of-squares tests are presented which overall support a stable relation for the period of interest.

Note that an income elasticity of one was not rejected by the data and thus we have imposed this restriction by including $(m-p-y)_{t-1}$ as a single regressor. Equation (3.1) is similar to the specifications of WL although it includes further lags of $\Delta^2 p_t$ and $(R-r)_t$ and thus has richer dynamics. The reason for the differences is again the change in the observation period and the fact that the starting point of our model reduction procedure was a model with four lags of the stationary variables whereas WL include two lags only. We have also used our extended data set to construct a model with at most two lags and ended up with the same specification as WL. Note that lags of Δpm_t were not significant at the 5% level in (3.1) and are therefore omitted. The deterministic terms are the same as in WL.

Normalizing on the coefficient of $(m-p-y)_{t-1}$ in (3.1) gives the following long-run relation:

$$(m-p)_t = y_t - 13.50\Delta p_t + 0.14S90q3_t + ec_t. \tag{3.2}$$

Adding the long-run impact of the interest rate differential and using the annual inflation rate $\pi_t = 4\Delta p_t$ instead of Δp_t gives the long-run money demand equation

$$(m-p) = y - 5.35(R-r) - 3.38\pi + 0.14S90q3.$$

Comparing this relation with the results of WL,

$$(m-p) = y - 4.84(R-r) - 3.72\pi + 0.15S90q3,$$

and WTL,

$$(m-p) = y - 4.32(R-r) - 3.57\pi + 0.13S90q3,$$

shows that the parameter estimates are very similar. In particular, an income elasticity of one is supported by the data in all three cases.

3.2 The system

Since the estimators of the cointegration parameters obtained from (3.1) are superconsistent we use $ec_t = (m-p-y)_t + 13.50\Delta p_t - 0.14S90q3_t$ from (3.2) as an additional stationary variable in the sequel in specifying the systems equations for $\Delta(m-p)_t$, $\Delta^2 p_t$, Δy_t and $(R-r)_t$ in our model. The starting point of the money demand equation is the same as in Section 3.1 whereas 'reduced form equations' with four lags of the variables $\Delta(m-p)_t$, Δy_t, $\Delta^2 p_t$, $(R-r)_t$, and the unlagged exogenous variable Δpm_t with additional four lags are specified for the remaining endogenous variables. Moreover, ec_{t-1}, $d_t(R-r)_t$ as well as the deterministic terms are included in the initial equations. As in the single equation analysis we then eliminate insignificant variables successively according to the lowest t-values but always keeping the error correction term in each equation until the end. Then it was eliminated if it turned out to be insignificant at the 5% level. This strategy eventually resulted in the equations presented in the following. Estimation is done in the full system using iterated three-stage least squares (3SLS).

The money demand equation is

$$\begin{aligned}\Delta(m-p)_t = &-\underset{(-7.1)}{0.111}\, ec_{t-1} - \underset{(-2.0)}{0.069}\, \Delta(m-p)_{t-4} - \underset{(-6.6)}{1.262}\, \Delta^2 p_t \\ &- \underset{(-2.8)}{0.251}\, \Delta^2 p_{t-4} - \underset{(-5.7)}{0.220}\, \Delta y_{t-1} - \underset{(-4.9)}{0.568}(R-r)_{t-1} \\ &+ \underset{(2.8)}{0.427}(R-r)_{t-3} - \underset{(-2.8)}{0.406}(R-r)_{t-4} - \underset{(-7.6)}{0.430}\, d_t(R-r)_t \\ &+ \underset{(10.7)}{0.187} - \underset{(-10.0)}{0.115}\, d_{1t} - \underset{(-10.0)}{0.077}\, d_{2t} - \underset{(-14.8)}{0.059}\, d_{3t} + \underset{(24.1)}{0.145}\, I90q3_t \\ &- \underset{(-3.6)}{0.021}\, I92q4_t - \underset{(-3.1)}{0.018}\, I93q3_t + \hat{u}_{mt} \qquad (3.3)\end{aligned}$$

$T = 84$ [1976(1)–1996(4)]

$\bar{R}^2 = 0.93$	$\text{SE} = 0.0061$	$\text{JB} = 0.81\ (0.67)$
$\text{LM}(1) = 0.34\ (0.56)$	$\text{LM}(4) = 0.31\ (0.87)$	$\text{LM}(8) = 0.56\ (0.81)$
$\text{ARCH}(1) = 0.01\ (0.91)$	$\text{ARCH}(2) = 0.03\ (0.97)$	$\text{ARCH}(4) = 0.21\ (0.93)$

The test statistics given here are computed from the residuals of the estimated system. The results are very similar to those of equation (3.1), that is, none of the diagnostic test statistics is significant at conventional levels and, hence, the residuals appear to be normally distributed as well as free of autocorrelation and autoregressive conditional heteroscedasticity. As expected, equation (3.3) is very similar to (3.1). The only material difference is that the fourth lag of $\Delta(m-p)_t$ is included in addition. It is also easy to check that the long-run effect of the interest rate spread is clearly negative, as theoretically expected. The negative coefficient of the error correction term implies that excess money lowers money growth, as one would expect in a stable model.

The income equation turns out to be

$$\begin{aligned}\Delta y_t = &\ \underset{(2.3)}{0.044}\, ec_{t-1} + \underset{(3.2)}{0.269}\, \Delta(m-p)_{t-1} + \underset{(2.5)}{0.172}\, \Delta(m-p)_{t-2} \\ &- \underset{(-3.7)}{0.323}\, \Delta y_{t-1} + \underset{(3.4)}{0.243}\, \Delta y_{t-4} - \underset{(-0.4)}{0.007} - \underset{(-8.2)}{0.083}\, d_{1t} \\ &- \underset{(-1.2)}{0.012}\, d_{2t} - \underset{(-1.9)}{0.008}\, d_{3t} + \underset{(9.0)}{0.108}\, I90q3_t + \hat{u}_{yt} \qquad (3.4)\end{aligned}$$

$T = 84$ [1976(1)–1996(4)]

$\bar{R}^2 = 0.92$	$\text{SE} = 0.012$	$\text{JB} = 2.45\ (0.29)$
$\text{LM}(1) = 0.00\ (1.00)$	$\text{LM}(4) = 1.52\ (0.20)$	$\text{LM}(8) = 1.18\ (0.32)$
$\text{ARCH}(1) = 1.47\ (0.23)$	$\text{ARCH}(2) = 1.11\ (0.34)$	$\text{ARCH}(4) = 1.05\ (0.39)$

Again the diagnostics do not indicate any problems with autocorrelation, conditional heteroscedasticity or nonnormality. The income equation includes the error correction term with the expected positive sign so that excess money stimulates growth in real income. There is quite a bit of interaction from the changes in the other variables of the system. Obviously, there is dynamic feedback between income and money with lags of both variables appearing in both equations. The deterministic terms are the same as in the money equation except for the impulse dummies $I92q4_t$ and $I93q3_t$ which are not needed in the income equation.

The inflation equation was found to be

$$\begin{aligned}\Delta^2 p_t = & -\underset{(-2.2)}{0.058}\,\Delta(m-p)_{t-1} + \underset{(2.8)}{0.089}\,\Delta(m-p)_{t-3} \\ & - \underset{(-11.3)}{1.086}\,\Delta^2 p_{t-1} - \underset{(-9.5)}{1.044}\,\Delta^2 p_{t-2} - \underset{(-6.9)}{0.747}\,\Delta^2 p_{t-3} - \underset{(-2.7)}{0.258}\,\Delta^2 p_{t-4} \\ & + \underset{(2.2)}{0.075}\,\Delta y_{t-3} + \underset{(3.6)}{0.096}\,\Delta y_{t-4} + \underset{(2.6)}{0.065}\,\Delta pm_{t-4} \\ & + \underset{(5.3)}{0.021} - \underset{(-4.6)}{0.034}\,d_{1t} - \underset{(-4.4)}{0.027}\,d_{2t} - \underset{(-4.8)}{0.031}\,d_{3t} + \hat{u}_{pt} \end{aligned} \tag{3.5}$$

$T = 84$ [1976(1)–1996(4)]

$\bar{R}^2 = 0.98$	SE = 0.0046	JB = 0.97 (0.62)
LM(1) = 0.05 (0.82)	LM(4) = 0.54 (0.71)	LM(8) = 0.67 (0.72)
ARCH(1) = 0.18 (0.67)	ARCH(2) = 0.75 (0.48)	ARCH(4) = 0.68 (0.61)

The diagnostic tests do not indicate any specification problems for this equation either. In addition to the own lags, the estimated equation also includes lags of income and money. Thus, there is obviously considerable interaction between inflation, money and income, as one would expect. However, the error correction term turned out to be insignificant in this equation and hence the inflation rate is weakly exogenous. Given that we have used unadjusted seasonal data the importance of the seasonal lags in the foregoing equations is not surprising. Moreover, as expected, the import prices have an impact on German inflation which has a delay of one year (four quarters), however. In this case the deterministic terms consist of an intercept and seasonal dummies only. The impulse dummy for the GMU period is not needed here because there is no break in the inflation rate due to the GMU (see Fig. 1).

Finally the equation for the interest rate spread is[7]

$$\begin{aligned}(R-r)_t = & \underset{(12.2)}{0.836}(R-r)_{t-1} - \underset{(-2.9)}{0.200}(R-r)_{t-4} + \underset{(2.2)}{0.055}\,\Delta pm_{t-4} \\ & + \underset{(3.9)}{0.014} + \underset{(2.8)}{0.004}\,d_{1t} + \underset{(2.9)}{0.004}\,d_{2t} + \underset{(2.1)}{0.003}\,d_{3t} + \hat{u}_{rt}\end{aligned} \tag{3.6}$$

[7] Note that we are using the interest rate spread as the dependent variable in equation (3.6) rather than its first differences. The latter variable would be consistent with the general model set-up in (2.2). As mentioned in the discussion of that model, because $(R-r)_t$ is a stationary variable, it is more natural to include it directly and not in first differences.

$T = 84$ [1976(1)–1996(4)]

$\bar{R}^2 = 0.67$	SE = 0.0043	JB = 6.44 (0.04)
LM(1) = 0.05 (0.83)	LM(4) = 0.43 (0.79)	LM(8) = 0.53 (0.83)
ARCH(1) = 1.80 (0.18)	ARCH(2) = 1.11 (0.34)	ARCH(4) = 0.86 (0.49)

Again the diagnostic tests do not indicate specification problems except that there is some evidence against normally distributed disturbances, a result which is quite common for financial data. Since the normal distribution is only of limited importance for our inference we do not regard this result as problematic. The interest rate spread is seen to depend on own lags and a lag of the import price inflation rate only. Since international influences have an impact on interest rates, as repeatedly argued by the Deutsche Bundesbank, it is not surprising that import price inflation enters the interest rate equation. Obviously, the interest rate spread is exogenous in the partial system consisting of $(m-p)_t$, y_t and Δp_t. Although the Bundesbank uses interest rates such as the discount rate, the lombard rate and especially the repo rate to control the money stock it is generally acknowledged that these rates influence the market rates and therefore the spread. Since we have not modeled the link between the policy variables and the spread the latter may be viewed as an indicator of monetary policy.

In the interest equation we again have an intercept term and seasonal dummies only as deterministic terms. Since there is no level shift due to the GMU in the interest rates it is not surprising that the corresponding dummy is not needed here. However, it may be a bit surprising that the seasonal dummies are significant in this equation. This may be due to the seasonal pattern of the import price inflation variable (see Fig. 1).

In our model the only instantaneous endogenous variable entering the right-hand side is $\Delta^2 p_t$ in the money demand equation. Thus most of the interaction between the variables enters in a dynamic way through the lags of the endogenous variables. Therefore it is of interest to analyze the interactions in more detail. They are difficult to see directly from the coefficients of the model. Therefore we will perform an impulse response analysis in the next section in order to get a better picture of the channels by which disturbances affect the system.

4. Impulse response analysis

In this section we will consider the effects of impulses hitting the system. For this purpose we remove all deterministic terms and the 'exogenous variables' pm_t and $d_t(R-r)_t$ from the system and trace the marginal effects of impulses to the different equations. Removing the exogenous variables means that they are treated as fixed in the impulse response analysis. The constancy assumption is justified in a linear model if they are really exogenous and, hence, they are not affected by impulses hitting the system.

Generally impulse responses of the levels variables of the ECM (2.2) may be obtained by solving for the levels variables. We write the resulting model as

$$A_0 z_t = A_1 z_{t-1} + \cdots + A_{p+1} z_{t-p-1} + \Phi x_t + \Xi D_t + u_t, \tag{4.1}$$

The responses to an impulse u_0 at time zero are then obtained by removing the terms Φx_t and ΞD_t and computing the forecasts for z_1, z_2, etc. conditionally on $z_0 = A_0^{-1}u_0$ and $z_t = 0$ for $t < 0$. Commonly the impulses u_0 are vectors with a unit in one position and zeros elsewhere. For instance, $u_0 = (1, 0, \dots, 0)'$ represents a unit impulse to the first equation.

This type of impulse response analysis has been criticized on the grounds that the residuals of a model may be correlated and hence isolated shocks to individual equations may not actually occur in the underlying system. Therefore the model cannot be expected to reflect the responses to such shocks adequately (see, e.g., Lütkepohl (1991) and Lütkepohl & Breitung (1997) for a more detailed discussion of impulse response analysis). Therefore it may be of interest to check the residual correlation matrix of our system which is

$$\hat{R} = \begin{bmatrix} 1.00 & 0.10 & 0.21 & -0.06 \\ 0.10 & 1.00 & 0.04 & 0.14 \\ 0.21 & 0.04 & 1.00 & -0.18 \\ -0.06 & 0.14 & -0.18 & 1.00 \end{bmatrix} \begin{matrix} \Delta(m-p) \\ \Delta y \\ \Delta^2 p \\ R-r \end{matrix}$$

Clearly, all off-diagonal elements are relatively small and the actual correlations may well be zero. Hence, the impulse response analysis presented in the following is not prone to the critique related to correlated residuals.

In our system there is one deviation from the standard impulse response set-up which needs special consideration. The original variables in z_t are $(m-p)_t$, y_t, Δp_t and $(R-r)_t$. Because we are interested in the behaviour of nominal money, the log price level p_t has to be regarded as a separate variable in the system and thus appears in levels and first differences. We therefore reparameterize the model such that we get a system similar to (4.1) but with endogenous variables $z_t^* = (m_t, y_t, \Delta p_t, (R-r)_t, p_t)'$ and a fifth equation $p_t = \Delta p_t + p_{t-1}$. Then we compute impulse responses for these variables and thereby get the responses of nominal money to impulses in the inflation rate equation etc. The resulting impulse responses of m_t, Δp_t and y_t are depicted in Fig. 3.

The dynamic interactions of the variables are largely in line with expectations. An exception may be the reaction of the inflation rate caused by an impulse in nominal money (see the first column in Fig. 3). Although a one-time impulse in the equation for nominal money has a lasting effect on the dependent variable, there is almost no reaction in the inflation rate. This behaviour of the system accords well with the fact that inflation has been low in Germany for many years although money growth often exceeded the Bundesbank's target zone. The reaction of income to a money impulse is quite plausible under these circumstances. An impulse in nominal money which is not accompanied by increased inflation or changes in other variables must have an effect on real income at least in the long-run given that we have a unit income elasticity in the cointegration relation.

An impulse in the inflation equation results in an initial decline in the money stock which may be a consequence of policy actions by the Bundesbank. As expected, in the long-run the nominal money stock has to account for a change in the price level and, hence, m increases due to an impulse in the inflation rate. The inflation variable itself reacts in a strongly seasonal way which may be a spurious effect, of course, because the impulse responses are

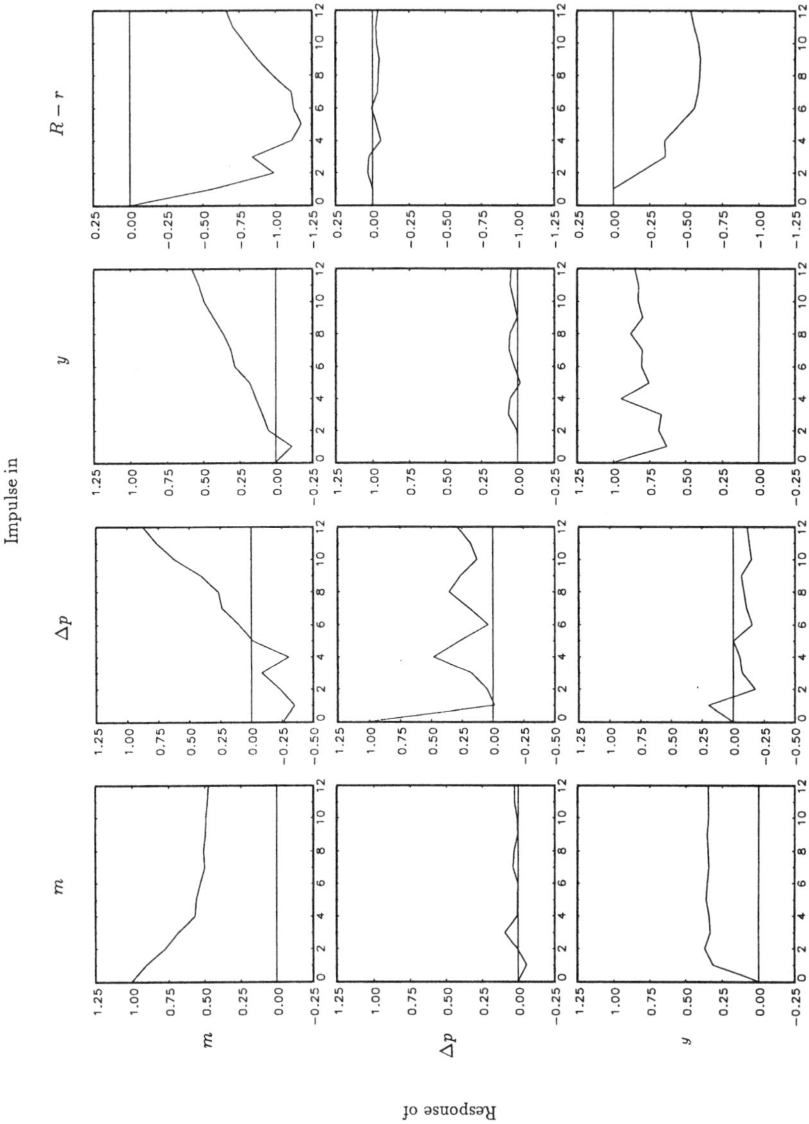

Fig. 3. Impulse responses of German money demand system

computed from estimated coefficients so that there is some uncertainty regarding the sizes of the actual effects.[8] Finally, after an initial income growth, an inflationary impulse leads to a long-term decline in the real income variable.

A one-time impulse in the income equation has a persistent effect on income, hence, it also drives up nominal money and leads to some inflation in the long-run. Again there is a strongly seasonal pattern in the response function of the inflation rate. Finally, an impulse in the interest rate differential and, hence, an increase in the opportunity costs of holding M3 money results in a decline of the nominal money stock, a long-term decrease in the inflation rate and a decline in real income. Hence, overall the reactions of the variables are plausible in the light of economic theory and they also conform with the assumed interactions which form the basis of the monetary policy conducted by the Bundesbank.[9] In contrast to the impulse response analysis presented by the Deutsche Bundesbank (1997) it seems, however, that in our system the reaction of the inflation rate to money shocks is not as pronounced as the reaction of money to inflation shocks. This result is in line with findings of Juselius (1996) for the post-1983 period where the empirical support for price inflation to be a monetary phenomenon is rather weak.

5. Conclusions

In this study we have constructed a small macroeconomic model for studying the dynamic relation between interest rates, money growth, real growth and inflation in Germany based on seasonally unadjusted, quarterly data for 1976 to 1996. Thus, our sample period covers the post-GMU period. A money demand equation for M3 is the central relation in the system. This relation includes GNP, the GNP deflator as a measure for the price level and an interest rate spread variable which represents the opportunity costs of holding money. Moreover, the system contains an import price index as an exogenous variable reflecting international influences. The model pays special attention to the cointegration properties of the variables and is set up as an ECM with a long-run money demand relation as its centerpiece. To find this relation we have first constructed a structural single equation ECM for money demand and then we have used the error correction term obtained in this way in building up a full dynamic system. Then an impulse response analysis is performed to analyze the dynamic interactions between the variables and in particular to study the monetary transmission process.

It turns out that shocks in the money growth variable do not have a very pronounced impact on inflation whereas there appears to be a quite strong effect of inflation shocks on money growth. Therefore, from this analysis it is not quite clear whether a strong and predictable relation between money and inflation really exists in Germany which can be exploited to control inflation. On the other hand, our empirical results clearly show that, for given influences

[8] We do not give confidence bands for our impulse responses because there are a number of problems related to the standard confidence bands which are often reported in the literature (see Benkwitz, Lütkepohl & Neumann (1997)). In particular, standard confidence bands lack a theoretical foundation for our system.

[9] In Fig. 3 we give only the first 12 impulse responses. Graphing more impulse responses did not lead to different conclusions.

from abroad, interest rates are exogenous and, hence, can be used as monetary policy instruments to control inflation and growth. However, using only these instruments, the typical trade-off exists. Higher interest rates reduce inflation but also cause a decline in real growth. In addition, it is also clear that interest rates are not under the full control of the Bundesbank but depend to some extent on international influences.

Appendix. Variables and data sources

Seasonally unadjusted quarterly data for the period from the first quarter of 1976 to the fourth quarter of 1996 were used for the following variables taken from the given sources. All data refer to West Germany until 1990(2) and to the unified Germany afterwards.

M3: nominal monthly values from *Monatsberichte der Deutschen Bundesbank*; the quarterly values are the values of the last month of each quarter. The variable m is log M3.

GNP: quarterly real gross national product from *Deutsches Institut für Wirtschaftsforschung, Volkswirtschaftliche Gesamtrechnung*. The variable y is log GNP.

Price index: GNP deflator (1991 = 100) from *Deutsches Institut für Wirtschaftsforschung, Volkswirtschaftliche Gesamtrechnung*. The variable p is the logarithm of the price index.

Average bond rate (Umlaufsrendite) (R): monthly values from *Monatsberichte der Deutschen Bundesbank*; the quarterly value is the value of the last month of each quarter.

Own rate of M3 (r): the series was constructed from the interest rates of savings deposits (rs) and the interest rates of 3-months time deposits (rt) from *Monatsberichte der Deutschen Bundesbank* as a weighted average as follows:

$$r = \begin{cases} 0.24rt + 0.42rs & \text{for } 1976(1)\text{–}1990(2) \\ 0.30rt + 0.33rs & \text{for } 1990(3)\text{–}1996(4) \end{cases}$$

The weights are chosen according to the relative shares of the corresponding components of M3. The quarterly value is the value of the last month of each quarter.

Import price index: PM (1991 = 100) from *Deutsches Institut für Wirtschaftsforschung, Volkswirtschaftliche Gesamtrechnung*. The variable pm is the logarithm of PM.

The data may be obtained from the internet, http://wotan.wiwi.hu-berlin.de/oekonometrie/engl/data.html

References

Benkwitz A, Lütkepohl H, Neumann M (1997) Problems related to bootstrapping impulse responses of autoregressive processes. Discussion Paper 85, Sonderforschungsbereich 373, Humboldt University Berlin

Deutsche Bundesbank (1995) Geldnachfrage und Währungssubstitution in Europa. Monatsbericht Januar 1995:33–49

Deutsche Bundesbank (1997) Überprüfung des Geldmengenziels. Monatsbericht August 1997:17–32
Goldfeld SM, Sichel DE (1987) Money demand: The effects of inflation and alternative adjustment mechanisms. Review of Economics and Statistics 69:511–515
Hansen G, Kim JR (1995) The stability of German money demand. Tests of the cointegration relation. Weltwirtschaftliches Archiv 131:286–301
Hansen G, Kim JR (1996) Money and inflation in Germany: A cointegration analysis, Empirical Economics 21:601–616
Hendry DF (1995) Dynamic econometrics. Oxford University Press, Oxford
Hendry DF, von Ungern-Sternberg T (1981) Liquidity and inflation effects on consumer's expenditure. In Deaton AS (eds.) Essays in the theory and measurement of consumer's behaviour, Cambridge University Press, Cambridge
Hubrich K (1998) System estimation of the German money demand – A long-run analysis. Empirical Economics, forthcoming
Hwang H (1985) Test of the adjustment process and linear homogeneity in a stock adjustment model of money demand. Review of Economics and Statistics 67:689–692
Issing O (1997) Monetary targeting in Germany: The stability of monetary policy and of the monetary system. Journal of Monetary Economics 39:67–79
Issing O, Tödter K-H (1995) Geldmenge und Preise im vereinten Deutschland. In: Duwendag D (ed.) Neuere Entwicklungen in der Geldtheorie und Währungspolitik, Duncker & Humblot, Berlin pp. 97–123
Juselius K (1996) An empirical analysis of the changing role of the German Bundesbank after 1983. Oxford Bulletin of Economics and Statistics 58:791–819
Juselius K (1998) Changing monetary transmission mechanisms within the EU. Empirical Economics 23
Kole LS, Meade EE (1995) German monetary targeting: A retrospective view. Federal Reserve Bulletin: 917–931
Lütkepohl H (1991) Introduction to multiple time series analysis. Springer-Verlag, Berlin
Lütkepohl H, Breitung J (1997) Impulse response analysis of vector autoregressive processes. In: Heij C, Schumacher H, Hanzon B, Praagman K (eds.) System dynamics in economic and financial models, John Wiley, Chichester, pp. 299–326
Scharnagl M (1998) The stability of German money demand: Not just a myth. Empirical Economics 23
Stock JH (1987) Asymptotic properties of least squares estimators of cointegrating vectors. Econometrica 55:1035–1056
Tullio G, de Souza E, Giucca P (1996) The demand for money functions in Europe and in Germany before and after the fall of the Berlin Wall. In: de Grauwe P, Micossi S, Tullio G (eds.) Inflation and wage behaviour in Europe, Clarendon Press, Oxford, pp. 310–338
Wolters J, Lütkepohl H (1997) Die Geldnachfrage für M3: Neue Ergebnisse für das vereinigte Deutschland. ifo Studien, 43:35–54
Wolters J, Teräsvirta T, Lütkepohl H (1998) Modelling the demand for M3 in the Unified Germany. Review of Economics and Statistics, 80:399–409

Money demand stability: Evidence from Spain

Juan Luis Vega*

European Central Bank, Postfach 16 03 19, D-60066 Frankfurt am Main, Germany

Abstract. Using several tests for structural stability in regressions with I(1) variables and for the existence of cointegration in models with regime shifts, the empirical evidence on the existence of a structural break in the Spanish long-run demand for broad money (ALP2) is analysed.

The results indicate that shifts affecting the demand for ALP2 in recent years have substantially altered its long-run properties. As to the cause of this structural break, emphasis is placed on the role played by the increasing openness of the Spanish financial system to international markets as obstacles to free capital movements have progressively disappeared.

Key words: Money demand, cointegration, stability, regime shift

JEL classification: E41, C22

1. Introduction

Ever since the article by Poole (1970), a stable and predictable relationship between the demand for money and its determinants has been considered a pre-requisite for the formulation of monetary policy strategies based on intermediate monetary targeting. Nevertheless, this stability hypothesis is far from being uncontroversial. Since the mid-70s, many researchers have extensively documented episodes of either *missing money* or *great velocity decline* in a number of countries. Explanations put forward have very often been

---

* This paper represents the views of the author and should not be interpreted as reflecting those of any institution. I am grateful to J. Ayuso, J. J. Dolado, F. Restoy and two anonymous referees for helpful comments. The data may be obtained from the internet, http://wotan.wiwi.hu-berlin.de/oekonometric/engl/data.html. This paper was written while the author was working at the Banco de España.

related to portfolio adjustments against a background of financial innovation and market deregulation.

During the eighties these apparent instabilities led many central banks to broaden the definition of monetary aggregates being monitored/targeted in order to take account developments in financial assets considered to be close substitutes for those already included in the definition of money. At the same time, major changes in the specification of existing empirical money demand functions were made, affecting both the dynamic specification and the range of explanatory variables in the empirical equations.

By the end of the decade, the concept of cointegration seemed to enable a reconciliation of the evidence of short-run instabilities co-existing with a stable long-run demand for money. However, no formal test statistics were available for the latter hypothesis. The recent publication of tests for structural stability in regressions with first-order integrated variables [Hansen (1992), Phillips and Quintos (1993) and Hansen and Johansen (1996)] and for the existence of cointegration in models with regime shifts [Gregory and Hansen (1996)] provide some useful tools for looking more closely at the issue of stability.

This article reviews evidence from Spain on structural breaks in the long-run demand for broad money function. The Spanish case is bound to be a good example for looking for such breaks. Since the Banco de España first announced growth targets for M3 in 1978 the monetary policy framework has been subject to numerous alterations. In 1984, changes were made in the central bank's operating procedures (from bank reserves to short-term interest rates) and in the monetary aggregate targeted (from M3 to ALP[1]). Since then, the definition of ALP has been modified on several occasions to accommodate financial innovation which increased the degree of substitutability between assets included and not included. In the late 1980's, in response to the increasing difficulty of pursuing a strategy based on short-term control of ALP, the exchange rate was assigned a higher weight in the Banco de España's reaction function and the monetary control strategy shifted towards a more gradualist bent in which short-term deviations from the monetary targets were considered less relevant for policy. Following the entry of the peseta in the EMS exchange rate mechanism, the monetary aggregate became less a target in itself than a reference which served to warn of possible medium- to long-term conflicts between domestic and external targets.

In spite of this changing monetary policy framework and the rapid pace of financial innovation and deregulation during the 80s, there is strong evidence with data spanning the period 1979–1989 of a cointegrating relationship between real balances, real income, inflation and interest rates which is interpretable as a demand for money function. Nevertheless, there is also a view, widely held by some analysts, that those historical relationships have deteriorated sharply in recent years. In this connection, both monetary policy and the Spanish financial system have witnessed important changes during the 1990's: reform of the reserve requirement system; heightened competition among fi-

[1] ALP stands for "liquid assets held by the public" and comprises financial assets included in M3 plus: outright purchases of short-term general government securities; endorsed bills and commercial paper guaranteed by deposit institutions; non-interbank private asset transfers; and, medium- and long-term securities issued by the Official Credit Institute and the specialized credit institutions.

nancial institutions; the extraordinary growth of mutual funds; the elimination of administrative obstacles to free capital movements; the broadening of the fluctuation bands of the ERM; and, the adoption in 1995 of inflation targets.

With this perspective, section 2 revisits the available empirical evidence on the existence of breaks in the Spanish long-run demand for broad money (ALP2). Section 3 draws the main conclusions.

2. Long-run demand for broad money: Cointegration and stability

Since the work by Dolado (1988), empirical studies on the estimation of money demand functions in Spain have – in congruence with international evidence in this respect stressed first, the existence of a long-run equilibrium relationship between integrated variables (cointegration) interpretable as a demand for real balances function; and further, the estimation of the dynamic process of adjustment to this equilibrium in the form of an error correction mechanism (ECM) model. Typically, demand equations are estimated as follows:

$$\Delta(m-p)_t = k - \alpha[(m-p) - m^d]_{t-1} + \delta_0(L)\Delta(m-p)_{t-1} + \delta_1(L)\Delta y_t + \delta_2(L)\Delta r_t^p + \delta_3(L)\Delta r_t^a + \delta_4(L)\Delta^2 p_t + \varepsilon_t \quad (1)$$

$$m_t^d = \alpha_0 + \alpha_1 y_t + \alpha_2 r_t^p + \alpha_3 r_t^a + \alpha_4 \Delta_4 p_t \quad (2)$$

where: m_t, p_t and y_t, are, respectively, the logarithms of the money stock, consumer-price index (CPI) and real GDP; r_t^p and r_t^a are vectors of interest rates on assets within (r_t^p) and outside (r_t^a) the definition of the monetary aggregate; and, $\Delta_4 p_t$ is the annual rate of inflation as measured by the CPI. Δ is the difference operator and $\delta_i(L)$ are finite-order polynomials in the lag operator. Following Cabrero et al. (1992), in the case of broad money ALP2[2] analysed below, r_t^p is proxied by the weighted average rate – net of taxes – of the assets included in the monetary aggregate and r_t^a by the internal rate of return – net of taxes – on medium- to long-term government debt. All series, bar real GDP, are seasonally unadjusted. Figures 1A and 1B plot the data[3].

Equation (1) represents the dynamic form of the demand for money, whose equilibrium specification, in terms of desired demand for real balances, is given by equation (2). Equation (2) in turn is, in view of the emphasis placed in recent times on the long-run properties of monetary aggregates, the main focus of this paper, whilst the parameters describing the short-run dynamics are treated here as *nuisance parameters* to which we shall not pay attention. More specifically, an attempt is made throughout the paper to analyse whether the passage of time makes it necessary to alter any of the conclusions which other authors have formulated on the long-run demand for real

[2] ALP2 comprises ALP plus short-term private securities (commercial paper).

[3] The order of integration of the variables in equation (2) has been studied in many of the references below. For the sample under review, it holds that money and prices are I(2), while real money, income, inflation and interest rates are I(1).

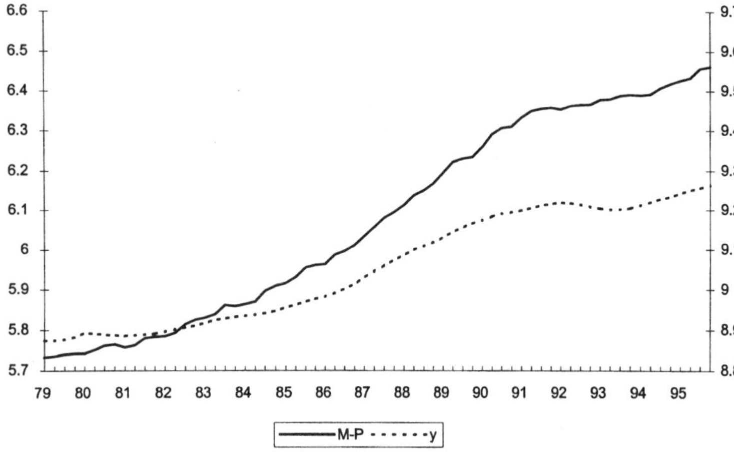

Fig. 1A. Logarithms of real broad money ALP2 (left scale) and real income (right scale)

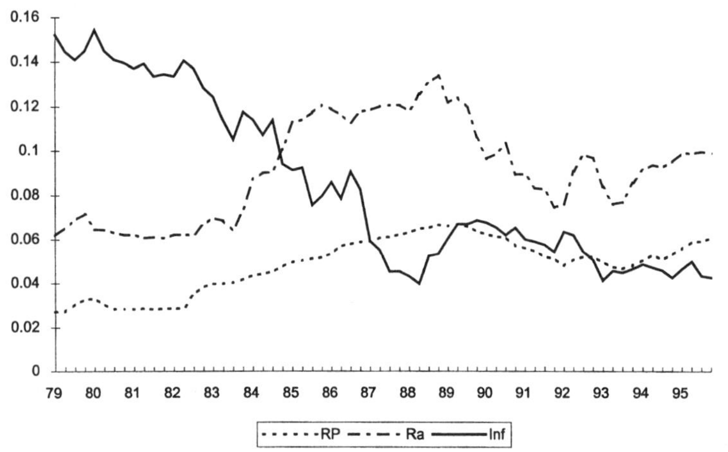

Fig. 1B. Inflation, and own and alternative interest rates on broad money ALP2

balances given by equation (2) and, if so, in which sense. In addition, the paper also aims at the application of estimation methods which, beyond the traditional result of superconsistency (Stock, 1987), allow for the use of standard (asymptotic) inference procedures on the long-run parameters.

As regards the empirical evidence available on the long-run demand for broad money in Spain, Cabrero et al. (1992) and Dolado and Escrivá (1992) determined, using data spanning the 80s, the existence of one (and only one) cointegrating vector interpretable as a long-run money demand function in the case of the monetary aggregate ALP2. At the same time, it was concluded that certain short-run circumstantial instabilities were co-existing with a high degree of stability of the long-run relationship, although no formal tests were performed in this latter respect. Other authors – Escrivá and Malo de Molina (1991) and Ayuso and Vega (1994) – have highlighted the same type of findings.

Table 1. The long-run demand for broad money ALP2: 1979/Q1–1988/Q4

$$(m-p)_t = \underset{(12.61)}{-7.64} + \underset{(23.03)}{1.51}y_t + \underset{(9.89)}{3.01}rp_t - \underset{(7.81)}{1.10}ra_t - \underset{(2.87)}{0.41}\Delta_4 p_t$$

ADF = −4.89**	PP = −5.20**	DHS = 1119.7***	$h_k = 0.061$
F-mean = 5.89	Lc = 0.38	F-sup = 16.30 ($\tau = 81/I$)	

Notes: All calculations were made using GAUSS-386. Paramaters are estimated using the fully modified proceudure of Phillips and Hansen (1990). *t*-ratios in brackets. ***, ** and * indicate rejections of the null at 1%, 5% and 10%, respectively. For some of the tests, the levels of significance (γ) and/or the estimated break points (τ), as appropriate, are reported in brackets.

These conclusions are substantiated by the evidence given in Table 1, which shows estimates of equation (2) for the period running from the first quarter of 1979 to the last quarter of 1988 as well as several residual-based tests that help evaluate the empirical evidence on the existence of a stable long-run relationship in that period. Estimation in the table is performed using Phillips and Hansen (1990) fully modified (FME) procedure, with the long-run variance-covariance matrix estimated, following suggestions by Andrews (1991) and Andrews and Monahan (1992), using a prewhitened quadratic spectral kernel with a first-order autoregression for the prewhitening and an automatic bandwidth estimator. The FME is, in this context, asymptotically equivalent to maximum-likelihood and provides, on the one hand, for the mitigation of second-order biases detected in static OLS estimates of cointegrating vectors, and on the other, for the use of standard (asymptotic) procedures for inference.

The ADF, PP and DHS statistics reported in Table 1 are, respectively: the augmented Dickey-Fuller test, the Phillips-Perron test and the Durbin-Hausman test proposed by Choi (1994). These are residual-based tests for the null of no cointegration, i.e. tests for the existence of a unit root in the residuals of the regression. Conversely, the h_k test (Leybourne and McCabe, 1993) directly tests for the null of cointegration[4], i.e. the stationarity of the estimated residuals. The reason for including the latter is to provide cover to some degree from the traditional criticism that unit root tests offer scant power in finite samples for rejecting the null. Although the lack of power is not a differential characteristic of these tests[5], the argument is that, in a situation in which the economic hypothesis of interest is the alternative one (cointegration), statistical tests will habitually tend not to reject the null (non-cointegration) unless there is substantial evidence against it. Thus, test h_k may be a good supplementary tool to the foregoing ones, whereby if both types of tests provide the same inference on the existence or not of cointegration, we may be relatively confident about the robustness of the result. Finally, the remaining tests in Table 1 (F-mean, Lc and F-sup) are those proposed in

[4] None of these tests has a standard distribution. Critical values for ADF and PP can be found in MacKinnon (1991); the asymptotic critical values for DHS and h_k are tabulated in the references quoted.

[5] See Gonzalo and Lee (1996).

Table 2. The long-run demand for broad money ALP2: 1979/Q1–1993/Q4

$$(m-p)_t = \underset{(32.38)}{-9.09} + \underset{(55.55)}{1.67}\, y_t + \underset{(7.75)}{3.43} rp_t - \underset{(6.66)}{1.43} ra_t - \underset{(0.81)}{0.09} \Delta_4 p_t$$

ADF = −0.26	PP = −1.10	DHS = 46.00	$h_k = 1.11^{***}$

ADF-LS = −1.89 ($\tau = 91/\text{III}$)	PP-LS = −2.28 ($\tau = 91/\text{III}$)
ADF-RS = −6.74* ($\gamma = 0.10; \tau = 89/\text{III}$)	PP-RS = −6.19 ($\gamma = 0.23; \tau = 89/\text{II}$)
ADF-RS$^{\alpha 1}$ = −4.78 ($\gamma = 0.58; \tau = 91/\text{II}$)	PP-RS$^{\alpha 1}$ = −5.24 ($\gamma = 0.34; \tau = 91/\text{II}$)
ADF-RS$^{\alpha 2, \alpha 3}$ = −5.48 ($\tau = 89/\text{III}$)	PP-RS$^{\alpha 2, \alpha 3}$ = −5.62 ($\tau = 89/\text{II}$)

Notes: See notes to Table 1.

Hansen (1992), and seek to evaluate explicitly the constancy of the long-run relationship.

The estimates shown in Table 1 are consistent with the empirical regularities reported in the references above: income-elasticity far above one, which is often interpreted as capturing wealth effects not explicitly taken into account in the specification of equation (2); the semielasticity with respect to the own rate higher than that of the alternative rate; and, the presence of inflation in the long-run relationship. As regards the evidence on cointegration, the ADF, PP and DHS tests strongly reject the hypothesis of non-cointegration in the period 1979Q1–1988Q4. Likewise, the h_k test provides the same inference, not rejecting – at standard confidence levels – the null of cointegration. Finally, none of the Hansen tests rejects the hypothesis of the existence of a long-run demand for broad money that is stable in the period analysed.

Table 2 shows the same long-run demand for ALP2 estimated over the extended sample 1979Q1–1993Q4. Contrary to the findings in Table 1, the evidence in favour of the cointegration hypothesis is now scant, suggesting a structural break in the ALP2 long-run demand function: the ADF, PP and DHS tests do not allow the null of non-cointegration to be rejected at standard levels of significance; likewise, the h_k test rejects cointegration at very high confidence levels.

With a view to examining in more detail the issue of structural breaks in the long-run relationship, Table 2 reports a number of additional statistics based on the work by Gregory and Hansen (1996). These statistics extend the traditional ADF and PP tests in order to allow, under the alternative hypothesis, the cointegration relationship to change at an unknown point in the sample, either the intercept (LS) or the entire vector of coefficients (RS)[6], including the intercept. In a setting of structural change, in which the power of the traditional ADF or PP tests falls sharply, these tests can detect cointegration while providing an estimation of the date ($\hat{\tau}$) at which the potential break occurs. The following outline – in which the generic name DF has been given to traditional tests and DF* to those proposed by these authors – may help in the joint interpretation of both types of tests:

[6] The asymptotic critical values of both tests are tabulated in the aforementioned reference.

Interpretation

H_0: non-cointegration	cointegration	structural change
DF does not reject DF* does not reject	non-cointegration	–
DF does not reject DF* rejects	cointegration	structural change may be significant
DF rejects DF* rejects	cointegration	no evidence on structural change
DF rejects DF* does not reject	cointegration	no evidence on structural change

Based on the foregoing outline, it is easy to interpret the tests proposed in Gregory and Hansen (1996) as proving useful only when the traditional tests do not enable the null hypothesis of non-cointegration to be rejected. In other cases, when DF rejects, rejection by DF* cannot be interpreted as evidence in favour of structural change, since the alternative contains as a particular case the standard model of cointegration with constant parameters. Likewise, when DF rejects but DF* does not, the result has to be interpreted in the light of the much lesser power of the latter when, in fact, there is no break. In both cases, tests for structural change in regressions with first-order integrated variables as proposed in Hansen (1992) or in Phillips and Quintos (1993) may allow the stability of the cointegration relationship to be evaluated.

One difficulty with the Gregory and Hansen tests lies in the existence, in finite samples, of biases against the null hypothesis (non-cointegration), as evidenced by the results of the Monte Carlo experiments conducted by these authors. To negotiate this obstacle, finite-sample critical values have, where necessary, been simulated[7]. For the RS tests in Table 2 these are: −7.93 (1%), −7.14 (5%) and −6.70 (10%), far higher in terms of absolute values than the asymptotic critical values tabulated in Gregory and Hansen (1993): −6.92, −6.41 and −6.17, respectively.

Turning to the results in Table 2, only with the ADF-RS test does some marginal evidence in favour of the existence of cointegration appear when the entire vector of parameters is allowed to change. Consistent with the previous findings in Table 1, the break point ($\hat{\tau}$) is positioned right at the end of the sample – around the second or third quarter of 1989 –, implying that the changes in the long-run parameters are estimated with few degrees of freedom. Nevertheless, the solution of letting all the parameters change proves unsatisfactory, in the sense that the evidence provided by the RS tests in favour of the hypothesis of two cointegration regimes is rather weak.

An additional possibility explored in Table 2 involves restricting the nature of the structural change to which the demand for ALP2 would have been subject; that is restricting the type of structural break under the alternative hypothesis in the Gregory and Hansen RS tests to the intercept and some of the slope coefficients. This would improve power properties of the tests and, moreover, it would enable more accurate hypotheses to be analysed on the nature of the possible structural change. The number of tests along these lines

[7] These critical values have been generated in GAUSS-386 using $n = 5000$ replications for $T = 60$ observations. Although n is relatively small for this type of exercise, it is empirically tested that the critical values calculated are sufficiently robust for the purposes of this paper.

analysed in Table 2 is, however, limited to competing hypotheses which analysts have used in recent years to signify disturbances that were affecting the demand for money[8].

First of all, since the detection of instabilities in the demand for ALP, it has been occasionally argued that the recent increase in the savings ratio and in resident private-sector wealth may be one of the underlying factors. From this viewpoint, the high long-run income elasticity estimated for this aggregate (1.51 in the equation in Table 1) would capture wealth effects not explicitly taken into account in equation (2). As a result, alterations in the income-wealth ratio would induce instability in the equation estimated and, more specifically, in the parameter that measures long-run income elasticity (α_1).

To test the role played by factors of this type, the ADF-RS$^{\alpha 1}$ and PP-RS$^{\alpha 1}$ tests in Table 2 restrict the possibilities of structural change under the alternative hypothesis to the intercept and to the parameter that affects income in equation (2)[9]. As with the RS tests, the correct critical values were simulated for the sample size at issue, giving the following result: −7.06 (1%), −6.32 (5%) and −6.01 (10%). The results of the tests reported in the table continue not to allow rejection of the null hypothesis of non-cointegration.

Second, it has also been suggested that a further factor behind this instability may have been the increase – by historical standards – in the sensitivity of the monetary aggregate to swings in interest rates. In principle, this idea does not challenge the evidence presented that a structural break affecting the demand for ALP2 occurred in or around 1989. Indeed, at the end of that year, ahead of the far-reaching reform of the reserve requirement ratio in the early months of 1990, the first skirmishes occurred in the so-called "war of the supercuentas" (high-yield deposit accounts). This episode was ultimately framed within a broader process of heightening competition among financial institutions to raise deposits. Similarly, this was the setting of the extraordinary growth of portfolio investment institutions in recent years.

Hence, the ADF-RS$^{\alpha 2,\alpha 3}$ and PP-RS$^{\alpha 2,\alpha 3}$ tests reported in Table 2 restrict the structural change to the intercept and to the parameters that affect the own and alternative interest rates in equation (2)[10]. Nor does the evidence drawn from these tests allow the rejection of the null hypothesis of non-cointegration when the alternative allows the change described in the parameters that affect both interest rates in the ALP2 long-run demand equation.

Lastly, a third factor which has been pointed out focuses on the gradual elimination of administrative obstacles to free capital movements and the resulting opening of the Spanish financial system to international markets that considerably broadened the resident private sector's investment and financing opportunities, increasing the range of alternative assets to those included in ALP2. From this standpoint, although the main liberalising impulse occurred in 1987, 1989 also proved to be an important year, with the lifting of quantitative limits on investment in securities issued on foreign markets. Subsequently, this process steadily intensified through a series of measures which

---

[8] See, in this connection, the Banco de España 1993 Annual Report or the article *Monetary Policy in 1994* in the January 1994 edition of the Banco de España Economic Bulletin.

[9] Evidently, this is an indirect test which is conditioned by the absence of a quarterly time series of private-sector wealth for the Spanish economy.

[10] Critical values have not been simulated for this case. However, such values must be greater in absolute terms than those relating to the RS$^{\alpha 1}$ tests.

Table 3. Long-run demand for broad money ALP2 (79/Q1–93/Q4): the role of foreign interest rates

a) general specification

$$(m-p)_t = \underset{(28.25)}{-9.08} + \underset{(48.12)}{1.67}y_t + \underset{(7.03)}{3.34}rp_t - \underset{(5.78)}{1.41}ra_t - \underset{(0.67)}{0.10}\Delta_4 p_t + \underset{(0.009)}{0.001}rx_t$$

ADF = −0.25	PP = −1.07	DHS = 40.26	$h_k = 1.32^{***}$
ADF-RS$^{\alpha 5}$ = −6.48* ($\gamma = 0.07; \tau = 89/\text{III}$)		PP-RS$^{\alpha 5}$ = −6.07 ($\gamma = 0.15; \tau = 89/\text{II}$)	

b) restricted specification

$$(m-p)_t = \underset{(16.76)}{-8.21} + \underset{(29.56)}{1.57}y_t + \underset{(9.77)}{2.74}rp_t - \underset{(5.97)}{0.85}ra_t - \underset{(3.00)}{0.34}\Delta_4 p_t - \underset{(7.95)}{1.39}rx_t^* + \underset{(8.37)}{0.124}S89/I$$

ADF = −4.81	PP = −5.54	DHS = 654.31	$h_k = 0.0766$

Notes: See notes to Table 1. The variables S89/I and rx_t^* take zero values before 1989 and, thereafter, the former variable takes one, and the latter the simple average of three-month interest rates in Germany and USA.

liberalised ecu-denominated deposits (September 1989) and the purchase of securities issued on money markets abroad (April 1990) and allowed residents to hold bank accounts in pesetas and foreign currency at non-resident banks (February 1992). Similarly, the decline in foreign exchange risk derived from the peseta's entry into the ERM on June 19 1989 may also have had a major impact in making foreign markets more accessible to the Spanish financial system.

In accordance with the foregoing, the set of variables in equation (2) has been extended so as to add an interest rate on foreign assets (rx_t). More specifically, the simple average of three-month Euromarket interest rates on the D-Mark and the dollar have been included in the following estimations[11]. As can be seen in Table 3 (top panel), this variable is not significant when the equation is estimated for the whole sample 1979/I–1993/IV, and, moreover, the ADF, PP, DHS and h_k tests continue not to allow any amendment to be made to the previous conclusions about the absence of cointegration. On the contrary, the results of the ADF-RS$^{\alpha 5}$ and PP-RS$^{\alpha 5}$ tests do offer some evidence in favour of cointegration, when the possibility of a change in the sensitivity of ALP2 to variations in the foreign rate is envisaged, rejecting[12] at 93% confidence level (the first test) and 85% (the second) the unit root hypothesis in the estimated residuals (non-cointegration). The break point ($\hat{\tau}$) continues to be estimated at around 1989 and, moreover, the foreign interest rate did not prove significant in the previous period.

In keeping with this last observation, the ALP2 long-run demand equation is re-estimated including only rx_t values as from the first quarter of 1989

[11] Strictly speaking, these interest rates should be adjusted for exchange rate depreciation expectations. The problem has been obviated with the argument that this component would be I(0), not affecting (asymptotically) the estimation of the long-run parameters.

[12] The critical values simulated for these tests are: −7.30 (1%), −6.65 (5%) and −6.29 (10%).

Table 4. The long-run demand for broad money ALP2 (79/Q1–93/Q4): results using different estimation procedures

Estimation method	y_t	rp_t	ra_t	$\Delta_4 p_t$	rx_t^*
SOLS	1.497	2.968	−1.052	−0.456	−1.382
FME	1.572	2.740	−0.851	−0.341	−1.387
	(0.053)	(0.280)	(0.143)	(0.114)	(0.174)
ECM	1.480	3.115	−1.333	−0.477	−1.111
$(k=2)$					
DOLS	1.579	2.913	−0.890	−0.400	−0.827
$(k=1)$	(0.079)	(0.384)	(0.228)	(0.193)	(0.314)
DGLS	1.553	3.058	−1.111	−0.425	−0.537
$(k=1)$	(0.083)	(0.398)	(0.238)	(0.185)	(0.324)
JOH	1.559	3.227	−1.149	−0.257	−1.561
$(k=2)$	(0.381)	(0.696)	(0.241)	(0.178)	(0.325)

Notes: Standard errors in brackets (autocorrelation and heteroskedasticity consistent for DOLS). If $x = (y, rp, ra, \Delta_4 p, rx^*)$ and $z = m - p$, the figures in the table refer to esitmates of the β's as follows:
1. OLS: ordinary least squares in the static regression: $z_t = \beta x_t + u_t$
2. ECM: OLS in: $\Delta z_t = \sum_{j=1}^{k} \Delta z_{t-j}\gamma_j + \sum_{j=0}^{k} \Delta x_{t-j}\delta_j - \alpha z_{t-1} + \alpha\beta x_{t-1} + u_{2t}$
3. DOLS: OLS in: $z_t = \beta x_t + \sum_{j=-k}^{k} \Delta x_{t-j}\gamma_j + u_{3t}$
4. DGLS: generalised least squares in regression (3), where it is assumed that u_{3t} follows an AR(1) process.
5. JOH: application of the Johansen procedure with unrestricted constant and no trend to the vector (z, x), assuming rx^* to be exogenous.

(rx_t^*)[13]. The results, which are shown in the bottom panel of Table 3, may be described as satisfactory, with the foreign interest rate playing a significant role and without there being substantial changes in the remaining parameters – others than the intercept – regarding the estimation to 1988/IV shown in Table 1[14]. The long-run semi-elasticity of ALP2 in relation to variations in the foreign rate is estimated at −1.39, which would imply a semi-elasticity of about −0.7 in relation to individual changes in German and US interest rates.

Nonetheless, the aforementioned results must be viewed with some caution. First, because the foreign interest rate semi-elasticity is estimated with few degrees of freedom and, therefore, with little accuracy. The robustness of the estimates is, however, analysed below. Second, as the intercept is allowed to vary, the possibility of other unspecified factors taking place from 1989 onwards and leading to a level shift in the demand function cannot be totally dismissed. However, the results from tests LS in Table 2 strongly suggest that such factors are not decisive in getting cointegration. In this connection, the role of the change in the intercept seems to be confined to compensate the abrupt negative jump which, otherwise, would have taken place in the demand function as a result of the inclusion of the variable rx_t^*. This, in turn,

[13] Using FME here rests on the assumption of rx_t^* being strongly exogenous.

[14] The ADF, PP, DHS and h_k values in the bottom panel of Table 3 are shown for illustrative purposes to enable comparison with the values obtained in the other tables. The relevant inference on cointegration is provided by the ADF-RS$^{\alpha 5}$ and PP-RS$^{\alpha 5}$ tests in the top panel of the table.

points to the effects of the opening up of the Spanish financial system being a more gradual process than that permitted in this paper[15].

Finally, Table 4 shows, along with the FME estimation, the result of the application to the equation in Table 3 (bottom panel) of various procedures for the estimation of cointegrating vectors: SOLS (static ordinary least squares: Engle and Granger, 1987), ECM (Hendry and Ericsson, 1991), DOLS (dynamic OLS: Saikkonen, 1991), DGLS (dynamic generalised least squares: Stock and Watson, 1993) and JOH (Johansen, 1988). Of these, the latter three, together with FME, are asymptotically efficient according to Saikkonen (1991), i.e. their asymptotic distribution is strictly more concentrated around the true value of the parameter. The details of the estimation are given in the notes to the table.

The estimations of the parameters of income, the own and alternative interest rates and inflation are fairly similar, irrespective of the estimation method used. On the contrary, the parameter that measures the semi-elasticity of ALP2 to variations in foreign interest rates, though significant in most cases, is that which displays the greatest variability between estimations, with values ranging from -1.387 (with FME) to -0.537 (with DGLS). That is perhaps a reflection of the limited observations available for its estimation. Conversely, the estimation of this parameter does prove robust to certain changes in the definition of the relevant foreign interest rate. Thus, for example, if the equation is re-estimated via FME using a weighted average foreign rate[16] instead of the simple average of the rates of the D-Mark and the dollar, the long-run semi-elasticity estimated (-1.279) is very similar to the previous case. Likewise, when German and US rates are included separately in the equation for an extended sample period ending in 1995Q4, a semi-elasticity somewhat higher to German rates is obtained (-1.14 versus -0.77), although some accuracy is lost in the estimation so that the equality of the coefficients continue not to be rejected.

To sum up the results in this section, it would appear necessary to modify the conclusions drawn by other authors on the ALP2 demand equation, particularly those concerning the existence of cointegration and the stability of the coefficients which define the long-run relationship. The empirical evidence analysed indicates that the shifts in the demand for broad money in recent years, far from being transitory episodes limited to the short run, have substantially changed the long-run properties of the aggregate. As to the meaning of this structural change, three hypotheses have been examined: the increase in the private-sector savings rate, the heightened sensitivity of money demand to changes in the own and alternative interest rates, and the growing openness of the Spanish financial system to international markets. It is the third hypothesis that seems to play a pivotal role in explaining the apparent instability of the traditional ALP2 demand equations. Thus, only when the returns alternative to those included in ALP2 are expanded to include, as from 1989, foreign interest rates is it possible to recover a long-run demand for broad money equation reasonably stable in recent years.

---

[15] The inclusion of learning-adjusted foreign rates [Hendry and Ericson, 1991] could prove to be useful in this context. We stick to step-functions, however, to allow for the use of the inference in Gregory and Hansen (1996).

[16] Specifically, the weighted average rate used is that appearing in the first column of Table 19.24 of the Banco de España's "Boletín Estadístico".

3. Conclusions

As pointed out in the Introduction, the stability of the demand for money is a key factor in assessing the viability of monetary policy strategies based on intermediate monetary targeting. However, the stability hypothesis is far from being uncontroversial. Since the mid-70s, many researchers have documented a number of episodes of both *missing money* and *great velocity decline* in various countries.

As regards Spain, the evidence for the stability of money demand is mixed. On the one hand, the equations estimated have been invariant against the changes made since 1978 in the basic monetary policy framework. The change from bank reserves to short-term rates as the operational target, or the greater weight attached to the exchange rate in the reaction function, does not appear to have caused significant shifts in the estimated empirical relationships. This has reinforced the structural interpretation of such relationships, as opposed to an alternative reduced-form interpretation. In this respect, the Lucas critique does not appear to have been empirically relevant in the case of the demand for money in Spain[17].

By contrast, the changes in the financial environment of the Spanish economy in recent decades seem to have had a powerful impact on the estimates in question. During the 80s, major portfolio adjustments by the public as a result of financial innovation and market deregulation led the Banco de España to broaden the definition of its intermediate target, which a shift from M3 to ALP as from 1984. In response to further financial innovation which increased the degree of asset substitutability, successive changes were made in ALP to include financial assets regarded as close substitutes for those already covered by the definition of money.

Early in the 90s, with the liberalisation of capital movements and the definitive opening up of the Spanish financial system to international markets, instability was again noted in the estimated relationships. Indeed, the empirical evidence analysed in the previous section indicates that the recent shifts in the demand for this aggregate – far from representing transitory, short-run episodes – had substantially changed its long-run properties.

Econometrically, in both cases it has been possible to re-specify the money demand equations so that they become stable again. This is done either by redefining the monetary aggregate, or by including new variables among its determinants. However, there are also other factors which cast doubt on whether this aggregate can provide a sufficiently solid basis for monetary policy design.

First, the evidence presented above focused on the parameters that define the long-run demand equation. Yet this should not obscure the fact that the description of the process of dynamic adjustment to the long-run path may often be of fundamental importance for monetary policy purposes, e.g., when a forecasting equation is needed. In the context of annual monetary planning, factors which are difficult to gauge and which have not been taken into account, notably expectations of exchange rate depreciation, may be crucial in interpreting short-run developments in the monetary aggregate. This was the case with the significant, if temporary, cross-border deposit shifts in the quarters of 1992 prior to the successive devaluations of the peseta. More generally,

[17] See Dolado (1988) for a detailed discussion.

the broadness of a monetary aggregate such as ALP, which includes financial assets that differ widely in the liquidity services they provide, greatly complicates interpretation of the aggregate's behaviour, as its demand combines strictly transactional motives with savings or portfolio motives.

Second, the inclusion of foreign variables, and more specifically foreign interest rates, among the determinants of money demand reduces the central bank's ability to influence the money stock through the control of its operational target, namely the short-term interest rate.

Finally, a monetary policy strategy which gives priority to medium- to long-run considerations in response to frequent short-run instabilities in the demand for money is not without problem. One difficulty is the extraordinarily complicated process of discriminating at an empirically level between one-off instabilities in the estimated equations and shifts in the long-run demand function. From the econometric standpoint, this problem becomes more acute at the end of the relevant sample period, precisely the time when the central bank has to explain monetary conditions and the prospects of meeting targets to the public. The monetary authorities are thus involved in an ongoing and increasingly complex task of interpreting developments in monetary aggregates on a case-by-case basis, which may ultimately erode the credibility of its commitment to the monetary target. An additional factor in this respect is the existence of a considerable lag between the time when the effects on the demand for money of a given change in the financial environment are first perceived and – once agents have fully adapted to the new context – the time when these effects may be estimated econometrically with reasonable precision and included in new specifications. During these intermediate periods, monetary policy operates with an increased degree of uncertainty. Such considerations, and others of a more institutional nature, led the Banco de España in 1995 to announce a change in monetary policy strategy and to adopt direct targets for inflation.

In short, as uncertainty about the behaviour of the monetary aggregate increases and it becomes less amenable to control, all these factors combine to erode the usefulness of broad money as an intermediate monetary target variable. However, despite these difficulties, the persistence of a stable long-run relationship between ALP2 and expenditure continues to justify its use as a privileged indicator in the analysis of monetary conditions.

References

Andrews DWK (1991) Heteroskedasticity and autocorrelation consistent covariance matrix estimation. Econometrica 59:817–858

Andrews DWK, Monahan JC (1992) An improved heteroskedasticity and autocorrelation consistent covariance matrix estimator. Econometrica 60:953–966

Ayuso J, Vega JL (1994) Agregados monetarios ponderados. Revista Española de Economía 11-1: 161–189, a version in English can be found as "Weighted monetary aggregates: The Spanish case", Working Paper 9303, Servicio de Estudios-Banco de España

Cabrero A, Escrivá JL, Sastre T (1992) Demand equations of the new monetary aggregates. Estudios Económicos 52, Servicio de Estudios-Banco de España

Choi I (1994) Durbin-Hausman tests for cointegration. Journal of Economic Dynamics and Control 18:467–480

Dolado JJ (1988) Innovación financiera, inflación y estabilidad de la demanda de ALP. Boletín Económico, Banco de España, abril

Dolado JJ, Escrivá JL (1992) La demanda de dinero en España: Definiciones amplias de liquides. Moneda y Crédito 195:111–134, a version in English can be found as "The demand for money in Spain: Broad definitions of liquidity, Working Paper 9107, Servicio de Estudios-Banco de España
Engle RF, Granger CWJ (1987) Cointegration and error correction: Representation, estimation and testing. Econometrica 55:251–276
Escrivá JL, Malo de Molina JL (1991) Implementation of Spanish monetary policy in the framework of European integration. Working Paper 9104, Servicio de Estudios-Banco de España
Gonzalo J, Lee T (1996) Relative power of t-type tests for stationarity and unit root processes. Journal of Time Series Analysis 17-1:37–48
Gregory AW, Hansen BE (1996) Residual-based tests for cointegration in models with regime shifts. Journal of Econometrics 70:99–126
Gregory AW, Nason JM, Watt DG (1996) Testing for structural breaks in cointegrated relationships. Journal of Econometrics 71, 1&2:321–341
Hansen BE (1992) Tests for parameter instability in regressions with I(1) processes. Journal of Business & Economics Statistics 10:321–335
Hansen H, Johansen S (1996) Recursive estimation in cointegrated VAR-models. Discussion Paper, Institute of Economics, University of Copenhagen
Hendry DF, Ericsson NR (1991) Modelling the demand for narrow money in the UK and the US. European Economic Review 35:833–881
Johansen S (1988) Statistical analysis of cointegration vectors. Journal of Economics Dynamics and Control 12:231–254
Leybourne SJ, McCabe BPM (1993) A simple test for cointegration. Oxford Bulletin of Economics and Statistics 55:97–103
MacKinnon JG (1991) Critical values for cointegration tests. In: Engle RF, Granger CWJ (eds.). Long run economic relationships, Oxford University Press, pp. 267–276
Phillips PCB, Hansen BE (1990) Statistical inference in instrumental variable regression with I(1) processes. Review of Economic Studies 57:99–125
Phillips PCB, Quintos CE (1993) Parameter constancy in cointegrating regressions. Empirical Economics 18:675–706
Poole W (1970) Optimal choice of monetary policy instruments in a simple stochastic macro model. Quarterly Journall of Economics 84:197–216
Saikkonen P (1991) Asympotically efficient estimation of cointegration regressions. Econometric Theory 7:1–21
Stock JH, Watson MW (1993) A simple estimator of cointegrating vectors in higher order integrated systems. Econometrica 61:783–820
Stock JH (1987) Asymptotic properties of least-squares estimators of co-integrating vectors. Econometrica 55:1035–1056

Friedman and Schwartz (1982) revisited: Assessing annual and phase-average models of money demand in the United Kingdom*

Neil R. Ericsson[1], **David F. Hendry**[2], **Kevin M. Prestwich**[3]

[1] Stop 24, Division of International Finance, Federal Reserve Board, 2000 C Street, N.W., Washington, DC 20551, USA (e-mail: ericsson@frb.gov)
[2] Nuffield College, Oxford OX1 1NF, UK (e-mail: david.hendry@nuffield.oxford.ac.uk)
[3] AMS—American Management Systems, 12601 Fair Lakes Circle, Fairfax, Virginia 22033, USA (e-mail: kevin_prestwich@mail.amsinc.com)

Abstract: Several studies have developed empirical models of U.K. money demand using the century of annual and phase-average data in Friedman and Schwartz (1982). The current paper evaluates key models from those studies, employing tests of constancy and encompassing. The evidence strongly favors an annual model from Ericsson, Hendry, and Prestwich (1998a), whereas models based on the phase-average data fare poorly.

Key words: constancy, encompassing, Friedman and Schwartz, money demand, phase averaging

JEL classification: E41, C52

---

* The first author is a staff economist in the Division of International Finance, Board of Governors of the Federal Reserve System, Washington, DC 20551 USA. The second author is Leverhulme Personal Research Professor of Economics at Nuffield College, Oxford OX1 1NF. The third author was a research assistant in the Division of International Finance at the Federal Reserve Board when this paper was initially drafted. The views in this paper are solely the responsibility of the authors and should not be interpreted as reflecting the views of the Board of Governors of the Federal Reserve System or of any other person associated with the Federal Reserve System. The first author gratefully acknowledges the generous hospitality of Norges Bank, where he revised some of the material herein. The second author gratefully acknowledges financial support from the U.K. Economic and Social Research Council under grant R000234954. We wish to thank Clifford Attfield, David Demery, and Nigel Duck for compiling the data in Attfield, Demery, and Duck (1995); and Neva Kerbeshian, Helmut Lütkepohl, Jaime Marquez, and two anonymous referees for helpful comments. All numerical results were obtained using PcGive Professional Version 9.0: see Doornik and Hendry (1996). The data may be obtained from the Internet at http://wotan.wiwi.hu-berlin.de/oekonometrie/engl/data.html

1. Introduction

Empirical modeling of the demand for money has been a central focus in the economics profession for many years. This interest is reflected in the sequence of studies by Friedman and Schwartz (1982), Hendry and Ericsson (1983), Longbottom and Holly (1985), Escribano (1985), Hendry and Ericsson (1991), Attfield, Demery, and Duck (1995), and Ericsson, Hendry, and Prestwich (1998a), which have developed various empirical models of U.K. money demand using the century of annual and phase-average data in Friedman and Schwartz (1982). Those models differ substantially in their empirical properties and in their purported implications for policy, so some model comparison is of value. The current paper evaluates the key models from those studies, employing tests of constancy and encompassing. The evidence strongly favors an annual model from Ericsson, Hendry, and Prestwich (1998a).

These various studies involve different models estimated over different sample periods and on different measures of the data (annual and phase-average). Two types of model comparison are common in the existing literature. First, a given model can be evaluated over different data periods with the same data measure, generating tests of constancy. Second, different models estimated over the same period and with the same data measure can be compared, as with standard encompassing tests. The current paper assesses both constancy and encompassing for four key models that use Friedman and Schwartz's data. It also evaluates these models by a new encompassing approach, comparing different models estimated over the same sample period but with different data measures. Tests of constancy and encompassing are natural to consider for evaluating these models. As Judd and Scadding (1982) document, constancy is a critical and often elusive feature of empirical money-demand equations. Likewise, encompassing is a key feature in a progressive research strategy and so is sensible to consider for extensions of datasets; see Mizon and Richard (1986) and Hendry (1995, Chapters 9 and 14) *inter alia*.

This paper is organized as follows. Section 2 describes the annual data, and Section 3 discusses the annual models. An annual model in Ericsson, Hendry, and Prestwich (1998a) encompasses previous annual models but not conversely, and that model has empirically constant coefficients. Section 4 defines the relationship between annual and phase-average data and reproduces Friedman and Schwartz's central empirical (phase-average) results on U.K. money demand. Section 5 derives some implications of phase averaging in order to compare the annual and phase-average results. Section 6 then compares annual models from Hendry and Ericsson (1991) and Ericsson, Hendry, and Prestwich (1998a) with phase-average models from Friedman and Schwartz (1982) and finds clear evidence supporting the annual models. Throughout, the analysis emphasizes the progressive nature of empirical research and the practical importance of coherent rather than mechanistic extensions of empirical models. Section 7 concludes.

2. The annual data

This section describes the annual data. The basic data series are annual values of the broad money stock (M), real net national income (I), the corresponding deflator (P), short-term and long-term nominal interest rates (RS and $R\ell$), population (N), and high-powered money (H), all for the United Kingdom. Data for 1871 through 1975 are from Friedman and Schwartz (1982). Attfield, Demery, and Duck (1995) extended those series over 1976–1993, constructing them from a variety of sources and splicing together several alternative definitions of money. The variables M and H are in £ million; I is in £ million for 1929; N is in millions; $P = 1.00$ in 1929; and RS and $R\ell$ are fractions. Ericsson, Hendry, and Prestwich (1998b, Appendix) give further details on the data, and Hendry and Ericsson (1991) and Ericsson, Hendry, and Prestwich (1998a) graph the data and provide some descriptive statistics.

Some constructed variables are of interest. First, under the quantity theory, the income elasticity is unity, so a key derived variable is velocity V $[= (I \cdot P)/M]$.

Second, there are dummy variables. Retaining the notation in Hendry and Ericsson (1991) and Ericsson, Hendry, and Prestwich (1998a), the variables D_1 and D_3 are zero-one dummies for World Wars I and II, and D_4 is a zero-one dummy for 1971–1975. The latter aims to capture the deregulation of the banking sector with the introduction of Competition and Credit Control in 1971. A similar period of deregulation occurs in 1986–1989. The dummy D_c proxies for both episodes of deregulation, being unity for 1971–1975 and 1986–1989, and zero otherwise.

Third, there are several measures for the opportunity cost of holding money M. Ideally, the measured opportunity cost would incorporate the own rate on money in addition to the outside rate, but a consistent and complete series on the own rate is not currently available. Three feasible alternatives have been advanced, as follows. Friedman and Schwartz (1982) advocated using a fraction of RS, denoted RN and calculated as $(H/M) \cdot RS$. This measure assumes that all components of M except for high-powered money H earn interest at the (outside) short-term rate RS. Hendry and Ericsson (1991) proposed using the short-term interest rate RS itself because, over Friedman and Schwartz's sample, very little of M2 earned interest, and the interest rate on the interest-bearing component of M2 was itself very low. Finally, Ericsson, Hendry, and Prestwich (1998a) suggested modifying Friedman and Schwartz's measure RN so as to account for the changes in the measurement of high-powered money and broad money that occurred over the extended sample. Proper measurement of RN requires the unspliced data, even while the modeled money series is spliced. To distinguish between measures using spliced and unspliced series, H and M denote spliced series, whereas H^a and M^a denote actual values (superscript ^{a} for actual). Specifically, H^a and M^a are not rescaled for the definitional changes in 1975 (for H) and 1987 (for M). Correspondingly, RN denotes $(H/M) \cdot RS$ (as above) with spliced series, and RN^a denotes $(H^a/M^a) \cdot RS$. Over 1871–1975, RS is virtually indistinguishable from RN and RN^a (aside from a scale factor) because H/M and H^a/M^a are essentially constant over that sample period. However, over 1975–1993, H/M and H^a/M^a plummet from 0.22 to 0.09 (for H/M) or 0.04 (for H^a/M^a), implying very different behavior of RS, RN, and RN^a.

Throughout, capital letters denote both the generic name and the level of a variable; logs are in lowercase; and "levels" often means the logarithm of the levels, with the context clarifying the usage. Uppercase delta Δ is the difference operator, defined as $(1 - L)$, where the lag operator L shifts a variable one period into the past. Hence, for x_t (a variable x at time t), $Lx_t = x_{t-1}$ and so $\Delta x_t = x_t - x_{t-1}$. More generally, $\Delta_j^i x_t = (1 - L^j)^i x_t$ for positive integers i and j. If i or j is not explicit, it is taken to be unity. Single and double asterisks (* and **) adjacent to values of statistics denote significance at the 5% and 1% levels respectively.

3. Constancy, encompassing, and the annual models

This section describes models constructed on the initial annual dataset (1871–1975) and then on the extended dataset (1871–1993), paralleling these models' historical development. This progression traces and summarizes the encompassing nature of the model sequence, where encompassing occurs both across samples for a given model (constancy) and across models for a given sample ("standard" encompassing).

Hendry and Ericsson (1983) developed a linear equilibrium correction model (EqCM) over 1878–1970.[1] Using the same data, Longbottom and Holly (1985) and Escribano (1985) obtained improved specifications, the first through the role of interest rates and the second through a nonlinear EqCM. Each of the two new models encompassed the model in Hendry and Ericsson (1983), but neither could encompass the other. Hendry and Ericsson (1991) developed a model that improved on all three of the previous models, encompassing each one; and they extended the sample through 1975. Because that improved model encompasses the earlier models, it serves like a sufficient statistic for those earlier models. So, for our present purposes, we ignore the earlier models and focus on the improved model, which is an empirically constant EqCM of broad money M, in which the quantity theory of money defines the long-run equilibrium and the data determine the dynamics:

$$\begin{aligned}\Delta(m-p)_t = {} & \underset{(0.06)}{0.47}\,\Delta(m-p)_{t-1} - \underset{(0.04)}{0.11}\,\Delta^2(m-p)_{t-2} - \underset{(0.04)}{0.59}\,\Delta p_t \\ & + \underset{(0.05)}{0.41}\,\Delta p_{t-1} - \underset{(0.005)}{0.017}\,\Delta rs_t - \underset{(0.017)}{0.078}\,\Delta_2 r\ell_t \\ & - \underset{(0.20)}{1.15}(\hat{u}_{t-1} - 0.2)\hat{u}_{t-1}^2 + \underset{(0.002)}{0.007} + \underset{(0.6)}{3.4}(D_1 + D_3)_t \\ & + \underset{(0.9)}{7.1}\,D_{4t} + \underset{(0.027)}{0.090}\,D_{4t}\Delta rs_t \qquad (1)\end{aligned}$$

$$T = 98\ [1878\text{–}1975] \quad R^2 = 0.88 \quad \hat{\sigma} = 1.478\% \quad Jt = 1.22 \quad Var = 0.05.$$

For each observation, the equilibrium correction residual $\hat{u}$ is calculated as:

$$\hat{u}_t = (m - p - i)_t - (-0.310 - 7.00RS_t) \qquad (2)$$

$$T = 98[1873\text{–}1970] \quad R^2 = 0.56 \quad \hat{\sigma} = 10.86\%,$$

[1] Although Hendry and Ericsson (1983), Longbottom and Holly (1985), Escribano (1985), and Hendry and Ericsson (1991) referred to their models as error correction models, technically speaking they are equilibrium correction models. See Hendry (1995, p. 213) for a discussion of the distinction between the two types of models.

where, for historical reasons, the coefficients in (2) are derived from a static Engle-Granger regression over 1873–1970.[2] Here and below, t is the annual time subscript; T is the number of annual observations; R^2 is the squared multiple correlation coefficient; $\hat{\sigma}$ is the standard deviation of the residuals, expressed as a percentage of real money and adjusted for degrees of freedom; *Jt* and *Var* are Hansen's (1992) statistics for testing joint parameter nonconstancy and variance nonconstancy; and OLS standard errors are in parentheses $(\cdot)$. The coefficients on the war dummies $(D_1 + D_3)$ and the deregulation dummy D_4 (and on D_c, below) have been scaled up 100-fold so that they are interpretable as percentages. The coefficient on $D_{4t}\Delta rs_t$ is *not* rescaled, so as to maintain units comparable to those of the coefficient on Δrs_t. While diagnostic tests are important in model evaluation, the papers cited above give a battery of such tests for (1)–(2) and the models examined below, so diagnostic tests (beyond those for constancy and encompassing) are not included herein.

Equations (1)–(2) use the annual data as compiled by Friedman and Schwartz (1982), which end in 1975. Attfield, Demery, and Duck (1995) and Ericsson, Hendry, and Prestwich (1998a, Section III) evaluate mechanistic extensions of this model over 1976–1993 and find strong evidence of parameter nonconstancy. However, the way in which a model is extended over a new sample bears directly on its statistical performance on that sample. To wit, a coherent economic extension of (1)–(2) over the same sample obtains constant coefficients, as shown in Ericsson, Hendry, and Prestwich (1998a, Section V). This economic extension is:

$$\begin{aligned}\Delta(m-p)_t = {} & \underset{(0.05)}{0.48}\,\Delta(m-p)_{t-1} - \underset{(0.04)}{0.10}\,\Delta^2(m-p)_{t-2} - \underset{(0.04)}{0.62}\,\Delta p_t \\ & + \underset{(0.05)}{0.40}\,\Delta p_{t-1} - \underset{(0.006)}{0.020}\,\Delta rn_t^a - \underset{(0.016)}{0.041}\,\Delta_2 r\ell_t \\ & - \underset{(0.33)}{2.26}(\tilde{u}_{t-1} - 0.2)\tilde{u}_{t-1}^2 + \underset{(0.002)}{0.004} + \underset{(0.5)}{3.9}(D_1 + D_3)_t \\ & + \underset{(0.7)}{5.2}\,D_{ct} + \underset{(0.026)}{0.100}\,D_{4t}\Delta rs_t \end{aligned} \quad (3)$$

$$T = 116[1878\text{–}1993] \quad R^2 = 0.87 \quad \hat{\sigma} = 1.622\% \quad Jt = 1.93 \quad Var = 0.82^{**}$$

$$Cov : F(10, 95) = 1.31 \quad Chow : F(20, 85) = 2.73^{**},$$

where $\tilde{u}$ is the Engle-Granger residual from:

$$\tilde{u}_t = (m - p - i)_t - (-0.318 - 6.67 RN_t^a) \quad (4)$$

$$T = 98[1873\text{–}1970] \quad R^2 = 0.59 \quad \hat{\sigma} = 10.57\%.$$

Equations (1) and (2) require two economic extensions to obtain (3) and (4). First, the deregulation dummy D_4 is extended as D_c when entering by itself in

[2] Due to increased numerical accuracy in recent versions of PcGive, the estimated intercept in (2) differs slightly from the one reported in Hendry and Ericsson (1991, equation (9)). See Ericsson, Hendry, and Prestwich (1998a, footnote 4) for details.

order to capture the deregulation in 1986–1989. Second, the measure of the opportunity cost (RS) is replaced by RN^a in order to capture the decline in the non-interest-bearing fraction of measured money during the last two decades.

The coefficients in (1) and (3) are virtually identical, confirming the constancy of these equations' coefficients. Forecasts and recursive estimates of (3) in Ericsson, Hendry, and Prestwich (1998a, Figures 7 and 8) and the insignificance of *Jt* and the Chow (1960) covariance statistic (*Cov*) underscore the constancy of (3)'s coefficients. That said, $\hat{\sigma}$ has increased by about 10%, and *Var* and the Chow (1960) predictive-failure statistic (*Chow*) reject, indicating that the nonconstancy present is due to omitted variables nearly orthogonal to the included variables. Equally, rejection by the predictive-failure and *Var* tests reflects these tests' high power to detect numerically modest changes in $\hat{\sigma}$. The long sample and the high variance of the data relative to that of the equation error are the proximate reasons for that high power. Overall, the model (3) performs well for this recent turbulent period in the U.K. economy, while its increased error variance reveals that further improvements are possible.

Formal encompassing tests of (1) and (3) strongly favor equation (3). For the samples considered (1878–1973, 1878–1975, and 1878–1993), the parameter-encompassing statistics are: $F(2,83) = 1.22$ [0.30], $F(2,85) = 5.28$ [0.0069], and $F(2,103) = 22.15$ [0.0000] for whether (1) encompasses (3); and $F(2,83) = 0.13$ [0.88], $F(2,85) = 0.17$ [0.85], and $F(2,103) = 0.45$ [0.64] for whether (3) encompasses (1). $F(\cdot,\cdot)$ denotes the asymptotic null distribution, and p-values are in brackets. This analysis and the more detailed results in Ericsson, Hendry, and Prestwich (1998a) establish that (3) encompasses key aspects of (1) on the extended sample through suitable measurement of the opportunity cost and proper adjustment for financial deregulation. Thus, the following sections turn to assessing these annual models in light of phase-average models.

4. Phase-average data and a model thereof

While the original data are annual, Friedman and Schwartz (1982) analyze phase averages of that annual data in order to focus on the longer-term movements in the data. This section describes what phase averaging is, and it documents Friedman and Schwartz's central phase-average model for U.K. money demand.

In phase averaging, the annual data are averaged separately over contraction and expansion phases of data-selected reference business cycles, where that averaging aims to remove the short-term fluctuations from the data. For a given annual series $\{x_t; t = 1, \ldots, T\}$, the corresponding phase-average series is constructed as:

$$\bar{x}_j = \frac{\frac{1}{2}x_{t_j} + x_{t_j+1} + \cdots + x_{t_j+c_j-1} + \frac{1}{2}x_{t_j+c_j}}{c_j} \qquad j = 1, \ldots, J, \tag{5}$$

where an overbar denotes phase averaging, j is the index for phase averaging, c_j is the phase length of the jth phase (in years), t_j is the first year of the jth phase, and J is the number of phase-average observations corresponding to T

annual observations. Beginning and ending years are weighted by one half and appear in adjacent phases as well. Friedman and Schwartz (1982, Chapters 3 and 4) phase-average 108 annual observations (1868–1975) on the logarithms of money, prices, incomes, and population, and the levels of the interest rates to obtain 38 phase averages for each series.

Friedman and Schwartz (1982, p. 282) present their central regression for U.K. money demand in their Table 6.14. We could closely replicate that equation:

$$(\bar{m} - \bar{p} - \bar{n})_j = \underset{(0.19)}{0.02} + \underset{(0.049)}{0.883}(\bar{\imath} - \bar{n})_j - \underset{(3.29)}{11.22}\,\overline{RN}_j - \underset{(0.29)}{0.21}\,G(\bar{p} + \bar{\imath})_j$$

$$+ \underset{(0.58)}{1.38}\,\overline{W}_j + \underset{(2.7)}{20.6}\,\overline{S}_j \qquad (6)$$

$$J = 36\ [1874\text{–}1973] \quad R^2 = 0.97 \quad \hat{\sigma} = 10.36\%.$$

The variable $G(\bar{p} + \bar{\imath})$ is the two-sided growth rate of nominal income, $\overline{W}$ is a dummy for "postwar adjustment", and $\overline{S}$ is a data-based dummy for "[a]n upward demand shift, produced by economic depression and war . . . " during 1921–1955, where quotes are from Friedman and Schwartz (1982, pp. 228, 281).[3] Friedman and Schwartz also consider a similar equation in rates of change, discussed below.

Hendry and Ericsson (1991) document evidence on the mis-specification of (6), including rejection of residual normality, price homogeneity, and constancy, the last by both Chow and covariance statistics. Hansen's statistics provide further evidence of nonconstancy: $Jt = 2.15^*$ and $Var = 0.23$. That said, comparison of (1) and (3) with (6) is still of interest because an otherwise apparently well-specified model may yet fail to encompass a model with known mis-specification. Sections 5 and 6 thus interpret and assess the phase-average results in light of their annual counterparts.

5. An interpretation of phase-average error variances

Encompassing statistics are relatively easy to calculate for annual models and for phase-average models. However, encompassing statistics for comparing annual models with phase-average models are as yet undeveloped, although the approach is clear. Using (5), the annual model is reduced to a phase-average representation, whose derived coefficients are compared with the coefficients of the estimated phase-average model. Except under highly restrictive assumptions, the required annual model is a full system of equations for money, prices, income, and interest rates, and not just a conditional money-demand equation. Construction of a full system is beyond the scope of this paper, as is a derivation of the formal encompassing statistic.

---

[3] The reported numbers in (6) differ slightly from those in Hendry and Ericsson (1991, equation (1)) because of rounding errors in the data. Hendry and Ericsson (1991, equation (1)) uses the phase-average data published in Friedman and Schwartz (1982), which are rounded, whereas (6) uses phase-average data calculated directly from the annual data in Friedman and Schwartz (1982).

Section 6 below offers two alternatives: it examines the error variances of annual and phase-average models, and it compares phase-average outcomes with annual outcomes transformed to phase averages. Examination of error variances is of interest because a necessary condition for encompassing is variance dominance, where one equation dominates another equation in variance if the former has a smaller error variance; see Hendry and Richard (1982). To assess variance dominance, the error variances from the two types of models must be in the same units. By re-examining the results in Friedman and Schwartz (1982), the current section shows how to ensure that the variances are in the same units.

In estimating their phase-average regressions, Friedman and Schwartz (1982) used weighted least squares to correct for the heteroscedasticity introduced by variable-length phase averaging. If unnormalized weights are applied in the phase-average regressions, the resulting equation standard errors are directly comparable to equation standard errors from annual regressions. However, to replicate the regressions in Friedman and Schwartz (1982), the weights must be normalized such that the average weight is unity for regressions in levels, and slightly less than unity for regressions in rates of change. Normalization is immaterial to the validity of the heteroscedasticity transform, but comparisons of the equation standard error for phase-average and annual regressions must account for the normalization factor, which rescales the phase-average equations by a non-unit scalar.

An example clarifies the implications of the normalization. Suppose an annual variable x_t is distributed as $IN(0, \sigma^2)$: that is, x_t is serially independent and normally distributed with mean zero and variance σ^2. From (5), the phase-average variable $\bar{x}_j$ is distributed as $N(0, \sigma^2/k_j^2)$, where $k_j^2 = 2c_j^2/(2c_j - 1)$. Even though the annual variable x_t is homoscedastic, the phase average $\bar{x}_j$ is not, as its variance depends upon the phase length c_j. To correct this heteroscedasticity, Friedman and Schwartz (1982) used weighted least squares regressions, where the weights depended on k_j. If the weights had been the $\{k_j\}$ themselves, then the weighted errors in the regression equation would have been distributed as (e.g.) $N(0, \sigma^2)$ for $\bar{x}_j$ regressed on a constant. However, Friedman and Schwartz (1982) [and Attfield, Demery, and Duck (1995) as well] used *normalized* weights κ_j (say), where $\kappa_j = k_j \backslash \bar{k}$ and the normalization factor $\bar{k}$ is the approximate sample mean of k_j. Because $\bar{k}$ simply rescales the entire weighted least squares regression, the choice between k_j and κ_j does not affect coefficient estimates, their standard errors, or their t-ratios. The equation standard error *is* affected, though, noting that $\kappa_j \bar{x}_j$ is distributed as $N(0, \sigma^2/\bar{k}^2)$. Thus, for a phase-average regression estimated by weighted least squares with normalized weights, the equation standard error must be multiplied by $\bar{k}$ to transform it into units comparable to those of the equation standard error from a regression with annual data.

Normalization has consequences for Friedman and Schwartz's phase-average regressions, both in levels and in rates of change. For the phase-average equation in levels [comparable to (6)], Friedman and Schwartz (1982, p. 282) report that $\hat{\sigma}$ is 5.54% from the regression with normalized weights. Because the mean of the unnormalized weights is $\bar{k} = 1.826$, the $\hat{\sigma}$ comparable to annual results is $5.54\% \cdot 1.826 = 10.12\%$. That is virtually 10.36%, the value for $\hat{\sigma}$ obtained in (6), using unnormalized weighted least squares. Second, for the phase-average equations with rates of change in (e.g.) Friedman and Schwartz (1982, Table 6.8), the normalization factor $\bar{k}$ is 8.00 exactly, which is close to 7.19, the average of the unnormalized weights. Thus, for the $\hat{\sigma}$ of 1.34% in the "final" rates-of-change equation in Friedman and Schwartz (1982, p. 282), the actual $\hat{\sigma}$ comparable to annual results is $1.34\% \cdot 8.00 = 10.72\%$.

6. Constancy and encompassing with different measures of data

Using the adjustments from Section 5, Section 6.1 compares estimated values of $\hat{\sigma}$ from annual and phase-average models for U.K. money demand to determine the direction of variance dominance.[4] Variance dominance is a property based on in-sample calculations, and variance dominance is necessary for encompassing. Section 6.1 also performs similar comparisons for out-of-sample calculations, where dominance in root mean squared error (RMSE) is necessary for forecast encompassing; see Ericsson (1992). Once comparable units and time periods are obtained, the annual models clearly dominate the phase-average models, both in variance and in RMSE. Then, Section 6.2 evaluates the models' statistical and numerical constancy. These combined results allow re-assessment of claims in Friedman and Schwartz (1991) and Attfield, Demery, and Duck (1995).

6.1 Encompassing and goodness of fit

Table 1 lists comparably scaled values of $\hat{\sigma}$ and RMSE for four equations: the phase-average equations in levels and rates of growth from Friedman and Schwartz (1982, p. 282), the initial annual model (1), and the translated annual model (3). This subsection compares these two measures of fit, both across models and across samples.

When estimated over the initial sample of 1878–1973 (equivalent to phases 2–36), the annual models (1) and (3) have virtually identical equation standard errors (1.424% and 1.406%) and substantially variance-dominate both phase-average equations, which have equation standard errors of 10.36% and 10.75% respectively. The annual models also variance-dominate the phase-average models when estimated over the new sample (1974–1993) and over the extended sample (1878–1993). Typically, a phase-average model's equation standard error is 7 or more times that of a corresponding annual model, reflecting just how much better the annual models explain the data relative to the phase-average models. Put slightly differently, roughly 98% of the residual variation in a phase-average model is explained by either annual model.

As this comparison shows, the EqCMs (1) and (3) fit far better than Friedman and Schwartz's phase-average equations in levels and rates of change. One potential explanation is the treatment of dynamics: (1) and (3) incorporate dynamics directly, whereas Friedman and Schwartz's equations

---

[4] The situation is further complicated by the *data-based* selection of the phases, contrasting with the annual model being fit and forecast to data at fixed 1-year intervals. However, Campos, Ericsson, and Hendry (1990) show that the dominant effects of Friedman and Schwartz's phase averaging appear to be captured by fixed-length phase averaging, so the analysis below ignores the consequences of endogenously selecting the phases.

Table 1. Estimated equation standard errors ($\hat{\sigma}$), RMSEs, and constancy statistics for phase-average and annual models

Statistic [phase observations in brackets]	Phase-average Data		Annual Data	
	Log-level model (6)	Growth-rate model	Initial model (1)	Translated model (3)
$\hat{\sigma}$				
[2–36] 1878–1973	10.36	10.74	1.424	1.406
[37–44] 1974–1993	21.70	28.37	2.915	2.644
[2–44] 1878–1993	10.95	12.67	1.931	1.622
RMSE: original data				
[37–42] 1974–1988	13.93	20.76	6.750	2.648
[37–44] 1974–1993	–	–	28.124	2.755
RMSE: Figure 1				
[1–36]	10.15	–	–	–
[2–36]	10.19	–	1.346	–
[37–42]	14.75	–	6.110	–
[37–43]	–	–	13.533	–
Chow statistic				
value	1.71	3.28*	5.40**	2.73**
p-value	0.1536	0.0139	0.0000	0.0007
degrees of freedom	(6, 30)	(6, 29)	(20, 85)	(20, 85)
Covariance statistic				
value	0.30	1.03	4.95**	1.31
p-value	0.8736	0.4065	0.0000	0.2342
degrees of freedom	(4, 32)	(4, 31)	(10, 95)	(10, 95)
Hansen statistic				
Jt	1.71	1.10	2.58	1.83
Var	0.28	0.58*	0.86**	0.78**

Notes:
1. All values of $\hat{\sigma}$ and RMSE are in percent.
2. Listed dates correspond to estimation periods (for $\hat{\sigma}$) and forecast periods (for the RMSE).
3. Phase observations appear in square brackets. For $\hat{\sigma}$, the listed phase observations are the literal equivalents to the years listed. Samples for the estimation of phase-average models are 1–36, 37–42, and 1–42 for the log-level model, and 2–36, 37–42, and 2–42 for the growth-rate model. For RMSEs, the listed phase observations are the literal equivalents to the years listed and are also the actual samples. Values of $\hat{\sigma}$ and RMSE for phase-average samples are converted to annual units for comparability.
4. Statistics for testing constancy are calculated over phases 1–42 and 2–42 for the phase-average equations in levels and growth rates and over 1878–1993 for the annual equations.

do not. That said, the latter do implicitly adjust for dynamics through phase averaging, which uses 64 degrees of freedom, contrasting with only 11 degrees of freedom for dynamics in (1) and (3). In that light, comparison of the two phase-average equations with the (static) annual Engle-Granger regressions (2) and (4) offers a stark inference. The equation standard errors for those four equations are essentially the same, implying that phase averaging failed entirely in its ostensible purpose—to remove the short-run fluctuations in the data.

The first set of RMSEs in Table 1 are obtained by estimating each model over its initial sample (e.g., phases 2–36, or 1878–1973) and forecasting over the remainder of the sample. For the longest matching forecast sample (phases

37–42, or 1974–1988), the annual equations dominate the phase-average equations in RMSE. The ratio of RMSEs for (6) and (3) is over 5, similar to the in-sample results. When the forecast sample is extended through 1993, the RMSEs for the annual models increase: marginally for (3) and dramatically for (1). The change in RMSE for (1) arises from that equation's poor measure of opportunity cost (*RS*) and a lack of accounting for data splicing. RMSEs for the phase-average models can be computed through only phase 42 (1985–1988) because one regressor in the phase-average models is the two-sided growth rate $G(\bar{p}+\bar{\imath})$. Its calculation for phase 43 requires $\bar{p}+\bar{\imath}$ for the (not yet complete) phase 44 (1991 onward). Still, the RMSE over 1974–1993 for the annual model (3) is much smaller than the equation standard errors and RMSEs of the phase-average models over any of the samples.

Choice of units for $\hat{\sigma}$ can affect inference. In Table 1, values of $\hat{\sigma}$ (and of the RMSE) for the phase-average and annual equations are in comparable units because the underlying phase-average regressions used unnormalized weighted least squares. By contrast, Friedman and Schwartz (1982, p. 282) used normalized weighted least squares, and Friedman and Schwartz (1991) did not account for that normalization in their comparisons of phase-average and annual models. Because of this technical mistake, Friedman and Schwartz (1991, pp. 46–47) stated that their regressions variance-dominate those in Hendry and Ericsson (1991). Rather, the converse is true, as Table 1 shows. On a related issue, because (1) and (3) are EqCMs, both are equations in log-levels, even though their dependent variables are growth rates. Thus, these equations' values of $\hat{\sigma}$ require no additional rescaling to be comparable to $\hat{\sigma}$ for (6), contrary to Friedman and Schwartz's (1991, footnote 9) claim.

The relationship between annual and phase-average data provides an additional method for evaluating the annual and phase-average models: transform the annual models' fitted and forecast values to phase averages and compare those values directly with those from the phase-average models. Figure 1 does precisely this for the initial annual model (1) and the phase-average model in levels, (6). Figure 1*a* plots the actual, fitted, and forecast values for velocity *v* over the extended sample (phases 1–43), and Figure 1*c* plots the corresponding residuals and forecast errors. Figures 1*b* and 1*d* are comparable to Figures 1*a* and 1*c* but plot values over the forecast sample alone. The phase-average model generally has larger errors than the annual model, an outcome consistent with the comparison of Figures 4 and 7 in Hendry and Ericsson (1991). The phase-average model's forecast error in phase 37 is particularly large, being nearly 20%. Using the transformed annual model (3) rather than the initial annual model (1) obtains an even more pronounced contrast between the annual and phase-average results.

The second set of RMSEs in Table 1 numerically summarize the graphical results in Figure 1.[5] As with the earlier comparisons, the annual model (1) always dominates the phase-average model (6) for matched samples, reflecting the superior performance of the annual model. Over phases 37–43, the RMSE for the annual model is 13.533% because of the large outlier in phase 43 (1988–1991). As noted above, the phase-average model cannot be tested for that phase.

---

[5] Because the annual model used the sample 1878–1970 due to lagged values, its phase-average fitted values begin in phase 2, not phase 1.

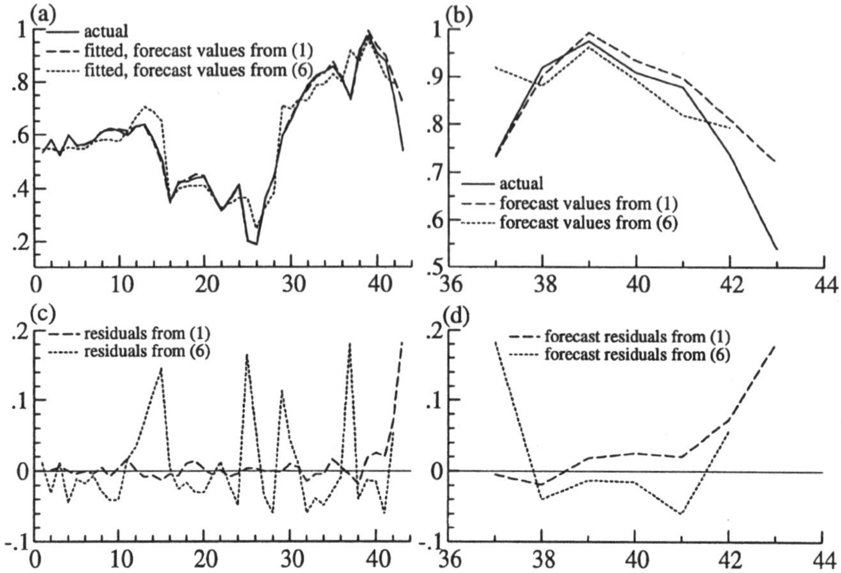

Fig. 1. Actual, fitted, and forecast values for velocity v from the annual equation (1) (--) and the phase-average equation (6) (---), and the corresponding residuals, all in a common phase mapping

6.2 Tests of constancy

Tests of constancy are an alternative metric for assessing the relative fit of models, so this subsection analyzes the constancy of the phase-average and annual models. The annual models (1) and (3) both fail the Chow predictive-failure and Hansen *Var* tests, and (1) fails the covariance test as well: see Table 1. These failures reflect the models' increased variances over the new and extended samples. By contrast, the phase-average models show little evidence of nonconstancy over the extended sample.

The apparent contradiction between variance dominance and constancy has an immediate resolution. Variance dominance and RMSE dominance compare the fit of different models across the same sample, whereas the Chow, covariance, and Hansen statistics compare the fit of a given model across different samples. Furthermore, the power of a constancy test depends not only on the magnitude of the change in the coefficients, but also on the fit of the model and on the number of observations available. The annual models fit the data well in sample, their coefficients are precisely estimated, and the forecast period has a large number of observations: 20 for 1974–1993, or about 20% the number in the initial dataset. Combined, these features ensure that the constancy tests have high power to detect even small nonconstancies in the annual models. Conversely, the phase-average models fit poorly in sample, equation (6) in particular is detectably nonconstant in sample even though that sample is small, and the number of observations forecast is small (only 6). Thus, further nonconstancies in the phase-average model are hard to detect statistically.

Put somewhat differently, the numerical and statistical forecast properties of a model need not be the same: the values of $\hat{\sigma}$, RMSE, and the Chow statistic demonstrate this distinction; see Ericsson (1992). The phase-average model appears constant, in fair part because it fits the data so poorly. The annual model is statistically detectably nonconstant because it fits the data so well.

The distinction between statistical and numerical properties has immediate implications for inferences, as did rescaling $\hat{\sigma}$ in Section 6.1. Specifically, the results in Table 1 and Figure 1 allow a re-assessment of Attfield, Demery, and Duck (1995), who tested for the constancy of (6) over phases 37–42 [1973–1988] and the constancy of (1) over 1976–1993. Using Chow and covariance tests, Attfield, Demery, and Duck (1995, Tables 1–8) found that (6) appears constant whereas (1) does not. In concluding, they claimed:

> ... the set of estimates based on the *phase-average* data and the approach adopted by [Friedman and Schwartz (1982)] appear to provide a reasonably good explanation of phase-average money holdings since 1975, at least until the very last phase now available. And some formal tests of stability suggest that these estimates are stable. In contrast, the estimates based on annual observations and the approach adopted by [Hendry and Ericsson (1991)] do not provide a satisfactory explanation for the annual observations after 1975 and appear to be highly unstable. (p. 10)

These inferences are incorrect or misleading, for four reasons. First, while the annual model (1) is statistically less constant than the phase-average model (6), the annual model provides a far better *explanation* of phase-average money than does the phase-average model; see Figure 1. Attfield, Demery, and Duck (1995) confuse goodness of fit and constancy, which are not equivalent concepts. Second, the phase-average models appear statistically constant in fair part because they fit the data so poorly. For the phase-average model in levels, tests of constancy out-of-sample are further contaminated because that model is known to be nonconstant in-sample; see Hendry and Doornik (1997). Third, in Attfield, Demery, and Duck (1995), comparison of annual and phase-average models is based on mismatched samples, biasing the constancy tests in favor of the phase-average models. Their Figures 1*a*, 1*b*, and 2 of the models' forecast errors seem impressive, but the worst performance of the annual model is over data that the phase-average model does not attempt to predict. Fourth, Attfield, Demery, and Duck (1995) ignore the economic consequences of redefining the dependent variable. In particular, they mechanically extended the annual model (1) when testing its constancy over 1976–1993. If that model is economically extended, as in (3), it performs quite respectably.

7. Conclusions

The central role of money demand relationships in economic policy has stimulated many empirical studies, including those cited above, which developed various empirical models of U.K. money demand using Friedman and Schwartz's annual and phase-average data. This paper evaluates key models from those studies, employing tests of encompassing and constancy. A historical sequence of annual models has led to an equilibrium correction model on data through 1993, where that model encompasses the earlier annual models. That model also captures salient features in the data from 1975 (the end of Friedman and Schwartz's sample) through 1993—a period with radical changes in economic policy. The model's performance on the new data depends directly upon sensible economic choices for extending the time series of those data to reflect their altered measurement. That said, the annual model, whether mechanistically or economically extended, explains the data far better than the phase-average models. This result holds over the fitted sample and forecast periods; and it holds regardless of whether outcomes are compared across the different datasets on a uniform metric, or whether the outcomes from the annual model are transformed into phase averages and then compared with the outcomes from the phase-average models. The remaining nonconstancy in the economically extended annual model indicates the high power of constancy tests in well-fitting models, and it points to the possibility of further progress in model specification.

References

Attfield CLF, Demery D, Duck NW (1995) Estimating the UK demand for money function: A test of two approaches. Mimeo, Department of Economics, University of Bristol, Bristol, England

Campos J, Ericsson NR, Hendry DF (1990) An analogue model of phase-averaging procedures. Journal of Econometrics 43, 3:275–292

Chow GC (1960) Tests of equality between sets of coefficients in two linear regressions. Econometrica 28, 3:591–605

Doornik JA, Hendry DF (1996) PcGive Professional 9.0 for Windows. International Thomson Business Press, London

Ericsson NR (1992) Parameter constancy, mean square forecast errors, and measuring forecast performance: An exposition, extensions, and illustration. Journal of Policy Modeling 14, 4:465–495

Ericsson NR, Hendry DF, Prestwich KM (1998a) The demand for broad money in the United Kingdom, 1878–1993. Scandinavian Journal of Economics 100, 1:289–324

Ericsson NR, Hendry DF, Prestwich KM (1998b) Friedman and Schwartz (1982) revisited: Assessing annual and phase-average models of money demand in the United Kingdom. International Finance Discussion Paper, Board of Governors of the Federal Reserve System, Washington, D.C., available on the WorldWide Web at www.bog.frb.fed.us/pubs/ifdp/1998/

Escribano A (1985) Non-linear error-correction: The case of money demand in the U.K. (1878–1970). Mimeo, University of California at San Diego, La Jolla, California

Friedman M, Schwartz AJ (1982) Monetary trends in the United States and the United Kingdom: Their relation to income, prices, and interest rates, 1867–1975. University of Chicago Press, Chicago

Friedman M, Schwartz AJ (1991) Alternative approaches to analyzing economic data. American Economic Review 81, 1:39–49

Hansen BE (1992) Testing for parameter instability in linear models. Journal of Policy Modeling 14, 4:517–533

Hendry DF (1995) Dynamic econometrics. Oxford University Press, Oxford

Hendry DF, Doornik JA (1997) The implications for econometric modelling of forecast failure. Scottish Journal of Political Economy 44, 4:437–461

Hendry DF, Ericsson NR (1983) Assertion without empirical basis: An econometric appraisal of 'Monetary trends in … the United Kingdom' by Milton Friedman and Anna Schwartz. In: Monetary trends in the United Kingdom, Bank of England Panel of Academic Consultants, Panel Paper No. 22, Bank of England, London, October, pp. 45–101

Hendry DF, Ericsson NR (1991) An econometric analysis of U.K. money demand in 'Monetary trends in the United States and the United Kingdom' by Milton Friedman and Anna J. Schwartz. American Economic Review 81, 1:8–38
Hendry DF, Richard J-F (1982) On the formulation of empirical models in dynamic econometrics. Journal of Econometrics 20, 1:3–33
Judd JP, Scadding JL (1982) The search for a stable money demand function: A survey of the post-1973 literature. Journal of Economic Literature 20, 3:993–1023
Longbottom A, Holly S (1985) Econometric methodology and monetarism: Professor Friedman and Professor Hendry on the demand for money. Discussion Paper No. 131, London Business School, London, England
Mizon GE, Richard J-F (1986) The encompassing principle and its application to testing non-nested hypotheses. Econometrica 54, 3:657–678

Broad money demand and financial liberalization in Greece*

Neil R. Ericsson[1], **Sunil Sharma**[2]

[1] Stop 24, Division of International Finance, Federal Reserve Board, 2000 C Street, N.W., Washington, DC 20551, USA (e-mail: ericsson@frb.gov)
[2] Research Department, International Monetary Fund, 700 - 19th Street, N.W., Washington, DC 20431, USA (e-mail: ssharma@imf.org)

Abstract: This paper develops a constant, data-coherent, equilibrium correction model for broad money demand (M3) in Greece over 1976–1994. The aggregate M3 was targeted until recently, and current monetary policy still uses such aggregates as guidelines. In spite of financial innovation, financial liberalization, and large fluctuations in the inflation rate, the estimated model is remarkably stable. Dynamics are important, with price and income elasticities being much smaller in the short run than in the long run. The model provides a better understanding of the portfolio consequences of financial innovation and the effects of monetary policy in Greece.

Key words: Cointegration, equilibrium correction, financial innovation, Greece, money demand

JEL classification: E41, E5

* The authors are staff economists in the Division of International Finance, Federal Reserve Board, Washington, DC 20551 USA, and the Research Department, International Monetary Fund, Washington, DC 20431 USA, respectively. They may be reached on the Internet at ericsson@frb.gov and ssharma@imf.org. The views expressed in this paper are solely the responsibility of the authors and should not be interpreted as reflecting those of the Board of Governors of the Federal Reserve System, the International Monetary Fund, or other members of their staffs. We wish to thank the Bank of Greece for providing the data; Sophocles Brissimis, Nicholas Paleocrassas, and George Simigiannis for offering insights into institutional aspects of the Greek financial system; and Richard Agénor, Caroline Atkinson, Adi Brender, Julia Campos, Dimitri Demekas, David Hendry, Katarina Juselius, Tim Lane, Helmut Lütkepohl, Jaime Marquez, Jürgen Wolters, and two anonymous referees for useful comments. An earlier version of this paper appeared as Ericsson and Sharma (1996). All numerical results were obtained using PcGive Professional Versions 8 and 9: see Doornik and Hendry (1994a, 1994b, 1996, 1997) and Hendry and Doornik (1996). The data may be obtained from the Internet, http://wotan.wiwi.hu-berlin.de/oekonometrie/engl/data.html

1. Introduction

Recent changes in the Greek financial system pose challenges for the conduct of Greek monetary policy. With the removal of external capital controls and of restrictions on deposit-taking institutions, the monetary authorities have moved from administratively set credit allocations and interest rates to open market operations. New financial products have complicated the interpretation of monetary aggregates and have prompted the monetary authorities to shift their focus from the growth of broad money (M3) to the exchange rate. Besides requiring redefinition of what constitutes "money", these products have altered the characteristics of assets that were previously included in monetary aggregates. Greece's differential taxation of financial products has further complicated the assessment of movements in monetary aggregates.

The purpose of this paper is to model the empirical relationship between broad money, prices, real output, and interest rates in Greece over 1976–1994, and to examine the constancy of this relationship, especially in light of recent changes in the financial system. In spite of its importance for forecasting and policy, constancy has proved elusive for estimated money demand functions of many countries; see Judd and Scadding (1982) for the United States. While nonconstant empirical equations do not preclude a stable underlying relation, they leave unresolved the question of whether the observed predictive failure arises from shifts in the underlying relation or whether it is simply a consequence of model mis-specification.

For Greek money demand, that question is moot. The estimated model is remarkably constant in spite of large fluctuations in the inflation rate, the introduction of new financial instruments, and liberalization of the financial system. The long-run demand for real money depends upon real income with a unit elasticity, and upon the own interest rate with a semi-elasticity of approximately five. Assets outside money affect money demand through a spread between their rate of return and the rate of return on broad money. The dynamics of money demand are important, with price and income elasticities being much smaller in the short run than in the long run.

This paper is organized as follows. Section 2 presents a historical perspective and discusses the economic theory of money demand and the data available. Section 3 analyzes integration and cointegration properties of the data, testing for cointegration and weak exogeneity in a six-variable vector autoregression. The evidence on cointegration ties back directly to the economic theory of money demand. The empirical weak exogeneity of prices, income, and interest rates provides the foundation for development of a parsimonious, empirically constant, single-equation equilibrium correction model for money demand in Section 4. Section 5 concludes.

2. Background

This section sets the backdrop for the empirical modeling in Sections 3 and 4. It summarizes important economic events over the sample period (Section 2.1), sketches the static theory-model for money demand (Section 2.2), and describes the data available and some of their basic properties (Section 2.3).

2.1 A historical perspective

In the 1970s, the Greek financial system was strictly regulated. Funds were allocated at administratively set interest rates, and foreign exchange transactions were controlled. Compulsory investment requirements for banks channeled funds into certain sectors of the economy at subsidized rates and supported below-market financing of the government.

Between 1980 and 1987, financial liberalization evolved gradually. Interest rates on government paper were raised to levels comparable with bank deposit rates. After a long hiatus, sales of Treasury bills directly to the public resumed in 1985. The sale of medium-term, Drachma-denominated, foreign exchange-linked bonds resumed the following year. Deregulation of the financial system accelerated, following the 1987 Report of the Committee for the Reform and Modernization of the Greek Banking System. Banks were allowed to offer certificates of deposit and bank bonds at market rates. Over the next several years, many credit restrictions were removed, and borrowing and lending rates were deregulated, with the minimum rate on savings deposits finally being abolished in 1993. Direct credit restrictions, reserve requirements on banks, and the minimum rate on savings deposits had all been important instruments of monetary control.

The banking law of August 1992 instituted additional financial reforms, including adoption of the relevant EC directives. In 1994, monetary financing of the government and privileged government access to the central bank were abolished, and constraints on bank intermediation were further reduced. Significant liberalization of external transactions proceeded in tandem with financial deregulation, with controls on capital movements being completely abolished in May 1994. For recent overviews of the Greek financial system, see Alogoskoufis (1995), Filippides, Kyriakopoulos, and Moschos (1995), Soumelis (1995), and Ericsson and Sharma (1996, Section II.1).

Financial deregulation, coupled with changing and differential taxation of financial instruments, complicated the assessment of movements in monetary aggregates. Extension of the withholding tax to earnings on repurchase agreements (repos) precipitated a massive flight out of that asset in 1994. This flight occurred for two reasons. First, because withholding tax was applied to repos but not government securities, the latter offered a more attractive return. Second, financial liberalization allowed the creation of products called synthetic swaps. These derivatives reduced the tax liability on interest from Drachma deposits by simultaneously swapping Drachmas for foreign currency (with a lower interest rate and hence a lower tax liability) and entering into a forward agreement to purchase Drachmas with the foreign currency deposit at maturity.

Because the financial sector was highly regulated and external capital movements were controlled over much of the sample, two points should be emphasized. First, the range of available financial instruments was very limited until 1985, when sales of Treasury bills to the public resumed. Even then, real assets constituted a substantial part of an investor's portfolio, so inflation (a proxy for their rate of return) may be an important determinant of money demand. Second, although government paper of various maturities became available in the late 1980s and early 1990s, the interest rates on these instruments were closely linked to the key one-year Treasury bill rate. Thus, that one-year rate is used to proxy the return on financial assets outside of M3.

2.2 Economic theory

Money is demanded for at least two reasons: as an inventory to smooth differences between income and expenditure streams, and as one among several assets in a portfolio; see Baumol (1952), Tobin (1956), and Friedman (1956). The transactions motive implies that nominal money demand (M^d) depends on the price level (P) and the volume of real transactions (Y). Holdings of money as an asset are determined by the return to money as well as returns on alternative assets, and by total assets (often proxied by income). Commonly, money demand is specified in log-linear form, albeit with the interest rates entering in their levels. Sections 3 and 4 below assume such a specification, in which the competing assets are Drachma (Dr) broad money as measured by M3, Drachma Treasury bills, and domestic goods. The corresponding rates of return are the net interest rates on time deposits RT^n and on repos RR^n (both being returns on components of M3), the interest rate on Treasury bills RB, and the inflation rate Δp. The superscript ^{n} denotes net of withholding tax, Δ is the first difference operator, and variables in lower case denote logarithms.[1] See Cagan (1956) on the inclusion of inflation in the money demand function. In light of the financial structure and data properties described elsewhere in this section, this choice of assets and returns seems reasonable. Thus, money demand may be written explicitly as:

$$m^d - p = \gamma_0 + \gamma_1 y + \gamma_2 RT^n + \gamma_3 RR^n + \gamma_4 RB + \gamma_5 \Delta p, \qquad (1)$$

where long-run price homogeneity is imposed. Anticipated signs of the coefficients $\{\gamma_i\}$ are $\gamma_1 > 0$ (specifically, $\gamma_1 = 1$ for the quantity theory of money), $\gamma_2 > 0$, $\gamma_3 > 0$, $\gamma_4 < 0$, and $\gamma_5 < 0$.

Equation (1) can be rewritten with a single interest rate and a set of spreads, where this reparameterization may be more interpretable economically. One such reparameterization is:

$$m^d - p = \gamma_0 + \gamma_1 y + \delta_2 RT^n + \delta_3 (RB - RT^n) + \delta_4 (RB - RR^n) + \gamma_5 \Delta p, \quad (2)$$

where $\delta_2 = \gamma_2 + \gamma_3 + \gamma_4$, $\delta_3 = \gamma_3 + \gamma_4$, and $\delta_4 = -\gamma_3$. The coefficient δ_2 captures the total levels effect of the interest rates, and the spreads capture the incremental effects of the own rates relative to the Treasury bill rate. The assumed signs of coefficients in (1) imply that $\delta_4 < 0$. The coefficients δ_2 and δ_3 are not uniquely signed without additional information. However, $\delta_2 > 0$ and $\delta_3 < 0$ seem likely, particularly if (for δ_2) Treasury bills are an imperfect substitute for M3 and because (for δ_3) the spread $RB - RT^n$ is nonzero during some periods when $RB - RR^n$ is zero or undefined.

In Greece, only one financial asset outside M3 has been generally available to the public: Treasury bills. Because the ratio of Treasury bills to M3 was small until 1990, we make the simplifying assumption that Treasury bills only became available to the public as an alternative to M3 beginning in 1991.

[1] The difference operator Δ is defined as $(1 - L)$, where the lag operator L shifts a variable one period into the past. Hence, for x_t (a variable x at time t), $Lx_t = x_{t-1}$ and so $\Delta x_t = x_t - x_{t-1}$. More generally, $\Delta_j^i x_t = (1 - L^j)^i x_t$ for positive integers i and j. If i or j is not explicit, it is taken to be unity.

Thus, in modeling money demand, the spread $(RB - RT^n)$ in (2) is replaced by a modified spread ST, which is zero through 1990 and $(RB - RT^n)$ thereafter. Repos are treated similarly. Because the fraction of repos in M3 was small during the first year that they were available (1991), we use a modified spread SR, defined as zero through 1991 and equal to $(RB - RR^n)$ thereafter. Thus, the money demand relation is re-specified as:

$$m^d - p = \gamma_0 + \gamma_1 y + \delta_2 RT^n + \delta_3 ST + \delta_4 SR + \gamma_5 \Delta p. \tag{3}$$

Economic theory offers little guidance in modeling the behavior of money out of equilibrium, beyond saying that adjustments to desired levels of money holdings are likely to take time due to adjustment costs. Further, undue restriction of dynamics may contaminate the estimation of the long-run specification itself. Sections 3 and 4 develop a dynamic equilibrium correction model (EqCM) of broad money demand, allowing the economic theory above to define the long-run equilibrium while determining short-run dynamics from the data.[2] Similar approaches to modeling money demand appear in Hendry and Ericsson (1991a, 1991b), Baba, Hendry, and Starr (1992), and Hendry (1995, Chapter 16).

2.3 The data

This subsection sequentially discusses the components of money, the corresponding rates of return, prices, and income. Money M is the broad measure M3 (Dr million), P is the consumer price index (1970 = 100, but based on 1988 consumption weights), the scale variable Y is real gross domestic product (GDP; Dr million, at factor cost in 1970 prices), and the rates of return are on assets within and outside of broad money (measured as fractions at annual rates). The data span the period 1975–1994 and were obtained from the Bank of Greece. All series are quarterly, seasonally unadjusted. The data were not seasonally adjusted because such pre-filtering may affect dynamics; see Wallis (1974) and Ericsson, Hendry, and Tran (1994). Rather, seasonality is captured explicitly in estimation by including seasonal dummies and (initially) seasonal lags in the set of regressors. Figures below appear as panels of graphs, with each graph labeled by a suffix $a, b, c, \ldots$, as follows: $\begin{bmatrix} a & b \\ c & \cdots \end{bmatrix}$. Ericsson and Sharma (1996, Appendix I) provide more extensive details on the data.

Broad money may be decomposed into several assets, with each asset offering a possibly different (own) rate of return. For Greece, the relevant components of M3 are currency in circulation (CC), private demand deposits (DD), private savings deposits (SD), time deposits (TD), bank bonds (BB), and repurchase agreements (repos, denoted REP). Figure 1*a* graphs these components, cumulatively, in units of 10^6 million Drachmas. Narrow money (M1) is the sum of the first two components ($CC + DD$), and M3 is the sum of all six components.

[2] Although the model constructed below is often called an error correction model, technically speaking it is an equilibrium correction model. Hendry (1995, p. 213) discusses the distinction between the two.

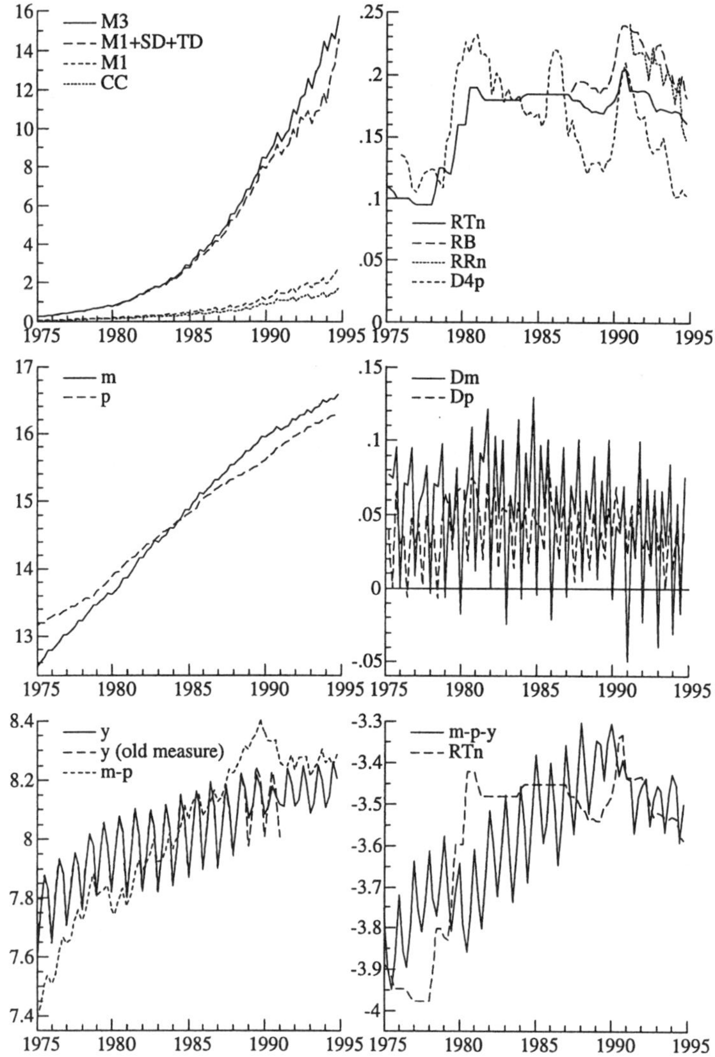

Fig. 1. Components of M3, various rates of return and annual inflation, nominal money and prices, their growth rates, real income (two measures) and real money, and inverse velocity and the net own rate

Each component of M3 has an associated nominal rate of return: zero for currency, *RD* for demand deposits, *RS* for savings accounts, *RT* for time deposits, and *RR* for repos.[3] Time deposits and repos offer the highest rates of

[3] The interest rate on bank bonds is not currently available. However, the fraction of bank bonds in M3 changes only very slowly over time and is never greater than 8%. Repos, introduced at the end of 1990, have become an increasingly important source of funds for deposit institutions. In 1992, the Bank of Greece redefined M3 to include bank bonds and repos, using this new measure to set its M3 targets. We use that new definition of broad money for the entire sample period.

return on the components of M3 described above, so *RT* and *RR* are natural proxies for the own (marginal) rate for M3. For that reason, and in order to limit the number of variables examined, *RD* and *RS* are excluded from the econometric modeling in Sections 3 and 4. Additionally, tax adjustment of interest rates appears economically and statistically important. In 1991Q1, the government introduced a withholding tax of 10 percent on interest from bank deposits, increasing it to 15 percent in 1992. In April 1994, this tax was extended to cover returns from repos. Figure 1*b* plots the corresponding net rates of return, denoted RT^n and RR^n. Since their introduction in 1990, repos have offered rates of return competitive with those on time deposits. Figure 1*b* also plots the Treasury bill rate *RB* and the annual rate of inflation $\Delta_4 p$, which are rates of return on alternative assets. For much of the period until mid-1986, all *ex post* real interest rates were negative. Thereafter, *ex post* real returns on time deposits were positive, except for a brief interlude around 1990 when inflation again reached 20 percent.

Figure 1*c* plots money and prices (m and p), with the latter adjusted to match the mean of the former. The price level is measured by the consumer price index because a quarterly series for the GDP deflator is not available. Figure 1*d* graphs the quarterly growth rates Δm and Δp, showing strong seasonality in both series.

Figure 1*e* plots real M3 ($m - p$), which grew at approximately 6% per annum through 1989 and remained relatively constant thereafter. Figure 1*e* also plots two published measures of real GDP: an initial series (y^{old}), available through 1991Q1; and a revised series (y), revised from 1987 onwards. To allow for the visible break in measured seasonality, estimation initially includes seasonal dummies for 1989 onwards in addition to seasonal dummies spanning the whole sample. In the final EqCM (7), the subsample seasonal dummies are excluded, as they are not statistically significant.

Figure 1*f* plots the net return on time deposits (RT^n) and the log of measured inverse velocity ($m - p - y$), where RT^n is adjusted in the figure so as to match the mean and range of ($m - p - y$). Inverse velocity is equivalent to imposing a unit income elasticity in (1) (or $\gamma_1 = 1$ in (3)). Seasonality aside, the inverse of velocity increased until 1990 and then fell somewhat. One potential explanation is the changes in the opportunity cost of holding money. Until virtually the end of the sample, the value of outstanding Treasury bills and repos is small relative to M3, so a simple representation of (3) involves the return on only one financial asset, M3 itself. While ($m - p - y$) and RT^n exhibit strong dynamic differences, their longer-term movements are similar, suggesting possible cointegration of the two variables; see Sections 3 and 4.

One alternative to holding M3 would be an asset denominated in a foreign currency. Its return is captured by the rate of depreciation of the exchange rate plus the interest rate on the asset. Notable devaluations occurred in January 1983 (of $15\frac{1}{2}$%) and October 1985 (of 20%). In a preliminary analysis, the depreciation rate and foreign interest rates (such as LIBOR) did not appear to matter, except that a dummy (denoted *DE*) for 1982Q4–1983Q1 helped capture the apparent anticipation and realization of the first major devaluation. Various capital controls were in place for much of the sample, and they may be responsible for the lack of significance of returns on foreign assets. Restrictions on capital movements were loosened significantly in May 1994, allowing new financial instruments such as synthetic swaps. Because data for the returns on synthetic swaps were not available, the analysis below includes a dummy (denoted DS), which is unity beginning with their introduction in 1994Q3.

3. Integration and cointegration

After conducting unit root tests on the variables of interest, we use Johansen's maximum likelihood procedure to test for cointegration among real money, real output, inflation, the interest rate on time deposits, and the spreads between the interest rates on Treasury bills, time deposits, and repos. In addition, we test various hypotheses about the long-run and feedback coefficients, and we test for the stationarity of individual variables in a multivariate setting. For further discussion of integration and cointegration, see Engle and Granger (1987), Ericsson (1992), Banerjee, Dolado, Galbraith, and Hendry (1993), and Johansen (1995).

Ericsson and Sharma (1996, Table 1) list the augmented Dickey-Fuller (1981) (ADF) statistics for the variables in our analysis. Empirically, all variables appear to be integrated of order two or lower. Real output y, real money $m-p$, the Treasury bill rate RB, and the spreads (ST and SR) appear to be I(1).[4] The statistical evidence is less conclusive for m, p, and RT. From its ADF statistic, RT might be I(2). However, its estimated second largest root is closer to zero than to unity, suggesting that RT is I(1) in fact. Nominal money and prices might be either I(1) or I(2), so they are transformed to real money and inflation, as in Ericsson, Campos, and Tran (1990) and Johansen (1992b) for U.K. data.

Based on these statistical properties of the data and on the economic and historical context discussed in Section 2, we test for cointegration among the variables $m-p$, y, Δp, RT^n, ST, and SR in a fourth-order vector autoregression. Table 1 reports the standard statistics and estimates from Johansen's procedure. The maximal eigenvalue and trace eigenvalue statistics (λ_{max} and λ_{trace}) both reject the null of no cointegration in favor of one cointegrating relationship at the 5% level. Figure 2j below plots the six (recursively estimated) eigenvalues, which are the basis for the maximum likelihood test statistics.[5] The eigenvalues are reasonably constant over time; and the largest eigenvalue is always substantially larger than the remaining five, implying that the finding of just one cointegrating vector is robust to the choice of sample.

Table 1 also reports the standardized eigenvectors and adjustment coefficients, denoted β' and α in a frequently used notation. The first row of β' is the estimated cointegrating vector, which can be written in the form of (3):

$$m-p = \hat{\gamma}_0 + 1.22y + 4.58RT^n - 3.07ST - 7.02SR - 3.38(4 \cdot \Delta p), \qquad (4)$$

where a circumflex ^ denotes the corresponding estimate. Each coefficient has its anticipated sign and is statistically significantly different from zero. The

---

[4] From an economic perspective, a spread might be I(0). However, financial innovation may shift the mean of the spread, thereby inducing an apparent unit root in the spread.

[5] To permit recursive estimation, the subsample seasonal dummies $D_{89t}Q_{t-i}$, the spreads ST_t and SR_t, and DE_t are perturbed slightly (by 0.0001) in various periods early in the sample. The recursive eigenvalues are calculated, conditional on full-sample estimates of the lagged dynamics.

Table 1. A cointegration analysis of Greek money demand data

Eigenvalues	0.596	0.284	0.265	0.222	0.125	0.033
Hypotheses	$r=0$	$r \leq 1$	$r \leq 2$	$r \leq 3$	$r \leq 4$	$r \leq 5$
λ_{max}	46.2**	17.0	15.7	12.8	6.8	1.7
95% critical value	39.4	33.5	27.1	21.0	14.1	3.8
λ_{trace}	100.2*	54.0	37.0	21.3	8.5	1.7
95% critical value	94.2	68.5	47.2	29.7	15.4	3.8
	Standardized eigenvectors β'					
	$m-p$	y	Δp	RT^n	ST	SR
	1	−1.22	13.53	−4.58	3.07	7.02
	−0.43	1	0.18	−0.23	−7.39	15.94
	−0.22	0.78	1	−0.73	−0.48	−5.66
	0.50	−1.95	−3.31	1	−0.41	−9.93
	0.23	−0.69	2.42	0.45	1	0.14
	−0.12	−0.07	0.96	0.20	0.43	1
	Standardized adjustment coefficients α					
$m-p$	−0.081	0.036	−0.072	0.023	−0.011	0.117
y	0.069	−0.070	−0.355	0.097	−0.022	−0.006
Δp	−0.038	−0.022	0.034	−0.032	−0.068	−0.061
RT^n	0.020	0.023	0.084	−0.005	−0.086	0.002
ST	−0.001	0.009	0.048	0.040	0.057	−0.016
SR	−0.003	−0.033	0.092	−0.000	−0.001	0.012
	Weak exogeneity test statistics					
	$m-p$	y	Δp	RT^n	ST	SR
$\chi^2(1)$	3.89*	1.92	2.20	1.62	0.01	0.06
	Statistics for testing the significance of a given variable in β'					
	$m-p$	y	Δp	RT^n	ST	SR
$\chi^2(1)$	26.4**	7.4**	41.7**	37.8**	7.9**	4.7*
	Multivariate statistics for testing stationarity					
	$m-p$	y	Δp	RT^n	ST	SR
$\chi^2(5)$	63.8**	60.4**	54.9**	54.6**	49.7**	48.7**

Notes

1. The vector autoregression includes four lags on each variable ($m-p$, y, Δp, RT^n, ST, SR), an intercept Q_t, centered seasonal dummies (Q_{t-1}, Q_{t-2}, Q_{t-3}), the devaluation dummy DE_t, the subsample seasonal dummies ($D_{89t}Q_t$, $D_{89t}Q_{t-1}$, $D_{89t}Q_{t-2}$, $D_{89t}Q_{t-3}$), and the dummy for synthetic swaps DS_t. The sample size is $T = 75[1976Q2 - 1994Q4]$.
2. The statistics λ_{max} and λ_{trace} are Johansen's maximal eigenvalue and trace eigenvalue statistics for testing cointegration, adjusted for degrees of freedom. The null hypothesis is in terms of the cointegration rank r and, e.g., rejection of $r = 0$ is evidence in favor of at least one cointegrating vector. The critical values are taken from Osterwald-Lenum (1992, Table 1). Throughout this paper, the superscripts * and ** denote that the 5% and 1% critical values are exceeded.
3. The system-based test statistics for weak exogeneity, significance, and stationarity are evaluated under the assumption that $r = 1$ and so are asymptotically distributed as $\chi^2(1)$, $\chi^2(1)$, or $\chi^2(5)$ if weak exogeneity, no long-run presence, or stationarity of the specified variable is valid.

restriction of unit income homogeneity is not rejected. The associated likelihood-ratio statistic is $\chi^2(1) = 0.57$ [0.45], where "$\chi^2(1)$" specifies the asymptotic distribution under the null hypothesis, "0.57" is the observed value of the statistic, and the asymptotic p-value is in brackets. See Johansen (1995) for the form of the test. Also, the coefficients on the spreads can be imposed to be equal: $\chi^2(1) = 1.16$ [0.28]. With that restriction, (4) can be reparameterized with a single spread, that of the Treasury bill rate relative to the average of the interest rates on time deposits and repos. Inflation (measured as an annual rate) has a semi-elasticity of about −3. While apparently large, this elasticity is similar to those obtained in studies of broad money demand for other countries; see (e.g.) Taylor (1986) and Wolters, Teräsvirta, and Lütkepohl (1998).

The variables analyzed above do *not* appear to be cointegrated when using Engle and Granger's (1987) procedure. Even if cointegration is assumed, the estimated coefficients are difficult to interpret economically. The explanation is straightforward. The Engle-Granger procedure imposes a common factor restriction on dynamics whereas the Johansen procedure does not, and invalid imposition of that restriction reduces power and leads to finite sample biases; see Banerjee, Dolado, Hendry, and Smith (1986) and Kremers, Ericsson, and Dolado (1992). For the Greek data, the common factor restriction is strongly rejected: $F(44, 36) \approx 4.37$ [0.0000].

The coefficients in the first column of α in Table 1 measure the feedback effects of the disequilibrium onto the variables in the vector autoregression. In particular, -0.081 is the estimated feedback coefficient for the money equation. Lagged excess money induces smaller current money holdings, albeit with slow adjustment. Numerically, the estimated coefficient is somewhat smaller in absolute value than those found for some other countries: -0.093 for the United Kingdom (M1), -0.26, -0.15, and -0.20 for the Netherlands, Germany, and France (all M2), and approximately -0.12 for Argentina (M3); see Hendry and Ericsson (1991b), Taylor (1986), and Kamin and Ericsson (1993).

The next row in Table 1 reports values of the statistic for testing weak exogeneity of a given variable for the cointegrating vector; see Johansen (1992a, 1992b). Output, inflation, the interest rate on time deposits, and the spreads are (individually) weakly exogenous. A joint test of their weak exogeneity is also statistically acceptable, as is a joint test of their weak exogeneity plus long-run unit income elasticity and equality of the spreads' coefficients: $\chi^2(5) = 8.70$ [0.122] and $\chi^2(7) = 9.78$ [0.20] respectively. With all seven restrictions imposed on the vector autoregression, the estimate of the cointegrating relation is:

$$m - p = \hat{\gamma}_0 + y + 5.08RT^n - 4.00ST - 4.00SR - 3.76(4 \cdot \Delta p). \qquad (5)$$

The restricted feedback coefficient is -0.140. All the coefficients in (5) satisfy the economic-theoretic restrictions postulated for (1) and (3). Valid weak exogeneity supports Section 4's analysis of the cointegrating vector in a single-equation conditional equilibrium correction model of money being without loss of information.

The penultimate row of Table 1 reports chi-squared statistics for testing the significance of individual variables in the cointegrating vector. Each variable is significant at the 5% level, and all but one (SR) are significant at the 1% level.

The final row of Table 1 reports values of Johansen's (1995, p. 74) multivariate statistic for testing the stationarity of a given variable. This statistic tests the restriction that the cointegrating vector contains all zeros except for a unity corresponding to the designated variable, where the test is conditional on there being one cointegrating vector. For instance, the null hypothesis of stationary real money implies that the cointegrating vector is $(1\ 0\ 0\ 0\ 0\ 0)'$. Empirically, all the tests reject stationarity with p-values of less than 0.01%. By being multivariate and so involving a larger information set, these statistics may have higher power than their univariate counterparts. Also, the null hypothesis may be more appealing, as it is one of stationarity rather than non-stationarity. That said, these rejections of stationarity parallel the *inability* to reject the null hypothesis of a unit root using the ADF statistic.

The results above from the Johansen procedure are robust to several potential concerns: the absence of a trend, the inclusion of the dummy variables *DE* and *DS*, the presence of the two spreads *ST* and *SR*, and residual properties. If a trend is included in the cointegrating vector, the test statistics λ_{max} and λ_{trace} still reveal a single cointegrating vector; and, that trend is insignificant in that cointegrating vector. Critical values for λ_{max} and λ_{trace} are affected by the inclusion of dummy variables. However, *DE* and *DS* are nonzero for only two periods each, so their effect is minimal. For 1976–1990, over which the spreads *ST* and *SR* are zero, the variables $(m-p)$, y, RT^n, and Δp are cointegrated with virtually the same coefficients as in (4). Thus, the spreads serve to augment the basic relationship between real money, real income, the own rate, and inflation. The vector autoregression is reasonably well specified over the full sample, although there is some indication of residual autocorrelation and nonnormality. The two spreads appear primarily responsible for these features, as the residuals from estimates over 1976–1990 are better behaved.

4. A dynamic model of money demand

In light of the results on cointegration and weak exogeneity using Johansen's procedure, this section develops a parsimonious, conditional, single-equation model for Greek broad money demand. Such a model is of interest for several reasons. A conditional money demand model may be constant, even when the reduced form vector autoregression for Johansen's procedure is nonconstant. As Judd and Scadding (1982) emphasize, constancy is particularly important for money demand equations. The graphs of the Greek data indicate changes in seasonal patterns for some variables, high variability of the inflation rate, and marked changes in the interest rates as financial markets were liberalized, suggesting the possibility of large structural breaks. Also, as a practical matter, a well-specified parsimonious model may be easier to obtain in a single-equation context than in a multiple-equation one. Section 4.1 develops the parsimonious EqCM from a general autoregressive distributed lag; Section 4.2 evaluates that EqCM's short- and long-run properties; and Section 4.3 examines its statistical properties, including parameter constancy.

4.1 General to specific modeling

Given the choice of variables and lag length in the vector autoregression above, a fourth-order autoregressive distributed lag (ADL) in m, p, y, RT^n, *ST*, and *SR* is a natural starting point for single-equation modeling. As with the vector autoregression, the ADL model was extended in three ways. First, the dummy variable *DE* for 1982*Q*4–1983*Q*1 was included to account for fluctuations in money demand associated with the $15\frac{1}{2}$ percent devaluation of the Drachma in early January 1983. Second, the dummy variable *DS* was included to proxy for the returns on synthetic swaps. Third, four seasonal dummies beginning in 1989 were included so as to allow for the change in seasonality of measured GDP. This subsection estimates that autoregressive distributed lag model, solves for its long-run properties, reinterprets it as an unrestricted EqCM, and reduces it to a parsimonious EqCM.

The long-run static solution to the estimated autoregressive distributed lag is:

$$m = \underset{(5.69)}{-4.31} + \underset{(0.11)}{1.01}\, p + \underset{(0.52)}{1.04}\, y + \underset{(2.59)}{4.56}\, RT^n - \underset{(1.29)}{3.87}\, ST - \underset{(5.22)}{7.05}\, SR. \tag{6}$$

The coefficients on p and y are numerically close to unity, and each is much less than a standard deviation away from unity, so the long-run solution to the ADL could likely be formulated in terms of the inverse velocity. Additionally, the coefficients on RT^n, ST, and SR are similar to the system estimates in (4), providing further (indirect) evidence of the validity of weak exogeneity.

Table 2 lists the estimated coefficients, standard errors, and test statistics for the EqCM representation of the fourth-order ADL, which is our starting point for the general-to-specific modeling of Greek money demand. The variable Q_t is the intercept; $\{Q_{t-i}, i = 1, 2, 3\}$ are centered seasonal dummies; D_{89t} is a step dummy, being zero through 1988 and unity from 1989Q1 onwards; and t is the quarterly time subscript. T, R^2, $\hat{\sigma}$, and dw are the sample size of the estimation period, the squared multiple correlation coefficient, the estimated equation standard error, and the Durbin-Watson statistic respectively; and the coefficients are estimated by least squares. The coefficient on $(m-p-y)_{t-1}$ is -0.127, close to that obtained by Johansen's procedure. Likewise, the estimated coefficients on p_{t-1} and y_{t-1} are close to zero, both numerically and statistically, implying that the hypothesis of long-run unit price and income homogeneity embedded in $(m-p-y)_{t-1}$ is reasonable. Formally, the restriction of long-run price and income homogeneity is not rejected (LM_h).

Table 2 and the regressions below include diagnostic statistics for testing against various alternative hypotheses: residual autocorrelation (dw and AR), skewness and excess kurtosis (*Normality*), autoregressive conditional heteroscedasticity ($ARCH$), RESET ($RESET$), heteroscedasticity (*Hetero*), and non-innovation errors relative to a more general model (*Inn*).[6] The null distribution is designated by $\chi^2(\cdot)$ or $F(\cdot,\cdot)$, the degrees of freedom are in the parentheses, and (for AR and $ARCH$) the lag order is the first degree of freedom. Statistically, the ADL appears reasonably well specified, with the exception of some autocorrelation that is possibly due to the considerable over-parameterization of the unrestricted ADL.

The unrestricted ADL is valuable for obtaining the long-run solution (6), but it has far too many parameters for many other uses. While no rules guarantee obtaining a successful parsimonious model from the ADL, some intuitive guidelines were helpful in simplification. First, the variables m, p, y, RT^n, ST, and SR were transformed to current and lagged differences and one (possibly lagged) level, as in Table 2. In addition, m_{t-1}, p_{t-1}, and y_{t-1} were transformed to the differential $(m-p-y)_{t-1}$ and the two log-levels, p_{t-1} and

[6] For references on the test statistics, see Durbin and Watson (1950, 1951), Godfrey (1978), and Harvey (1981, p. 173); Jarque and Bera (1980) and Doornik and Hansen (1994); Engle (1982); Ramsey (1969); White (1980, p. 825) and Nicholls and Pagan (1983); and Hendry and Doornik (1996), which also provides extensive discussions of all these statistics.

Table 2. The unrestricted equilibrium correction representation for broad money conditional on prices, real output, and interest rates

Variable	Lag i			
	0	1	2	3
Δm_{t-i}	−1.0	−0.262	0.586	0.300
	(–)	(0.140)	(0.114)	(0.137)
Δp_{t-i}	−0.485	−0.592	−0.180	−0.094
	(0.132)	(0.146)	(0.128)	(0.126)
Δy_{t-i}	0.007	0.118	−0.030	0.003
	(0.078)	(0.087)	(0.077)	(0.064)
ΔRT^n_{t-i}	−0.164	0.228	−0.038	0.300
	(0.272)	(0.266)	(0.248)	(0.240)
ΔST_{t-i}	−0.451	−0.156	0.737	0.625
	(0.287)	(0.292)	(0.259)	(0.241)
ΔSR_{t-i}	1.044	1.153	1.298	0.485
	(0.659)	(0.571)	(0.491)	(0.360)
$(m-p-y)_{t-i}$		−0.127		
		(0.049)		
p_{t-i}		0.001		
		(0.014)		
y_{t-i}		0.006		
		(0.067)		
RT^n_t, S_t, SR_t	0.581	−0.987	−0.404	
	(0.163)	(0.477)	(0.790)	
Q_{t-i}	−0.549	−0.057	−0.006	−0.024
	(0.814)	(0.029)	(0.030)	(0.033)
DE_t, DS_t	−0.033	−0.023		
	(0.007)	(0.015)		
$D_{89t}Q_{t-i}$	0.006	0.002	−0.031	−0.001
	(0.005)	(0.016)	(0.016)	(0.016)

$T = 75[1976Q2–1994Q4]$ $R^2 = 0.9845$ $\hat{\sigma} = 0.7776\%$
$dw = 2.39$ $LM_h : F(2,36) = 0.01$
$AR : F(5,31) = 2.94^*$ $ARCH : F(4,28) = 0.78$
$Normality : \chi^2(2) = 1.26$ $RESET : F(1,35) = 3.37$

Notes
1. The dependent variable is Δm_t. Even so, the equation is in levels, not in differences, noting the presence of lagged levels.
2. The variables $\{Q_{t-i}\}$ are the centered seasonal dummies, except that Q_t is the intercept.

y_{t-1}, thereby reparameterizing these variables as the log of inverse velocity and two possibly redundant lags. Combined, the two types of transformations helped obtain a relatively orthogonal set of regressors, making interpretation and simplification easier. Second, shorter lag lengths were preferred to longer ones. Third, because of their economic importance, variables directly involved in the long-run solution were not deleted. See Ericsson, Campos, and Tran (1990), Hendry and Ericsson (1991a, 1991b), and Hendry (1995) for more discussion on reparameterizations and general-to-specific modeling.

Applying the transformations above and following these informal guidelines, the following parsimonious, economically interpretable, and statistically acceptable EqCM was obtained; see Ericsson and Sharma (1996, Appendix II) for details.

$$\begin{aligned}\Delta m_t = & \underset{\substack{(0.071)\\ [0.078]}}{-0.117}\,\Delta m_{t-1} + \underset{\substack{(0.075)\\ [0.095]}}{0.671}\,\Delta m_{t-2} - \underset{\substack{(0.059)\\ [0.066]}}{0.394}\,\Delta_2 p_t \\ & + \underset{\substack{(0.024)\\ [0.030]}}{0.072}\,\Delta y_t - \underset{\substack{(0.149)\\ [0.320]}}{0.488}\,\Delta ST_t + \underset{\substack{(0.107)\\ [0.140]}}{0.603}\,\Delta_2 ST_{t-2} - \underset{\substack{(0.006)\\ [0.012]}}{0.026}\,DE_t \\ & - \underset{\substack{(0.011)\\ [0.013]}}{0.086}(m-p-y)_{t-1} + \underset{\substack{(0.053)\\ [0.061]}}{0.410}\,RT^n_t - \underset{\substack{(0.140)\\ [0.171]}}{0.675}\,S_t \\ & - \underset{\substack{(0.042)\\ [0.052]}}{0.320} - \underset{\substack{(0.007)\\ [0.008]}}{0.060}\,Q_{t-1} - \underset{\substack{(0.007)\\ [0.008]}}{0.040}\,Q_{t-2} - \underset{\substack{(0.008)\\ [0.009]}}{0.003}\,Q_{t-3} \end{aligned} \tag{7}$$

$$T = 75[1976Q2\text{–}1994Q4] \quad R^2 = 0.9712 \quad \hat{\sigma} = 0.8128\% \quad dw = 2.30$$

$$AR: F(5,56) = 2.04 \quad ARCH: F(4,53) = 0.57$$

$$Normality: \chi^2(2) = 0.85 \quad RESET: F(1,60) = 0.71$$

$$Hetero: F(22,38) = 0.44 \quad Inn: F(25,36) = 1.23.$$

OLS standard errors appear in parentheses $(\cdot)$, and jackknife heteroscedasticity-consistent standard errors appear in square brackets $[\cdot]$; see White (1980), Messer and White (1984), and MacKinnon and White (1985) on the latter. The variable S is $(ST + SR)/2$, the average of the two spreads, and so is also $RB - (RT^n + RR^n)/2$. Equation (7) can be written with $\Delta(m-p)_t$ as the dependent variable and with RT^n, S, and Δp in the equilibrium correction term, in which case that term is:

$$-0.086[m - p - y - 4.75RT^n + 7.81S + 3.57(4 \cdot \Delta p)]_{t-1}; \tag{8}$$

see Hendry and Ericsson (1991b, equation (15)).

4.2 Short- and long-run properties of the model

Both short- and long-run properties can be derived from (7). The coefficient on the equilibrium correction term is highly significant statistically, confirming that a long-run (cointegrating) relationship exists between broad money, prices, real output, the net interest rate on time deposits, and the spreads. The size of this coefficient implies that adjustment to disequilibria via the equilibrium correction term is slow. The mean lags for p, y, RT^n, ST, and SR are 19, 5, 5, 8, and 5 quarters respectively; their median lags are all somewhat shorter, being 12, 5, 4, 7, and 4 quarters respectively.[7] In (7), current inflation has a

[7] For computational convenience, the mean and median lags were calculated by estimating equation (7) without imposing long-run unit income and price elasticities, long-run equality of elasticities for ST and SR, equal coefficients on Δp_t and Δp_{t-1}, and equal coefficients with opposite sign for ST_{t-2} and ST_{t-4}. Because these restrictions are empirically acceptable and the corresponding coefficients are precisely estimated, the derived mean and median lags from the less restricted equation should not differ much from those for (7).

negative and numerically small coefficient, implying that in essence the EqCM is modeling Δm_t in the short run, although real money (and velocity) is being determined in the long run through the equilibrium correction term. Such a relationship is consistent with *Ss*-type models of money demand, in which short-run factors determine movements in nominal money given desired bands, and longer-run factors (including the price level) determine the bands themselves.

The solved steady-state long-run money demand function from (7) is:

$$m - p = -3.70 + y + 4.75RT^n - 7.81S - 3.57(4g), \qquad (9)$$

where money and prices are assumed to grow at the same rate ($\Delta m = \Delta p \equiv g$), and where $4g$ is the annualized nominal growth rate. This long-run relationship between inverse velocity and (for the most part) RT^n is visually apparent in Figure 1*f* above, noting that $S = 0$ until 1991. Long-run unit elasticities for prices and output are not rejected; and the estimated semi-elasticity of the nominal net interest rate on time deposits is 4.75, implying an elasticity of about 0.7 when annual interest rates are 15 percent. Inverse velocity depends negatively on the inflation rate. Given the limited range of financial assets available and the underdeveloped nature of the capital market, the presence of inflation in (9) is not surprising: real assets have been an important component of an investor's portfolio.

Equations (4), (5), (6), and (9) present estimates of the long-run money demand relation under somewhat different assumptions. Equations (5), (6), and (9) assume weak exogeneity, with (9) also relying on a valid simplification from Table 2. Equation (4) does not assume weak exogeneity, but its estimates may be more sensitive than (6) and (9) to mis-specification in the equations for income, inflation, and the interest rates. That said, all four estimated long-run solutions are remarkably similar, as are their corresponding feedback coefficients for the money equation. Such robustness is an argument in favor of the validity of both weak exogeneity and the additional simplifications entailed by (7) relative to Table 2.

Another fruitful comparison is of actual real money holdings ($m - p$), the static solution ((9) with $g = 0$), and the dynamic steady state (9). Figure 2*a* plots all three, where the right-hand side variables in (9) are evaluated at current values, albeit with income and inflation as annual averages in order to remove the pronounced seasonality in those variables. The static equilibrium path consistently lies above actual real money. This discrepancy reflects the uniformly positive inflation rate over the sample, which contrasts with the zero inflation rate assumed in the static solution. Real money and the dynamic steady state are quite similar: deviations between them are typically 10% and never more than 25%, with deviations lasting a year or two at a time; see Figure 2*b*. By contrast, Ericsson, Hendry, and Tran (1994) find that disequilibria in U.K. *narrow* money holdings over roughly the same sample are often more than 25% and sometimes even exceed 50%. Such large disequilibria probably reflect the small costs of being out of equilibrium as much as the size of the shocks that created the disequilibria; cf. Hendry (1995, p. 582).

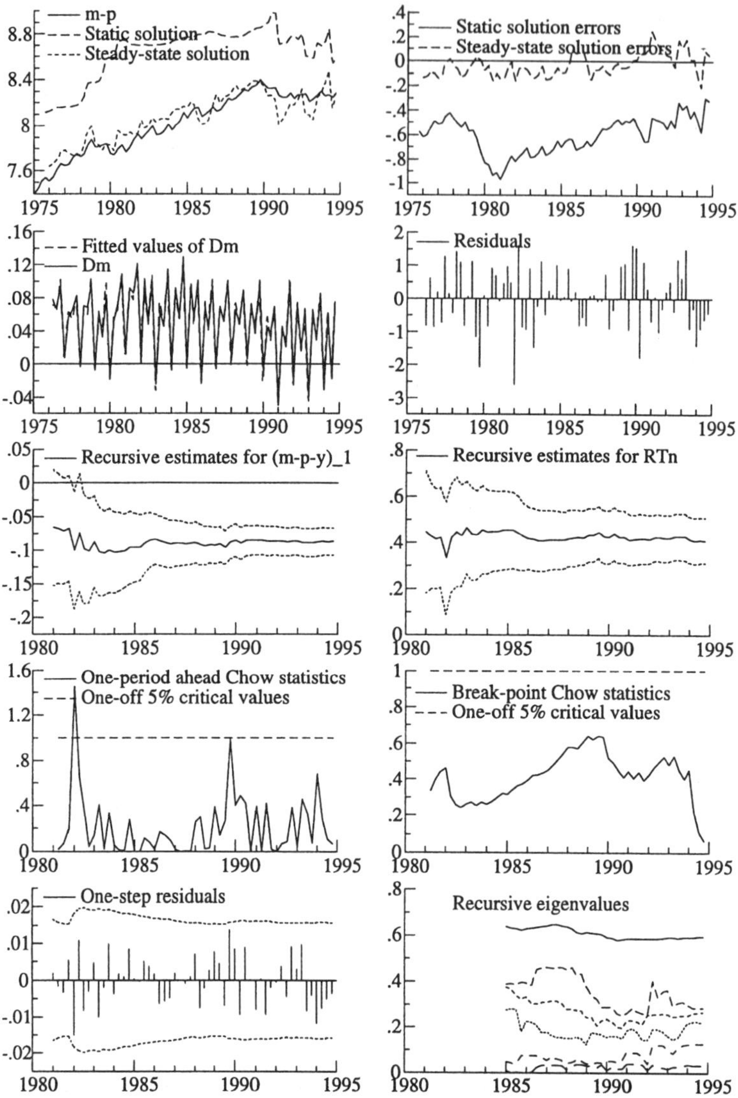

Fig. 2. Static and dynamic long-run solutions for $(m-p)_t$, the corresponding errors, fitted and actual values for Δm_t, the corresponding residuals, recursive estimates for $(m-p-y)_{t-1}$, recursive estimates for RT_t^n, 1-step Chow statistics, break-point Chow statistics, and 1-step residuals with $0 \pm 2\hat{\sigma}_t$, all for (7); and recursive eigenvalues from the VAR

4.3 Statistical properties of the model

Statistically, the EqCM in (7) appears reasonably well specified. Figures 2*c* and 2*d* respectively plot the fitted and actual values of Δm_t and the corresponding residuals, showing how well (7) explains the data. The restrictions in (7) are not rejected relative to the unrestricted EqCM in Table 2 (*Inn*), and no diagnostic test is significant. Lagrange multiplier tests for a variety of omitted variables in (7) are likewise not rejected. Specifically, F-statistics for testing the significance of $\{RD^n_{t-i}, i = 0, \ldots, 4\}$, $\{RS^n_{t-i}, i = 0, \ldots, 4\}$, $\{e_{t-i}, i = 0, \ldots, 4\}$, DS_t, and $\{D_{89t} \cdot Q_{t-i}, i = 0, \ldots, 3\}$ are $F(5,56) = 1.51$ [0.20], $F(5,56) = 0.24$ [0.94], $F(5,56) = 0.31$ [0.90], $F(1,60) = 0.89$ [0.35], and $F(4,57) = 1.52$ [0.21] respectively; and a test of their joint significance yields $F(20,41) = 0.86$[0.64]. The variables RD^n and RS^n are the interest rates on demand deposits and savings deposits, net of withholding tax; and e is the logarithm of a trade-weighted nominal effective exchange rate index.

Parameter constancy is a critical issue for money demand equations. Figures 2*e* and 2*f* show the recursively estimated coefficients of the key variables $(m - p - y)_{t-1}$ and RT^n_t in (7) and plus-or-minus twice their recursively estimated standard errors, denoted $\hat{\beta}_t$ and $\hat{\beta}_t \pm 2ese(\hat{\beta}_t)$ in a frequently used notation. Coefficients vary only slightly relative to their *ex ante* standard errors, and both $(m - p - y)_{t-1}$ and RT^n_t are highly significant by 1985. Recursive estimates of the other coefficients in (7) are also empirically constant.[8]

Figure 2*g* plots the sequentially estimated one-period ahead Chow (1960) statistics, and Figure 2*h* plots the break-point Chow (1960) statistics for the sequence {1981*Q*2–1994*Q*4, 1981*Q*3–1994*Q*4, 1981*Q*4–1994*Q*4, ..., 1994*Q*3–1994*Q*4, 1994*Q*4}. While two of the fifty-five one-period ahead Chow statistics (i.e., about 4%) are statistically significant, none of the break-point Chow statistics are significant at even their one-off 5% levels. That is, no split of the sample would obtain a rejection. Figure 2*i* plots the one-step residuals and plus-or-minus twice the corresponding equation standard errors, and the latter vary little numerically.

4.4 *Remarks*

Several remarks on the interpretation of the above results may be helpful. Issues include model constancy and policy, inversion of the estimated money demand equation, forecasting, and encompassing of other empirical models.

The empirical constancy of (7) suggests that the *process* determining broad money demand in Greece has remained largely unchanged during the 1980s and 1990s, even while inflation and interest rates have varied and financial liberalization has occurred. In particular, the explanation for the recent stagnation of real money demand lies in what has happened to actual income, inflation, and interest rates. Holdings of broad money balances appear to be endogenously determined by the private sector, while the government controls and/or regulates interest rates and the financial market's structure. With the money stock being endogenous, it cannot be controlled by the government, although the government can target it through its policies for interest rates and financial structure *inter alia*. Thus, policy (including financial liberalization) appears to affect agent behavior through the variables entering the conditional model, albeit not through the parameters of that model.

---

[8] See Ericsson and Sharma (1996, Figures 17–21). In estimating (7) recursively, the coefficients on ΔST_t, $\Delta_2 ST_{t-2}$, S_t, and DE_t are taken as given at their full-sample estimates. This modification is helpful because these variables become nonzero only well after the initial subsample used for recursive estimation. Treating their coefficients as known may bias the Chow statistic towards rejection because extra degrees of freedom are assumed in calculating that statistic. However, that bias did not matter in practice.

Relatedly, the constancy of (7) in the presence of financial deregulation is partial evidence against the Lucas critique applying here; see Hendry (1988) and Engle and Hendry (1993). However, such robustness does not justify one common procedure in policy analysis: inversion of the estimated money demand function to obtain the price level or the interest rate as a function of money. Inversion of a conditional money demand model such as (7) obtains coefficients that are not functions of the inverse coefficients of the money demand model alone. As discussed in Ericsson and Sharma (1996), the estimated coefficients of the inverted equation are also difficult to interpret economically. Further, while the money demand equation (7) is empirically constant, its inversion need not be so.

Ex ante forecasting requires specifying the paths for the right-hand side variables—output, inflation, and interest rates. If multi-step ahead forecasts of money demand are constructed conditional on those future paths of the right-hand side variables, Granger noncausality from m to p, y, RT^n, ST, and SR is assumed. In general, weak exogeneity and Granger noncausality are separate conditions, so the latter should also be tested before producing conditional forecasts. If Granger causality is present, joint forecasting is required: see Hendry and Mizon (1993), Juselius (1993), and Hendry and Doornik (1994).

In principle, statistical comparison of models (encompassing) can help identify weaknesses of the models being tested, and so indicate directions for their improvement. Two practical difficulties prohibit calculating encompassing tests against other researchers' models: no other empirical models of Greek money demand currently exist that use the new measure of M3, and encompassing statistics for comparing models of different aggregates have not yet been developed. That said, learning-adjusted returns on new assets and Treasury bills may better capture individuals' actual responses than the existing specification; see Hendry and Ericsson (1991b) and Baba, Hendry, and Starr (1992).

5. Conclusions

The estimated conditional model of broad money demand in Greece is remarkably stable and otherwise well specified over the period 1976–1994. The model's empirical constancy holds in the face of financial liberalization and large fluctuations in the inflation rate. Even so, the fundamental changes currently underway in the Greek financial system could affect money demand and, as a consequence, further complicate the conduct of monetary policy. With greater capital mobility, returns on foreign assets (and hence foreign interest rates and the exchange rate) are likely to influence money demand, as did the increased availability of Treasury bills in the early 1990s. The presence of the spreads in the estimated EqCM already suggests the potential empirical role of new alternative assets in the demand for broad money.

References

Alogoskoufis G (1995) The two faces of Janus: Institutions, policy regimes and macroeconomic performance in Greece. Economic Policy 20:147–184 (with discussion)

Baba Y, Hendry DF, Starr RM (1992) The demand for M1 in the U.S.A., 1960–1988. Review of Economic Studies 59, 1:25–61

Banerjee A, Dolado JJ, Galbraith JW, Hendry DF (1993) Co-integration, error correction, and the econometric analysis of non-stationary data. Oxford University Press, Oxford

Banerjee A, Dolado JJ, Hendry DF, Smith GW (1986) Exploring equilibrium relationships in econometrics through static models: Some Monte Carlo evidence. Oxford Bulletin of Economics and Statistics 48, 3:253–277

Baumol WJ (1952) The transactions demand for cash: An inventory theoretic approach. Quarterly Journal of Economics 66, 4:545–556

Cagan P (1956) The monetary dynamics of hyperinflation. Chapter 2 in: Friedman M (ed.) Studies in the quantity theory of money, University of Chicago Press, Chicago, pp. 23–117

Chow GC (1960) Tests of equality between sets of coefficients in two linear regressions. Econometrica 28, 3:591–605

Dickey DA, Fuller WA (1981) Likelihood ratio statistics for autoregressive time series with a unit root. Econometrica 49, 4:1057–1072

Doornik JA, Hansen H (1994) An omnibus test for univariate and multivariate normality. Discussion Paper No. W4&91, Nuffield College, Oxford, England

Doornik JA, Hendry DF (1994a) PcFiml 8.0: Interactive econometric modelling of dynamic systems. International Thomson Publishing, London

Doornik JA, Hendry DF (1994b) PcGive 8.0: An interactive econometric modelling system. International Thomson Publishing, London

Doornik JA, Hendry DF (1996) GiveWin: An interface to empirical modelling. International Thomson Business Press, London (Version 1.0)

Doornik JA, Hendry DF (1997) Modelling dynamic systems using PcFiml 9.0 for Windows. International Thomson Business Press, London

Durbin J, Watson GS (1950) Testing for serial correlation in least squares regression. I. Biometrika 37, 3 and 4:409–428

Durbin J, Watson GS (1951) Testing for serial correlation in least squares regression. II. Biometrika 38, 1 and 2:159–178

Engle RF (1982) Autoregressive conditional heteroscedasticity with estimates of the variance of United Kingdom inflation. Econometrica 50, 4:987–1007

Engle RF, Granger CWJ (1987) Co-integration and error correction: Representation, estimation, and testing. Econometrica 55, 2:251–276

Engle RF, Hendry DF (1993) Testing super exogeneity and invariance in regression models. Journal of Econometrics 56, 1/2:119–139

Ericsson NR (1992) Cointegration, exogeneity, and policy analysis: An overview. Journal of Policy Modeling 14, 3:251–280

Ericsson NR, Campos J, Tran H-A (1990) PC-GIVE and David Hendry's econometric methodology. Revista de Econometria 10, 1:7–117

Ericsson NR, Hendry DF, Tran H-A (1994) Cointegration, seasonality, encompassing, and the demand for money in the United Kingdom. Chapter 7 in: Hargreaves CP (ed.) Nonstationary time series analysis and cointegration, Oxford University Press, Oxford, pp. 179–224

Ericsson NR, Sharma S (1996) Broad money demand and financial liberalization in Greece. International Finance Discussion Paper No. 559, Board of Governors of the Federal Reserve System, Washington, D.C., July, available on the WorldWide Web at www.bog.frb.fed.us/pubs/ifdp/1996/559/default.htm; and IMF Working Paper No. WP/96/62, International Monetary Fund, Washington, D.C., June

Filippides AA, Kyriakopoulos PE, Moschos DM (1995) Bank of Greece monetary policy instruments. Bank of Greece Economic Bulletin 6:55–63

Friedman M (1956) The quantity theory of money—A restatement. Chapter 1 in: Friedman M (ed.) Studies in the quantity theory of money, University of Chicago Press, Chicago, pp. 1–21

Godfrey LG (1978) Testing against general autoregressive and moving average error models when the regressors include lagged dependent variables. Econometrica 46, 6:1293–1301

Harvey AC (1981) The econometric analysis of time series. Philip Allan, Oxford

Hendry DF (1988) The encompassing implications of feedback versus feedforward mechanisms in econometrics. Oxford Economic Papers 40, 1:132–149

Hendry DF (1995) Dynamic econometrics. Oxford University Press, Oxford

Hendry DF, Doornik JA (1994) Modelling linear dynamic econometric systems. Scottish Journal of Political Economy 41, 1:1–33

Hendry DF, Doornik JA (1996) Empirical econometric modelling using PcGive 9.0 for Windows. International Thomson Business Press, London

Hendry DF, Ericsson NR (1991a) An econometric analysis of U.K. money demand in 'Monetary trends in the United States and the United Kingdom' by Milton Friedman and Anna J. Schwartz. American Economic Review 81, 1:8–38
Hendry DF, Ericsson NR (1991b) Modeling the demand for narrow money in the United Kingdom and the United States. European Economic Review 35, 4:833–881 (with discussion)
Hendry DF, Mizon GE (1993) Evaluating dynamic econometric models by encompassing the VAR. Chapter 18 in Phillips PCB (ed.) Models, methods, and applications of econometrics: Essays in honor of A. R. Bergstrom, Blackwell Publishers, Cambridge, Massachusetts, pp. 272–300
Jarque CM, Bera AK (1980) Efficient tests for normality, homoscedasticity and serial independence of regression residuals. Economics Letters 6, 3:255–259
Johansen S (1992a) Cointegration in partial systems and the efficiency of single-equation analysis. Journal of Econometrics 52, 3:389–402
Johansen S (1992b) Testing weak exogeneity and the order of cointegration in UK money demand data. Journal of Policy Modeling 14, 3:313–334
Johansen S (1995) Likelihood-based inference in cointegrated vector autoregressive models. Oxford University Press, Oxford
Judd JP, Scadding JL (1982) The search for a stable money demand function: A survey of the post-1973 literature. Journal of Economic Literature 20, 3:993–1023
Juselius K (1993) VAR modelling and Haavelmo's probability approach to macroeconomic modelling. Empirical Economics 18, 4:595–622
Kamin SB, Ericsson NR (1993) Dollarization in Argentina. International Finance Discussion Paper No. 460, Board of Governors of the Federal Reserve System, Washington, D.C.
Kremers JJM, Ericsson NR, Dolado JJ (1992) The power of cointegration tests. Oxford Bulletin of Economics and Statistics 54, 3:325–348
MacKinnon JG, White H (1985) Some heteroskedasticity-consistent covariance matrix estimators with improved finite sample properties. Journal of Econometrics 29, 3:305–325
Messer K, White H (1984) A note on computing the heteroskedasticity consistent covariance matrix using instrumental variable techniques. Oxford Bulletin of Economics and Statistics 46, 2:181–184
Nicholls DF, Pagan AR (1983) Heteroscedasticity in models with lagged dependent variables. Econometrica 51, 4:1233–1242
Osterwald-Lenum M (1992) A note with quantiles of the asymptotic distribution of the maximum likelihood cointegration rank test statistics. Oxford Bulletin of Economics and Statistics 54, 3:461–472
Ramsey JB (1969) Tests for specification errors in classical linear least-squares regression analysis. Journal of the Royal Statistical Society, Series B, 31, 2:350–371
Soumelis G (1995) Greece: Reforming financial markets. OECD Observer 193:40–41
Taylor MP (1986) From the general to the specific: The demand for M2 in three European countries. Empirical Economics 11, 4:243–261
Tobin J (1956) The interest elasticity of transactions demand for cash. Review of Economics and Statistics 38, 3:241–247
Wallis KF (1974) Seasonal adjustment and relations between variables. Journal of the American Statistical Association 69, 345:18–31
White H (1980) A heteroskedasticity-consistent covariance matrix estimator and a direct test for heteroskedasticity. Econometrica 48, 4:817–838
Wolters J, Teräsvirta T, Lütkepohl H (1998) Modelling the demand for M3 in the unified Germany. Review of Economics and Statistics, 80:399–409

Stability of money demand in Switzerland: A comparison of the M2 and M3 cases*

Michel Peytrignet, Christof Stahel

Swiss National Bank, PO Box, CH-8022 Zurich, Switzerland (e-mail: peytrignet.michel@snb.ch)

Abstract. Long-run parameters of money demand functions for Switzerland's M2 and M3 aggregate are estimated and their stability investigated. For both aggregates a single stable cointegrating vector is found. Around these long-run relationships a single-equation model for $\Delta m2$ and a single-equation model for Δcpi is built respectively for M2 and M3, and both estimated models are found to be stable. Testing forecast performance, the Δcpi model seems to be superior to the $\Delta m2$ model, providing some positive signs that the M3 model is stable in the sense that it does not suffer from a structural break during the period of estimation.

Key words: Demand for Money, cointegration, sequential reduction

JEL classification: E52; E41; C32

1. Introduction

The stability of monetary aggregates is an issue particularly important for a central bank which implements a quantitative monetary policy based on intermediate monetary targeting. Even though the Swiss National Bank (SNB) targets the seasonally-adjusted monetary base on a medium-term horizon (5 years), broadly-defined monetary aggregates are additional indicators

* We would like to thank Jürgen Wolters and two anonymous referees for their comments and Neil Ericsson, David Hendry, Katarina Juselius, Helmut Lütkepohl, Grayham Mizon and the other participants of the Workshop on Money Demand in Europe, Berlin, October 10–11, 1997, where an earlier version of the paper was presented, for their suggestions. The data may be obtained from the internet, http://wotan.wiwi.hu-berlin.de/oekonometrie/engl/data.html. The views expressed here are those of the authors and do not reflect the views of the Swiss National Bank.

which are very useful for a central bank on the condition that their demand are stable.

This paper summarizes the most recent results obtained on the stability of money demand defined on the broad monetary aggregates M2 and M3 in Switzerland. Neither the stability of the monetary base nor of M1 is inquired in this paper. The reasons are the structural shocks which affected both aggregates since the late eighties. M1, M2 and M3 are defined (cf. Fluri, 1995) as follows:

$$\text{M1} = \text{Currency} + \text{Demand Deposits} + \text{Transactions Accounts}$$

$$\text{M2} = \text{M1} + \text{Savings Deposits} - \text{Pension Funds Accounts}$$

$$\text{M3} = \text{M2} + \text{Time Deposits}$$

For each of the latter two aggregates, we first identify a long-run money demand function in a cointegration framework linking the log of the money aggregate with the log of CPI, the log of real GDP and the log of the return on government bonds. Second, around the long-run money demand function we develop a short-run I(0) set up.

The return on government bonds is an adequate measure of the opportunity cost of holding money in the form of M2 or M3 in Switzerland (cf. Fischer and Peytrignet, 1990). This does not suggest that government bonds are close substitutes for money but that the rate of return on these long bonds may be interpreted as a proxy for a "permanent" forward-looking short-term rate if the rational expectation theory of the term structure of interest rate is assumed to hold.

We are investigating money demand in Switzerland with quarterly, seasonally unadjusted data, because we believe that the available standard adjustment procedures that are frequently employed will eventually not only remove the seasonal pattern but may also alter the dynamic adjustments and the exogeneity status within a set of variables (cf. Ericsson et. al., 1994). Instead of, we introduce a set of centered seasonal dummies to capture the seasonal pattern.

Because each individual series is found I(1), a cointegration analysis is required[1]. In this paper, we use the procedure developed by Johansen (1988) and Johansen and Juselius (1990). The stability of the cointegrating vector parameters is inquired with the help of a descriptive generalized version of recursive analysis we develop by using a simplified version of the Stock and Watson (1993) dynamic ordinary least squares (DOLS) procedure.

2. The long-run analysis of M2 and M3

In this section, we elaborate long-run statistical models for M2 and M3 which are tested until they represent adequate descriptions of the unknown underly-

[1] The results are not reported here, but can be found for instance in Peytrignet and Fischer (1991). The unit root properties of M2 and M3 together with CPI, GDP and the long-term interest rate are tested with the Dolado-Jenkinson (1987) procedure as well as with the augmented Dickey-Fuller (1979) tests with various lag lengths.

ing data generation processes (DGP). These will be our benchmark models on which economic theory could validly be tested[2]. Following Juselius (1991) and Urbain (1993), we assume that the unknown DGP can be marginalized with respect to all variables, and their past values, which are deemed to be irrelevant for the purpose of our study. In other words, we assume that the DGP can be simplified with the help of economic considerations and restricted to a set of four variables. In particular, we model the joint probability distribution of $Z = (m\ cpi\ gdp\ rb)'$ with the help of the following VECM representation[3]:

$$\Delta Z_t = \Pi Z_{t-k} + \Gamma_1 \Delta Z_{t-1} + \cdots + \Gamma_{k-1} \Delta Z_{t-k+1} + \mu_t + \Phi D_t + \varepsilon_t, \tag{1}$$

where the Γ_i are given by

$$\Gamma_i = -(I - \Pi_1 - \cdots - \Pi_i), \quad (i = 1, \ldots, k-1) \tag{2}$$

and

$$\Pi = -(I - \Pi_1 - \cdots - \Pi_k). \tag{3}$$

Π and Γ_i, $i = 1, \ldots, k-1$, are unrestricted coefficient matrices, μ_t represents the deterministic component of the VECM, possibly a constant and a time trend that could be unrestricted or restricted to the cointegrating space, and D_t is a set of centered seasonal dummies with Φ the corresponding coefficient matrix.

By looking at the graphs of the series in appendix A, it is obvious that if no particular trend characterizes the evolution of *rb*; *m2*, *m3*, *cpi* and *gdp* typically are trended. Hence, an unrestricted drift seems to be justified a priori in the VECM to reflect the deterministic trends in the data. However, whether these deterministic trends cancel out in the cointegrating space remains an open issue. If this was not the case, a linear time trend should be included in the cointegrating space. The cointegration of the variables in Z_t implies that Π is of reduced rank r, $r \in \{1, \ldots, p-1\}$, where p is the dimension of the system. The rank r and the form of the deterministic term in the VECM will be tested below following Johansen (1995).

In this study, we use a sample of quarterly data from 77:1 to 97:1. The starting date was retained in order to minimize the importance of the transition between the end of the Bretton Woods fixed exchange rate system to the new regime of flexible exchange rates. This change of regime produced enormous adaptation and transition problems in Switzerland. During this period, the SNB introduced measures for restraining capital movements in order to diminish the tendency for the Swiss franc to appreciate and to minimize the consequences for the Swiss economy.

For the M2 model we found that $k = 6$ is adequate to minimize the auto-

---

[2] The computations in the paper are performed with CATS in RATS written for RATS v. 4.20, PC-Give and PC-Fiml v. 8/9. and Matlab v. 4.

[3] Small letters indicate the (natural) logarithm of the corresponding variables and m is either the M2 or M3 aggregate. $\Delta \equiv (1 - L)$ is the (one-) difference operator, where $(1 - L)x_t \equiv x_t - x_{t-1}$. Π_i are the coefficient matrices in the corresponding VAR representation.

Table 1. Statistical properties of the VAR residuals

	M2 model		M3 model	
lag-length, k	6		5	
		p-value		p-value
Ljung-Box	233.565	0.02	271.305	0.02
LM(1)	11.484	0.78	19.309	0.25
LM(4)	22.947	0.12	17.660	0.34
Normality	26.565	0.00	10.014	0.26

Both models are estimated with $r = 4$ over the sample 77:1 – 97:1. The Ljung-Box Test is approximately $\chi^2(192)$ distributed for the M2 model and $\chi^2(224)$ for the M3 model. All LM tests are $\chi^2(16)$ distributed. p-values represent the marginal significance levels.

correlation in the residuals and that $k = 5$ is sufficient to remove it in the M3 model. Summary statistics on the analysis are gathered in table 1. The remaining non-normality in the M2 model may not be to serious a problem since the asymptotic properties of the method depend on the *i.i.d.* assumption of the errors only (cf. Johansen, 1995). The hypothesis of no ARCH effect in each of the four equations of the M2 and the M3 model can be rejected respectively at most at the 4.5% and 35.5% marginal significance level.

Regarding the independence assumption of the residuals, we find that at the 2% level, the Ljung-Box test rejects the null hypothesis of no autocorrelation in the residuals of the M2 and the M3 model up to the 18th and 19th order, respectively. But the LM test, both with one and four lags, is unable to reject the null. Investigating this problem further using the small sample approximation of an F-test that is offered in PcFiml we accept the hypothesis of no autocorrelation.

However, in interpreting the results which follow, we should keep in mind that non-normality, ARCH effects and residual autocorrelation are perhaps weaknesses of the M2 model and that there might be some time-dependence left in residuals of the M3 model.

Next, we have to specify and test for the deterministic structure μ_t of the VECM. The results of the trace test for the M2 and M3 model are gathered together with the critical values in table 2 using Johansen's notation for the deterministic component.

Because the choice of r is not independent of the structure of μ_t, we follow the strategy of choosing jointly r and μ_t as proposed by Johansen (1995)[4]. According to the results in table 2, we accept an unrestricted constant, $\mu_t = \alpha\beta_0 + \alpha_\perp\gamma_0$, in the VECM and the existence of one cointegrating vector for the M2 model. If we believed in the existence of two cointegrating relations, we jointly have to accept a constant that is restricted to the cointegrating space and hence that the individual series are not trended. This is almost certainly in contradiction with a visual inspection of the data. According to the results for the M3 model, we also jointly accept an unrestricted constant

[4] Johansen (1995) shows that these hypothesis can be nested going from the more restricted to the less restricted case. We are aware of the possible problems arising from this specific to general approach but have no other discriminating tool at hand.

Table 2. M2 and M3 model trace tests

Trace test	$\mu_t = \alpha\beta_0$	c.v.	$\mu_t = \alpha\beta_0 + \alpha_{\perp}\gamma_0$	c.v.	$\mu_t = \alpha\beta_0 + \alpha_{\perp}\gamma_0 + \alpha\beta_1 t$	c.v.
M2 model						
0	74.43	56.06	55.49	50.35	71.12	66.25
1	39.98	37.61	27.68	32.56	41.77	45.42
2	13.21	22.05	9.33	17.52	23.40	27.75
M3 model						
0	82.43	56.06	63.30	50.35	81.11	66.25
1	42.20	37.61	31.03	32.56	44.42	45.42
2	15.85	22.05	4.82	17.52	12.43	27.75

The critical values (c.v.) are the 97.5% values and are taken respectively from table 1*, table 1 and table 2* in Osterwald-Lenum (1992). The estimation for the M2 model is based on $k = 6$ and the eigenvalues are 0.3099, 0.2170, 0.1026 and 0.0159. The estimation for the M3 model is based on $k = 5$ and the eigenvalues are 0.3460, 0.2917, 0.0558 and 0.0059.

Table 3. Long-run estimates of the M2 and the M3 model

	M2 model				M3 model			
β	*m2*	*cpi*	*gdp*	*rb*	*m3*	*cpi*	*gdp*	*rb*
	1	−1.105	−1.039	0.809	1	−0.974	−1.685	0.365
st'deviation	–	0.084	0.143	0.047	–	0.070	0.122	0.041
α	$\Delta m2$	Δcpi	Δgdp	Δrb	$\Delta m3$	Δcpi	Δgdp	Δrb
	−0.248	−0.004	−0.055	−0.422	0.004	0.149	−0.021	−0.612
t-value	−3.788	−0.120	−1.384	−1.386	0.089	5.382	−0.430	−1.762

When $r = 1$, no additional constraint is necessary to identify the cointegrating vector. Hence, the computation of the standard deviations of the parameters is justified. For a discussion of identification in the context of VECM, see Urbain (1993, p. 33) and Johansen and Juselius (1994).

and one cointegrating vector, whereas the same argument as above holds against the existence of two long-run relations and a restricted constant[5].

The long-run estimates of the M2 and the M3 model are presented in table 3, where Π has been decomposed into two matrices, α and β, with full column rank such that $\Pi = \alpha\beta'$. In particular, the cointegrating vector β along with the loading factors α, the standard deviations and t-values are all tabulated as they are taken from CATS in RATS.

The parameters of the cointegrating vectors have the signs and magnitudes economic theory predicts for long-run money demand functions for such aggregates as M2 and M3. All of them are highly significant, but only one loading factor in each model is statistically different from zero. This indicates that the respective cointegrating vector should enter only in the short-run equation of Δm in the M2 model and in the short-run equation of Δcpi in the M3 model. In turn, this implies that CPI, real GDP and the return on gov-

[5] Estimating the M3 model with one cointegrating vector and a linear trend in the cointegrating relation led to complete nonsense results.

Table 4. Long-run estimates of the M2 and the M3 model with weak exogeneity restrictions imposed

	M2 model				M3 model			
β	*m2*	*cpi*	*gdp*	*rb*	*m3*	*cpi*	*gdp*	*rb*
	1	−1.095	−1.028	0.784	1	−1.042	−1.537	0.317
st'deviation	–	0.087	0.147	0.049	–	0.077	0.134	0.045
α	$\Delta m2$	Δcpi	Δgdp	Δrb	$\Delta m3$	Δcpi	Δgdp	Δrb
	−0.296	–	–	–	–	0.151	–	–
t-value	−4.531	–	–	–	–	6.007	–	–

ernment bonds are weakly exogenous with respect to the long-run parameters of the M2 model and similar that M3, real GDP and the return on government bonds are weakly exogenous with respect to the long-run parameters of the M3 model. Such propositions will formally be tested below. However, before proceeding with testing the exogeneity assumption, we have to reassure that we have no autocorrelation in the residuals after imposing the reduced rank restriction $r = 1$.

For the M2 model the results calculated with $r = 1$ show that normality remains a problem ($\chi^2(8) = 36.67$), the null of non-autocorrelation is no more rejected neither by the Ljung-Box test (L-B, $\chi^2(204) = 216.39$, p-val $= 0.26$) nor by either of the two LM tests (LM(1): p-val $= 0.97$ and LM(4): p-val $=$ 0.26). Some ARCH effect in the $\Delta m2$ equation remains a problem however ($\chi^2(6) = 17.25$). For the M3 model no ARCH effect seems to be present, but normality is still a troublesome assumption ($\chi^2(8) = 21.38$) and autocorrelation at lag 1 has been introduced with the reduced rank restriction (LM(1): p-val $= 0.03$). Again, on the grounds of Johansen's argument (1995, p. 29), we proceed with our analysis with these reduced rank systems.

Now we are in the position to test the assumption of weak exogeneity of *cpi*, *gdp* and *rb* with respect to the long-run parameters in the M2 model and of *m*3, *gdp* and *rb* with respect to the long-run parameters in the M3 model. The restrictions cannot be rejected in both model. For the M2 model the LR test for $\alpha_{cpi} = \alpha_{gdp} = \alpha_{rb} = 0$ produces $\chi^2(3) = 2.67$ corresponding to a p-value of 45% and for the M3 model the LR test for $\alpha_{m3} = \alpha_{gdp} = \alpha_{rb} = 0$ gives $\chi^2(3) = 2.37$ with a p-value of 50%. The estimates of the restricted models are presented in table 4.

The cointegrating vectors β of the M2 and the M3 model look like money demand functions for the corresponding money aggregate. Again, before we proceed in exploring the economic content of the models any further, we have to check the stability of these long-run parameters.

The stability of these parameters can be checked visually by using recursive estimations. In Peytrignet (1996), we developed a generalized version of recursive analysis which can be applied, theoretically, on any estimators. As a matter of simplicity, we restrict ourselves in computing only a variant of DOLS which omits to correct the autocorrelation in the errors with AR terms. With this simplification the estimator is much easier to calculate and continues to be consistent.

The formula for our simplified DOLS looks as follows

$$m_t = \mu + \Phi D_t + \theta_{cpi} cpi_t + \theta_{gdp} gdp_t + \theta_{rb} rb_t + d_{cpi}(L)\Delta cpi_t + d_{gdp}(L)\Delta gdp_t + d_{rb}(L)\Delta rb_t + \varepsilon_t \quad (4)$$

where $d_x(L)$ are two-sided polynomials in L, μ is an unrestricted constant and D_t is a set of centered seasonal dummies.

To check the stability of $\theta_{x'}$ we estimate this formula recursively. More precisely, in order to complete the traditional recursive method which computes the long-run parameters in keeping the starting date of the samples fixed and letting only vary the end date of the samples, we take into account the fact that other recursive methods exist in the literature, in particular the ones mentioned in Lütkepohl et al. (1995). We modify their approach in letting varying both the start and the end dates of the samples. The results are gathered in a 3D-graph which shows the estimation of the long-run parameter θ_x on all the possible sub-samples allowed by the data. On such a graph, which is only descriptive, the periods of instability of the parameters can easily be detected. In particular, large movements of the whole surface indicate permanent shocks whereas local peaks and troughs indicate temporary breaks. Forward and backward recursive estimations are gathered in 2D-graphs and shown along with the 3D-graphs. The link between the graphs can be described as follows: For each parameter, the second graph shows the traditional forward recursive estimates. This represents the intersection of the surface with the *y,z* plan in the 3D-graph. The third graph shows the backward recursive estimate of the parameter which is the intersection of the surface with the *x,z* plan in the 3D-graph. Along the diagonal, the results of rolling regressions can be read with samples of the same size but different starting dates.

The recursive estimations of θ_{cpi}, θ_{gdp} and θ_{rb} for the M2 model are shown in figure 1 through figure 3[6]. This collection of graphs shows that the long-run parameters for the M2 model are reasonably stable on all sub-samples. If we extend the sample at the beginning to start with the first quarter of 1973, the parameters show some large instability around this extension of the sample probably stemming from the collapse of the Bretton Woods fixed exchange rate regime and its adjustment process in the economy to flexible exchange rates. Thus, it is worthwhile to keep the first quarter 1977 as the starting date of our analysis.

The recursive estimations of θ_{cpi}, θ_{gdp} and θ_{rb} for the M3 model look stable as well and are presented in figure 4 through figure 6. Note that the three parameters show higher stability as the ones for the M2 model, but estimating with the larger sample that starts in 1973:1 results in unstable parameters at the beginning of the sample like within the M2 model.

Given the above results for the M2 and the M3 model, the next step is to analyze if econometric restrictions inspired by economic theory can be imposed on the models without threatening their stability. Using Johansen's procedure, we test if the long-run parameters of CPI can be restricted to unity. A unit price elasticity implying that economic agents have no money illusion in the long

[6] In order to allow the comparison between M2 and M3, the scale of the graphs have been normalized on the values between 0 and 2.5 for the price and the real GDP parameters and between −1.2 and 0 for the interest rate coefficient. The parameters are estimated under the assumption that the two-sided polynomial is of degree 2. The results are practically unchanged with degree 4.

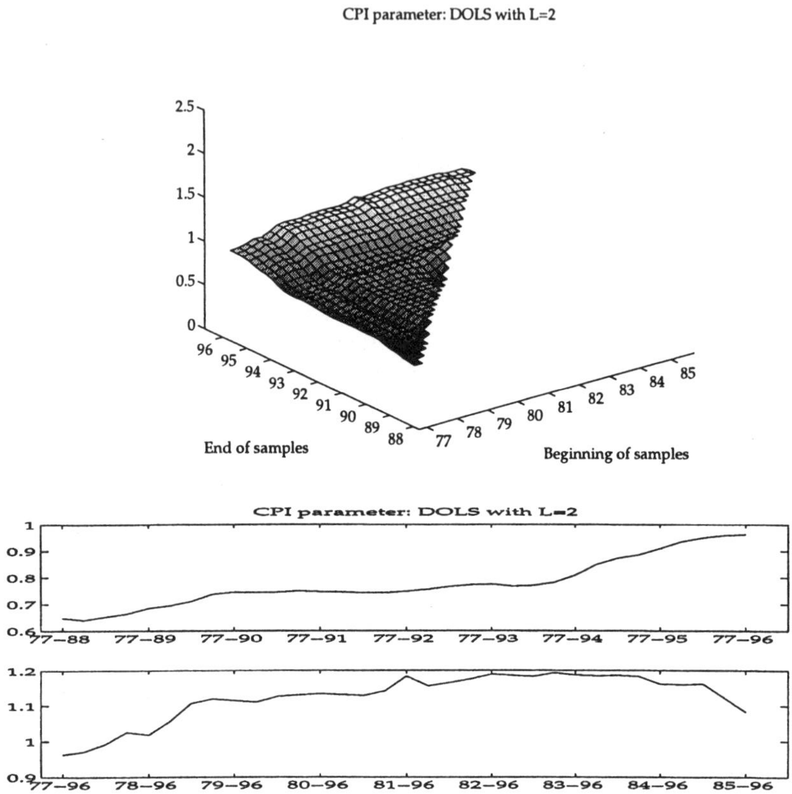

Fig. 1. DOLS-estimation of θ_{cpi} in the M2 model

run seems to be an economic restriction that both the M2 and the M3 model should be consistent with. Moreover, from the inspection of the above graphs, it seems to be possible to further restrict the income elasticity in the M2 model to unity implying a direct relationship between the velocity of $m2$ and the interest rate. The tests are conducted in the VECM framework without and with imposing the restrictions of the single-equation hypothesis, i.e. all but one of the adjustment coefficients being zero as found above. Only restricting the parameters of the cointegrating vector as discussed above is neither rejected in the M2 nor in the M3 model with $\chi^2(2) = 4.32$ (p-val. 0.12) and $\chi^2(1) = 0.03$ (p-val. $= 0.87$), respectively. Imposing the additional single-equation hypothesis does not change the results; the test statistics are respectively $\chi^2(5) = 7.93$ (p-val. 0.16) and $\chi^2(4) = 2.51$ (p-val. $= 0.64$) for the M2 and the M3 model. The estimation results under the single-equation hypothesis are presented in table 5.

An income elasticity of 1.6 in the M3 model is reasonable, since the only difference between M2 and M3 is the inclusion of the time deposits which are growing much faster than GDP. Therefore, the coefficient representing the income elasticity must be larger than one in this model.

Restricting the price and income parameters in the M2 model to unity, the DOLS recursive 3D-graph, figure 7, shows a stable long-run interest rate parameter.

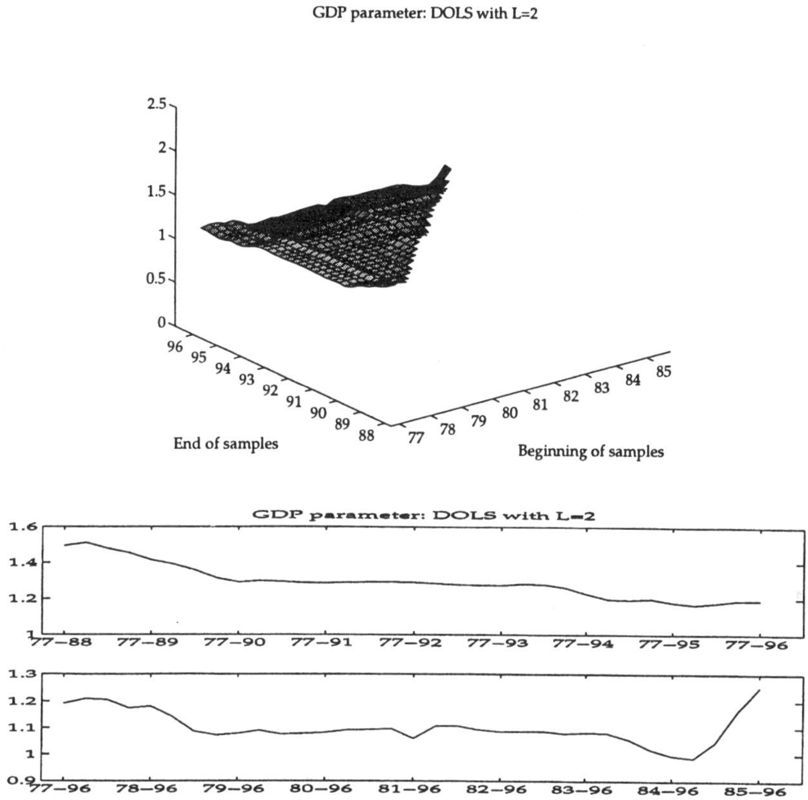

Fig. 2. DOLS-estimation of θ_{gdp} in the M2 model

Imposing a unit price elasticity in the M3 model does alter the stability of the income and interest rate parameters somewhat as can be seen from the recursive 3D-graphs, figure 8, shown below.

The introduced instability concerns all the samples ending after the fourth quarter of 1994, no matter what starting date and particularly the samples beginning after the first quarter of 1984[7].

Since the long-run relation in the M2 and the M3 models seem to be acceptably stable, we proceed with the above results and reduce the above I(0) systems to single equations model.

2. A short-run model for M2 money demand

Taking the M2 model residuals from the estimated cointegrating relation in table 5, *ecm*2, we can construct a single-equation I(0) model in applying a reduction process *à la* Hendry (1986), going from the general to the specific. To be more detailed, we start modeling a VECM as in (1), but instead of re-

[7] This instability is probably due to the GDP data in 1996 and 1997, which is still provisional and is expected to be significantly revised.

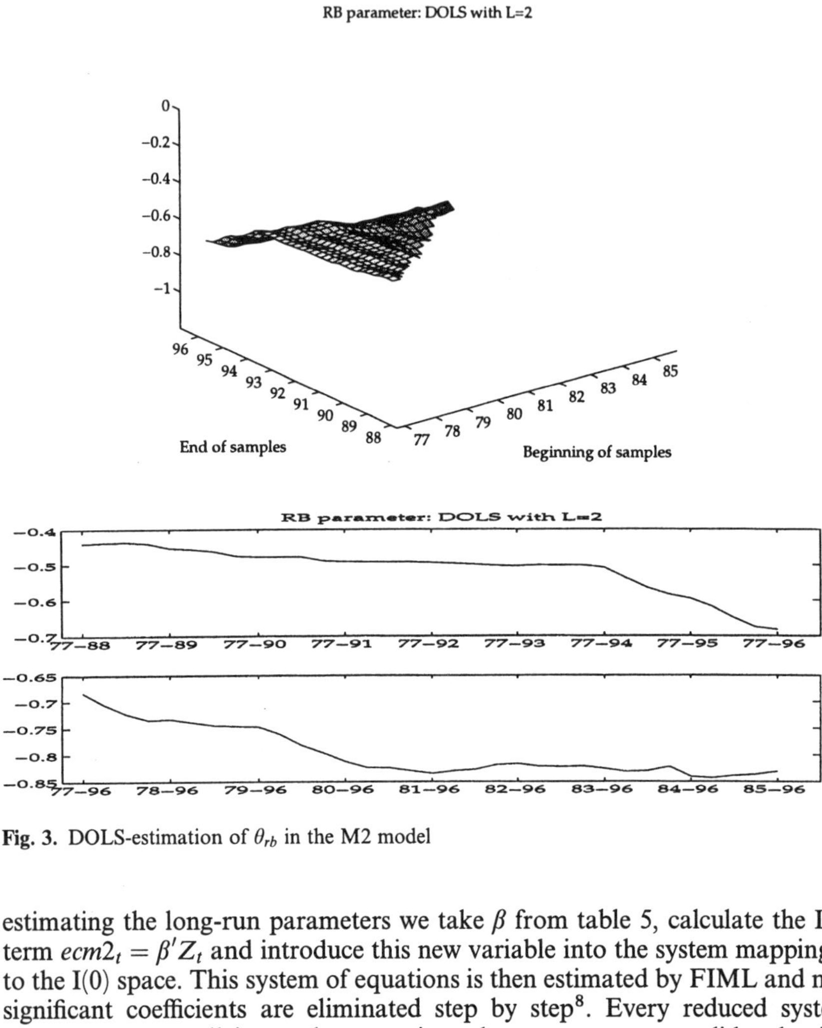

Fig. 3. DOLS-estimation of θ_{rb} in the M2 model

estimating the long-run parameters we take β from table 5, calculate the I(0) term $ecm2_t = \beta' Z_t$ and introduce this new variable into the system mapping it to the I(0) space. This system of equations is then estimated by FIML and non significant coefficients are eliminated step by step[8]. Every reduced system must encompass all its predecessors in order to represent a valid reduction step. The final parsimonious system should be reducible to a single-equation model as the above long-run analysis implies. Within this single-equation model the reduction process is further employed resulting in a parsimonious short-run model.

We have argued in the introduction that the rate of return on the long bond may be interpreted as a proxy for a "permanent" forward-looking short-term rate. However, using this rate only we will not be able to explain shifts in the portfolio of economic agents due to short-run interest rate differentials; in particular, we can not explain the shifts into or out of time deposits that occur because of nonparallel shifts in the term structure. In order to capture this, we include the first difference of the three month Euro-Swiss franc interest rate, $\Delta r3m$, into the model.

[8] To make sure the order in which non-significant variables are deleted is not important, we employ different deleting schemes.

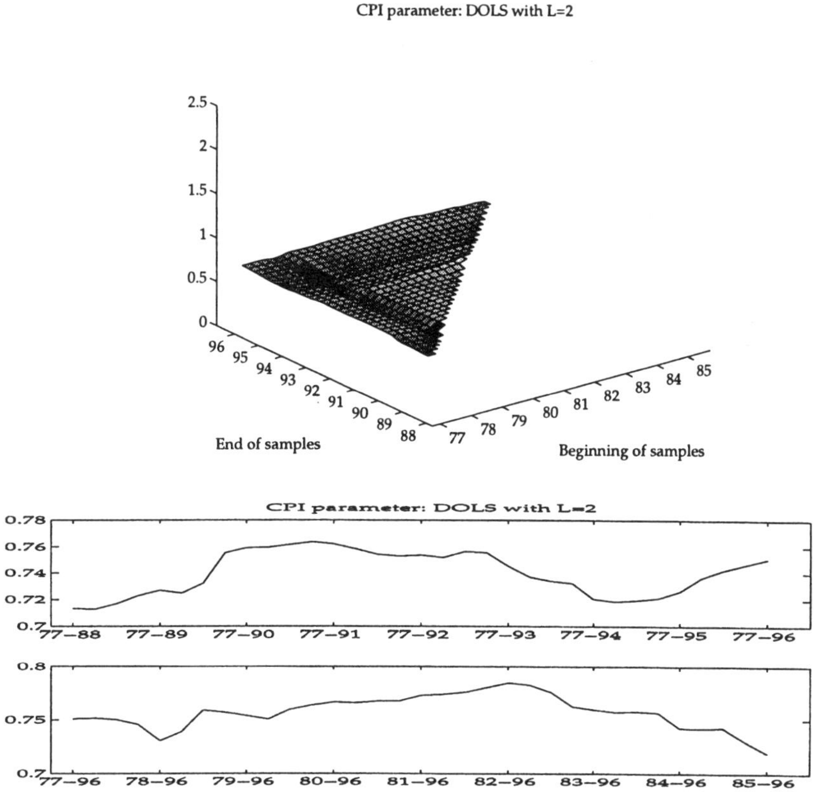

Fig. 4. DOLS-estimation of θ_{cpi} in the M3 model

After an eight step reduction process for M2, we obtain the following specification (White (1980) standard deviations are in parentheses):

$$\begin{aligned}\Delta(m2-cpi)_t = {} & \underset{(0.0024)}{0.0292} - \underset{(0.0045)}{0.0254}\,Q1 - \underset{(0.0032)}{0.0209}\,Q2 - \underset{(0.0031)}{0.0388}\,Q3 \\ & + \underset{(0.0663)}{0.3493}\,\Delta(m2-cpi)_{t-1} - \underset{(0.0249)}{0.1440}\,ecm2_{t-1} \\ & - \underset{(0.0213)}{0.1273}\,\Delta rb_t - \underset{(0.0034)}{0.0116}\,\Delta r3m_t - \underset{(0.1637)}{0.6570}\,\Delta cpi_t \end{aligned} \tag{5}$$

$R^2 = 0.900$ $\sigma = 0.96\%$ Sample: 77:2–97:1 DW $= 1.99$

AR(6,65) = 0.36[0.90] ARCH(6,59) = 0.53 [0.78]
AR(1,70) = 0.00 [0.99] ARCH(1,69) = 0.07 [0.79]
Norm(2) = 1.93 [0.38] Chow(40,31) = 1.87 [0.04]

Het(13,57) = 1.13 [0.36] Reset(1,70) = 0.84 [0.36]
Het2(38,32) = 1.44 [0.14] Reset(3,73) = 1.09 [0.36]
Chow(8,63) = 1.56 [0.15] Chow(4,67) = 0.27 [0.89]

The p-value are in brackets. All tests are F-tests except Norm which is χ^2.

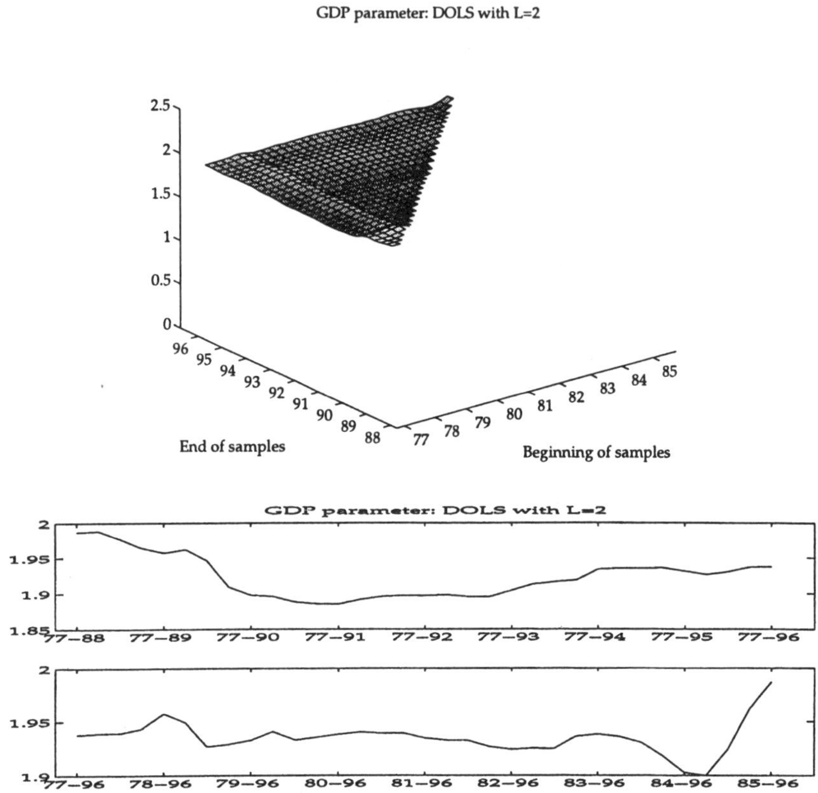

Fig 5. DOLS-estimation of θ_{gdp} in the M3 model

Equation (5) passes all the PC-Give tests. The one-step forecasting performances are summarized by three Chow tests with respectively 40, 8 and 4 periods left for forecasts. With 40 periods of forecasts, the performance of the model deteriorates, in particular for the years 1988–1989 when the SNB revised the liquidity prescriptions for the banking system after the introduction of the new electronic interbank payment system SIC.

To summarize, both the long- and the short-run parameters of the M2 model seem to be reasonably stable. The assumption of weak exogeneity of the three month Euro-Swiss franc interest rate and the possible omission of a second long-run relationship between the two included interest rates will be tackled in further research extending the model to include the term structure.

3. A short-run model for the inflation rate

Since we found *m*3, *gdp* and *rb* to be weakly exogenous for the long-run parameters of the M3 model, we are in a position to reduce the system to a single-equation model for the inflation rate, Δcpi, employing the same method as we did for the M2 model. However, Switzerland is a small open economy

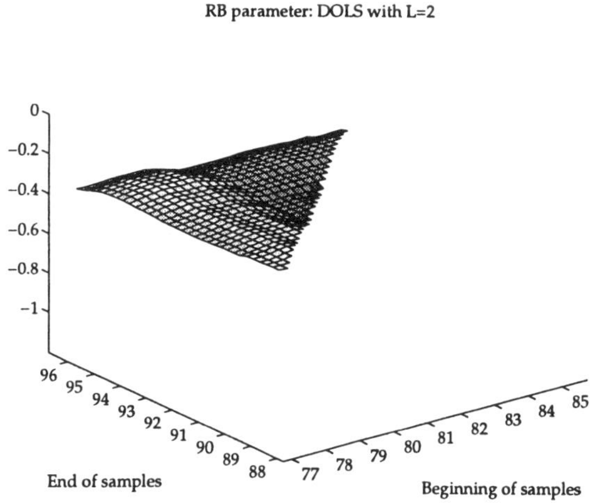

and changes in the country's consumer price index depend in the short-run to some extent on the inflation rates of its most important trade partners. Since Germany is one of the largest ones, its inflation rate should play a valuable role in the determination of the Swiss rate. More precisely, from a purchasing power parity point of view the exchange rate corrected German inflation rate (CPIDER) should matter. Adding this variable as weakly exogenous to the VECM (1) and taking the M3 model residuals from the estimated cointegrating relation in table 5, *ecm*3, to construct a single-equation I(0) model we implicitly make the assumptions that *cpider* is actually weakly exogenous and does not enter the cointegrating relation of the money demand function for *m*3. After a 24 step reduction process we arrive at the following I(0) model:

$$\begin{aligned}\Delta cpi_t = {} & \underset{(0.1032)}{0.6651} + \underset{(0.0845)}{0.2246}\, \Delta cpi_{t-4} - \underset{(0.0231)}{0.0887}\, \Delta gdp_t \\ & + \underset{(0.0201)}{0.0754}\, \Delta cpider_t + \underset{(0.0120)}{0.0770}\, ecm3_{t-1} \end{aligned} \tag{6}$$

$R^2 = 0.566$ $\sigma = 0.44\%$ Sample: 78:1–97:1   DW = 1.64

AR(6,66) = 1.78 [0.12]	ARCH(6,60) = 2.64 [0.02]
AR(1,71) = 0.23 [0.15]	ARCH(1,70) = 0.43 [0.51]
Norm(2) = 1.50 [0.47]	Chow(40,32) = 0.40 [0.99]
Het(8,63) = 0.99 [0.45]	Reset(1,71) = 0.46 [0.50]
Het2(14,57) = 0.87 [0.60]	Reset(3,69) = 3.09 [0.03]
Chow(8,64) = 0.59 [0.78]	Chow(4,68) = 1.21 [0.31]

The p-value are in brackets. All tests a F-tests except Norm which is χ^2.

The model is data congruent conditional on the test battery contained in PcGive. The only problems could emerge from an ARCH effect in the re-

Table 5. Long-run estimates of the M2 and the M3 model with weak exogeneity and unit elasticity restrictions imposed

	M2 model				M3 model			
β	*m2*	*cpi*	*gdp*	*rb*	*m3*	*cpi*	*gdp*	*rb*
	1	−1	−1	0.681	1	−1	−1.599	0.321
st'deviation	–	–	–	0.049	–	–	0.049	0.042
α	$\Delta m2$	Δcpi	Δgdp	Δrb	$\Delta m3$	Δcpi	Δgdp	Δrb
	−0.228	–	–	–	–	0.162	–	–
t-value	−4.167	–	–	–	–	5.982	–	–

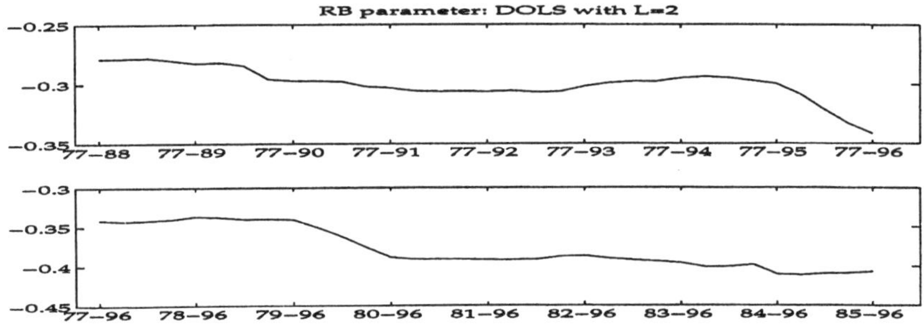

Fig 6. DOLS-estimation of θ_{rb} in the M3 model

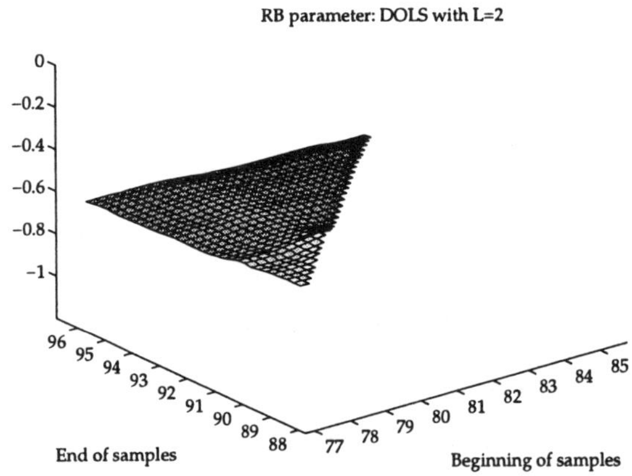

Fig 7. DOLS-estimation of θ_{rb} in the M3 model

siduals and a possible mis-specification, that is shown by the low p-value of the broader RESET test. However, the coefficients are strongly significant and have the right signs, given that the cointegrating vector is normalized on *m*3.

Note, that the forecasting performance of the single-equation model for the Swiss inflation rate is good for 40, 8 and 4 quarters and from this point of view has better performance than the single-equation model (5) for *m*2.

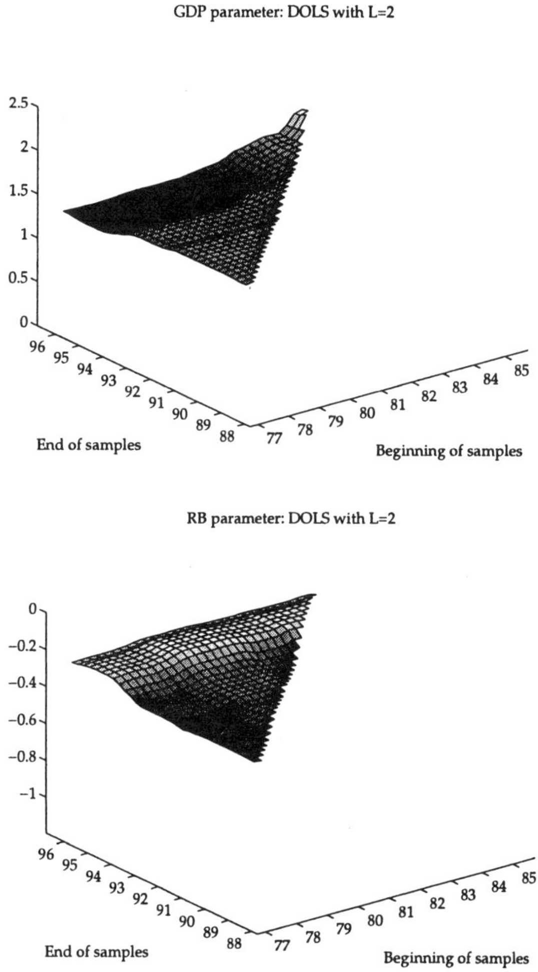

Fig. 8. DOLS-estimation of θ_{gdp} and θ_{rb} in the M3 model

4. Conclusions

This paper presents a report on the most recent results obtained on the stability of the broadest defined monetary aggregates the SNB computes for Switzerland. We first estimate the long-run parameters of money demand functions for the M2 and M3 aggregates and investigates their stability. For both aggregates a single stable cointegrating vector is found. In the sequel, a single-equation model for $\Delta m2$ is built around the long-run relationship found for M2. Third, a single-equation model for Δcpi is built around the corresponding cointegrating vector for M3. For both models the estimates are found to be stable. Finally, the forecast performance of the Δcpi model seems to be superior to the $\Delta m2$ model, providing some positive signs that the M3 model is stable in the sense that it does not suffer from a structural break during the period of estimation.

However, the results in the analysis pose two further questions. First, what is the difference between the two aggregates M2 and M3 that makes it possible to end up with a short-run model for *m*2 and one for *cpi*, respectively? And second, can we draw any general monetary policy implications from the results?

The only difference between M2 and M3 is the inclusion of time deposits in the latter. Since we have not modeled portfolio adjustments between M2's components and the time deposits induced by shifts in the term structure, it is possible that any long-run disequilibrium is fed into the monetary aggregate *m2*, hence overshadowing the adjustment process for *cpi*, as found in the M3 case.

As we have mentioned above, the SNB targets the seasonally-adjusted monetary base on a medium-term horizon, but the recent instability of this aggregate renders its practical use rather difficult. The above findings on the long-run stability property of the demand for *m*3 suggests that this aggregate could play a more active role as an additional indicator in the SNB's monetary policy framework. However, in order to rely more extensively on this broad monetary aggregate further research has to be undertaken.

Appendix A

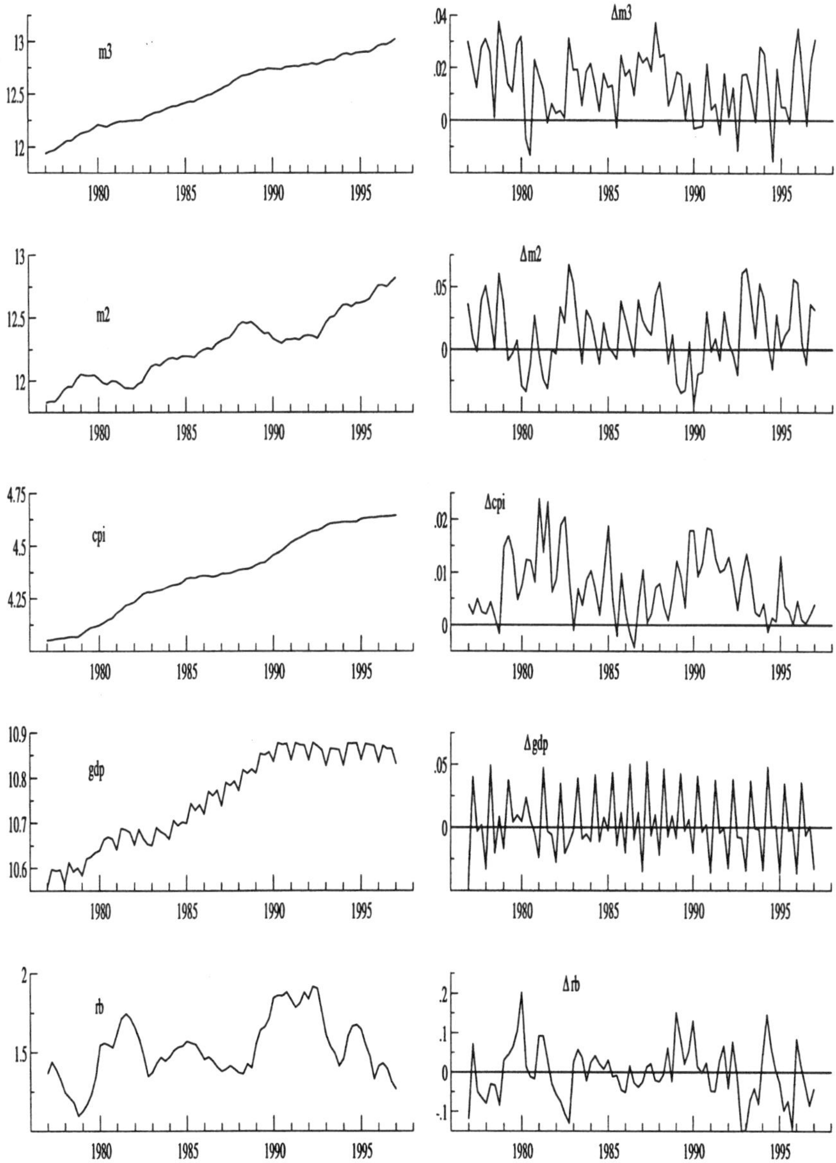

References

Dickey DA, Fuller WA (1979) Distribution of the estimators for autoregressive time-series with a unit-root. Journal of American Statistical Association 74:427–31

Dolado JJ, Jenkinson T (1987) Cointegration: A survey of recent developments. Applied Economics Discussion Paper Number 39, University of Oxford

Ericsson NR, Hendry DF and Tran H (1994) Cointegration, seasonality, encompassing and the demand for money. Chapter 7 in: Hargreaves CP (eds.) Nonstationary times series analysis and cointegration, Oxford University Press, Oxford

Fischer A, Peytrignet M (1990) Are larger monetary aggregates interesting? Some exploratory evidence for Switzerland using feedback models. Schweizerische Zeitschrift für Volkswirtschaft und Statistik 126:505–20

Fluri R (1995) Grundlagen zur Revision der Geldaggregate im Jahre 1995. Geld, Währung und Konjunktur 1:76–88

Hendry DF (1986) Econometric modelling with cointegrated variables: An overview. Oxford Bulletin of Economics and Statistics 48:201–12

Johansen S (1988) Statistical analysis of cointegration vectors. Journal of Economic Dynamics and Control, 12:231–54

——— (1995) Likelihood-based inference in cointegrated vector autoregressive models. Oxford University Press, Oxford

——— Juselius K (1990) Maximum likelihood estimation and inference on cointegration – with applications to the demand for money. Oxford Bulletin of Economics and Statistics 52:169–210

——— (1994) Identification of the long-run and the short-run structure. An application to the ISLM model. Journal of Econometrics 63:7–36

Juselius K (1991) Long-run relations in Australian monetary data. Discussion Papers #91-18, Institute of Economics, University of Copenhagen, Denmark

Lütkepohl v H, Moryson M, Wolters J (1995) Stabilitätsanalyse der bundesdeutschen Geldnachfrage anhand alternativer Ansätze zur Modellierung variierender Regressionskoeffizienten. Kredit und Kapital 28:107–33

Osterwald-Lenum M (1992) A note with quantiles of the asymptotic distribution of the maximum likelihood cointegration rank test statistics. Oxford Bulletin of Economics and Statistics 54:461–72

Peytrignet M (1996) Stabilité économétrique des agrégats monétaires suisses. Monnaie et conjoncture 3:251–78

——— Fischer A (1991) Agrégats monétaires suisses: M1 exogène ou endogène?. Monnaie et conjoncture 3:247–81

Stock JH, Watson MW (1993) A simple estimator of cointegrating vectors in higher order integrated systems. Econometrica 61:783–820

Urbain J-P (1993) Exogeneity in error correction models. Lecture Notes in Economics and Mathematical Systems, Vol. 398, Springer-Verlag, Berlin

White H (1980) A heteroskedasticity-consistent covariance matrix estimator and a direct test for heteroskedasticity. Econometrica 48:817–38

Changing monetary transmission mechanisms within the EU

Katarina Juselius[1,2]

[1] Institute of Economics, University of Copenhagen, DK-1169 Copenhagen, Denmark
[2] European University Institute, Economics Department, Via die Roccettini 9, I-50016 San Domenico, Italy (e-mail: juselius@datacomm.iue.it)

Abstract. The paper presents a comparative analysis of monetary transmission mechanisms and changes in them after the "second *ERM*" in March 1983. The empirical model investigates the determination of money, income, prices, and interest rates in Germany, Denmark, and Italy based on the cointegrated *VAR* model. It provides empirical results on the macroeconomic effects of joining the *ERM* and financial deregulation.

Key words: Cointegration, long-run impact, money demand, *IS–LM*, monetary policy, capital liberalization

JEL classification: C32, E41, E52

1. Introduction

The paper addresses policy questions motivated by the planned European Monetary Union. While trade liberalization in the European Common Market started as early as in 1957, the intra-European movements of goods and labor were, nevertheless, largely restricted by government regulations and trade barriers. Against the background of rather disappointing European macroeconomic performance in the seventies (after the first oil shock) and the first part of the eighties, European governments set out to abolish the remaining regulations on the movement of goods, capital and labor. The final goal of the integration process is the creation of the European Monetary Union as one currency area.

Whether the EMU is desirable or not is related to the macroeconomic and microeconomic costs and benefits of the planned union. Lower interest rates, stable low inflation rates, more disciplinary pressure on politicians are often mentioned as examples of expected positive effects. Less scope for domestic policy to smooth economic fluctuations in the presence of asymmetric shocks is probably the most important negative effect. For further detail, see for instance the excellent review by Kenen (1995).

When it comes to a quantitative assessment of the macroeconomic consequences of joining or not, the empirical evidence has either been scarce or unreliable. To evaluate the costs of the lost monetary autonomy one needs to know whether monetary policy in the past has been effective in achieving its goal, i.e. curbing inflation in a period of expansionary demand and, possibly, stimulating real growth in a recession. Against the background of the recent experience of the long lasting recession in Europe, with modest real growth rates, high rates of unemployment, low inflation rates and high real interest rates, this question seems particularly important.

The increased economic integration as a result of the EEC (later EC), EMS and ERM has considerably changed the scope for macroeconomic policy, but the consequences have not always been well understood. A possible explanation is that available theories are generally based on steady-state behavior, or assume fast market adjustment towards steady-state, whereas actual macroeconomic behavior in periods of transition seems to be characterized by slow adjustment to new steady-states.

It is our prior hypothesis that the effectiveness of monetary policy can be related to the balance, or lack of it, in other important sectors of the economy, such as the labor sector, the foreign sector, and the government sector. For instance, at the beginning of the eighties most countries joining the *EMS* and the *ERM* were not on the *PPP* steady state relative to each other. Because the adjustment to the *PPP* has historically been very slow, we expect the *PPP* position of an *ERM* country to be of relevance for the efficiency of the pursued monetary policy for the following reasons:

For a relatively high *PPP* country the equilibrium correction of prices is likely to be very slow due to downward nominal rigidities. For a narrow band *ERM* country the adjustment of nominal exchange rates is only possible to a very limited extent. Restoring the *PPP* balance can, therefore, be expected to take a long time. In the period of transition to a sustainable *PPP* level, inflation is likely to remain low independently of the pursued monetary policy. On the other hand, for a relatively low *PPP* country the price adjustment is likely to be more flexible and monetary policy should be more effective.

In capital deregulated countries with narrow exchange rate bands, monetary policy using interest rate control is likely to be less effective. Assuming that the price of capital is largely determined by the world demand and supply, means that the level of long-term interest rate is outside domestic monetary influence. Even if monetary control of short-term interest rates is possible in the short run, controlling the adjustment of the short-term rate to the market determined long-term interest rate would be difficult in the absence of capital regulations.

We investigate three European countries: Germany, Denmark, and Italy. At the beginning of the *EMS* Germany and Denmark represent high *PPP* countries, whereas Italy is a low *PPP* country. Denmark and Germany adopted the narrow bands of the *ERM* in 1979 and both countries were more or less capital deregulated at the beginning of 1983. Italy joined the *EMS* from the beginning but with broader exchange rate bands. It maintained some control on capital movements until the end of the eighties. Denmark represents a very small open economy, strongly dependent on the German economy. Germany is large and very influential, whereas Italy is large, but less influential. In many respects the two periods and the three countries resemble a "designed experiment".

At the start of the *EMS* we expect monetary policy to be less effective in deregulated, high *PPP*, narrow *ERM* countries, whereas low *PPP*, capital regulated, broad *ERM* countries are likely to exhibit a higher degree of monetary effectiveness.

The purpose of this paper is, therefore, to study empirically the long-run and short-run adjustment behavior of money, prices, income and interest rates and its effect on monetary policy in the three above mentioned European countries. The empirical analyses of how monetary transmission mechanisms have worked and possibly changed after the increased monetary integration in Europe are based on the cointegrated *VAR* model and span approximately the last 20 years.

Section 2 gives the economic background, section 3 discusses some methodological questions relevant for the comparative aspects of the study, section 4 discusses issues related to the statistical and econometric part of the study, section 5 presents the empirical model and its basic characteristic features. In sections 6, 7, and 8 the main comparative results are presented and discussed. Section 9 summarizes and concludes.

2. Economic background

Section 2.1 summarizes the most important institutional events. Section 2.2 reviews the *IS–LM* model as a background for the specification and interpretation of the long-run structure of the empirical model and section 2.3 discusses the elements and the transmission mechanisms of monetary policy.

2.1. Reforms and interventions

The sample period covers the post Bretton Woods period from 1971 to the end of 1994. In the first part of this period the "snake in the tunnel" exchange rate agreement was in effect. It was replaced in March 1979 by the European Monetary System based on the new currency unit *ECU*. The *ERM* of the *EMS* became effective with West Germany and Denmark adopting a band of $\pm 2.25\%$, and Italy of $\pm 6\%$ until Jan 1990 when it was changed to $\pm 2.25\%$.

The ERM agreement of March 1983 put a stop to the previously frequent realignments, and divides the sample into a more flexible and less flexible European exchange rate regime.

In September 1992 the speculative currency attack on the European currencies forced Italian lira out of the *ERM*.

In August 1993 Denmark adopted a band of $\pm 15\%$, whereas Germany kept the previous band of $\pm 2.25\%$. The *ERM* system had for practical purposes broken down.

Because capital deregulation has been a gradual process extending over many years, it is hard to give an exact date for when the capital market worked more or less without friction. Nevertheless, we consider Germany reasonably deregulated at the beginning of 1980, Denmark at the beginning of 1983, Italy at the end of 1989.

The following country-specific interventions had a strong impact on the system:

Denmark: In 1975:3 the value added tax was temporarily removed, and restored during the next two quarters; several permanent value-added tax reforms in 1977:4, 1978:4 and 1980:3.

Germany: In October 1990 East and West Germany were reunified. In anticipation of this, there was a large change in money stock in 1990:3

Italy: In 1974:4 there was a drastic drop in money stock and real GDP as a result of the introduction of credit and exchange control in combination with very tight fiscal policy; in 1976:1 the exchange market was closed; in 1981:2 the Central Bank was "divorced" from the Treasury; in 1986:2 there was a drastic reduction (3%) of the discount rate; in 1992:3 Italy left the *ERM*.

2.2. *A stochastic formulation of the theoretical relations*

The empirical analysis focuses on the dynamics of "excess money" and its effects on prices, income and interest rates. The specification of the long-run structure is based on the *IS–LM* model augmented with the short-run Phillips curve (Laidler, 1985), whereas the short-run adjustment structure is empirically determined. Because the inflation rate is $I(1)$ empirically, we include nominal growth rates in the theoretical framework, thereby allowing for dynamic steady-states. The empirical connection between economic steady-states and cointegration is discussed below for each relation. This section draws strongly on Juselius (1996 and 1998).

Money demand, m^d, is assumed to be the sum of the transactions, precautionary, and speculative demand for money and related to the level of real income, y, price, p, the opportunity cost of holding money relative to bonds, $R_m - R_b$, and to real stock, Δp. Assuming log-linearity and long-run price and income homogeneity the hypothetical long-run money demand relation becomes:

$$m_t^d - y_t - p_t - a_1(R_{mt} - R_{b_t}) - a_2 \Delta p_t = u_{m_t} \tag{2.1}$$

where u_{m_t} is a residual and lower cases denote logarithmic values and upper cases levels.

For (2.1) to qualify as a demand for money relation $a_1 \geq 0$, $a_2 \leq 0$, and $u_{m_t} \sim I(0)$. The stationarity can for instance be achieved by $a_2 = 0$, $m_t - p_t - y_t \sim I(0)$ and $(R_{m_t} - R_{b_t}) \sim I(0)$; or by $m_t - p_t - y_t \sim I(1)$ and $(R_{m_t} - R_{b_t}) \sim I(1)$, but $\{(m_t - p_t - y_t) - a_1\ (R_{m_t} - R_{b_t})\} \sim I(0)$.

Money supply is related to changes in foreign reserves, and to the price or quantity control rules adopted by the Central Bank. Since interest rate control has been predominantly used in particular in the latter period, we expect the Central Banks to raise short-term interest rates (relative to the level of long-term interest rates) if inflation is above the target rate π^*. Therefore, the following relation between the interest rate spread and the deviation of inflation rate from the target inflation rate is assumed to be empirical evidence of the

Central Bank reaction rule:

$$R_{m_t} - R_{b_t} - a_3(\Delta p_t - \pi^*) - R_0 = u_{CB_t} \tag{2.2}$$

where R_0 is a constant, $a_3 > 0$ and the residual $u_{CB_t} \sim I(0)$ for (2.2) to qualify as a monetary policy rule. Note, that (2.2) does not exclude other CB rules like inflation relative to the *PPP*, or inflation relative to the real *GDP* growth.

Aggregate income. The *IS* relationship of the model predicts that trend-adjusted real aggregate income is negatively related to the long-term real interest rate. In addition trend-adjusted real income can be cointegrated with inflation. See for instance Hendry and Mizon (1993) and Juselius (1996). If unemployment and output gap are negatively cointegrated, the latter can be interpreted as a short-run Phillips curve relationship. The following specification of the real income relation accounts for both possibilities:

$$y_t - a_4 * trend - a_5 R_{b_t} - a_6 \Delta p_t = u_{y_t} \tag{2.3}$$

where $a_4 \geq 0$, $a_5 < 0$, $a_5 = -a_6$ and $u_{y_t} \sim I(0)$ would be consistent with the *IS* curve, whereas $a_5 = 0$ and $a_6 > 0$ would be consistent with the short-run Phillips curve.

The stationarity of u_{y_t} can, for instance, be achieved by $y_t - a_4 * trend \sim I(0)$ and $(a_5 R_{b_t} - a_6 \Delta p_t) \sim I(0)$; or by $y_t - a_4 * trend \sim I(1)$ and $R_{b_t} \sim I(1)$, but $(y_t - a_4 * trend - a_5 R_{b_t}) \sim I(0)$.

Interest rates. The Fisher parity predicts that the short-term interest rate depends on expected inflation:

$$R_{m_t} - \mathscr{E}_t(\Delta p_{t+1}) = u_{Rm_t}, \tag{2.4}$$

where $\mathscr{E}_t(\Delta p_{t+1})$ is the expected inflation at time t. The expectations hypothesis predicts that the long-term interest rate is the average of expected short-term interest rate for the entire time to maturity. Assuming that deviations between expectations and actual realizations are stationary, this would lead to a stationary spread, i.e.

$$R_{b_t} - R_{m_t} = u_{Rb_t} \tag{2.5}$$

Empirical support requires that $u_{Rm_t} \sim I(0)$, and $u_{Rb_t} \sim I(0)$ implying one common stochastic trend driving both the inflation rate and the interest rates. In open economies without restrictions on capital and goods the Fisher open parity predicts stationarity of both domestic and foreign real interest rates, as well as interest and inflation spread.

Prices. Previous empirical findings (Juselius, 1996, 1998) suggest that $\Delta p \sim I(1)$, and, hence, that prices are integrated of second order, i.e. $p \sim I(2)$. This statistical observation gives the rationale for distinguishing between the long-run determination of the price level and the medium-run determination of the inflation rate. In the long run the quantity theory of money predicts that the price level is related to $m - y$, i.e. to monetary expansion in excess of real productivity growth. If $m - p - y \sim I(1)$, we expect the inflation rate to adjust to deviations from this steady state. According to the short-run Phillips curve, inflation increases with excess aggregate demand. Finally, if Central Bank policy is effective we expect inflation to fall when monetary policy is strict and rise when it is loose. In terms of cointegration (2.1)–(2.3) contain these hypotheses as special cases.

Instruments:		**Targets**		**Goals**
• Reserve requirements on private banks		• Money stock		• inflation rate
• Central bank interest rates	→	• Market interest rates	→	• GDP growth(?)
• Open market operations				
• Interventions in the foreign currency market		• Exchange rates		• purchasing power parity

Fig. 2.1. Elements of monetary policy

2.3. Monetary transmission mechanisms

Figure 2.1 provides a broad overview of the basic elements of monetary policy. See also Juselius (1996). In practise the distinction between instruments and targets is not always clear-cut, neither the meaning of a transmission mechanism. To facilitate the subsequent empirical discussion we will present a simple example of a transmission mechanism following a monetary expansion m:

$$\begin{array}{ccccccccc} (+) & & (-) & & (-) & & (+) & & (+) \\ (m - m^*) & \rightarrow & R_s & \rightarrow & R_l & \rightarrow & (y - y^*) & \rightarrow & \Delta p \end{array}$$

The economy now experiences excess liquidity, $m - m^*$, where m^* is the steady-state value given by (2.1). First we would expect a fall in the short-term market interest rates, and, then according to (2.2), a similar fall in the long-term interest rates. The fall in market interest rates will cause an increase in aggregate (investment) demand, $(y - y^*)$, where the steady-state value y^* is given by (2.3). Finally, excess aggregate demand for goods and labor causes prices to rise. A reverse transmission mechanism takes place if the Central Bank raises interest rates.

In practise the mechanisms are neither so straightforward nor so simple. The effects of central bank policy actions are usually blurred by other events and, hence, difficult to identify empirically. The time lag before monetary policy actions become fully effective can be long and varying. Because the macroeconomy is continuously subject to other shocks than monetary policy shocks it is often econometrically difficult to isolate the former from the latter.

Nevertheless, recent advances in time-series econometrics have provided powerful methods to address these questions empirically. In the next sections we will discuss the results of four different econometric investigations with the aim of providing a balanced picture of the monetary transmission mechanism both in the short run and the long run.

3. Some methodological considerations

In a comparative study, similarity in model design and in empirical investigation is mandatory. The cointegrated *VAR* model defined in the next section has a general structure and its assumptions can be checked against the data. Based on an empirically well-specified model the verification of the most important factors influencing the transmission mechanisms of monetary policy takes place in four stages: (*i*) testing the number of cointegration relations and the long-run weak exogeneity properties (*ii*) testing cointegration properties between variables, (*iii*) testing the dynamics of short-run adjustment of the cointegrating relations and (*iv*) testing the long-run impact of unanticipated "shocks" to the system.

3.1. *Some general characteristics of the model*

An important question is in what sense increased economic integration and the association with the *ERM* have changed the macroeconomic transmission mechanisms. Empirically we can investigate this by distinguishing between (*i*) changes in the long-run coefficients β and (*ii*) changes in the adjustment coefficients α. Within the first group we further distinguish between changes in the intercept and the incoefficients of the variables. Of specific interest are zero, nonzero coefficient changes, i.e. changes in cointegrating properties signalling changes in the functioning of the markets.

For instance, in capital deregulated countries we would expect (2.4)–(2.5) to hold, i.e. nominal interest rates and inflation to adjust to each other, implying one stochastic trend. Hence, cointegration would be found between pairs of two variables. Market regulations usually means friction and slower adjustment. If regulations are binding, such "regulation" shocks can have permanent (long-lasting) effects and, hence, produce new stochastic trends that differ from the stochastic market trend. Hence, cointegration would now only be found between three or more variables.

To obtain information on this we will ask questions like:

- Has the number of cointegration relations increased with increased economic integration?
- Are the number of cointegration vectors the same between regimes and between countries?
- Are any of the variables weakly exogenous for the long-run parameters, i.e. is there absence of long-run feed-back effects?
- Are the same variable(s) weakly exogenous between regimes and between countries.

3.2. *Cointegration properties and common stochastic trends*

If two variables share the same stochastic trend(s) we will find cointegration between them. If there exists another stochastic trend affecting only one of the variables, cointegration is lost unless a new variable containing this trend is introduced. This is further spelled out in Section 4.2. Information on cointegration between minimal sets of variables is therefore useful in pointing out which variables share a common stochastic trend, i.e. which variables are stochastically tied together. In Section 6 we will ask this type of questions, for example:

(*i*) is monetary expansion cointegrated with inflation/interest rates?
(*ii*) is the interest rate spread stationary?

(*iii*) are real interest rates stationary?
(*iv*) is demand pressure (trend-adjusted real income) and inflation rate/interest rate stationary?

The empirical analysis of these questions provides information about the direct relationship between, say, a policy instrument variable and a target or a goal variable. These relationships are quite likely to change relative to the degree of openness of the economies. As indicated in (2.1), velocity and interest rate spread could be stationary in a deregulated open economy. On the other hand, in a more regulated regime velocity and interest rate spread could be $I(1)$ but cointegrate to $I(0)$, i.e. share the same stochastic "regulation" trend.

3.3. *Short-run adjustment effects*

Cointegration properties provide important but not sufficient information about the economically interesting relations. We also need information on the weights of the stationary relations and how they combine within the system. For a full understanding of the short-run adjustment mechanisms we need to ask questions like:

(*v*) Does money stock adjust to changes in velocity and interest rate spread?

Let $\alpha_{1m}(m-p-y)+\alpha_{2m}(R_m-R_b)$ be two components entering the money stock equation. If $\alpha_{1m}<0$, and $\alpha_{2m}>0$, then this can be interpreted as evidence of adjustment to a long-run money demand relation.

(*vi*) Is inflation affected by excess monetary expansion?

Let $\alpha_{1\Delta p}(m-p-y)$ be a component in the inflation equation. If $\alpha_{1\Delta p}>0$, then this can be interpreted as evidence of monetary effects on inflation.

(*vii*) Are there real income effects from monetary expansions in the short-run?

Let $\alpha_{1y}(m-y-p)$ be a component in the real income equation. If $\alpha_{1y}>0$, then this can be interpreted as evidence of short-run real income effects from a monetary expansion.

(*viii*) Does the long-term interest rate adjust to the short-term interest rate?

Let $\alpha_{1Rb}(R_b-R_m)$ be a component in the bond rate equation. If $\alpha_{1Rb}<0$, then this can be be interpreted as evidence of the long rate adjusting to the short rate.

(*ix*) Does excess aggregate demand cause interest rates to rise?

Let $\alpha_{1R}(y-b*trend)$ be a component in the interest rate equation. If $\alpha_{1R}>0$ then it can be interpreted as evidence of demand pressure effects on interest rates.

(*x*) Does excess money (liquidity) cause interest rates to go down?

Let $\alpha_{1R}(m-p-y)$ be a component in the interest rate equation. If $\alpha_{1Rb}<0$, it can be interpreted as evidence of short-run liquidity effects.

By investigating the short-run adjustment effects we can get information on whether for instance an expansion/contraction of money supply has a predictable short-run effect on economic activity. If the estimate $\hat{\alpha}_{2m}$ suggests that demand for the monetary aggregate is interest insensitive, then the *LM* curve is rather steep and changes in money supply will have large effects. The questions (*viii*)–(*x*) are relevant for understanding the transmission mechanisms from central bank interest rates to short-term market rates and further to the long bond rate. The question (*vii*) is important for the transmission from the monetary sector to the real sector of the economy. These questions are investigated in Section 7.

3.4. Long-run impact

The direct effect of monetary policy is usually considered small in the short run, but claimed to be much larger in the long run. Therefore, in addition to the short-run effects we also need information about the long-run impact of "monetary shocks".

(*xi*) Has an unexpected "shock" to money stock a long-run impact on inflation? on real income? on interest rates?

(*xii*) Has an unexpected "shock" to the short-term interest rate a long-run impact on inflation? on money stock? on real income?

These questions are investigated in Section 8.

4. Econometric considerations

Section 4.1 defines briefly the cointegrated $I(1)$ model as parameter restrictions on the unrestricted VAR model. Section 4.2 discusses the preferred model and its cointegration and common trends implications.

4.1. The statistical model

The Vector Error Correction model with a constant term, centered seasonal dummies, and intervention dummies is chosen as the empirical model:

$$\Delta x_t = \Gamma_1 \Delta x_{t-1} + \Pi x_{t-2} + \Phi D_t + \mu + \varepsilon_t,$$

$$\varepsilon_t \sim N_p(0, \Sigma), t = 1, \ldots, T \tag{4.1}$$

where x_t is a $(p \times 1)$ vector of variables in the system, and the parameters $\{\Gamma_1, \Pi, \Phi, \mu, \Sigma\}$ are unrestricted.

The hypothesis that x_t is $I(1)$ is formulated as the reduced rank of $\Pi = \alpha\beta'$ and the full rank of $\alpha'_\perp \Gamma \beta_\perp$, where α, β are $p \times r$ matrices, $\alpha_\perp$, $\beta_\perp$ are $p \times (p-r)$ matrices orthogonal to α, β, respectively and $\Gamma = I - \Gamma_1$.

The moving average representation of the model defines x_t as a function of ε_t, the initial values X_0, and the variables in D_t. For the $I(1)$ model it is given by

$$x_t = C\sum_1^t \varepsilon_i + C\mu t + C\Phi\sum_1^t D_i + C^*(L)(\varepsilon_t + \mu + \Phi D_t) + B \tag{4.2}$$

where $C = \beta_\perp(\alpha'_\perp \Gamma \beta_\perp)^{-1}\alpha'_\perp$, $C^*(L)$ is an infinite polynomial in the lag operator L and B is a function of the initial values.

4.2. Combining cointegration and common trends analysis

Juselius (1998) demonstrated that the case $(r = 3, p - r = 2)$ can be considered plausible for a reasonably deregulated economy. For a more regulated economy we might have slower market adjustment and, hence, the case $(r = 2, p - r = 3)$ might be preferable.

Two independent stochastic trends imply two types of "autonomous" disturbances u_{1t} and u_{2t}, measured for instance by $\hat{u}_{1t} = \hat{\alpha}'_{\perp 1}\hat{\varepsilon}_t$ and $\mu_{2t} = \hat{\alpha}'_{\perp 2}\hat{\varepsilon}_t$ where $\hat{\varepsilon}_t$ is the vector of residuals from (4.1). Conceptually u_{1t} and u_{2t} could be considered a real and a nominal disturbance, respectively, u_{1t} could be related to a shift in the aggregate supply curve and u_{2t} to a shift in the aggregate demand curve. In this case the nonstationary part of (4.2) can be formulated as:

$$m - p = b_{11}\sum u_{2i} + b_{12}\sum u_{1i} + \cdots$$

$$y = b_{21}\sum u_{2i} + b_{22}\sum u_{1i} + \cdots$$

$$R_m = b_{31}\sum u_{2i} + b_{32}\sum u_{1i} + \cdots \tag{4.3}$$

$$R_b = b_{41}\sum u_{2i} + b_{42}\sum u_{1i} + \cdots$$

$$\Delta p = b_{51}\sum u_{2i} + \cdots$$

This representation assumes that both m and p are $I(2)$, i.e. contain one stochastic $I(2)$ trend, $\sum\sum u_{2i}$, such that Δp (and Δm) is only affected by one stochastic trend, $\sum u_{2i}$.

It appears from (4.3) that $(m - p - y) \sim I(0)$ implies $b_{11} - b_{21} = 0$ and $b_{12} - b_{22} = 0$, i.e. the two stochastic trends influence real money stock and real aggregate income with the same weights. Similarly, $(R_m - R_b) \sim I(0)$ implies that $b_{31} - b_{41} = 0$ and $b_{32} - b_{42} = 0$.

Assume now that the real trend is captured by a linear trend and that $\sum u_{1i}$ describes a "regulation" trend only affecting $m - p$ and R_m, i.e. $b_{22} = b_{42} = 0$. In this case $(m - p - y) \sim I(1)$ and $(R_m - R_b) \sim I(1)$, but together they are cointegrating.

Note also, that $R_m - \Delta p \sim I(0)$ if $b_{31} = b_{51}$ and $b_{32} = 0$, implying that R_m in this case is affected only by the stochastic nominal trend. If $R_m - \Delta p \sim I(1)$, either $b_{31} \neq b_{51}$ or $b_{32} \neq 0$ implying in the latter case that R_m is affected by both stochastic trends and, hence, cannot cointegrate with Δp.

The case $(y - b_4 * trend - b_5\Delta p) \sim I(0)$, i.e. $b_{21} - b_5 b_{51} = 0$ and $b_{22} = 0$, implies that the stochastic trend in real aggregate income originates solely from nominal disturbances.

Thus, the econometric investigation should combine the statistical information in the data with the economic understanding of the problem such that all statements can be checked for their internal logical consistency. This is closely related to the concept of economic scenarios discussed in Juselius (1998).

5. The empirical model

The cointegrated *VAR* model (4.1) with two lags and a linear trend in the cointegration space motivated by the short-run Phillips curve relation (2.3) was chosen as the baseline model. To facilitate comparisons we analyze a similar data vector for all three countries, i.e.

$$x_t' = [m - p, y, \Delta p, R_m, R_b]_t$$

where m is the log of the broad monetary aggregate M3 for Germany and M2 for Italy and Denmark, p is the log of the implicit price deflator except for Italy where it is the log of the *CPI*, y is real *GDP*, (seasonally adjusted for Italy, otherwise seasonally unadjusted), R_m is an interest rate measuring the average yield on the components of money stock, R_b is the yield on long-term bonds. The interest rates are divided by 400 to make the estimated coefficients comparable with logarithmic quarterly changes. For a more detailed discussion of the measurements see Juselius (1996, 1998) and Gennari and Juselius (1998).

The sample periods are slightly different for the four countries and span 1975:3–1994:4 for Germany, 1974:1–1994:4 for Italy, and 1975:1–1993:4 for Denmark. For Germany there is a shift dummy in the cointegration space at the reunification 1990:3 and for Denmark at 1983:1 signifying the lifting of capital restrictions (Juselius, 1996, 1998). The model contains centered seasonal dummies $s1$, $s2$, $s3$ and an unrestricted constant term. For Germany an additional set of seasonal dummies is needed to account for the change in the seasonal pattern after the reunification. The following impulse dummies were needed to account for the country-specific institutional events explained in Section 2.2: Germany II: DUM902; Denmark: Dvat, D752, D923; Italy: D744, D761, D812, D862, D923.

The graphs of the data are shown in Appendix. The calculations have been performed with the software program CATS for RATS, Hansen and Juselius (1994).

5.1. *Inference on parameter constancy*

Recursive test procedures (Hansen and Johansen (1993)) indicated major changes in both β and α at around 1983 for Germany (Juselius, 1996) and for Italy (Gennari and Juselius, 1998), but for Denmark the model was surprisingly constant when a step dummy at 1983:1 was included in the cointegration space (Juselius, 1998).

The instability in the model parameters at about 1983 is likely to be related to the so called "second *ERM*" in March 1983, when the *ERM* countries agreed to stop the previous quite frequent realignments. For Germany and Denmark it meant a change from a more flexible to an almost fixed *ERM*. For Italy the change of regime started in 1981:2 with the divorce between the Central bank and the Treasury. The actual transition took place over an extended period, and 1983 works probably reasonably well as a dividing date between the two regimes.

The significance of a regime change at 1983 was tested with an *LR* test, approximately distributed as $\chi^2(v)$, where v is the total number of estimated parameters in the cointegrated VAR model under the null of constant parameters. Due to the large numbers of parameters, the power of the test is probably low. Nevertheless, a large test statistic signals major changes in the model and can provide a motivation for splitting the sample.

Because the *VAR*-model is based on two lags, the effective sample size for the conditional data vector is two observations less than for x_t. When splitting the sample at 1983:1 we can either use 1983:1–2 as initial values or condition on 1982:3–4. The sum of the effective sample size of each sub-period is $T-2$ in the first case, but T in the second case, where T is the effective size of the full sample. Choosing the latter option the following test statistics were obtained:

$$\textit{Germany}: \quad \chi^2(117) = 346.0 \quad > \quad \chi^2_{.95} \simeq 147$$

$$\textit{Denmark}: \quad \chi^2(109) = 128.7 \quad < \quad \chi^2_{.95} \simeq 139$$

$$\textit{Italy}: \quad \chi^2(109) = 300.6 \quad > \quad \chi^2_{.95} \simeq 139$$

It appears that the null of parameter constancy is strongly rejected both for Germany and Italy, whereas for Denmark the assumption of parameter constancy seems appropriate when a shift in the cointegrating relations at 1983:1 has been allowed for (cf. Juselius, 1998).

Because of the many reforms at around 1983, the choice of sample split at 1983:1 is only indicative. Based on sensitivity analyses the following effective sample periods were chosen for further analyses:

Germany I: 1975:4-82:4 and Germany II: 1984:1-1994:4

Italy I: 1974:3-83:1 and Italy II: 1983:3-94:4.

5.2. *Misspecification tests and cointegration rank*

As a general check of the model we report in Tables 5.1–5.3 some multivariate and univariate misspecification tests for each sub-sample and country. A significant test statistic is given in bold face. We also report the estimated eigenvalues of the Π matrix, as well as the five largest roots of the characteristic polynomial.

As discussed in Section 4.3, the cointegration rank can be seen as an indication of how well markets adjust and, therefore, of market regulation. When the economy is more or less deregulated we expect two unit roots in the model. Our preferred hypothesis is, therefore, $\{r = 3, p - r = 2\}$, but in more regulated periods we expect r to be lower.

Following the arguments in Juselius (1998) the choice of cointegration rank is based on three different sources of information: (*i*) the eigenvalues of Π and the trace tests, (*ii*) the five largest roots of the model, and (*iii*) the t-values of the adjustment coefficients of the second and third eigenvector.

Table 5.1 shows no sign of misspecification for the German models. The degrees of freedom are low, particularly in the first period, and the results should be interpreted with this in mind. The R^2 is high except for the bond rate, which in Section 5.3 is found to be weakly exogenous. However, some of the large roots of the unrestricted model remain after restricting the rank to $r = 2$ and $r = 3$. Inspection of the α_{ir} coefficients showed significant adjustment to $\beta_r'x$ both for $r = 2$ and 3. All this is typical evidence that some variable(s) contain a near $I(2)$ unit root. For Germany I long-run price homogeneity was not empirically acceptable, but imposed nevertheless. Hence, $m - p$

Table 5.1. Misspecification tests and characteristic roots for Germany

Germany I					
Multivariate tests:					
Residual autocorr. LM_1	$\chi^2(25) = 21.04$			p-val.	0.69
LM_4	$\chi^2(25) = 25.54$			p-val.	0.43
Normality: LM	$\chi^2(10) = 13.41$			p-val.	0.20
Univariate tests:	Δm	Δy	Δp	ΔR_m	ΔR_b
ARCH(2)	2.95	3.77	0.06	1.29	0.89
Jarq. Bera(2)	0.17	0.50	2.97	0.22	0.48
R^2	0.79	0.98	0.99	0.67	0.36
Eigenvalues of the Π-matrix:	0.89	0.69	0.52	0.32	0.20
Modulus of 5 largest roots					
Unrestricted model:	0.88	0.88	0.85	0.76	0.76
$r = 3$	1.00	1.00	0.89	0.89	0.76
$r = 2$	1.00	1.00	1.00	0.88	0.69
Germany II					
Multivariate tests:					
Residual autocorr. LM_1	$\chi^2(25) = 26.57$			p-val.	0.38
LM_4	$\chi^2(25) = 36.58$			p-val.	0.06
Normality: LM	$\chi^2(10) = 9.63$			p-val.	0.47
Univariate tests:	Δm	Δy	Δp	ΔR_m	ΔR_b
ARCH(2)	0.71	1.74	1.45	2.96	0.56
Jarq. Bera(2)	1.34	0.09	0.56	3.34	0.78
R^2	0.95	0.97	0.99	0.72	0.40
Eigenvalues of the Π-matrix:	0.80	0.59	0.35	0.28	0.12
Modulus of 5 largest roots					
Unrestricted model:	0.96	0.96	0.94	0.94	0.74
$r = 3$	1.0	1.0	0.83	0.75	0.75
$r = 2$	1.0	1.0	1.0	0.77	0.76

Table 5.2. Misspecification tests and characteristic roots for Denmark

Multivariate tests:					
Residual autocorr. LM_1	$\chi^2(25) = 17.4$			p-val.	0.86
LM_4	$\chi^2(25) = 21.3$			p-val.	0.67
Normality: LM	$\chi^2(10) = 18.2$			p-val.	0.05
Univariate tests:	Δm	Δy	Δp	ΔR_m	ΔR_b
ARCH(2)	1.92	2.16	1.79	2.45	0.31
Jarq. Bera(2)	0.88	3.97	1.12	**9.12**	3.69
R^2	0.82	0.41	0.77	0.53	0.55
Eigenvalues of the Π-matrix:	0.57	0.35	0.26	0.11	0.06
Modulus of 5 largest roots					
Unrestricted model:	0.88	0.88	0.76	0.76	0.54
$r = 3$	1.0	1.0	0.81	0.68	0.68
$r = 2$	1.0	1.0	1.0	0.77	0.45

Table 5.3 Misspecification tests and characteristic roots for Italy

Italy I					
Multivariate tests:					
Residual autocorr. LM_1	$\chi^2(25) = 16.39$			p-val.	0.90
LM_4	$\chi^2(25) = 26.64$			p-val.	0.37
Normality: LM	$\chi^2(10) = 9.73$			p-val.	0.46
Univariate tests:	Δm	Δy	Δp	ΔR_m	ΔR_b
ARCH(2)	3.86	0.42	1.00	4.72	2.32
Jarq. Bera(2)	2.35	**9.89**	1.50	0.22	2.77
R^2	0.95	0.86	0.82	0.84	0.75
Eigenvalues of the Π-matrix:	0.77	0.67	0.50	0.26	0.09
Modulus of 5 largest roots					
Unrestricted model:	0.93	0.93	0.89	0.89	0.83
$r = 3$	1.0	1.0	0.88	0.88	0.79
$r = 2$	1.0	1.0	1.0	0.81	0.81
Italy II					
Multivariate tests:					
Residual autocorr. LM_1	$\chi^2(25) = 26.50$			p-val.	0.38
LM_4	$\chi^2(25) = 29.97$			p-val.	0.23
Normality: LM	$\chi^2(10) = 16.94$			p-val.	0.36
Univariate tests:	Δm	Δy	Δp	ΔR_m	ΔR_b
ARCH(2)	1.29	1.27	1.62	0.74	0.22
Jarq. Bera(2)	1.91	4.15	4.45	2.21	6.02
R^2	0.95	0.64	0.82	0.76	0.72
Eigenvalues of the Π-matrix:	0.62	0.42	0.40	0.20	0.15
Modulus of 5 largest roots					
Unrestricted model:	0.97	0.97	0.64	0.64	0.61
$r = 3$	1.0	1.0	0.82	0.71	0.71
$r = 2$	1.0	1.0	1.0	0.57	0.56

may not be $CI(2, 1)$, thus leaving an $I(2)$ component in real money stock. Because the stationarity of the "concentrated" VAR model remains valid, asymptotic inference still holds. Nevertheless, estimates based on the small sample of this study should be interpreted with some caution.

Because the third cointegration vector was strongly significant in the inflation and short-term interest equation we continue the analysis with the preferred case $r = 3$.

Denmark was found to have approximately constant parameters over the two sample periods and the misspecification tests reported in Table 5.2 are, therefore, for the full sample. There are no obvious signs of misspecification. The roots of the characteristic polynomial suggest two unit roots consistent with the preferred hypothesis and we continue with this assumption.

The misspecification tests in Table 5.3 for Italy are acceptable, except for a minor problem with normality in the first period. The roots of the characteristic polynomial suggest that $r = 2$ might be preferable to $r = 3$ in the first period. As for Germany I, long-run price homogeneity was not acceptable, but imposed nevertheless. Because $\beta_3' x_{t-1}$ exhibited strongly significant adjustment in money, income and inflation, we proceed with the preferred case

Table 5.4. Testing for weak exogeneity

r	$m-p$	y	Δp	R_m	R_b	$\chi^2(r)$
			Germany I			
2	9.25	19.09	27.81	**1.22**	**2.67**	5.99
3	10.17	25.66	33.77	11.31	**5.02**	7.81
			Germany II			
2	16.66	29.50	5.40	12.33	**5.35**	5.99
3	20.69	30.79	9.37	16.00	**5.95**	7.82
			Denmark			
2	10.36	**0.70**	39.33	**0.71**	**0.56**	5.99
3	19.35	**1.98**	50.05	11.47	**0.72**	7.82
			Italy I			
2	13.84	12.42	**2.21**	9.96	10.02	5.99
3	27.40	23.91	14.39	10.97	11.56	7.82
			Italy II			
2	**0.39**	10.63	6.84	**0.60**	6.24	5.99
3	**6.05**	20.89	12.78	**7.03**	17.75	7.82

$r = 3$ based on similar arguments as for Germany I. For the second period the preferred case seems appropriate.

Altogether, the models for Germany I and Italy I left a few quite large roots in the model. Because similarity in model design is important in a comparative study and because the statistical information in the data did not strongly suggest otherwise, we continue with the case $r = 3$ and $k = 2$. Nevertheless, there was some empirical support for $r = 2$ in the first periods, indicating less market adjustment and more regulations.

5.3. *Weak exogeneity for the long-run parameters β*

Because the choice of r was not completely straightforward, we report the test results of weak exogeneity for both $r = 2$ and 3. The test of weak exogeneity, $R\alpha = 0$, where R is a unit vector, is approximately distributed as $\chi^2(r)$. The results are reported in Table 5.4, where insignificant test values are indicated with bold face.

For Denmark and Germany the bond rate is found to be weakly exogenous for the long-run parameters β independently of the choice of r. If $r = 2$ the short-term interest rate would also become weakly exogenous in Germany I, indicating slow adjustment in the first more regulated period. For Denmark real income, in addition to the bond rate, is weakly exogenous, implying no long-run effects from monetary policy on real income.

For Italy II the short-term rate is found to be weakly exogenous independently of the choice of r, whereas Italy I has no weakly exogenous variables for $r = 3$. For $r = 2$ inflation would be weakly exogenous. The results for Italy I differ from the others and merit a closer inspection. The estimates in Section 7, Table 7.4 show that the bond rate is not adjusting to the short-term rate, whereas the latter is adjusting to the bond rate. In this sense Italy I is similar to Denmark and Germany. The rejection of the bond rate as weakly exogenous is because it is significantly affected by the output gap. This probably reflects the strong ties between the Italian Central Bank and the Treasury in the first period.

For Italy II both money stock and short-term interest rate are weakly exogenous, i.e., the Central Bank of Italy seems to have been able to exert both price and quantity control. This (exceptional) central bank autonomy can possibly be explained by the fact that Italy removed the restrictions on capital movements as late as 1989, left the *ERM* in 1992 and generally adopted the broad *ERM* bands. Another plausible explanation is that the econometric verification of money demand adjustment might have failed empirically because of measurement errors in Italian real GDP due to the probably considerable size of the black economy. This might have led to a systematic underestimation of real GDP.

Altogether, the finding of weak exogeneity is not invariant to the choice of r. Assuming $r = 2$ both the short-term deposit rate and the long-term bond rate had been weakly exogenous for Germany I and Denmark. In this case the two interest rates would have acted as two independent driving trends and, thus, provided very strong evidence against the expectation's hypothesis. Assuming $r = 3$ the role of the long-term bond rate as an important driving force remains in the model. This is particularly so in the capital deregulated economies with strong bands on exchange rates. The classification of short-term interest rate as "endogenously" adjusting to the bond rate, or as weakly exogenous, depending on the choice of r, demonstrates how crucial this choice is.

6. Comparing cointegration properties

Section 4.2 showed that two common stochastic trends produce cointegration between sets of either two or three variables. Using this the strength of cointegration between the variables discussed in Section 3.2 have been systematically investigated.

The investigated hypotheses are of the form $\beta = \{H\phi_1, \psi_1, \psi_2\}$, i.e. we test whether a single restricted relation lies in $sp(\beta)$, while leaving the other relations unrestricted. For a derivation of the test procedure, see Johansen and Juselius (1992). The results for all countries and periods are reported in Tables 6.1–6.4, where $\tilde{x}$ implies "trend adjusted x", p-values are given in square brackets, "yes" means cointegration, and "yes, but" means cointegration but no support for the hypothetical *ISLM* reaction pattern of Section 2.3. Bold face means both empirical and theoretical support. An extensive presentation of the results can be found in Juselius (1996, 1998), and Gennari and Juselius (1998).

6.1. Is monetary expansion cointegrated with inflation?

In Table 6.1 we compare the cointegration properties of inflation, the goal variable, with the intermediate target variables: trend-adjusted velocity and trend-adjusted real income, respectively. For instance, if monetary expansion always leads to inflation we would expect inflation to cointegrate positively with trend-adjusted velocity. Germany I, Italy I and II show evidence of this,

Table 6.1. Comparing cointegration of inflation with money expansion and demand pressure, respectively

	$\widetilde{vel} - a_2 \Delta p \sim I(0)$	$\tilde{y} - a_6 \Delta p \sim I(0)$
Germany I	**yes [0.32]**	**yes [0.45]**
Germany II	yes, but $a_2 < 0$ [0.18]	**yes [0.56]**
Denmark	no	yes, but $a_6 < 0$ [0.53]
Italy I	**yes [0.88]**	**yes, [0.12]**
Italy II	**yes [0.34]**	no

Table 6.2. Comparing cointegration of interest rate with money expansion and demand pressure, respectively

	$\widetilde{vel} + a_1 R_m \sim I(0)$	$\tilde{y} + a_5 R_m \sim I(0)$	$\tilde{y} + a_5 R_b \sim I(0)$
Germany I	$\widetilde{vel} \sim I(0)$	no	no
Germany II	yes?, [0.07]	yes, but $a_5 < 0$, [0.92]	yes, but $a_5 < 0$, [0.38]
Denmark	**yes [0.41]**	no	no
Italy I	yes, but $a_1 < 0$, [0.08]	yes, but $a_5 < 0$, [0.15]	no
Italy II	yes, but $a_1 < 0$, [0.99]	no	yes, but $a_5 < 0$, [0.06]

whereas in Germany II there is significant cointegration but with the "wrong" sign.

As discussed in section 2.3, monetary expansion can also be inflationary through demand pressure. Therefore, positive cointegration between inflation and trend-adjusted real income can also indicate monetary transmission effects. In Germany I and II, and Italy I we found empirical support for this. In Denmark there is cointegration but with the "wrong" sign, and in Italy II there is no cointegration.

Altogether, Germany I and Italy I and II seem to provide empirical support for inflation being related to monetary expansion. In Germany II and Denmark, the deregulated high *PPP* countries, no such evidence was found. Instead, trend-adjusted real income was negatively related to inflation.

6.2. *Is short-term interest rate negatively cointegrated with monetary expansion?*

The cointegration results reported in Table 6.2 do not give much support to a negative transmission effect between interest rate and monetary expansion, as the standard mechanism of the ISLM model would predict. Cointegration is found, but the coefficients have the "wrong" signs, with the exception of Denmark. In the latter case the negative effect disappears when the bond rate is included. See Table 7.1.

Similarly, theory predicts on one hand that increasing interest rates would lower the demand for investments and, hence, decrease real aggregate demand, i.e. the *IS* effect but, on the other hand, that excess aggregate demand would increase interest rates. To distinguish between the two cases, the ad-

Table 6.3. Comparing bivariate cointegration properties of inflation and interest rates

	$\Delta p \sim I(0)$	$R_m - \Delta p \sim I(0)$	$R_b - \Delta p \sim I(0)$	$R_m - R_b \sim I(0)$
Germany I	no	no	no	yes?, [0.10]
Germany II	no	**yes, [0.69]**	**yes, [0.20]**	no
Denmark	no	no	no	no[1)]
Italy I	no	no	no	no
Italy II	no	yes?, [0.05]	yes?, [0.10]	yes?, [0.08]

[1)] If we relax the restriction $(1, -1)$ there is strong evidence that $R_m - 0.5R_b$ is $I(0)$.

Table 6.4. Comparing trivariate cointegration properties between interest rates and inflation rate

	$R_m - a_3 R_b - (1 - a_3)\Delta p \sim I(0)$	$(R_m - R_b) - a_3 \Delta p \sim I(0)$
Germany I	no [0.06]	$\mathbf{a_3 = 1.84}$ **[0.11]**
Germany II	$a_3 = -0.45$ [0.73]	$\mathbf{a_3 = 0.83}$ **[0.41]**
Denmark	no [0.04]	no
Italy I	$\mathbf{a_3 = 0.58}$ **[0.29]**	$\mathbf{a_3 = 1.49}$ **[0.44]**
Italy II	no [0.03]	no [0.04]

justment structure has to be examined as well. Here we focus on cointegration properties and leave the assessment of the adjustment to the next section.

Germany I and Denmark exhibit no evidence of direct cointegration between the output gap and any of the interest rates. Germany II shows strong support for *positive* cointegration, whereas in Italy this is only weakly supported. Altogether the demand pressure effect on interest rates seems predominant.

6.3. *Are interest rates and inflation cointegrated?*

The Fisher parity (2.4) and the term structure of interest rates (2.5) predict one nominal stochastic trend. The cointegration results presented in Table 6.3 show no convincing evidence for both real interest rates and the interest rate spread to be jointly stationary in any country or period.

Both for Germany I and Italy I the adjustment to the Fisher parity and the term structure is very weak, supporting the hypothesis that cointegration is more difficult to find in a regulated than in an unregulated economy. Strong evidence of the Fisher parity is only found in Germany II. Weak support of interest parity is found in Germany I and Italy II, whereas for Denmark there is strong support for the stationarity of the modified spread $R_m - 0.5R_b$.

The finding of two stochastic trends driving inflation and the interest rates, makes it relevant to look at cointegration properties between all three variables. The results are reported in Table 6.4.

We first test the hypothesis of homogeneity between short-term interest rate relative to the long-term bond rate and the inflation rate, and then the

Central Bank policy rule (2.2), i.e. whether the interest rate spread is related to inflation. The homogeneity hypothesis is supported for Italy I[1], whereas support for the Central Bank policy rule is found in Germany I + II and Italy I.

Credit regulations, controls on capital movements, etc. is *ceteris paribus* likely to lower adjustment towards perceived steady-states and might explain the finding of two stochastic trends between inflation and the two interest rates. However, this explanation seems more plausible in the first period, but is not so obvious in the more recent period.

For Denmark the strong dependency on Germany explains the difficulty of pursuing an independent monetary policy. For Italy II the results suggest that the interest rate spread is only weakly stationary, i.e. the adjustment between the short-term and the long-term interest rates and the inflation rate is less pronounced in the second period then in the first. This can be explained by the increased Central Bank independence after the divorce from the Treasury, and by Italy maintaining restrictions on capital movements and relatively flexible exchange rates.

7. Comparing the combined effects

In this section we compare the combined cointegration effects as measured by the row estimates of $\Pi = \alpha\beta'$ for $r = 3$. We have chosen Π instead of the identified α and β because the rows of Π, contrary to α and β, are invariant to linear transformations in the sense that $\Pi = \alpha PP^{-1}\beta' = \tilde{\alpha}\tilde{\beta}'$, where P is a nonsingular $r \times r$ matrix. Bold face is used to indicate a significant t-value.

In Table 7.1. we compare the first rows of Π which measures the combined cointegration effect on *money stock*. For Germany II, Denmark, and possibly Italy II money stock seems to adjust to money demand with plausible opportunity cost effects (cf. (2.1)). For Italy I money stock is not significantly adjusting to velocity but the coefficients of interest rates and inflation are consistent with money demand. As already mentioned long-run price homogeneity could not be established in this period because money stock corrected for real GDP has grown much faster than prices.

With the exception of Germany I, money stock seems to be a realization of the demand for money with own interest rate as the most important determinant. Only in Germany II and Denmark, i.e. the financially deregulated economies, is the long-term bond rate strongly significant in the money demand relation. Inflation has a negative (demand) effect on money stock in Denmark and Italy I. In Germany I alone there is evidence of the Central Bank policy rule determining money stock.

In particular, the strong own interest rate effects on money demand, implies that an increase in central bank interest rate is not likely to decrease the equilibrium level of money stock, if the private bank deposit rates follow central bank interest rates. Agents are willing to hold more money, and, hence, the increase in money stock is not inflationary. This can explain the previous finding that inflation and monetary expansion were negatively cointegrated in Germany II, Denmark and Italy I.

In Table 7.2. we compare the second row of Π, measuring the combined

[1] The stationarity of real interest rates in Germany II explains the negative coefficient of a_3.

Table 7.1. Comparing real money stock relations of the Π matrix

	$m-p$	y	Δp	R_m	R_b	*Trend*	*Dummy*
Germany I	0.12	−0.04	**2.27**	**−1.74**	**2.26**	−0.001	–
Germany II	**−0.26**	**0.28**	−0.36	**1.39**	**−5.86**	−0.001	*0.02*
Denmark	**−0.30**	**0.30**	−0.03	**5.32**	**−4.76**	–	0.04
Italy I	−0.03	*−0.28*	**−1.19**	**5.17**	**−2.77**	**0.002**	–
Italy II	−0.20	**0.45**	−0.95	**3.80**	−0.65	−0.000	–

Table 7.2. Comparing real income relations of the π matrix

	$m-p$	y	Δp	R_m	R_b	*Trend*	*Dummy*
Germany I	**0.45**	**−0.49**	**1.22**	−0.37	*0.90*	**−0.003**	–
Germany II	**0.22**	**−1.43**	**2.15**	−0.01	**7.64**	**0.008**	**0.09**
Denmark	0.02	−0.05	−0.18	−1.70	0.94	–	−0.00
Italy I	**0.12**	**−0.29**	−0.28	**−1.19**	**0.74**	**0.002**	–
Italy II	0.07	**−0.15**	**1.31**	**−2.08**	**−0.66**	0.000	–

Table 7.3. Comparing inflation relations of the π matrices

	$m-p$	y	Δp	R_m	R_b	*Trend*	*Dummy*
Germany I	*0.06*	**−0.13**	**−2.30**	**1.65**	**−1.93**	−0.00	–
Germany II	**0.05**	*0.13*	**−0.87**	0.26	0.04	**−0.001**	**−0.017**
Denmark	0.02	**−0.15**	**−1.66**	*1.71*	−0.40	–	−0.006
Italy I	−0.05	**0.23**	**−1.04**	**−1.26**	−0.64	*0.001*	–
Italy II	**0.11**	−0.02	**−0.69**	**0.83**	0.03	**−0.001**	–

cointegration effect on *real income*. There are significant real money effects in Germany and Italy I, signifying a potential role of monetary policy to influence real growth in economies with monetary autonomy. There are negative short-term interest rate effects on real *GDP* (though significantly so only for Italy I and II) consistent with the *IS* relation, whereas the long-term bond rate is mostly positively related to trend-adjusted real income. Only Italy II provides some evidence of a negative *real* interest rate effect. The real income-inflation effects confirm the demand pressure/short-run Phillips curve effects of Table 6.1.

In Table 7.3 we report the estimates of the third row of Π, measuring the combined cointegration effects on *inflation*. Germany II and Italy II exhibits significantly positive real money effects and in Italy I there is evidence of demand pressure effects on inflation, consistent with the results in Table 6.1. Except for Italy I the short-term interest rate is positively related to inflation, suggesting that increases in the short-term interest rate do not necessarily decrease inflation in the short-run. The long-run impact is investigated in the next section.

Table 7.4 reports the estimates of the *interest rate* rows of the Π matrix. Since the bond rate was weakly exogenous except for Italy, the bond rate

Table 7.4. Comparing interest rate relations of the Π matrix

	$m-p$	y	Δp	R_m	R_b	*Trend*	*Dummy*
			Deposit rate relations R_m				
Germany I	−0.01	**0.07**	*−0.18*	**−0.38**	**0.52**	**−0.00**	
Germany II	**0.01**	**0.02**	0.05	**−0.18**	**0.23**	**−0.00**	**−0.004**
Denmark	*−0.01*	0.00	0.00	**−0.31**	*0.10*	–	**0.002**
Italy I	**0.01**	**−0.01**	**0.07**	**−0.14**	**0.14**	**0.00**	–
Italy II	**−0.01**	**0.01**	0.02	0.04	−0.02	0.00	–
			Bond rate relations R_b				
Italy I	**−0.02**	**0.07**	**−0.11**	0.03	**−0.20**	**−0.00**	
Italy II	**0.05**	0.01	0.06	0.18	**−0.39**	**0.00**	–

equations are only reported for this country. Among the most striking results is the very weak (almost non-existing) effect of inflation combined with the significant effect of the long-term bond rate. The only exception is Italy II for which the short-term interest rate is essentially weakly exogenous. Interest rates show minor demand pressure effects and, for Italy, liquidity effects.

A comparison of the estimates of the *short-term rate* and *bond rate* equations for Italy I and II suggests a change in the transmission mechanisms between the two periods. In the first period the short-term rate adjusts to the long-term bond rate, but not vice versa, whereas in the second period the long-term bond rate adjusts to the short-term interest rate[2], but not vice versa. The increased central bank independence can explain this result.

Altogether, the presence of free capital movements combined with narrow exchange rate bands might explain the weak exogeneity of the bond rate (absence of long-run feedback effects) and the adjustment of short-term interest to the long-term rate. Italy II with restrictions on capital movement all through the eighties and with broad exchange rate bands is the only exception to this finding.

8. Comparing the long-run impact

In this section we investigate the long-run impact of unanticipated "shocks" to the system. Because the conditional expectation $E_{t-1}\{\Delta x_t \mid \Delta x_{t-1}, \beta x_{t-1}\}$ has optimal properties as a predictor of Δx_t, we choose the residuals $\hat{\varepsilon}_{it}$ from (4.1) as estimates of the unanticipated shocks associated with variable x_i. The estimates of $C = \beta_\perp(\alpha'_\perp \Gamma \beta_\perp)^{-1}\alpha'_\perp$ in (4.2), where the orthogonal complements $\beta_\perp$ and $\alpha_\perp$ are based on the unrestricted estimates of α and β, are reported in Tables 8.1–8.3. The coefficients are calculated for the non-standardized residuals and the standard errors are reported separately. The average linear growth in real money stock and real income over the period estimated by $C\mu$ in (4.2) are reported under the heading "trend". Standard errors of estimates are calculated using results in Paruolo (1997). Significant coefficients with a p-value of 0.05 or less are indicated with bold face, whereas those with a p-value of approximately 0.30–0.05 are indicated with italics.

[2] For $r = 2$ this effect is strongly significant.

Table 8.1. The long-run impact matrix, C, for Germany

	$\Sigma\hat{\varepsilon}_{m_i}$	$\Sigma\hat{\varepsilon}_{y_i}$	$\Sigma\hat{\varepsilon}_{\Delta p_i}$	$\Sigma\hat{\varepsilon}_{Rm_i}$	$\Sigma\hat{\varepsilon}_{Rb_i}$
			Germany I		
$\hat{\sigma}_\varepsilon$	0.0075	0.0048	0.0027	0.0013	0.0011
$m-p$	**2.05**	*−0.99*	*1.90*	0.86	*−8.45*
y	**1.97**	*−0.86*	*1.72*	−0.22	−5.04
Δp	**0.11**	*−0.04*	*0.09*	−0.05	−0.16
R_m	0.21	−0.00	0.07	*−1.03*	**2.43**
R_b	−0.03	0.08	−0.10	*−0.78*	**2.37**
trend	0.0100	0.0033	−0.0002	−0.0004	−0.0002
			Germany II		
$\hat{\sigma}_\varepsilon$	0.0047	0.0071	0.0029	0.0005	0.0008
$m-p$	−0.76	−0.35	−0.78	*15.37*	**−23.11**
y	1.13	0.53	1.33	−3.14	10.74
Δp	0.24	0.11	0.29	−0.09	1.61
R_m	0.42	0.20	0.51	0.30	2.24
R_b	0.17	0.08	0.20	−0.81	*2.02*
trend	0.0067	0.0067	0.0003	0.0002	0.0000

The results reported in Table 8.1. for Germany I and II differ considerably. In the first period unanticipated shocks to real money have a significant long-run effect on inflation, but also on real *GDP*. Hence, monetary expansion seems to have affected long-run (or medium long-run) real growth contrary to conventional monetary beliefs. In the second period the significance of monetary shocks drops considerably.

In the first period inflationary shocks tend to increase money stock, in the second the effect is negative (though not significantly so) consistent with a money demand effect. In the first period there is some evidence of inflationary shocks having long-run effects on real *GDP*, but essentially no effects on interest rates.

Of the two interest rates, the unanticipated shocks to the bond rate have a much stronger long-run impact on real money stock. Consistent with the weak exogeneity results, shocks to the bond rate are driving the short-term interest rate, but not vice versa.

To summarize, monetary shocks seem to have become less important and shocks to the bond rate more important. The linear trend estimates show that real money stock grew much faster than real *GDP* in the first period, whereas the growth rates are identical in the second period.

The empirical results of Italy I and II are reported in Table 8.2. Similarly to Germany I, unanticipated shocks to real money stock seem to have a long-run impact on inflation and real *GDP* in both periods, as well as on short interest rate in the first period. Unanticipated shocks to the short interest rate have a strong and positive impact on real money stock and on inflation in both periods. The impact on real *GDP* is negative in the second period and not significant in the first. The short-term rate is driving the long-term bond

Table 8.2. The long-run impact matrix, C, for Italy

	$\Sigma\hat{\varepsilon}_m$	$\Sigma\hat{\varepsilon}_y$	$\Sigma\hat{\varepsilon}_{\Delta p}$	$\Sigma\hat{\varepsilon}_{Rm}$	$\Sigma\hat{\varepsilon}_{Rb}$
			Italy I		
$\hat{\sigma}_\varepsilon$	0.0100	0.0043	0.0061	0.0005	0.0012
$m-p$	**0.96**	**−1.35**	*1.44*	**33.36**	0.21
y	**0.30**	−0.29	0.32	**10.62**	1.10
Δp	0.00	**−0.07**	**0.07**	−0.06	**−0.54**
R_m	**0.02**	−0.01	−0.01	*0.75*	**0.30**
R_b	−0.00	**0.09**	**−0.09**	0.02	**0.67**
trend	0.0007	0.0061	0.0001	0.0002	0.0004
			Italy II		
$\hat{\sigma}_\varepsilon$	0.0104	0.0037	0.0022	0.0003	0.0011
$m-p$	**0.29**	**1.08**	*1.57*	6.45	*−2.50*
y	**0.38**	**0.64**	0.44	−4.90	−1.48
Δp	0.02	**0.28**	**0.55**	**4.13**	−0.65
R_m	−0.02	*0.09*	*0.24*	**2.39**	−0.21
R_b	0.04	**0.23**	**0.40**	**2.48**	*−0.54*
trend	0.0079	0.0051	−0.0001	−0.0002	−0.0002

Table 8.3. The long-run impact matrix, C, for Denmark

	$\Sigma\hat{\varepsilon}_m$	$\Sigma\hat{\varepsilon}_y$	$\Sigma\hat{\varepsilon}_{\Delta p}$	$\Sigma\hat{\varepsilon}_{Rm}$	$\Sigma\hat{\varepsilon}_{Rb}$
$\hat{\sigma}_\varepsilon$	0.021	0.015	0.0127	0.0011	0.0014
$m-p$	0.03	**0.58**	−0.17	−0.44	**−14.45**
y	0.13	**1.12**	−0.14	−4.05	−2.60
Δp	−0.01	**−0.09**	0.01	−0.31	*0.40*
R_m	−0.00	0.01	−0.00	−0.13	**0.68**
R_b	−0.01	**0.05**	0.01	−0.38	**1.51**
trend	0.0026	0.0031	−0.0003	−0.0000	0.0001

rate and inflation in the second period, whereas in the first period it is the other way around.

The results of Denmark are reported in Table 8.3. The lack of any significant long-run effects from monetary shocks are striking, as are the significant effects of unanticipated shocks to real *GDP* on all variables in the system. In particular, the significant, though small, coefficients of real income shocks to the interest rates, signifies the demand pressure effects on nominal interest rates. Another important result is the strong and significant effect of unanticipated shocks to the bond rate on almost all variables of the system. There are positive effects from the bond rate to inflation, but essentially no effects from inflation to nominal interest rates.

To summarize: The results seem to support the prior hypothesis that monetary policy has become rather ineffective in both Germany and Denmark, both being relatively high *PPP* countries at the start of the *EMS* with strong bands on the exchange rates in the second period. Unanticipated shocks to the bond rate have important long-run effects in all countries and periods except Italy II, the only country that maintained capital regulation until late in the eighties. These findings point to the importance of understanding the role of capital liberalization for European monetary transmission mechanisms.

9. Summary and Conclusions

The purpose of the paper was to compare the dynamic adjustment effects of excess demand/supply of money, excess aggregate demand, and Central Bank reaction rule on price inflation, money growth, real income growth and changes in interest rates in the period before and after 1983 for three European countries, Germany, Denmark, and Italy.

In the post 1983 period we found strong empirical support for money demand determining real money stock. Most of the money demand relations exhibited strong positive own interest rate effects and negative bond rate effects. The more deregulated the economy, the stronger was the bond effect. Therefore, money stock did not seem to be an appropriate monetary target in particular in the deregulated economies with narrow exchange rate bands.

The short-run monetary expansion effects on inflation were mostly small and insignificant. The long-run impact of monetary expansion on inflation and real GDP growth was quite strong and significant for Germany I and Italy I + II, but not for Denmark and Germany II. There was essentially no evidence of shocks to the short-term interest rate having a long-run impact on inflation in any country or period.

The latter result is related to the weak exogeneity of the bond rate in the narrow bands *ERM* regimes and the adjustment of the short-term interest rate to the bond rate. Italy II is the only exception to this. Altogether, in economies with free capital movements and narrow exchange bands, the level of the bond rate seems to be internationally determined and, hence, outside domestic monetary control. Hence, the argument that monetary policy is effective through the control of short-term interest rates does not get support in this period, except possibly in the short run.

We found no empirical support for the Fisher parity, not even for inflation to have any significant effect on the interest rates.

The empirical results seem mostly to support the prior assumption that the scope for pursuing an independent monetary policy in Germany was significantly larger in the period before 1983 than after, that it was very small for Denmark both before and after, and that monetary policy worked reasonably well for Italy in both periods, though in the first period the strong ties to the Treasury aggravated short-term interest control.

Altogether, the increased economic integration within the *EC* seems to have produced major changes in the macroeconomic transmission mechanisms and significantly decreased the scope for domestic monetary policy. In the first period, with higher domestic monetary autonomy, we found significant long-run monetary effects on inflation but also on real GDP growth. This suggests that the macroeconomic costs of giving up monetary independence within the *EMS* have been considerable. These costs are likely to persist in the planned EMU, in particular if we assume that asymmetric shocks will be frequent and that there will be no compensating fiscal transfer within a near future.

Acknowledgments. This paper has benefitted from very detailed and useful comments from two unknown referees, from Mike Artis, and the participants at the workshop in Copenhagen, October, 4–5th 1997 and in the conference on European money demand in Berlin, October 10–11th 1997. Financial support from the Danish Social Sciences Research Council is gratefully acknowledged.

Appendix: The data

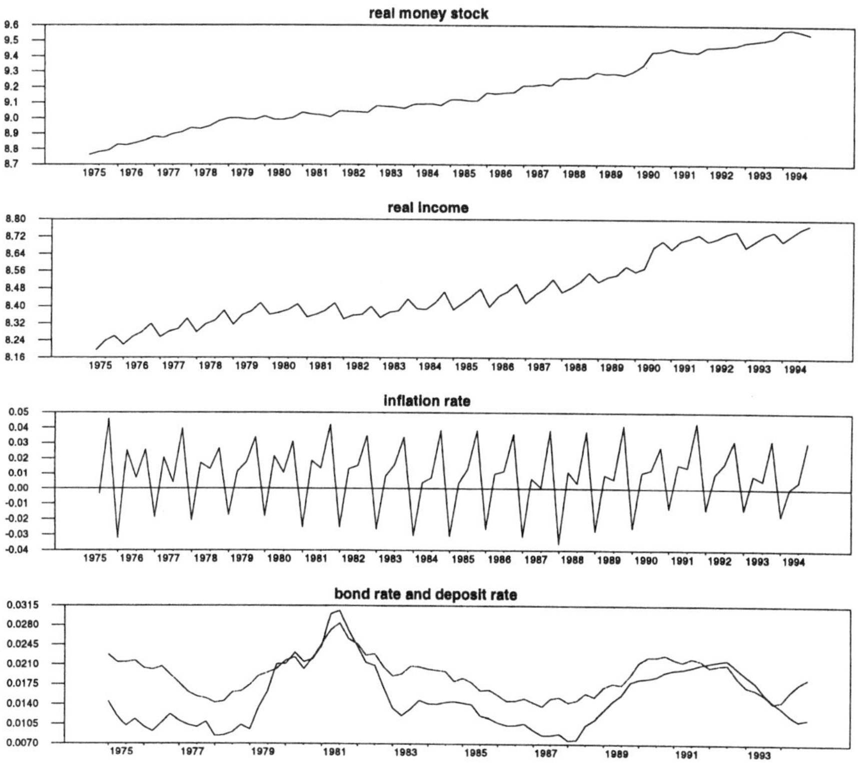

Fig. 9.1. The graphs of the German data

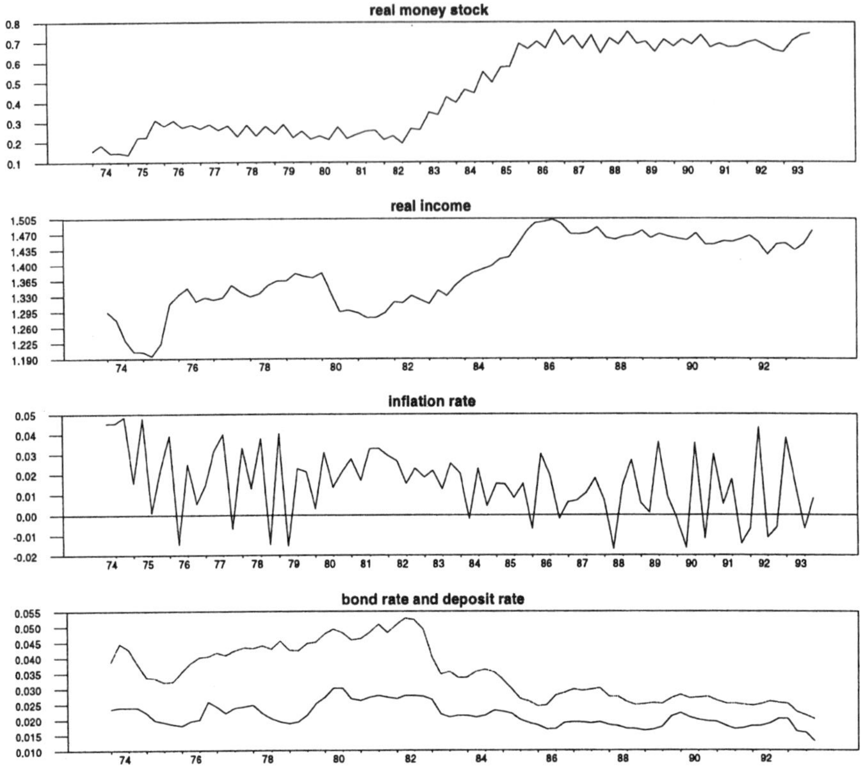

Fig. 9.2. The graphs of the Danish data

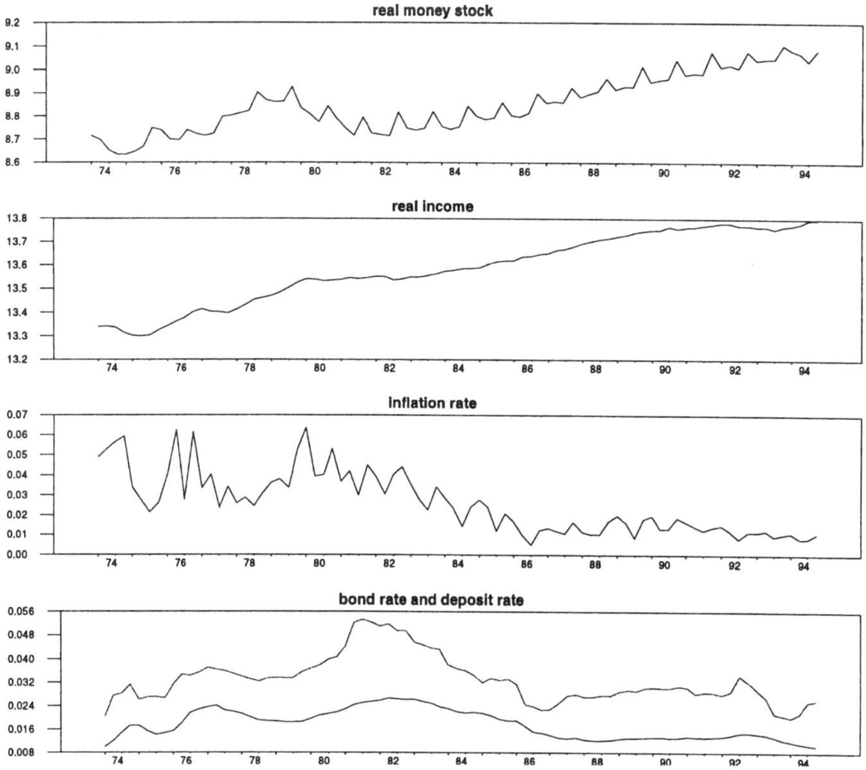

Fig. 9.3. The graphs of the Italian data

References

Gennari E, Juselius K (1998) Monetary transmission mechanisms in Italy. Unpublished manuscript at the European University Institute

Hansen H, Johansen S (1993) Recursive estimation in cointegrated VAR-models. Preprint 1, Institute of Mathematical Statistics, University of Copenhagen

Hansen H, Juselius K (1994) CATS in RATS. Manual to Cointegration Analysis of Time Series, Estima, Evanstone, IL

Hendry DF, Mizon GE (1993) Evaluating econometric models by encompassing the VAR. In: Phillips PC (ed.) Models, methods and applications of econometrics, Basil Blackwell, Oxford

Johansen S, Juselius K (1992) Testing structural hypotheses in a multivariate cointegration analysis of the *PPP* and the UIP for UK. Journal of Econometrics 53:211–244

Juselius K (1996) An empirical analysis of the changing role of the German Bundesbank after 1983. Oxford Bulletin of Economics and Statistics 58:791–819

Juselius K (1998) A structured VAR under changing monetary policy. Forthcoming in Journal of Business and Economic Statistics

Kenen PB (1995) Economic and monetary union in Europe. Cambridge University Press

Laidler DEW (1985) The demand for money. Theories and evidence. Harper and Row. New York

Paruolo P (1997) Asymptotic inference on the moving average impact matrix in cointegrated I(1) VAR systems. Econometric Theory 13:79–118

Long run money demand in the EU: Evidence for area-wide aggregates

Gabriel Fagan, Jérôme Henry*

European Monetary Institute, MESD Stage Three Division, Postfach 10 20 31, D-60020 Frankfurt am Main, Germany (e-mail: gf.gfagan.hg.eunet.de)

Abstract: Long-run properties of EU-wide money aggregates are analysed. For each of the three aggregates considered – Currency, M1 and M3H – it is possible to obtain cointegrating relationships with GDP and interest rates (long or short term market interest rates). Results are not improved when traditional aggregates, obtained by aggregating existing national aggregates, are extended by the inclusion of various measures of Cross-Border Holdings. Specific attention is also paid to aggregation issues and the relative performance of area-wide and national equations. The results show that aggregation bias is not a major problem and that the relatively good area-wide performance is largely a consequence of a statistical averaging effect.

Key words: Money demand, cross-country comparisons, European Union, aggregation, monetary targeting

JEL classification: E41, E52

1. Introduction

There is a general consensus that the empirical properties of the demand for money are an important consideration in influencing the choice of monetary

---

* Both authors are in the Stage Three Division of the Monetary, Economics and Statistics Department of the European Monetary Institute. The authors would like to thank colleagues at the EMI and participants at an EMI conference on EU money demand, held in 1995, for helpful comments and suggestions. Comments received from participants in the 1997 Econometric Society European Meeting and in the Workshop on Money Demand at Berlin Humboldt Universität in 1997 are also gratefully acknowledged. The final version benefited from comments by the editors and two anonymous referees. Opinions expressed in the paper are only those of the authors and do not necessarily represent the views of the EMI.

policy strategy. In particular, in the context of the preparations of monetary policy in Stage 3 "it is recognised that the long-term stability of money demand in the euro area is a crucial factor determining the effectiveness and scope of monetary targeting" (EMI, 1997). Against this background, the present paper presents the results of recent empirical research which has been carried out within the EMI on area-wide money demand in the EU14 countries (i.e. all EU countries excluding Luxembourg[1]). The main focus is on the long-term relationship between various measures of money, on the one hand, and real income, interest rates and prices on the other.

Although there are numerous studies of money demand for individual EU countries, interest in the properties of EU-wide money demand is only a comparatively recent phenomenon but has grown considerably and a number of empirical studies addressing this topic have been produced.[2] These studies have estimated equations for various country groupings and various area-wide measures of money, i.e. equations for aggregates comprising a composite of national money stocks, suitably aggregated, specified as a function of real income and prices in the area as a whole and average interest rates. The aggregates considered have ranged from narrower aggregates such as M1 to extended M3H aggregates including cross-border deposits. While the underlying specifications have been relatively uncomplicated – with real money balances being typically expressed as a function of real income and either short or long term market interest rates – the equations generally have very satisfactory properties from the point of view of both economic and statistical considerations. Indeed, it is frequently argued that such area-wide equations have, in general, superior empirical properties (e.g. a high degree of stability, relatively good equation fit etc.) than comparable equations for individual countries. The reasons for this apparently superior performance remain unclear but a number of hypotheses have been put forward to explain it, including the internalisation of currency substitution and the effects of cross-border trade and capital flows in the area-wide aggregate.

The present paper seeks to build on, and to extend, the existing literature in a number of respects. Firstly, as noted in Browne, Fagan and Henry (1997), considerable difficulties have been encountered in a number of EU countries when attempting to derive an appropriate empirical measure of the money stock; in order to throw some light on this issue in an area-wide context, the present paper presents empirical results for three aggregates – "Notes and Coins" (NC), M1 and M3H.[3] In addition, following Monticelli (1996), we also consider a number of 'extended' broad money aggregates which include various measures of cross-border holdings. Secondly, in carrying out an area-wide analysis, the issue of how to combine national data to form area-wide aggregates arises. In this respect, different methods have been proposed including fixed base period exchange rates, PPP exchange rates and current exchange rates. In order to assess this issue two aggregation methods are

[1] Due to data availability problems, data for Luxembourg were not included in the calculation of area-wide aggregates.

[2] See Browne, Fagan and Henry (1997) for a survey of such studies.

[3] M1 was first studied by Bekx and Tullio (1989), whereas Monticelli and Strauss-Kahn (1992) preferred to focus on M3. The use of weighted-sum aggregates – as in Spencer (1997) – has not been considered for reasons of data problems, regarding e.g. the availability of own interest rates for all components of the money stocks in the various countries.

employed and compared, namely current exchange rates and a fixed-weight index method (see Appendix 1).[4] Thirdly, while most studies have employed cointegration approaches based on the two-step least squares method, there now exists a much wider range of econometric techniques which may also be used in the context of cointegration.[5] Therefore, in order to assess the robustness of the results, the long-run properties of money demand are analysed according to a variety of econometric methods.

Finally, a key issue which must be addressed if area-wide equations are found to perform as well as, or better than, national equations is the reason for this superior performance. This issue is of crucial importance from the point of view of Stage 3. For example, it has been argued that the superior performance of area-wide equations is a 'statistical fluke' which reflects specific circumstances in Stage 2, such as desynchronisation of financial innovation and other negatively correlated idiosyncratic shocks to money demand in individual countries [Arnold (1994)]. In this view, the adoption of a single monetary policy and increasing financial integration will radically change this situation, leading to a much greater degree of synchronisation of shocks across countries, possibly leading to a much less stable money demand function than that estimated using area-wide data from Stage 2. Given the importance of this issue, the present paper devotes considerable attention to an investigation of the properties of area-wide money demand. This is achieved by a comparison of some of the area-wide equations with comparably specified national equations.

The remainder of this paper is structured as follows. Section 2 provides an overview of the data and aggregation methods employed. In Section 3 the results of an examination of the long run time-series properties of the data in the context of multivariate cointegration analysis of systems comprising real money, real income and interest rates are presented. The objective of this analysis is to assess whether a long-run relation between various measures of money and income and interest rates exists and is stable. Building on the insights provided by the multivariate analysis, Section 4 presents the results of single-equation approaches for estimation of long-run money demand functions. In this section we also consider aggregates containing cross border holdings. In Section 5 the performance of area-wide long-run equations is examined in more detail by comparison with correspondingly specified national equations in order to throw light on possible sources of the 'superior' performance of area-wide equations. Section 6 concludes.

2. Data sources and aggregation methods

2.1 Sources

As noted earlier, there is considerable uncertainty surrounding the appropriate definition of the money stock and a range of monetary aggregates have been examined in the various EU-wide and national studies, although the majority of the recent ones have tended to focus on broad money. Against this back-

[4] See Falk and Funke (1995) or Monticelli and Strauss-Kahn (1992) for similar approaches.

[5] Bearing in mind, however, that small sample problems may arise in terms of the interpretation of the resulting estimates.

ground, this paper also looks at the properties of a number of different aggregates, in particular a broad aggregate M3H, a narrow aggregate M1 and notes and coins held by the public, denoted NC. In all cases, the area-wide aggregate corresponds to the EU14 group of countries. In addition, extended broad money aggregates incorporating cross border holdings are also examined.

The principal source for the data on monetary aggregates is the 'building blocks' database compiled by the EMI Statistics division from data submitted by national central banks. Where the data did not cover a sufficiently long time span, they were linked to related national series available in the building blocks or BIS databank. Breaks in time series were dealt with by adjusting backdata to give a continuous historical series (e.g. the adjustment for German unification was performed rescaling the whole span of data at a pan-German level).[6] Data on cross border holdings were obtained from the BIS. Other data – real GDP, GDP deflators, short-term money market rates and long-term bond yields – are taken mainly from the BIS databank. In some cases, additional data from the IMF, the OECD or national accounts have also been used. The data employed in this study is quarterly, seasonally adjusted covering the period 1981Q1 to 1994Q4. All econometric tests have been carried out using the RATS package.

2.2 Aggregation

In order to compute area-wide aggregate variables it is necessary to employ a consistent method of compiling area-wide variables. In existing empirical work on area-wide money demand, different aggregation methods have been employed and it is fair to say that, up to now, there is no consensus as to the appropriate method (see Appendix 1 for a short discussion of some of the available methods). Thus, in order to assess the sensitivity of the results to differences in aggregation methods, two aggregation methods are employed here:

- Current exchange rate: The nominal money and output series, as well as deflators for each country were converted into Ecu. The first two series were then aggregated to yield area-wide nominal money and output in Ecu. As to prices, the area-wide variable is a weighted average of the deflators with the weights being the share of each country's nominal GDP in area-wide GDP. Real money and income were calculated by dividing the nominal series by the calculated area-wide GDP deflator.[7] Interest rate data were compiled as weighted averages of the corresponding national variables.
- Indices: Countries nominal and price variables were transformed into logarithms. The aggregation was performed with fixed weights, taken from GDP at PPP exchange rates for 1993. Real variables were derived from the dif-

[6] As mentioned in Browne et al. (1997), the German long-run money demand function is generally found to be stable. However, Falk and Funke (1995) have shown that German unification could have caused some temporary instability in the area-wide EU demand for money function. The rescaling method used here is equivalent to the introduction of an intercept dummy in the area-wide equation in order to take into account German unification.

[7] Prior to aggregation, all deflators were rebased, taking 1985 as a common base year.

ference between nominal ones and the aggregate GDP deflator. Using logarithms along with fixed weights yields the interesting result that the area-wide real variables are exactly equal to the weighted average of corresponding national variables, which is not the case with the first method (see Appendix 1). Moreover, they do not incorporate relative exchange rates effects, as opposed to the ones computed with the other method. The same fixed weights were used to compute the area-wide interest rates. The advantages of the index method are twofold: firstly, it facilitates comparison of the area-wide and national equations and, secondly, the measure of price inflation implied by this method – i.e. a weighted average of national inflation rates – corresponds to the usual definition employed by various international organisations including the EMI.

3. The long-run trends in the variables

As pointed out in Browne, Fagan and Henry (1997), theoretical and data availability considerations have led to relatively simple specifications of area wide money demand. Following this tradition, the present analysis focuses on a model in which real money balances are related to real income and market interest rates, whereby the short and long term interest rates are the opportunity costs of respectively the narrow and broad aggregates. In this context, it is useful to start the analysis of the long-run properties of the data within the multivariate framework put forward by Johansen (1991). This makes it possible to consider a variety of models, other than the single-equation one according to which money would be a function of exogenous variables. Monticelli and Strauss-Kahn (1992) and Wesche (1997) have also used this approach.

The multivariate analysis presented in this section is carried out for each of the aggregates – M3H, M1, NC – and using data compiled by both the exchange rate method and the index method. For each aggregate, vector autoregression (VAR) models are estimated and the Johansen technique is applied, to test for the number of cointegration vectors and, when there is cointegration, to estimate the parameters of these long-run relations.

In order to assess the robustness of the results to the list of variables considered, different systems were estimated, first, a bivariate system involving real money and real income – in logarithms – and, then, increasing the number of variables by including long and short-term interest rates (see Table 1).[8] In all cases, the deterministic component is an unrestricted constant, corresponding to a model with drift, therefore without any trend component in the long-run system. Theoretically, the number of long-run relations found may be an increasing function of the number of variables.

Another parameter which may affect the results is the lag length. *A priori*, the impact of changing the lag length on the number of cointegrating vectors is not known [see Hall (1991)]. It is possible nevertheless to select an optimal lag length, on the basis of standard information criteria (Akaike, Hannan-

[8] M3R denotes real M3, M1R real M1, NCR real currency, YR real GDP, LR long-term interest rate, and SR short-term interest rate. Cointegration within the bivariate system (SR, LR) has also been examined but the results are not reported, since, in all cases, no stable long-run relation could be found.

Table 1. Number of cointegration vectors found

Aggregation method		Exchange rate method		Index method	
Lags: Sample		1 80:2–94:4	2 80:3–94:4	1 80:2–94:4	2 80:3–94:4
Aggregate	*System*				
M3HR	YR	1	**1**	2	**1**
	YR LR	1	**1**	1	**2**
	YR LR SR	1	**1**	1	**1**
M1R	YR	0	**1**	0	**0**
	YR SR	1	**0**	1	**0**
	YR SR LR	**1**	1	**2**	1
NCR	YR	**1**	0	**1**	0
	YR SR	**1**	1	**1**	1
	YR SR LR	**1**	2	**1**	2

The data above indicate the number of cointegration vectors found (at the 10% level) in VAR systems.
The results corresponding to the lag selected on that basis are the figures in bold.

Quinn, Schwarz) or of Likelihood-Ratio tests. In practice, these almost always point to lag 1 or 2, although occasionally up to 4 lags could be suitable. Preference has been given to the Hannan Quinn criterion. Results are reported only for 1 or 2 lags, since models with 4 lags would be overparametrised in view of the limited sample available.

In addition, restrictions on the cointegration relations have been systematically implemented, in order to interpret these long-run relations: first, the *just-identifying restrictions*, and then, the *over-identifying restrictions* [see Johansen and Juselius (1994)].[9] Additional information has also been derived, concerning the weak exogeneity hypothesis [see Johansen (1992)], under which some variables do not react to a deviation from the long-run equilibrium, i.e. to a deviation from the cointegration relations (see Box 1 for illustrations of the sequence of tests which has been carried out).

[9] For instance when two relations are found in the system comprising money, output and an interest rate, they are strictly equivalent to two relations, involving money and output, on the one hand, and output and the interest rate, on the other. These can be respectively interpreted as the transaction money demand and some IS curve. This is the just-identifying restriction step, which does not need to be tested, since it is simply tantamount to re-arranging the original system. The over-identifying restriction, on the contrary, needs to be tested, e.g. for a second relation corresponding to a stationary interest rate.

Table 1 presents in summary form the number of cointegration vectors found (at the 10% level) in different systems. These results appear relatively robust to a change in the aggregation method. However, as expected, results are sensitive both to the number of variables included in the system and to the lag lengths. Nevertheless, no systematic link seems to exist between the cointegration rank, on the one hand, and the number of variables in the system – which is at odds with econometric theory – or the lag length employed, on the other.

The main finding is that a long-run relation between money and output can often be identified when money is measured by Notes and Coins or M3H, with income elasticities respectively around 1 and 1.5 in the identified system. This result holds for both aggregation methods, and is especially true for the broader aggregate. This does not apply to M1, for which, in many cases, no cointegrating relation can be found. In many cases, interest rates can be excluded from the long-run equation. However, the long-term residual derived from the money-income relation varies between ±10% for Notes and Coins and between ±5% for M3H, which would lead to a somewhat imprecise modelling of money, even for a long-run model. This suggests testing further the importance of interest rates using alternative estimation techniques. In any case, it appears from tests such as the ones reported in Boxes 1.1 to 1.3 (one example is given for each aggregate) that it is impossible to exclude from the long-run vectors both interest rates for either M1 or Notes and Coins.

4. Fully modified estimation of long-run money demand functions

4.1 Results for traditional aggregates

Building on the insights from the analysis contained in the previous section, this section presents the results of single-equation analysis of long run money demand for three aggregates (M3H, M1 and Notes and Coins). The estimation of a long-run equation linking real money to its determinants use the fully modified estimator proposed by Phillips and Hansen (1990), which has not been used, to our knowledge, in the other papers looking at EU-wide money demand. The advantage of this technique is that it corrects for biases which arise from autocorrelation in the long-run residual and also for the fact that the explanatory variables may not be weakly exogenous, i.e. past values of the residual from the long-run relations may be correlated with current values of the explanatory variables. As can be seen from the results reported in Boxes 1.1 to 1.3, it is very often the case that GDP as well as money are not weakly exogenous with respect to the long-run parameters.[10] Moreover, it allows for standard inference, since the estimated long-run parameters have an asymptotic normal distribution.[11]

---

[10] In practice, however, the endogeneity of GDP depends very much on the aggregation method or on the lag length chosen.

[11] ECM formulations have not been estimated, so that only residual-based tests are reported. In practice, tests on the *t*-ECM type, as suggested in Kremers, Ericsson, and Dolado (1992) would presumably be difficult to interpret since they would depend on the additional variables to be employed in the short-run model, even more so because of the small sample used.

Box 1.1: An example of multivariate analysis for real Notes and Coins (real GDP, long-term rate, short-term rate)

1 lag, exchange rate method, unrestricted constant term, 1980:2–1994:4
Trace test for less than one relation = 58.6, critical value at 90% = 43.8, *rejected* at 10%
Trace test for less than two relations = 15.5, critical value at 90% = 26.7, *accepted* at 10%
Freely estimated single long-run vector: NCR = 0.93YR + 0.6LR – 1.7SR
χ^2 Test for the long-run exclusion of the long-term rate: *accepted p-value* 70%, $\chi^2(1)$
χ^2 Test for the joint long-run exclusion of the short and long-term rate: *rejected p-value* 0%, $\chi^2(2)$
Derived restricted long-run vector: NCR = 0.97YR – 2.1SR
In this restricted model:
χ^2 Test for weakly exogenous long-term rates: *accepted*, p-value = 89% level, $\chi^2(2)$
χ^2 Test for weakly exogenous short and long-term rates: *accepted*, p-value = 65% level, $\chi^2(3)$
χ^2 Test for only money being not weakly exogenous: *rejected*, p-value = 8% level, $\chi^2(4)$

Box 1.2: An example of multivariate analysis for real M1 (real GDP, long-term rate, short-term rate)

1 lag, index method, unrestricted constant term, 1980:3–1994:4
Trace test for less than one relation = 68.3, critical value at 90% = 43.8, *rejected* at 10%
Trace test for less than two relations = 28.3, critical value at 90% = 26.7, *rejected* at 10%
Trace test for less than three relations = 5.0, critical value at 90% = 10.6, *accepted* at 10%
Just-identified long-run vectors: M1R = 0.91YR – 0.5SR and YR = 0.99M1R – 0.7LR
χ^2 Test for the long-run exclusion of the long-term rate: *accepted p-value* 23%, $\chi^2(2)$
χ^2 Test for the exclusion of the long-term rate and I(0) short-term rate: *rejected p-value* 8%, $\chi^2(3)$
Derived restricted long-run vectors: M1R = 0.94YR and YR = –16.5SR
Rearranged equivalent system: M1R = 0.94YR and M1R – Y1R = SR
In this restricted model:
χ^2 Test for weakly exogenous short-term rate: *accepted*, p-value = 11%, $\chi^2(4)$
χ^2 Test for only money being not weakly exogenous: *rejected*, p-value = 0%, $\chi^2(6)$

Box 1.3: An example of multivariate analysis for real M3H (real GDP, long-term rate, short-term rate)

2 lags, exchange rate method, unrestricted constant term, 1980:3–1994:4
Trace test for less than one relation = 55.0, critical value at 90% = 43.8, *rejected* at 10%
Trace test for less than two relations = 24.2, critical value at 90% = 26.7, *accepted* at 10%
Freely estimated single long-run vector: M3HR = 1.59YR – 0.7LR + 0.6SR
χ^2 Test for the long-run exclusion of the long-term rate: *accepted p-value* 11%, $\chi^2(1)$
χ^2 Test for the joint long-run exclusion of the short and long-term rate: *accepted p-value* 16%, $\chi^2(2)$
Derived restricted long-run vector: M3HR = 1.62YR
In this restricted model:
χ^2 Test for weakly exogenous short- and long-term rates: *accepted*, p-value = 12% level, $\chi^2(4)$
χ^2 Test for only money being not weakly exogenous: *rejected*, p-value = 0% level, $\chi^2(5)$

Table 2. Fully modified estimates of long run money demand equations for real balances (EU14 aggregates compiled using the exchange rate method)

	Coefficient on variable:			Diagnostic statistics:				
	YR	LR	SR	ADF	PP	LC	MeanF	SupF
M3HR	1.61 (102.7)			−4.7 (3.3)	−3.8	0.2 (0.7)	2.6 (7.8)	10.4 (17.8)
M3HR	1.58 (69.7)	−0.20 (1.8)		−5.3 (3.8)	−4.1	0.3 (0.8)	3.1 (9.1)	7.3 (19.7)
M3HR	1.55 (67.5)	−0.59 (2.7)	0.32 (1.9)	−5.4 (4.0)	−4.2	1.1 (1.0)	8.6 (10.4)	20.0 (21.4)
M1R	0.86 (29.5)			−2.5 (3.3)	−3.3	0.3 (0.7)	3.6 (7.8)	7.2 (17.8)
M1R	0.88 (28.4)		0.24 (1.7)	−2.8 (3.8)	−3.1	0.6 (0.8)	6.1 (9.1)	11.7 (19.7)
M1R	0.92 (30.1)	0.79 (2.7)	−0.30 (1.5)	−2.3 (4.0)	−3.7	1.3 (1.0)	22.6 (10.4)	48.2 (21.4)
NCR	1.02 (5.8)			−1.6 (3.3)	−2.1	0.3 (0.7)	3.6 (7.8)	7.2 (17.8)
NCR	1.06 (8.2)		−.02 (0.04)	−1.8 (3.8)	−2.3	0.3 (0.8)	3.8 (9.1)	9.9 (19.7)
NCR	1.17 (12.6)	2.9 (3.3)	−1.9 (2.8)	−2.8 (4.0)	−3.2	1.6 (1.0)	22.4 (10.4)	55.1 (21.4)

Figures below the coefficients are the asymptotic t-ratios. ADF, PP refer respectively to the Augmented Dickey-Fuller [cf. Engle and Granger (1987) and Engle and Yoo (1987)] and Phillips-Perron (1988) tests for the null of no-cointegration. The columns LC, MeanF and SupF report Hansen's (1992) tests for stability of the long-run equation. The 5% critical values for these tests are presented in parentheses below the test statistics. The equations are estimated over the period 1981Q1 to 1994Q4.

The estimated long run equations for the EU14 countries are reported in Table 2. The results refer to aggregates calculated using the current exchange rate method. The results for the index variables are generally similar and available from the authors on request. This section presents an overview of the main results for the three types of monetary aggregates.

4.1.1 M3H

From the estimates of the long-run demand for broad money reported in Table 2, a number of conclusions are suggested. Firstly, the ADF and PP statistics are consistent with the results obtained in the previous section, providing evidence that real M3H and real income are cointegrated. Application of Hansen's (1992) three tests for the stability of the long-run relation confirm that the estimated long-run relation is stable over the sample period. When interest rates are added to the equation, cointegration is retained and, for the most part, the equations retain their stability properties. However, the significance of the interest rate terms is relatively low, again consistent with the previous results.

Overall, the results suggest that for the M3H aggregate, the income elasticity is significantly above unity, being of the order of 1.5 – in line with the results from the multivariate analysis – which is consistent with the Friedman (1956) argument of money being a luxury good, but such a finding may also reflect the impact of financial innovation or developments in trended variables such as financial wealth (see e.g. Gerdesmeier (1996) on that issue). It is also more or less in line with what is reported in other work, e.g. Monticelli (1996) or Cassard, Lane and Masson (1994) for EU9 and ERM grouping of countries, respectively. Estimated interest elasticities are, however, relatively small in comparison with existing studies. The positive sign on the short-term interest rate in the equation could be due to the fact that this variable is picking up the effect of the 'own' rate on money while the long-term rate acting as a measure of the opportunity cost.

4.1.2 M1

Irrespective of the inclusion of interest rates in the specification, the results in Table 2 suggest that there exists no cointegrating relation between M1 and the other tested variables, as was found earlier on the basis of the tests in the multivariate framework. There is only one exception to this finding, which is the money-GDP equation, for which cointegration seems to hold, but only on the basis of the Phillips and Perron test. Moreover, there are some signs of stability, as indicated by the Hansen tests, and, finally the long-run coefficient is very similar to the multivariate estimate, so that income elasticity is very close to one, again reaching conclusions similar to those found in the literature, cf. Bekx and Tullio (1989) or Artis, Bladen-Hovell, and Zhang (1993) for EMS countries.

4.1.3 Notes and coins

The results presented in Table 2 point to the lack of cointegration for the EU14 countries between notes and coins and real income, whether or not interest rates are included in the equation. These results are not fully consistent with the multivariate results presented in the previous section, according to which income and this narrow money could cointegrate. Paradoxically, although cointegration between these latter two variables is rejected, both by the ADF and the PP test, the stability test do not reject the null of constant coefficients. Moreover, the income elasticity is very close to one, which is also the case when the multivariate analysis is carried out. These conflicting findings suggest that a clear-cut conclusion regarding the relevance of this aggregate for monetary policy purposes may be difficult to reach. In any case, measurement issues for such aggregate are also problematic enough – e.g. due to foreign use – to prevent its extensive use in such a context. This may also explain why results concerning this aggregate have not been reported previously.

4.2 Extended broad money aggregates: Cross-border holdings

So far attention has been focused on area-wide simple-sum monetary aggregates, obtained by the addition of national money stocks, which in many case also comprise deposits in foreign currency held by residents at banks located within the country. However, by definition, such aggregates exclude resident's deposits held at credit institutions located outside their own countries (even if the country where the deposits are located are inside the area), i.e. "cross-border holdings". For example, deposits of French residents held at banks in Germany are not included in the simple sum aggregate for the EU14 countries. Given the growing importance of cross-border holdings in EU countries over the last decade, it is necessary to examine the impact of the exclusion of these assets from area-wide aggregates on the estimated equations. Area-wide money demand functions for extended broad monetary aggregates, incorporating cross-border holdings, have been examined by Monticelli (1993, 1996).[12] As pointed out in these studies, in an area-wide contest, cross-border holdings have in general three distinguishing criteria:

- R: the residency of the holder (restricted to deposits of residents in area, or not)
- L: the locations of the credit institution at which the deposits are held (restricted to deposits at institutions located in area, or not), and
- C: the currency in which the deposits are denominated (restricted to deposits denominated in one of the area's currencies, or not).

Focusing first on deposits owned by residents of the area, four extended aggregates for area-wide broad money can be computed:

- M^R: the broadest category, is equal to the traditional simple sum aggregate plus all cross-border deposits owned by residents of the area, regardless of location of the credit institution and regardless of the currency of denomination;
- M^{RL}: the traditional simple sum aggregate plus cross-border deposits at credit institutions *within* the area, regardless of currency denomination;
- M^{RC}: the traditional simple sum aggregate plus cross-border deposits denominated in currencies of the area, regardless of the their location;
- M^{RLC}: the 'narrowest' extended aggregate, comprising the traditional simple sum aggregate plus cross-border deposits at credit institutions within the area, denominated in currencies of the countries included in the area.

An additional extended aggregate considered (M^C) includes deposits in area currencies owned both by residents and non-residents. These extended aggregates are compared with M^T, the traditional simple sum aggregate which does not included cross border holdings.

Monticelli (1993, 1996) found that traditional broad aggregates performed as well as, if not better than, extended aggregates and, within the class of

[12] Angeloni, Cottarelli, and Levy (1992) have also examined a number of aggregates incorporating Cross-Border-Deposits, but with a view to analysing their properties in terms of 'information content' rather than money demand stability. On the basis of this informational criterion, the conclusion is that extended aggregates dominate standard ones.

Table 3. Properties of extended aggregates including cross-border holdings in the EU14

				Coefficient on:	
	Trace	ADF	PP	YR	LR
M^R	26.8	−2.7	−2.6	1.93	−0.8
M^{RL}	28.6	−2.9	−2.8	1.84	−0.8
M^{RLC}	28.6	−2.9	−2.8	1.84	−0.8
M^C	26.5	−2.6	−2.7	1.68	−0.5
M^I	32.3	−3.8	−3.1	1.66	−0.5

For description of the alternative aggregates, see main text. The Trace statistic refers to the Johansen (1991) Trace test for cointegration in a trivariate system comprising real money balances, real income and the long term interest rate. Critical values are 26.8 (10%) and 29.7 (5%) respectively. ADF and PP refer respectively to the Augmented Dickey Fuller (1979) and Phillips-Perron (1988) single equation tests for the null of no-cointegration with 5% critical values of 3.8, taking the sample size of 50 observations in Engle and Yoo (1987). The estimated long-run coefficients are reported in the following two columns. The equations are estimated over the period 1984Q1 to 1994Q4.

extended aggregates, narrower measures tended to perform better than the very broad measures.

Data on a consistent basis on EU residents' cross border holdings are available from 1984:1 onwards. In order to facilitate comparison of the different aggregates and across countries in a consistent way, the empirical analysis is carried out over this period for each aggregate. Area-wide variables were computed using current Ecu exchange rates. For each aggregate, the following procedure was carried out. First, in a trivariate system comprising real money balances, real GDP and long term interest rates, the Johansen procedure was employed to test for the presence of cointegration. Using the same data, cointegration tests were also carried out in a single equation contest. Both procedures yield three tests of cointegration (the Trace test, the ADF and PP tests). Long-run equations were estimated using the Fully Modified Estimator. The results of the analysis are summarised in Table 3 which presents the three cointegration tests and the coefficients on real income and long term interest rates in the long-run equation.

On the basis of the evidence contained in Table 3, the following conclusions are appropriate. Firstly, while there is evidence in favour of cointegration, it is generally not overwhelming for all aggregates. In general, the Johansen Trace test provides evidence of cointegration at the 10% level (at the 5% level for the traditional aggregates). On the basis of this test, the evidence in favour of cointegration increases, as the aggregate considered is narrowed.

However, single equation tests (ADF and PP) provide a more ambiguous picture. The ambiguity of the evidence overall is probably attributable to the relatively small span of data employed here, inevitable given the data constraints. In terms of the coefficient sizes, long-run income elasticities are generally larger than unity, being generally larger for broader aggregates. Interest elasticities have the right sign in all cases and do not appear to differ markedly across aggregates within each country grouping.

Overall, the results obtained are consistent with earlier findings, namely that extended aggregates including cross border holdings do not outperform traditional simple sum aggregates and, within the class of extended aggregates, 'narrower' versions tend to yield better results. A possible explanation for this result is that cross border deposits may be held mainly for reasons such as portfolio considerations and avoidance of taxes and regulations. Thus they may be less likely to represent transactions balances and, accordingly, less closely linked to domestic expenditures than deposits held domestically.

5. Factors underlying the 'superior' performance of the area-wide equation

As noted earlier, a number of previous studies have found that area-wide money demand equations have superior properties – measured by the size of the residual standard error, stability properties etc. – than many national equations. This conclusion is also supported by some of the empirical results presented here. Therefore, in this section we attempt to examine this issue in more detail by comparing the long-run area-wide equation with correspondingly specified national equations.

In assessing the relationship between national and area-wide equations, the index method of aggregation is particular convenient since the area-wide variables, by construction, are weighted averages of the corresponding national variables. While the results obtained apply exactly to the index variables, they also apply, approximately, to the equations for variables aggregated using the exchange rate method[13].

Recall that, using the index method, area-wide variables (for money, income and prices) are constructed as follows:

$$\mathrm{Log}(X) = \sum w_i \,\mathrm{Log}(x_i) \tag{5.1}$$

or, for interest rates:

$$X = \sum w_i x_i \tag{5.1'}$$

where a capital letter denotes the area-wide variable, a lower case letter the national variable and the w_i are the weights employed.

[13] Empirical analysis showed that the logarithms of area-wide variables defined as the sum of national variables expressed in ECU are well approximated by a weighted sum of the logarithms of the national variables, as in equation (5.1). For example, a regression of the log of area-wide M3 on the logs of national M3s yielded a standard error of 0.03%, implying that the error of approximation is of a trivial magnitude in the case at hand. See also Wesche (1996) on aggregation issues.

Now consider the typical national semi-lograthmic equation:

$$\mathrm{Log}(m_i) = \alpha_i + \beta_i \, \mathrm{Log}(y_i) + \varphi_i r_i + u_i \tag{5.2}$$

where m_i denotes the real money stock in country i, y_i real GDP, r_i the interest rate and u_i the equation residual. The parameters α, β and φ may vary across countries. Multiplying across by the weights and aggregating across countries yields an expression for the area wide money stock:

$$\begin{aligned}\mathrm{Log}(M) &= \sum w_i \, \mathrm{Log}(m_i) \\ &= \sum w_i\alpha_i + \sum w_i\beta_i \, \mathrm{Log}(y_i) + \sum w_i\varphi_i r_i + \sum w_i u_i\end{aligned} \tag{5.3}$$

Further note that the national variables can always be expressed as being equal to the corresponding area-wide variable plus an 'error-term':

$$\mathrm{Log}(y_i) = \mathrm{Log}(Y) + v_i \tag{5.4}$$

$$r_i = R + \varepsilon_i \tag{5.5}$$

In view of the definition of the area-wide variables given by (5.1) and (5.1′), the residual terms in (5.4) and (5.5) must satisfy the following restrictions:

$$\sum w_i v_i = 0 \tag{5.6}$$

$$\sum w_i \varepsilon_i = 0 \tag{5.7}$$

Equation (5.3) may be now be rewritten as:

$$\begin{aligned}\sum w_i \, \mathrm{Log}(m_i) = {} & \sum w_i\alpha_i + \mathrm{Log}(Y)\sum w_i\beta_i + R\sum w_i\varphi_i \\ & + \sum w_i\beta_i v_i + \sum w_i\varphi_i\varepsilon_i + \sum w_i u_i\end{aligned} \tag{5.8}$$

or

$$\mathrm{Log}(M) = \alpha' + \beta' \, \mathrm{Log}(Y) + \varphi' R + \sum w_i\beta_i v_i + \sum w_i\varphi_i\varepsilon_i + \sum w_i u_i \tag{5.9}$$

which expresses area-wide money stock (M) as a function of area-wide income (Y) and interest rates (R) where α', β' *and* φ' are by definition the weighted averages of the national coefficients. The residual of the equation comprises a component due to possible aggregation bias:

$$\sum w_i\beta_i v_i + \sum w_i\varphi_i\varepsilon_i \tag{5.10}$$

and a pure residual term, which is the weighted average of the national residuals:

$$\sum w_i u_i \tag{5.11}$$

Note the contribution of the aggregation bias term to the area-wide equation variance will be zero if the coefficients are equal across countries [Maddala, (1977)], since if the equation coefficients are equal across countries, then (5.10) can be rearranged as:

$$\beta \sum w_i v_i + \varphi \sum w_i \varepsilon_i \tag{5.12}$$

which, in view of (5.6) and (5.7) is zero. Similarly, if the right-hand side (RHS) variables in the national equations move very closely together and thus with the area-wide variables. In this case, the variance of extra terms (5.10) would tend to be small and thus the aggregation bias would be limited even though the coefficients could differ significantly across countries (Indeed, in the limiting case where the RHS variables were perfectly correlated across countries, no aggregation bias would arise).[14] In the absence of either equality across countries of the coefficients or of the variables, however, an aggregation bias will be present which will tend to inflate the variance of the residual area-wide equation in comparison with the residual variances of the national equations.

In the absence of any aggregation bias the residual of the area-wide equation will be given by the last term in (5.9). By definition, letting **w** denote the vector of weights and **V** the variance/covariance matrix of the national residuals (u_i), the variance of this term is given by:

$$\mathbf{w}'\mathbf{V}\mathbf{w} \tag{5.13}$$

In general one would expect this variance to be lower than the typical variance of the individual country equation residuals due to a *statistical averaging* effect. For example, in the case of a two-country aggregate, the variance of the area-wide residual is given by:

$$\sigma_u^2 = w_1^2 \sigma_{u_1}^2 + w_2^2 \sigma_{u_2}^2 + 2 w_1 w_2 \operatorname{cov}(u_1 u_2) \tag{3.7}$$

If the covariance are zero, it is clear that the aggregate residual will have a variance which is certainly lower than the average individual country variance[15]. If the covariances are negative, the area-wide variance will be reduced even further; on the other hand, positive covariances will tend to increase the area-wide variances.

In practice, the performance of the area-wide equation compared to the national equations will depend on the relative effects of the aggregation bias and the statistical averaging effect with the former tending to inflate the area-wide variance while the latter tends to reduce it. In order to explore the extent to which these factors are at work in the case at hand, we employ an area-wide long-run money demand equation for the EU14 countries (using the index method, since this aggregates nicely for our purposes) and we also estimate

[14] Regarding cointegration, i.e. the long-run relations, Gonzalo (1992) shows that the equality between cointegrating vectors across countries is not required for cointegration to hold at the aggregate level. In other words, there is no need for money demand to be the same across countries to ensure that a long-run EU money demand function exists, provided that there exist a sufficient number of cointegration relations between money stocks or GDPs in the EU countries.

[15] Since by definition, the sum of the weights is unity, the sum of the squared weights cannot exceed unity.

Table 4. Long run real M3H demand equations in individual countries and in the EU

	YR	LR	CONST	%SER	ADF	PP
AT	1.1 (14.3)	−2.49 (−3.8)	−4.55 (−4.5)	5.2	−2.5	−2.3
BE	1.97 (12.0)	−0.37 (−0.6)	−17.07 (−7.3)	7.5	−3.4	−3
DK	1.19 (2.5)	−2.69 (−2.7)	−6.01 (−1.0)	9.8	−3.4	−3
DE	1.16 (29.9)	−1.95 (−5.0)	−5.76 (−11.2)	3.2	−2.4	−2.8
GR	2.6 (5.9)		−26.8 (−4.2)	22.8	−0.6	−1.4
ES	1.36 (13.7)	−0.64 (−1.2)	−9.03 (−5.6)	6.7	−1.7	−2.2
FI	1.89 (5.7)	−9.92 (−5.5)	−12.75 (−3.4)	20	−2.1	−2.6
FR	1.7 (11.8)	0.19 (−0.4)	−13.46 (−6.6)	5.4	−2.4	−2.8
IE	1.7 (6.9)	6.63 (−5.3)	−10.31 (−4.7)	16.3	−4	−4
IT	−0.07 (0.5)	−0.88 (−2.3)	16.82 −6.1	6.4	−1	−2.6
NL	2.09 (26.0)	−1.63 (−2.8)	−16.27 (−17.0)	5.9	−3	−3.6
PT	0.34 (2.2)	−2.58 (−4.1)	6 −2.7	10.7	−1.7	−2.4
SE	−0.52 (2.8)	−2.43 (−3.0)	15.07 −6.3	8.1	−2.8	−2.7
UK	2.85 (12.1)	−0.19 (−0.2)	−24.63 (−8.8)	12.5	−2.6	−1.7
EU14	1.43 (68.8)	−0.49 (−4.6)	−9.74 (−32.2)	1.1	−4.5	−3.8

(asymptotic t-ratios in parentheses)

long run national equations for each country and compare the results obtained from the aggregated and disaggregated approaches. The equations, which were estimated using the Fully Modified Estimator over the period 1981:1 to 1994:4, together with the residual covariance/correlation matrices are presented in Tables 4 and 5.

Comparing the area-wide with the national equations, it is notable that the area-wide equation appears to perform better on a statistical basis, as indicated by the lower standard deviation and the stronger evidence for cointegration (measured by the ADF and PP statistics). Looking at the results across countries, it is clear that the coefficients are quite different from country to country. Income elasticities vary from 2.9 in the UK to −0.5 in Sweden while the estimated elasticities with respect to long-term interest rates vary from −2.7 in Denmark to +6.6 in Ireland. This suggests the possibility of a significant aggregation bias. However, as noted above, equality of coefficients is a sufficient but not necessary condition for the absence of aggregation bias. In particular – if the right hand side variables follow similar paths across countries (which, in a highly integrated block of countries such as those considered here, is not implausible) – then aggregation bias may be very small despite the sharp difference in coefficients.

Table 5. Correlation matrix of long-run equation residuals

	AT	BE	DK	DE	ES	FI	FR	GR	IE	IT	NL	PT	SE	GB
AT	1.00	−0.33	0.28	0.15	−0.32	−0.08	−0.09	0.68	−0.25	0.57	0.63	−0.28	0.21	−0.24
BE		1.00	0.08	0.54	−0.02	−0.36	0.06	−0.10	0.21	−0.21	−0.23	−0.22	0.17	−0.22
DK			1.00	−0.13	−0.25	0.01	0.25	0.20	−0.43	0.27	−0.07	−0.29	−0.12	0.05
DE				1.00	−0.16	−0.31	−0.40	0.26	0.11	0.11	0.14	−0.32	0.48	−0.52
ES					1.00	−0.06	0.08	−0.15	0.10	−0.24	−0.15	0.40	0.18	0.21
FI						1.00	0.23	−0.57	−0.64	−0.10	−0.10	0.62	0.18	0.75
FR							1.00	−0.20	−0.01	0.21	−0.13	0.18	−0.27	0.39
GR								1.00	0.16	0.53	0.64	−0.65	−0.04	−0.68
IE									1.00	−0.09	−0.04	−0.28	−0.36	−0.46
IT										1.00	0.25	−0.38	0.14	−0.33
NL											1.00	−0.19	0.04	−0.19
PT												1.00	0.17	0.62
SE													1.00	0.04
GB														1.00

In order to assess the extent to which aggregation bias is present in the case at hand we carry out the following procedure: firstly, we use the area-wide equation to generate within-sample projections of area-wide real money balances (the aggregated approach); secondly, we use the national equations to project national money stocks and compile the results into an area-wide projection using the weights employed in the construction of the area-wide aggregate (the disaggregate approach). A comparison of the residuals of the area-wide approach with those generated by the disaggregate approach therefore provides an estimate of the extent of the aggregation bias. In fact, the residual of the area-wide equation (1.1%) is slightly less than that of the disaggregate approach (1.2%). This confirms that the aggregation problem refered to above is not a problem in the present case.

As regards, the statistical averaging effect, some evidence in this respect can be gleaned from the correlation matrix of the national residuals which is shown in Table 5. In some cases, there are indeed negative correlations between the residuals. A notable case is the negative correlation between the French and German residuals (correlation coefficient = −0.40)[16]. Such correlations would tend to contribute per se to a lower overall variance as well as a more stable equation. On the other hand, in many cases, the correlations are positive. In order to assess the overall impact of these cross-country covariances on the area-wide residual standard error we employ the formula for the residual variance (namely $\mathbf{w'Vw}$ as shown above) under three different hypotheses:

- the actual covariances as presented in Table 5;
- all covariances are zero; this implies setting the non-diagonal elements of V to zero; and
- the country residuals are perfectly positively correlated. This is something of a 'worst case' scenario, in which the statistical averaging effect would be nullified.

The results are as follows:

Standard error with actual covariances:[17]	1.2%
Standard error with zero covariances:	1.4%
Standard error with perfect positive correlation:	3.6%

This shows that the covariance terms do contribute modestly to a lower residual variance in the area-wide equation; however, the reduction in the variance is small with the standard error falling from 1.4% to 1.2%. Secondly, in

[16] A striking example of the operation of statistical averaging was observed in 1993. As a result of the issue of the "Balladur Bonds" and privatisations, M3 in France actually *fell* by 2.6% between the last quarters of 1992 and 1993. In contrast, in Germany over the same period, monetary growth, at 7.4%, exceeded the target range on foot of factors such as tax changes and the low level of long-term interest rates. Thus in both countries large deviations – though of opposite sign – from long run money demand equations were recorded. In the EU14 context, these two factors partly cancelled each other out, resulting in a less marked departure from estimated long-run equilibrium than at the national level.

[17] Note this differs from the 1.1% figure cited in the earlier Table. This reflects the fact that the data in the earlier Table refer to the aggregate area-wide equation whereas the 1.2% estimate here relates to the standard error from the disaggregate approach.

the event that the correlations between the national residuals were to become perfectly positive (everything else remaining the same), then the standard error of the area-wide equation would increase significantly to 3.6%. However, even at this level, the standard error would compare favourably with national equations, being smaller than the standard errors of each of the individual countries, with the exception of Germany (i.e. 3.2%).

The main conclusions of this analysis may be summarised as follows. Firstly, even though the coefficients of national equations appear to differ markedly, the evidence suggests that aggregation bias is relatively small. Secondly, the statistical averaging appears to be the principal source of the 'better' performance (measured by residual standard deviations) of the area-wide equation. In this respect, the contribution of covariances to the reduction in area-wide residual variance is quite small. Thirdly, even if the covariances were to become quite large (in the limiting case of perfect positive correlation), the variance of the area-wide residual, though increasing significantly, would still compare relatively favourably with those of national equations, being about the same magnitude as is the case of Germany.

These statistical results have important economical implications. Firstly, a number of reasons which have been put forward to explain the better performance of the area-wide equation such as currency substitution, the operation of the ERM system etc. [see Browne, Fagan and Henry (1997)] are not strictly necessary to explain the result. The currency substitution hypothesis, for example, suggests that shocks to one country's money demand due to currency substitution will be offset, at least to some extent, by shocks to money demand in other EU countries. Such shifts, which may contribute to instability in individual country equations, will therefore tend to be at least partially if not fully internalised within an area-wide aggregate. From a technical point of view, this hypothesis implies a negative correlation between residuals across countries. As shown above, however, covariance terms contribute little to the reduction in variance for the area-wide equation, implying that even if currency substitution is playing a role, it contribution to the superior performance of area-wide equations is quite limited. Thus, there is no need to invoke such explanations as currency substitution in order to explain the apparently superior performance of area-wide equations, although such phenomena are not necessarily ruled out by these results.

Secondly, it has been argued that results for area-wide money demand in Stage 2 are of little relevance for Stage 3 [e.g. Arnold (1996)] since the superior performance is a statistical 'fluke' due to the fact that shocks to money demand across countries were desynchronised during the period, implying that shocks to national money demands were relatively independent during the sample periods considered. In contrast, the exiting empirical evidence for the US suggest that shocks to money demand are highly correlated across regions. Once Stage 3 starts, however, it is argued that the existence of a single monetary policy together with increasing financial integration will result in such shocks becoming increasingly synchronised across countries (as is currently the case in the US) resulting in a deterioration of the area-wide equation's performance. This conclusion appears to be reasonable in principle. Nonetheless, it is worth pointing out that even if, following the move to monetary union, the shocks to national money demands were to become *perfectly* correlated, the variance of the area-wide long-run equation, though rising significantly above its current level, would still be of a reasonable magnitude compared to current national equations, being comparable to that of the German equation.

Of course, none of these arguments rule out the possibility that other factors – such as finanical innvoation, portfolio substitution etc. – could, in the event, lead to a deterioration in the performance of existing area-wide empirical relationships. The experience of a number of individual countries, where apparently stable equation performed poorly soon after the sample period, suggests that caution is required in attempting to derive conclusions about the prospective situation in Stage 3 on the basis of empirical studies carried out some four years before the move to monetary union.

6. Conclusions

Given the importance of the long-run properties of money demand for the choice of monetary policy strategy, the present paper has presented some empirical evidence regarding area-wide measures of the money stock. The evidence presented related to various aggregate – Notes and Coins, M1, M3H and extended aggregates incorporating cross-border holdings. The analysis has been carried out for area-wide aggregates composed of 14 EU countries.

A number of conclusions are suggested by the results obtained.

Firstly, in terms of the choice of aggregate, the evidence suggests that notes and coins do not have a stable long-run relation with the income and interest rate variables examined here. In contrast, the aggregates M1 and M3H do appear to have such a long run relation, although the strength of the evidence on the relative importance of the two aggregates varies depending on the estimation technique employed.

Secondly, as regards the issue of extended measures of broad money, incorporating cross-border holdings, the evidence here suggests that traditional measures of broad money perform as well as, if not better than, extended measures, a finding which is consistent with the results obtained in earlier area-wide studies. This latter result may be attributable to the fact that cross border deposits are held mainly for portfolio purposes and thus may be less closely linked to domestic expenditures than the more traditional aggregates.

Thirdly, the results of a comparison of national and area-wide M3H equations showed that a) aggregation bias is not a major problem despite the marked differences in equation coefficients across countries; and b) the lower residual variance of the area-wide equation is attributable to the phenomenon of statistical averaging which implies that, apart from special circumstances, a country-weighted average equation should perform better than individual country equations. These results suggest that traditional explanations for the superiority of area-wide equations – such as currency substitution – are not required (although they cannot be excluded). However, simulations revealed that even in the face of a substantial increase in residual covariances across countries (due, for example, to increased synchronisation of shocks) the area-wide equation would nonetheless continue to compare respectably with national equations, with a residual variance of the same order of magnitude as in the German case.

Finally, it is stressed that attempts to derive implications for monetary policy in Stage 3 from the present results is extremely hazardous given the fact that 1999 is some four years beyond the end of the sample period considered here. It cannot, for example, be ruled out that a number of factors – such as financial innovation and the impact of the regime shift involved in moving to the single currency – could lead to changes in portfolio allocation behaviour thereby undermining the stability of the area-wide equations. Nonetheless, for those cases where satisfactory results have been obtained, the estimates reported here present a useful starting point for further analysis as well as a 'benchmark' for the analysis of area-wide monetary developments in the EU.

Appendix 1: Aggregation of monetary aggregates and other variables

Two different methods can basically be used, the description of which follows. For each of them, the focus is on the relation that has to exist between the aggregation of nominal variables and deflators, so as to guarantee sensible series when expressed in real terms.

1) Levels in ECUs at current exchange rates

A first concept is nominal money in ECUs, which has been used for instance in Monticelli and Strauss-Kahn (1992). It provides an actual measure of nominal money Mn:[18]

$$Mn_Z = \sum_z e_i . Mn_i$$

where $i \in Z$ stands for each country in the subset Z and e_i is the *current* exchange rate in ECUs.

The weight of each country is then defined implicitly and depends on the exchange rate vis-à-vis ECU and therefore other EU currencies. With respect to a given base year (for time $t = 0$) the relative change in this indicator is exactly the one we get with a Laspeyres index for Z's monetary wealth in ECUs, i.e.:

$$\sum_Z \frac{Mn_i^0}{Mn_Z^0}\left(\frac{Mn_i}{Mn_i^0}\right)$$

Define the equivalent in terms of real money M as:

$$M_Z = \frac{Mn_Z}{P_Z}$$

where P_Z is the ECU deflator for subset Z.

In order to have consistent weighting schemes on prices and nominal money, P_Z needs to be computed with weights defined by the share of each

[18] In all cases, the subscript for time t is omitted but it has to be taken into account that both the variables and the weights can change over time, as is the case here obviously. This would not be the case with the usual Laspeyres or Paasche indexes, for which the weight is fixed at respectively its initial and final values in nominal terms. The Divisia index could be used, resorting to the average between the two.

country at time t in the nominal money stock in ECUs. Therefore,

$$P_Z = \sum_Z \frac{e_i . Mn_i}{Mn_Z} P_i$$

where P_i is the ECU deflator for country i (i.e. $P_i = e_i . P_{id}$, rebased).

Individual prices $P_{i,d}$ in domestic currency have to be converted into a common one, otherwise the real money aggregate will be depending on the exchange rate changes. Moreover, in order to keep the derived real money index equal to nominal money for the base year, we need to rebase all of the prices expressed in ECUs on the same base year. Such a method could nevertheless lead to distorsions in the real money stock series, which is no longer a simple expression of the individual real money stock. Indeed, it can be proved that its inverse is equal to a weighted average of the individual inverse real money stocks, the weights being equal to the squared weights for prices.[19]

This method can be applied to any other nominal aggregate, like output data. Starting from nominal output, one can derive a deflator with weights based on nominal output expressed in ECUs and then compute a series for real output.[20] The aggregation technique is then similar for output and money. Of course, so doing the statistics provided by individual countries on real output will not be taken into account, although, contrary to real money, they are usually part of the official country data.

2) Indexes in log-levels

Alternatively, one can use variables expressed in logarithms, so that the change would be measured by a geometric instead of an arithmetic average.[21] Define the log-level index for any series X as follows:

$$\ln X_Z = \sum_Z w_i \cdot \ln X_i$$

where w is the weighting vector and X could be money, output or prices.[22]

Weights w can be chosen so as to be consistent accross all indicators for a given subset Z, the most suitable common weighting scheme being GDP weights at PPP exchange rates in ECUs (i.e. the one used by the EMI when

[19] With such a method, the corresponding real aggregate is not simply the weighted average of the individual real variables, e.g. in general $P . X \neq Xn$ where all three zone variables have been affected the same weighting scheme. One has to bear in mind that here one of these three series has to be defined implicitly for such an accounting identity to hold.

[20] For instance, real output Q_Z is defined as:

$$Q_Z = \frac{Qn_Z}{\sum z_i e_i P_{id}} \quad \text{where } z_i = \frac{e_i Qn_i}{Qn_Z} \quad \text{and} \quad Qn_Z = \sum e_i Qn_i$$

[21] A third suggestion [*cf.* Bayoumi & Kenen (1992)] is the construction of an index based on the growth rates rather than on the levels. However, such an approach would be redundant with the latter, since it is always possible to derive from variables in growth rates a level indicator, by cumulating from a given point in time the changes in any given variable.

[22] Regarding interest rates, one would rather use the arithmetic average formula, directly computed in levels.

aggregating countries for interest rates, inflation and output).[23] This method yields another concept of monetary aggregate, both for real and nominal money, i.e. with $X = M$ or Mn. In this case, an index for money is used rather than its actual measure, in financial terms.

The advantage of such a method is mainly that the value index is actually equal to the product of the price by the quantity indexes. Moreover, individual contributions to the global growth rate remain unchanged, which was not true with the first suggested method where the larger countries have a bigger contribution.

References

Angeloni I, Cottarelli C, Levy A (1992) Cross-border deposits and monetary aggregates in the transition to EMU. Banca d'Italia Temi di discussione, No 163

Artis MJ, Bladen-Hovell RC, Zhang W (1993) A European money demand function. In: Masson PR, Taylor MP (eds.) Policy issues in the operation of currency unions, Cambridge, pp. 240–263

Arnold IJM (1996) Money demand stability in the EMU: Lessons from the US. working paper Nijenrode University, Breukelen

Arnold IJM (1994) The myth of a stable European money demand. Open Economies Review 5:245–259

Bayoumi TA, Kenen PB (1992) Using and EC-wide monetary aggregate in stage two of EMU. IMF Working Paper WP/92/56

Bekx P, Tullio G (1989) A note on the European monetary system, and the determination of the DM-Dollar exchange rate. Cahiers Economiques de Bruxelles 123:329–343

Browne F, Fagan G, Henry J (1997) Money demand in EU countries: A survey. EMI Staff Paper

Cassard M, Lane T, Masson PR (1994) ERM money supplies and the transition to EMU. IMF Working Paper No 94/1

Dickey D, Fuller W (1979) Distribution of the estimators for autoregressive time series with a unit root. Journal of the American Statistical Association 74, 366:427–431

EMI (1997) The single monetary policy in stage three: Specification of the operational framework. European Monetary Institute

Engle R, Granger C (1987) Co-integration and error correction: Representation, estimation and testing. Econometrica 55, 2:251–276

Engle R, Yoo S (1987) Forecasting and testing in co-integrated system. Journal of Econometrics, 35, 1:143–159

Falk M, Funke N (1995) The stability of money demand in Germany and in the EMS: Impact of German unification. Weltwirtschaftliches Archiv 131(3):470–488

Friedman M (1956) Studies in the quantity theory of money, A restatement. Studies in the Quantity Theory of Money; Chicago University Press, pp. 3–21

Gerdesmeier D (1996) The role of wealth in money demand. Deutsche Bundesbank, Discussion Paper No 96/5

Gonzalo J (1992) Cointegration and aggregation. working paper; Economics Department, University of California, San Diego (revised version of WP No 9133, UCSD)

Hall SG (1991) The effects of varying length VAR models on the Maximum Likelihood Estimates of cointegrating vectors. Scottish Journal of Political Economy 34(4):317–323

[23] Additionally, the simpler way to compute the above mentioned weights is to start from the weights for EU, normalised on their sum over Z, according to the following rule:

$$w_i = \frac{wEU_i}{\sum_{Z} wEU_j}$$

where wEU are the weights for EU15 and j covers the countries included into Z.

Hansen BE (1992) Tests for parameter instability in regressions with I(1) processes. Journal of Business and Economic Statistics 10(3):321–335
Johansen S (1991) Estimation and hypothesis testing of cointegration vectors in Gaussian vector autoregressive models. Econometrica 59:1551–1580
Johansen S (1992) Cointegration in partial systems and the efficiency of single equation analysis. Journal of Econometrics 52(3):389–402
Johansen S, Juselius K (1994) Identification of the long-run and the short-run structure: An application to the ISLM model. Journal of Econometrics 63(1):7–36
Kremers JJM, Ericsson NR, Dolado JJ (1992) The power of cointegration tests. Oxford Bulletin of Economics and Statistics, pp. 325–348
Maddala (1977) Econometrics. McGraw Hill
Monticelli C, Strauss-Kahn M-O (1992) European integration and the demand of broad money. Bank for International Settlements, Basle, BIS Working Papers, No. 18
Monticelli C (1993) All the money in Europe? – An investigation of the economic properties of EC-wide extended monetary aggregates. BIS Working Paper, No 19
Monticelli C (1996) EU-wide money and cross-border holdings. Weltwirtschaftliches Archiv 132:215–235
Perron P (1989) The great crash, the oil price shock, and the unit root hypothesis. Econometrica 57(6):1361–1401
Phillips PCB, Hansen BE (1990) Statistical inference in instrumental variables regression with I(1) processes. Review of Economic Studies 57:99–125
Phillips PCB, Perron P (1988) Testing for unit roots in time series regressions. Biometrika 75:335–346
Spencer P (1997) Monetary integration and currency substitution in the EMS: The case for a European monetary aggregate. European Economic Review 41:1403–1419
Wesche K (1997) The stability of European money demand: An investigation of M3H. Open Economies Review 8:371–392
Wesche K (1996) Aggregation bias in estimating European money demand functions. Bonn University, SFB 303, Projektbereich B, Discussion Paper No B-393

Wealth and the demand for money in the European Union*

Martin M. G. Fase[1,2], **Carlo C. A. Winder**[1]

[1] Econometric Research and Special Studies Department, De Nederlandsche Bank NV, P.O. Box 98, 1000 AB Amsterdam, The Netherlands (e-mail: c.c.a.winder@dnb.nl)
[2] University of Amsterdam, Faculty of Economics and Econometrics, Roetersstraat 11, 1018 WB Amsterdam, The Netherlands

Abstract. This study presents the results of an empirical analysis of the demand for money in the European Union as a whole over the period 1971–1995, with a particular focus on the impact of financial wealth. The empirical evidence shows a substantial impact of wealth on the demand for M2 and M3, whereas no influence of wealth on the demand for M1 is found. This finding may explain the remarkable increase of the broad monetary aggregates over the last decade or so. This means that taking into account the growth of wealth, the monetary expansion has been fairly modest. The evidence thus indicates that the strong increase of M2 and M3 should be attributed to portfolio investment considerations rather than to an expansionary monetary policy.

Key words: Demand for money, financial wealth, narrow and broad money

JEL classification: E41, E52

1. Introduction

Under the Maastricht Treaty, the member states of the European Union have agreed to adopt a single European currency and in 1999 at the latest a common monetary policy aimed at price stability. Since this historical moment is rapidly approaching and because of the far-reaching nature of this commitment, the monetary authorities will have to decide soon which monetary policy strategy will be pursued. Price stability has been endorsed by all member states as the ultimate policy objective. The discussion focuses on the issue whether intermediate monetary targeting or direct inflation targeting should be chosen.

* Helpful comments by two anonymous referees, the participants in the Workshop on Money Demand at the Humboldt Universität and Hans Lunsing are gratefully acknowledged.

Monitoring monetary aggregates is important in both monetary strategies but will undoubtedly play a more prominent role in intermediate monetary targeting. The choice for a specific strategy will be crucial for the presentation of monetary policy measures and thus will affect directly the degree of transparency, accountability and credibility of the European central bank. Obviously, the choice between the two strategies will also be determined by an assessment of their effectiveness in achieving price stability. For a strategy of intermediate monetary targeting to be effective, a number of conditions have to be satisfied. The most important are the stability of the demand for money and the controllability of the money stock. Hence, it is not surprising that the demand for money has again been a major research topic in recent years (see e.g. Bekx and Tullio, 1989, Kremers and Lane, 1990, Monticelli and Strauss-Kahn, 1992, Fase, 1994, 1995, Fase and Winder, 1993, 1994). The present study aims to contribute to the discussion by analysing the demand for money in the European Union as a whole, with a particular focus on the impact of financial wealth. In this respect, our analysis differs from earlier studies which have thus far neglected wealth as a determinant of the demand for money.

A stylized feature of the monetary developments in the European Union is the strong increase of notably the broad monetary aggregates M2 and M3, particularly since the beginning of the 1980s. This growth has exceeded the growth of nominal output to a considerable extent. According to the monetarist view on inflation, this monetary expansion should have led to an upward tendency in inflation rates, but the 1980s have actually shown a sharp reduction of inflation. In order to assess the merits of an intermediate monetary targeting policy, it is highly desirable to have an economic explanation for this strong increase of the monetary aggregates. This study will argue that the development of financial wealth provides an explanation for this phenomenon. Taking account of wealth leads to the conclusion that the actual monetary expansion has been fairly modest and that the strong increase of the broad monetary aggregates should be attributed to portfolio investment considerations rather than an expansionary monetary policy.

This paper is organized as follows. The next section briefly discusses the data and presents some tentative empirical evidence concerning the impact of wealth on the demand for money. Section 3 discusses the theoretical framework and the empirical results for the European Union as a whole. Section 4 is devoted to an assessment of the findings. First, we will present evidence on the stability of the demand for money. Next, we will discuss the results of the cointegration analysis, and the section concludes with a further assessment of the role of wealth. Section 5 contains some concluding remarks. The estimation results are set out in appendix A.

2. Construction of data and preliminary analysis

For the present study, the database used in Fase and Winder (1993, 1994), containing data for all EU countries before the most recent accessions for the monetary aggregates M1, M2 and M3, gross domestic product at current and 1985 prices, short and long-term interest rates, has been extended with information for Austria, Finland and Sweden. Hence, data for all present members of the European Union with the exception of Luxembourg, have been used to construct EU-wide variables. The sample period is 1971:I–1995:IV. In order to obtain a comprehensive picture of the monetary developments we did not restrict the analysis to one monetary aggregate but considered a broad spectrum, i.e. three money concepts: M1, M2 and M3. To investigate the impact of wealth on the demand for money we also constructed wealth data for all individual countries. Fase and Winder (1997) discuss in detail the procedure to construct these data. Following the seminal study of Brainard and Tobin (1968) we considered net financial wealth of the non-monetary private sector as the relevant wealth variable. This is defined as the differential between total assets – the sum of M1, quasi-money, claims on the banking sector and on the government and net foreign assets – and the claims of the monetary authorities and the banking sector on the private sector. A more general wealth concept, which includes not only financial wealth but also non-financial components like the capital stock, houses and perhaps durable consumption goods, has not been considered, because data for these debt instruments are not readily available. One may argue that for money demand behaviour portfolio investment considerations are dominant. In view of this, focusing on financial wealth is justified. However, even if a broader wealth concept would be more appropriate, the results in the present study remain valid if it is assumed that financial wealth is a good proxy for total wealth.

For the construction of EU-wide data, several options are available (see Winder, 1997)[1]. In order to express the data on monetary aggregates, nominal income and financial wealth of the individual countries in a common currency, we used the exchange rates against the DM in 1985. Next, the EU-wide variables are calculated as the sum of these national variables. The figures of the countries' national products in 1985 prices have also been converted into 1985 DM prices using the exchange rates against the DM in 1985. EU output in 1985 prices has been obtained by summing these transformed data on national products in 1985 prices. The price index for EU has been calculated as the ratio between EU output at current and constant prices. The short and long-term interest rates for the EU have been calculated as weighted averages of the corresponding interest rates in the individual countries. As weights we used the shares of the national products of the individual countries in aggregated nominal EU output.

The remainder of this section is devoted to a preliminary analysis of the impact of wealth on the demand for money. Particularly, the issue will be addressed whether the development over time of wealth offers an explanation for the monetary expansion experienced in the European Union over the last twenty years. To throw some light on this issue the development of the wealth-income ratio and the liquidity ratio, i.e. the money stock as a percentage of output in nominal terms, are depicted in the charts of figure 1. The shaded bars in the charts denote the periods in which the short-term interest rate was higher than the long-term interest rate for more than two succesive quarters, i.e. the yield curve had a decreasing – or inverse – slope.

Figure 1 shows that the wealth-income ratio increased strongly in the first half of the 1980s. For the period 1987–1993 this ratio was as a matter of fact constant and from 1993 onwards it has shown a steady increase. In contrast,

---

[1] Fase and Winder (1997) discuss the results for alternative aggregation methods, showing that the stylized facts of the data to be disucssed in this section, are shared by the data according to alternative conversion methods.

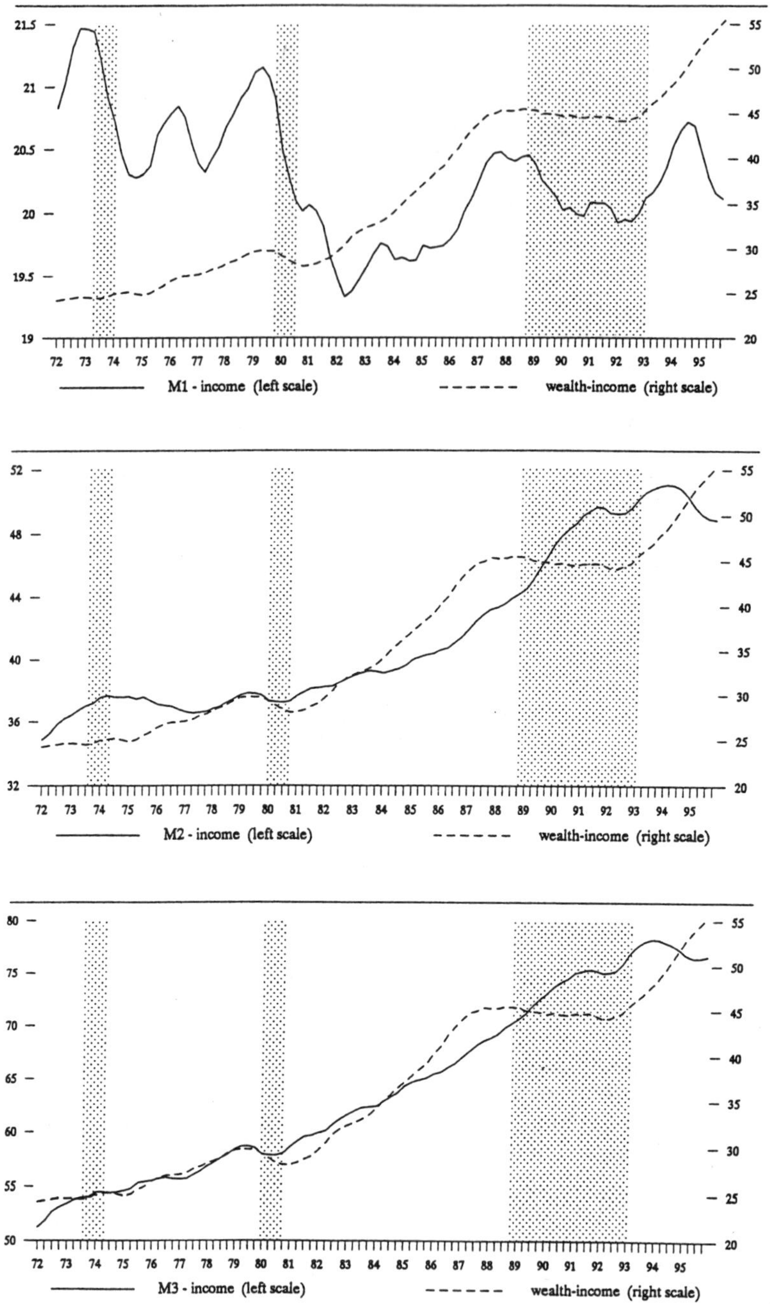

Fig. 1. Liquidity ratios and wealth-income ratio

the wealth-income ratio was relatively constant during the 1970s. Obviously, wealth developed far from proportionally to nominal income, thus causing serious doubts about the often-made assumption in the relevant literature that income can be used as a proxy for wealth. The liquidity ratios in figure 1 illustrate the monetary expansion in the European Union, which has occurred especially for the broader monetary aggregates M2 and M3. A salient feature of the charts in figure 1 is the diverse developments of the liquidity ratios. The M1 ratio has been rather volatile, though between relatively narrow margins, but has been lower in the 1980s and 1990s than in the 1970s. In contrast, the M2 and M3 ratios have increased steadily over the period considered, though at the end of the sample period a stabilization or even small decrease is in evidence. The rise of the M2 ratio was relatively modest during the 1970s and accelerated from the beginning of the 1980s onwards. The M3 ratio, on the other hand, showed a more steady rise during the sample period[2].

A striking feature of figure 1 is the similar development of the M2 and M3 ratios on the one hand and the wealth-income ratio on the other hand. The development of the M1 ratio is much less in line with that of the wealth-income ratio. Obviously, the decrease of the M1 ratio in the beginning of the 1980s is not related to the development of wealth. The resulting pattern for the broader monetary aggregates, however, supports the hypothesis that the relatively strong increase of wealth offers an explanation for the rising M2 and M3 ratios. In particular during the period 1972–1987 the liquidity ratios for M2 and M3 evolved in parallel with the wealth-income ratio. In the period 1987–1992 the wealth-income ratio stabilized, whereas the M2 and M3 ratios showed a continuing increase. It is likely that this further rise was related to interest rate developments. In all EU countries the short-term interest rate increased sharply in this period leading to inverse yield curves. The resulting shift from capital market investments to near money led to high growth rates for the broad monetary aggregates, and hence to a further increase of the M2 and M3 ratios. Periods with an inverted yield curve are denoted in figure 1 by shaded bars, showing that in two other subperiods the short-term interest rate exceeded the long-term rate. The effect of interest rate developments in these periods on the liquidity ratios is much less clear-cut, perhaps because the length of these subperiods was considerably shorter than the period around 1990. The adverse development of the liquidity ratios for the broad aggregates and the wealth-income ratio during the period 1987–1993, however, seems to be related to the movements in interest rates, illustrating that account must be taken by other determinants of the demand for money than income and wealth in order to assess the monetary developments. The theory of the demand for money offers an analytical framework for such a more comprehensive analysis. The results of this analysis will be discussed in the next section.

[2] The development of the EU aggregates conceals substantial differences between the individual countries. As documented in Fase and Winder (1993) monetary expansion has occurred especially in the northern EU countries, notably in Denmark, the Netherlands and the United Kingdom, whereas the southern countries offer a relatively stable picture. Differences between the demand for money relationships for the individual countries give rise to an aggregation bias in the estimates of EU-wide demand for money equations. Aggregation may on the other hand reduce the specification bias. As a result of the trade-off between aggregation and specification bias, EU-wide estimates may perform better than single-country ones (see Kremers and Lane, 1990 and Filosa, 1995).

3. Theoretical framework and empirical results

In line with Friedman's reformulation of Fisher's quantity theory and the closely related portfolio approach of e.g. Tobin, the postulated long-run demand for money relationship reads as

$$M \propto P^{\alpha_1} y^{\alpha_2} w^{\alpha_3} \exp(\alpha_4 rs + \alpha_5 rl + \alpha_6 \dot{p}) \tag{1}$$

with M the desired nominal money stock in a steady-state situation, P the price level, y real income, w real wealth, $\dot{p}$ the inflation rate while rs and rl represent the short-term and long-term interest rates. The price elasticity equals α_1, while α_2 and α_3 represent the income and wealth elasticities; α_4, α_5 and α_6 measure the relative change of money demand as a result of a one percentage point increase of the short-term interest rate, the long-term interest rate and the inflation rate respectively. These parameters are therefore the semi-elasticities with respect to the short and long-term interest rates and inflation. The often made assumption of price homogeneity, i.e. $\alpha_1 = 1$, is not imposed as an *a priori* restriction, but considered as an empirically testable hypothesis. If this restriction is valid, the steady-state relationship of equation (1) relates real money balances to the explanatory variables, with y reflecting the impact of the transactions volume and wealth the scale variable reflecting portfolio investment considerations. An alternative interpretation of this latter determinant is that it is a proxy for the influence of the money demand resulting from financial transactions (see also Friedman, 1971). These transactions are not accounted for appropriately by the income variable. The interest rates and the inflation rate represent the substitution processes between financial and physical assets. The short-term interest rate is the appropriate yield on near money. For the narrow monetary concept M1 α_4 should therefore be negative, while for the broader aggregates M2 and M3 a positive sign is plausible on theoretical grounds. The semi-elasticities α_5 and α_6 should be negative for M1, M2 as well as M3. Including both the short and long-term interest rate in the analysis ensures that the influence of the slope of the yield curve on the demand for money is also taken into account.

Equation (1) is the maintained hypothesis and describes the steady-state demand for money relationship. When deviations from this long-run equilibrium occur, adjustment processes occur to restore equilibrium. These short-run adjustment processes are modelled by means of lagged values of the variables in equation (1), leading to an error correction equation in which the short and long-run properties of the demand for money are described jointly. Following Friedman (1971) and earlier studies carried out at the Netherlands' Bank, a cyclical indicator, conj, has also been included to describe these short-run adjustment processes (see e.g. Fase and Kuné (1974) and Den Butter and Fase (1981)).

In our discussion of the empirical results we will focus on the long-run properties implied by the estimated demand for money relationships. In order to gain insight into the properties of the demand for money, a discussion of the steady state is obviously most revealing. To this end, the estimates of the parameters of the steady-state demand for money relationships for the various monetary aggregates are summarized in table 1. The detailed estimation results for M1, M2 and M3 are reported in appendix A. A number of restrictions on the parameters of the long-run demand for money relationship

Table 1. Estimates of parameters of long-run money demand relationship

Monetary aggregate	α_1	α_2	α_3	α_4	α_5	α_6
M1	1	0.8619	0	−0.0086	−0.0052	−0.0052
		(15.14)		(2.89)	(1.74)	(1.74)
M2	1	0.7479	0.2521	0.0126	−0.0195	−0.0195
		(11.25)	(3.79)	(1.99)	(3.44)	(3.44)
M3	1	0.6590	0.3410	0.0107	−0.0133	−0.0133
		(12.19)	(6.31)	(2.28)	(2.91)	(2.91)

Explanatory note: *t*-values are given in parentheses.

have been imposed. Examples are the restriction that the price elasticity equals one or the restriction that the sum of the income and wealth elasticity is equal to one. In the estimated equations we have also imposed the restriction that the long-run semi-elasticities with respect to the long-term interest rate and the inflation rate are equal. All these restrictions constitute testable hypotheses, which can be tested by means of *t*-tests. The results of the *t*-statistics for the respective hypotheses are reported in Fase and Winder (1997) and indicate that all restrictions imposed are justified from a statistical point of view.

Table 1 shows that wealth has a significant impact on the demand for M2 and M3. For M1 no influence of wealth was found, a result that had already been suggested by figure 1. The income elasticity of the demand for M1 is higher than for M2 and M3, indicating that M1 balances are mainly held for transaction purposes. For M2 and M3, the restriction has been imposed that the income and wealth elasticity add to 1. This finding corresponds with the results reported for various individual European countries. Examples are the Bundesbank (1995) and Gerdesmeier (1996) for Germany, Hall et al. (1989) for the United Kingdom, and Fase and Winder (1996) for Belgium and the Netherlands (see also Sterken, 1992). Fase and Winder (1996) found for both Belgium and the Netherlands that the wealth elasticity of the demand for M2 was sligthly higher than for M3. The results in table 1 show that for the European Union as a whole the wealth elasticity of M3 is somewhat higher. Table 1 shows furthermore that for all monetary aggregates considered price homogeneity applies.

With respect to the semi-elasticities of the short and long-term interest rate and the inflation rate, table 1 shows that all the estimates obtained have the theoretically plausible sign and are, with the exception of the semi-elasticities of M1 with respect to the long-term interest rate and inflation, significantly different from 0. For both M1, M2 and M3 the results of the econometric specification analysis give rise to impose the restriction that the inflation and long-term interest rate semi-elasticities are equal. Testing these restrictions shows that in all three cases the hypothesis that these semi-elasticities are equal cannot be rejected (see Fase and Winder, 1997). Table 1 shows also that the demand for M2 is more sensitive to changes in the interest rates and the inflation rate than the demand for M1 and M3. M1 balances have relatively low interest rates and inflation semi-elasticities, a finding that corresponds with the notion that these balances are mainly held for transaction purposes.

An alternative way to assess the estimation results is to consider the properties of near money. The elasticities found for M1, M2 and M3 imply elas-

Table 2. Long-run elasticities

Monetary aggregate	Price	Income	Wealth	Short-term interest rate	Long-term interest rate	Inflation
M1	1	0.862	0	−0.082	−0.053	−0.035
M2	1	0.748	0.252	0.120	−0.199	−0.129
M3	1	0.659	0.341	0.102	−0.136	−0.088
M2–M1	1	0.636	0.501	0.319	−0.343	−0.223
M3–M1	1	0.562	0.504	0.190	−0.175	−0.114
M3–M2	1	0.494	0.506	0.068	−0.019	−0.012

ticities of the demand for M2-M1, M3-M1 and M3-M2 and these elasticities must of course be economically plausible. This offers the opportunity to assess the mutual consistency of the results obtained for M1, M2 and M3. Therefore, the elasticities of the various near money concepts are presented in table 2 together with the elasticities for M1, M2 and M3. The price, income and wealth elasticities follow from table 1, whereas the elasticities with respect to the short and long-term interest rate and the inflation rate have been calculated by multiplying the semi-elasticities given in table 1 by the sample means of the corresponding variables.

Table 2 shows that the elasticities of the various near money concepts have an economically plausible sign and a reasonable size, implying that the results for M1, M2 and M3 are mutually consistent. The price elasticities of the various near monies are equal to 1, reflecting the similar properties of M1, M2 and M3. The income elasticities of the various near money concepts are smaller than for M1, with the demand for short-term time deposits and foreign currency deposits, i.e. M2-M1, having a higher income elasticity than the demand for short-term saving deposits, i.e. M3-M2. A striking feature of table 2 is the similar values of 0.50 for the wealth elasticities of the demand for the various near monies. The sum of the income and wealth elasticity equals 1 for M3-M2. This result reflects the corresponding property for the demand for M2 and M3. For the other two near money concepts the sum of the income and wealth elasticity is slightly larger than 1, reflecting that the income elasticity of M1 is smaller than 1, while the income and wealth elasticities for M2 and M3 add to 1.

The general picture following from table 2 for the interest rates and inflation elasticities of M1, M2 and M3 is similar to that found for the semi-elasticities discussed before. This is not surprising given the way these elasticities are calculated. A notable feature of table 2 is that the demand for M2-M1 is particularly sensitive to changes in the interest rates and the inflation rate, while the interest rates and inflation elasticities of the demand for M3-M2 are very small.

4. An assessment

In order to assess the results reported in the preceding section we examine three issues. In the first subsection we will present empirical evidence on the stability of the demand for money. The next subsection assesses the robustness of the empirical results by means of a cointegration analysis. Subsection 4.3

will further analyse whether the development over time of wealth offers an explanation for the monetary expansion that has occurred in the European Union since the beginning of the 1980s.

4.1 Stability of the demand for money

An important assessment criterion, both from a policy and an economic viewpoint, is the degree of stability of the demand for money. Several methods are available to assess stability. Here we consider three methods. The first concerns the residuals of the estimated equations. The standard error of the residuals of the estimated demand for money equations, reported in appendix A, are 0.67%, 0.80% and 0.58% for M1, M2 and M3 respectively. The size of these standard errors is rather low for all monetary aggregates considered, indicating that the overall fit is satisfactory. According to this measure of stability, the demand for M3 is more stable than the demand for M1 and M2, a finding that is in line with the results in Fase and Winder (1993) for the individual countries of the European Union. The residuals reflect the noise inherent in the estimated equations and may be useful to determine the width of the target zone if a policy of monetary targeting is pursued. However, this measure is less useful as a criterion to assess possible misspecification of the equations chosen.

Therefore, we have examined the stability over time of the estimated demand for money equations. This procedure involves re-estimation of the specifications for sub-periods and testing for parameter stability by means of Chow tests. To this end, the equations have been re-estimated for the sample periods before and after the German unification in 1990 using 1990:III as a breaking point. The hypothesis that the parameters in both subperiods are constant can be tested with an F-test, the F-statistic having an $F(13,69)$ distribution for M1, M2 as well as M3. The values obtained are 2.27, 1.25 and 1.48 for M1, M2 and M3 respectively. Only for M1 the F-statistic is significant at a 0.05 significance level, suggesting that the M1 equation is not stable. For M2 and M3 the hypothesis that the parameters are constant during both subperiods considered cannot be rejected. As a further test of stability we have also considered the constancy of the long-run parameters before and after German unification. From a policy viewpoint the long-run properties of the demand for money are more important than the short-run dynamics. The Chow statistic is in this case $F(3,79)$ distributed. This test yields the values 0.74, 0.65 and 0.20 for M1, M2 and M3 respectively. These results are all insignificant at a 0.05 significance level, indicating that the hypothesis that the long-run parameters are constant during the subperiods considered cannot be rejected. These results also indicate that the instability of the M1 equation found by the Chow test for constancy of all parameters, is related to non-constancy of the parameters describing the short-run dynamics of the M1 equation[3].

As a final procedure to assess the stability of the demand for money we considered recursive estimation procedures, which are particularly useful to

[3] In the misspecification analysis, we tested also for residual autocorrelation, normality of the disturbance terms and heteroscedasticity of the ARCH-type. The results are discussed in Fase and Winder (1997) and show that there is no evidence of misspecification.

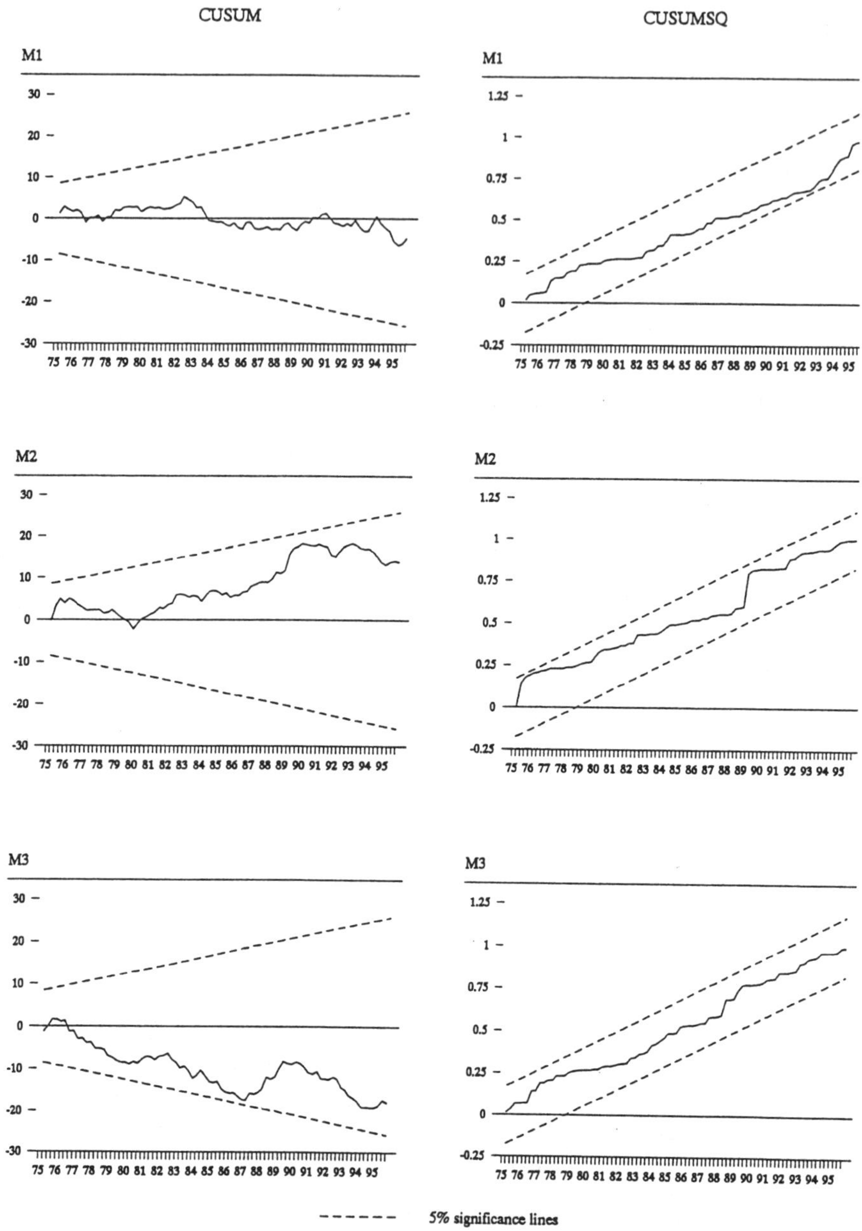

Fig. 2. Recursive residuals

detect structural changes. More specifically, we calculated the cumulative sum (CUSUM) and the cumulative sum of the squares (CUSUMSQ) of the recursive residuals[4]. Figure 2 depicts for M1, M2 and M3 the CUSUM and

[4] The CUSUM and CUSUMSQ have been calculated conditionally on the dummy variable incorporated to account for the effect of the German unification (see appendix A).

CUSUMSQ graphically, together with the 5% significance lines. For all monetary aggregates considered, both the CUSUM and CUSUMSQ do not cross the significance lines, suggesting that there is no evidence of parameter instability. This finding is encouraging and supports the earlier preliminary result that stability increases with the size of the economic geographical area considered using Divisia aggregates (see e.g. Fase, 1995). An explanation for this remarkable result found again in this paper is that the degree to which the supply of money is exogenous – strictly speaking a condition for the estimation of a single demand for money equation – is perhaps dependent on the capacity to absorb shocks which certainly increases with the size of the economy.

4.2 Results of a cointegration analysis

In order to assess the robustness of the empirical results found, a cointegration analysis has been carried out. One way to examine cointegration is to apply Johansen-type tests. Since these tests require the specification of a VAR model rather than a single equation approach, the Johansen procedure has not been applied. Instead, we estimated the equation

$$\begin{aligned}\Delta \ln(M/P) \propto\ & \alpha \ln(M/P)_{-1} + \beta_1 \ln y_{-1} + \beta_2 \ln w_{-1} + \beta_3 rs_{-1} + \beta_4 rl_{-1} \\ & + \beta_5 \dot{p}_{-1} + \sum_{i=1}^{4} \alpha_i \Delta \ln(M/P)_{-i} + \sum_{i=0}^{4} \beta_{1i} \Delta \ln y_{-i} \\ & + \sum_{i=0}^{4} \beta_{2i} \Delta \ln w_{-i} + \sum_{i=0}^{4} \beta_{3i} \Delta rs_{-i} + \sum_{i=0}^{4} \beta_{4i} \Delta rl_{-i} \\ & + \sum_{i=0}^{4} \beta_{5i} \Delta \dot{p}_{-i} \end{aligned} \tag{2}$$

One way to test the null hypothesis of no cointegration is to consider the t-statistic of $\hat{\alpha}$, t_{ecm} (see Kremers et al., 1992). Under specific assumptions this statistic is normally distributed. If these assumptions are violated, the Dickey-Fuller critical values can be used. Boswijk (1994) has shown that the Wald-statistic for the null hypothesis $\alpha = \beta_1 = \beta_2 = \beta_3 = \beta_4 = \beta_5 = 0$ can also be used to test for cointegration. This statistic does not have the familiar χ^2-distribution, but Boswijk reports the relevant critical values. If cointegration occurs, equation (2) also yields consistent estimates of the long-run parameters, which are, under specific exogeneity conditions, asymptotically normally distributed (see also Inder, 1993).

In the present study, we have estimated equation (2) and subsequently removed the most insignificant ones of the differentiated explanatory variables. The results obtained for the ultimate equation are reported in table 3. In case of M1, the model with and without wealth as an explanatory variable has been considered, since in the M1-equation discussed before wealth is absent. Table 3 shows that in all four cases considered the results for the t_{ecm} and the Wald-statistic are supportive for the cointegration hypothesis. The long-run properties of the demand for money implied by the estimated equations are

Table 3. Results of cointegration analysis

Monetary aggregate	Cointegration test		Elasticities		Semi-elasticities		
	t_{ecm}	Wald	Income	Wealth	Interest Rates		Inflation
					short	long	
M1	−2.50	23.32	0.6959	0.0661	−0.0023	−0.0166	−0.0003
			(2.61)	(0.63)	(0.46)	(2.16)	(0.06)
M1	−3.31	21.06	0.8835	0	−0.0013	−0.0159	0.0003
			(16.71)		(0.33)	(2.82)	(0.09)
M2	−3.61	45.88	0.6481	0.2826	0.0267	−0.0528	−0.0117
			(1.15)	(1.29)	(2.32)	(3.22)	(1.15)
M3	−2.81	53.82	0.6091	0.3838	−0.0094	0.0121	−0.0141
			(1.49)	(2.44)	(1.20)	(1.16)	(2.31)

Explanatory note: t-values in parentheses.

also given in table 3. If wealth is included in the M1-equation, we obtain a very small and insignificant estimate of the wealth elasticity, a finding which is in line with the result in the former section that wealth does not have an impact on the demand for M1. If wealth is excluded from the M1-equation, the income elasticity is estimated to be 0.88, which is very close to the estimate of 0.86 reported before. A remarkable result obtained for M2 and M3 is that the estimate of the sum of the income and wealth elasticity is close to 1. The M2-equation yields an estimate of 0.93, whereas for M3 an estimate of 0.99 results. These findings constitute empirical support for the result in the former section that the income and wealth elasticity of M2 as well as M3 sum to 1. The estimates of the long-run semi-elasticities with respect to the short and long-term interest rates and inflation obtained with the mechanic procedure carried out, have a similar magnitude as the findings reported before. In three out of nine cases the point estimates have the wrong sign, but these estimates are not significantly different from zero. In all other cases the estimates of the semi-elasticities have the theoretically plausible sign. All in all it can be concluded that the results in table 3 yield supportive evidence for the findings reported before.

4.3 Further assessment of the role of wealth

The empirical results in section 3 revealed a substantial impact of wealth on the demand for M2 and M3, whereas for M1 no influence of wealth could be found. The tentative analysis in section 2 showed a parallel development of the M2 and M3 ratios on the one hand and the wealth-income ratio on the other hand, suggesting that the increase of wealth offers an explanation for the rising liquidity ratios observed in the 1980s.

In the spirit of Fisher's quantity theory, liquidity ratios – or their inverse, i.e. the velocities of money – are often used as a simple indicator to assess monetary developments. It is a well-known fact that these ratios are fairly rough measures because substitution processes resulting from changes of interest rates and inflation may cause large fluctuations in the money stock. Another reason to consider the liquidity ratios with some caution is that the assumption of a unit income elasticity of the demand for money may be violated. In this regard it may be recalled that for M1 the income elasticity is estimated to be 0.86. Moreover, the results in the present study show that wealth also exerts a major influence on the demand for money. Obviously, this influence should be taken into account when assessing the monetary developments.

The long-run demand for money relationship (1) implies

$$M \propto P^{\alpha_1-\alpha_2-\alpha_3} Y^{\alpha_2} W^{\alpha_3} f(rs, rl, \dot{p})$$

with Y and W nominal income and nominal wealth respectively and $f(rs, rl, \dot{p}) = \exp(\alpha_4 rs + \alpha_5 rl + \alpha_6 \dot{p})$. Thus,

$$\frac{M}{Y} \propto P^{\alpha_1-\alpha_2-\alpha_3} Y^{\alpha_2-1} W^{\alpha_3} f(rs, rl, \dot{p}),$$

showing that the liquidity ratio also depends on wealth. If the price elasticity α_1 equals 1 and the income and wealth elasticity sum to 1, i.e. $\alpha_2 + \alpha_3 = 1$, we have

$$\frac{M}{Y} \propto \left(\frac{W}{Y}\right)^{1-\alpha_2} f(rs, rl, \dot{p}).$$

The relationship between the liquidity ratios and the wealth-income ratio has been considered in figure 1. With the above restrictions concerning the price, income and wealth elasticities, we also have

$$M/(Y^{\alpha_2} W^{1-\alpha_2}) \propto f(rs, rl, \dot{p}).$$

Since the interest rates and inflation do not display trend-like behaviour, it may be expected that the same property holds for $M/(Y^{\alpha_2} W^{1-\alpha_2})$. It may therefore be interesting to consider this ratio for the monetary aggregates. It goes without saying that this ratio is a purely descriptive statistic[5]. In figure 3 this statistic has been depicted together with the liquidity ratio for each of the money concepts considered, using the estimates of the long-run income elasticities given in table 1. Since the wealth elasticity of M1 is 0, the ratio $M/(P^{1-\alpha_2} Y^{\alpha_2})$, with α_2 being the long-run income elasticity, has been depicted. If the income and wealth elasticity add to 1, the modified ratio is independent of the unit in which the money stock, income and wealth are expressed. This situation applies to M2 and M3. If the elasticities do not add to 1, as is the case for M1, the level of the modified ratio depends on the unit in which the variables are expressed. Thus, it makes a difference whether M1 and income are expressed in millions or billions of German marks. It can easily be shown, however, that the development over time is not influenced by the choice of unit. It is only the level that is affected. Therefore, the chart for the

[5] If W is proportional to Y, $M/(Y^{\alpha_2} W^{1-\alpha_2})$ will – apart from a constant – be equal to the liquidity ratio and therefore develop in parallel with the liquidity ratio.

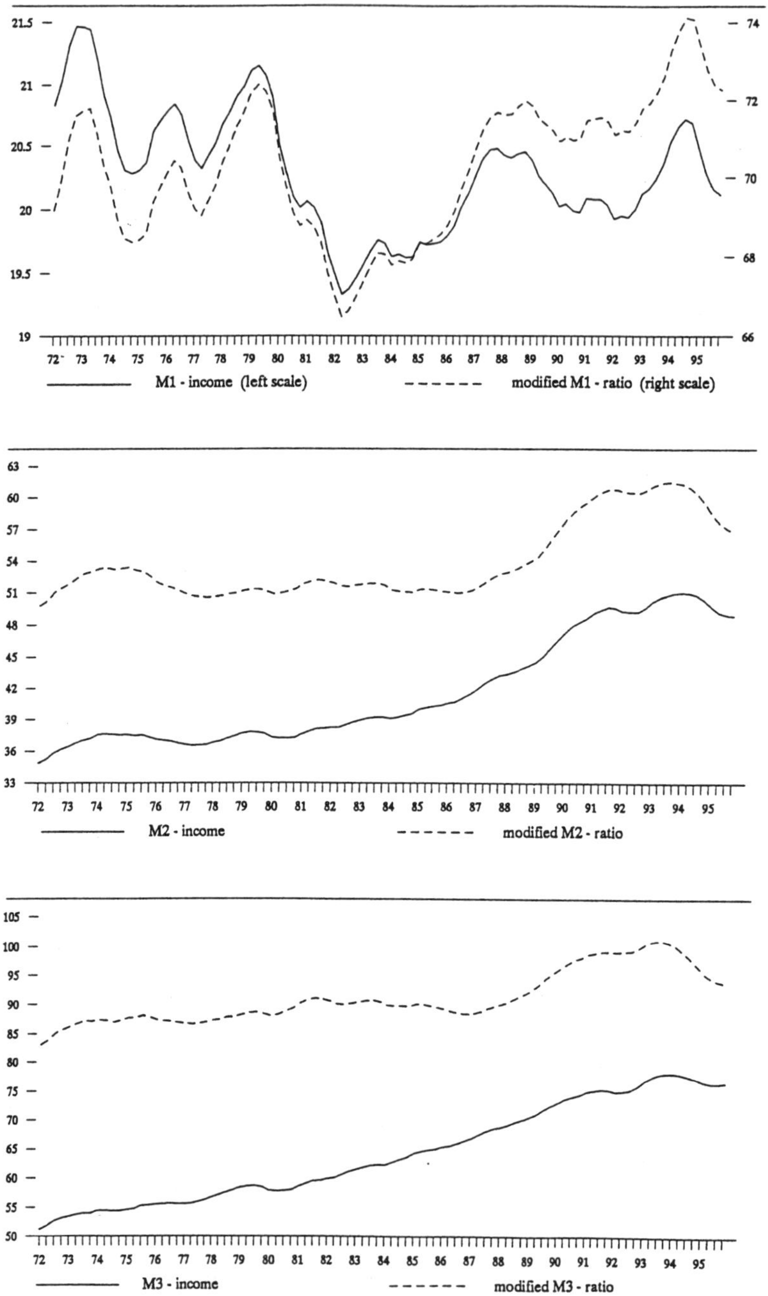

Fig. 3. Liquidity ratios and modified ratios

M1 ratio and the corresponding modified ratio is depicted with a double scale. For M2 and M3 a single scale suffices.

Figure 3 shows that the modified M2 and M3 ratios were relatively constant over the 1970s and 1980s. The charts display an increase of these ratios at the end of the 1980s, notably for the modified M2 ratio. This relatively strong increase of M2 and M3 is probably related to the influence of the inverted yield curve, which initiated shifts from capital market investments to liquid assets (see also section 2). Like the M1 ratio, the modified M1 ratio was rather volatile, albeit between relatively narrow margins. A salient feature of the modified M2 and M3 ratios in figure 3 is that no upward tendency is present during the 1980s. This result indicates that no excessive monetary expansion occurred, a conclusion that is in line with the modest development of the inflation rates during the 1980s. The relatively stable monetary developments according to these modified ratios may therefore be taken as a justification of the reserved policy reactions of the monetary authorities to the growth of the liquidity ratios[6].

5. Concluding remarks

This study presented the results of an empirical analysis of the demand for money in the European Union as a whole over the period 1971–1995, with a particular focus on the impact of financial wealth. In order to obtain a comprehensive picture of the monetary developments we did not restrict the analysis to a single monetary aggregate, but considered M1, M2 as well as M3. The empirical evidence shows a substantial impact of wealth on the demand for M2 and M3. In contrast, no influence of wealth on the demand for M1 could be found, indicating that portfolio investment considerations are less important for M1 balances. The empirical results show also that for M2 and M3 the income and wealth elasticity add to 1, and that M2 is more sensitive to changes in interest rates and inflation than M1 or M3. An extensive specification analysis indicated that the demand for the three money concepts considered for the European Union as a whole is stable. This finding is important because it is one of the main conditions for a policy of monetary targeting.

In the European Union, the broad monetary aggregates M2 and M3 have increased much more strongly than nominal output, in particular since the beginning of the 1980s. In the spirit of the monetarist view on inflation, according to which – loosely speaking – inflation is the result of too much money chasing too few goods, this monetary expansion should have led to an upward tendency in inflation. The 1980s have actually shown, however, a substantial reduction of the inflation rates. The analysis in the present study indicates that the strong growth of financial wealth in the 1980s offers an ex-

[6] Fase and Winder (1997) argue that the use of Divisia aggregates offers an alternative way to account for the impact of portfolio investment considerations on the demand for money. Correction of M2 and M3 for these portfolio investment balances according to the methodology put forward by Divisia (1925, 1926) shows that money growth relative to income growth has been modest during the 1980s, yielding supportive evidence for the hypothesis that the sharp increase of the liquidity ratios for the broad money concepts can be attributed to the increase of the volume of liquid assets held for portfolio investment purposes (see Fase and Winder, 1997).

planation for the sharp increase of the M2 and M3 ratio. Taking into account the development of wealth leads to the conclusion that the monetary expansion has been fairly modest, and thus that the strong increase of M2 and M3 should be attributed mainly to portfolio investment considerations.

Though the development of financial wealth offers an explanation for the strong increase of the broad monetary aggregates, it cannot be ignored that the resources embodied in the wealth position of the private sector – as far as the household sector is concerned – is a source of future consumption. The developments since the beginning of the 1980s indicate that these accumulated resources have not been used for consumption on a large scale. For the near future, it is likely that this will not be the case either. Demographic factors like the ageing of the population and austerity policies of the governments, including a re-shaping of the social welfare system, may well be an impetus for further increases of wealth. The fact that wealth may be used for actual spending objectives is, however, a reason for the monetary authorities to monitor the development of the wealth position of the private sector. This applies also if wealth is not yet used for current consumption, but is intended for future consumption. The results in our study show that wealth has a substantial impact on the demand for money. For an adequate assessment of the monetary developments it is therefore useful to take into account the development of wealth.

Appendix A: Estimation results

This appendix presents the estimated demand for money equations for the European Union as a whole. The notation of the variables is the same as in the main text. Since the data are not seasonally adjusted, seasonal dummies s_1, s_2 and s_3 are included in the estimation equations. Moreover, we included a dummy variable D_{903} with the value 1 in 1990:III and 0 in the other periods to account for the effect of the German unification. The *t*-values of the estimates, shown in brackets in the following equations, are adjusted for the possible presence of heteroscedasticity. $\bar{R}^2$ denotes the multiple correlation coefficient adjusted for degrees of freedom and *SE* is the standard error of the residuals.

$$
\begin{aligned}
\Delta \ln(M1/P) = {} & -\underset{(3.19)}{0.1833}(\ln(M1/P)_{-1} - \ln y) - \underset{(2.90)}{0.0253} \ln y - \underset{(2.16)}{0.0016}\, rs_{-1} \\
& - \underset{(2.17)}{0.0010}\, rl_{-1} - \underset{(2.17)}{0.0010}\, \dot{p} - \underset{(2.57)}{0.0064}\, \Delta \,\mathrm{conj}_{-2} - \underset{(2.46)}{0.0032}\, \Delta rs_{-1} \\
& - \underset{(3.49)}{0.0049}\, \Delta \dot{p} + \underset{(2.96)}{0.2648}\, \Delta \ln(M1/P)_{-4} + \underset{(2.74)}{0.1457}\, \Delta \ln y_{-4} \\
& + \underset{(2.69)}{0.1850} - \underset{(0.04)}{0.0004}\, s_1 + \underset{(1.51)}{0.0072}\, s_2 + \underset{(0.59)}{0.0048}\, s_3 + \underset{(9.80)}{0.0202}\, D_{903}
\end{aligned}
$$

Estimation period : 1972:I–1995:IV $\quad \bar{R}^2 = 0.89 \quad SE = 0.0067$

$$\Delta \ln(M2/P) = \underset{(5.28)}{-0.0866}(\ln(M2/P)_{-2} - \ln y_{-1}) + \underset{(2.58)}{0.0218}(\ln w - \ln y_{-1})$$
$$+ \underset{(1.87)}{0.0011}\, rs - \underset{(3.33)}{0.0017}\, rl_{-2} - \underset{(3.33)}{0.0017}\, \dot{p}_{-2} - \underset{(2.95)}{0.0052}\, \Delta\, \mathrm{conj}_{-3}$$
$$- \underset{(2.92)}{0.0058}\, \Delta rl_{-1} + \underset{(3.07)}{0.2355}\, \Delta \ln(M2/P)_{-4} + \underset{(3.70)}{0.2430}\, \Delta \ln y$$
$$- \underset{(2.10)}{0.0982}\, \Delta \ln w_{-3} + \underset{(4.53)}{0.0533} + \underset{(1.26)}{0.0114}\, s_1 + \underset{(0.72)}{0.0042}\, s_2$$
$$+ \underset{(1.40)}{0.0117}\, s_3 + \underset{(9.84)}{0.0236}\, D_{903}$$

Estimation period : 1972:I–1995:IV $\bar{R}^2 = 0.68$ $SE = 0.0080$

$$\Delta \ln(M3/P) = \underset{(5.77)}{-0.1032}(\ln(M3/P)_{-2} - \ln y) + \underset{(3.55)}{0.0352}(\ln w_{-1} - \ln y)$$
$$+ \underset{(2.14)}{0.0011}\, rs - \underset{(3.09)}{0.0014}\, rl - \underset{(3.09)}{0.0014}\, \dot{p} - \underset{(4.70)}{0.0040}\, \mathrm{conj}_{-1/2}$$
$$- \underset{(2.58)}{0.0034}\, \Delta(rl - rs)_{-2} + \underset{(3.26)}{0.1805}\, \Delta \ln y_{-4} + \underset{(3.99)}{0.1121}\, \Delta \ln w$$
$$- \underset{(1.92)}{0.0634}\, \Delta \ln w_{-3} + \underset{(5.94)}{0.0943} + \underset{(2.95)}{0.0228}\, s_1 + \underset{(0.72)}{0.0034}\, s_2$$
$$+ \underset{(1.65)}{0.0121}\, s_3 + \underset{(16.16)}{0.0331}\, D_{903}$$

Estimation period : 1972:I–1995:IV $\bar{R}^2 = 0.77$ $SE = 0.0058$

References

Bekx P, Tullio G (1989) A note on the European Monetary System and the determination of the DM-dollar exchange rate. Cahiers économiques de Bruxelles 123:329–343

Boswijk HP (1994) Testing for an unstable root in conditional and structural error correction models. Journal of Econometrics 63:37–60

Brainard WC, Tobin J (1968) Pitfalls in financial model building. American Economic Review 58:99–122

Butter FAG, Fase MMG (1981) The demand for money in EEC countries. Journal of Monetary Economics 7:201–230

Deutsche Bundesbank (1995) Uberprüfung des Geldmengenziels und Neuordnung der Mindestreserve. Monatsberichte Juli 1995

Divisia F (1925, 1926) L'indice monétaire et la théorie de la monnaie. Revue d'Economie Politique 39:842–861, 980–1008, 1121–1151; and 40:49–87

Fase MMG (1994) In search for stability: an empirical appraisal of the demand for money in G7 and EC countries. De Economist 142:421–454

Fase MMG (1995) Divisia aggregates and the demand for money in core EMU. to appear In: Belongia MT (ed.) Theory and practice of Divisia monetary aggregates. St. Martin/MacMillan, New York/London

Fase MMG, Kuné JB (1974) De vraag naar liquiditeiten in Nederland – 1952–1971. De Economist 122:326–356
Fase MMG, Winder CCA (1993) The demand for money in The Netherlands and other EC countries. De Economist 141:471–496
Fase MMG, Winder CCA (1994) Money demand within EMU – an analysis with the Divisia measure. De Nederlandsche Bank Quarterly Bulletin September 1994:25–55
Fase MMG, Winder CCA (1996) Wealth and the demand for money: Empirical evidence for The Netherlands and Belgium. De Economist 144:569–589
Fase MMG, Winder CCA (1997) Wealth and the demand for money in the European Union. BIS Conference Papers 4:340–362
Filosa R (1995) Money demand stability and currency substitution in six European countries (1980–1992). BIS Working Paper no. 30
Friedman M (1971) A theoretical framework for monetary analysis. National Bureau of Economic Research, Colombia University Press, New York
Gerdesmeier D (1996) Die Rolle des Vermögens in der Geldnachfrage. Deutsche Bundesbank Diskussionspapier 5/96
Hall SG, Henry SGB, Wilcox JB (1989) The long run determination of the UK monetary aggregates. Bank of England Discussion Papers nr 41
Inder B (1993) Estimating long-run relationships in economics – a comparison of different approaches, Journal of Econometrics. 57:53–68
Kremers JJM, Ericsson NR, Dolado JJ (1992) The power of cointegration tests. Oxford Bulletin of Economics and Statistics 54:325–348
Kremers JJM, Lane TD (1990) Economic and monetary integration and the aggregate demand for money in the EMS. IMF Staff Papers 37:777–805
Monticelli C, Strauss-Kahn M (1992) European integration and the demand for broad money. BIS Working Paper no. 18
Sterken E (1992) The financial transactions motive in the Dutch money demand equation. Kredit und Kapital 25:386–405
Winder CCA (1997) On the construction of European area-wide aggregates – a review of the issues and empirical evidence. Irving Fisher Committee on Central-Bank Statistics, IFC Bulletin 1:15–23

Workshop "Money demand in Europe"

List of participants

Holger Bartel
Graduiertenkolleg Freie Universität und Humboldt-Universität Berlin

Alexander Benkwitz
SFB 373, Humboldt-Universität Berlin

Andreas Beyer
Københavns Universitets

Jörg Breitung
Humboldt-Universität Berlin

Imke Brüggemann
Freie Universität Berlin

Herbert S. Buscher
Zentrum für Europäische Wirtschaftsforschung (ZEW)

Pu Chen
Universität Bielefeld

Henning Dankenbring
Graduiertenkolleg Freie Universität und Humboldt-Universität Berlin

Øyvind Eitrheim
Bank of Norway

Neil Ericsson
The Federal Reserve Washington

Carsten Folkertsma
De Nederlandsche Bank

Werner Gaab
Universität (GH) Essen

Dieter Gerdesmeier
Deutsche Bundesbank

Gerd Hansen
Christian-Albrechts-Universität Kiel

Uwe Hassler
Freie Universität Berlin

David Hendry
Nuffield College Oxford

Jérôme Henry
European Monetary Institute

Helmut Herwartz
Humboldt-Universität Berlin

Kirstin Hubrich
SFB 373, Humboldt-Universität Berlin

Katarina Juselius
Københavns Universitets

Reiner König
Deutsche Bundesbank

Peter Kuhbier
Freie Universität Berlin

Ulrich Leuchtmann
Universität Bielefeld

Bernd Lucke
Freie Universität Berlin

Helmut Lütkepohl
Humboldt-Universität Berlin

Grayham E. Mizon
European University Institute Florenz

Dieter Nautz
SFB 373, Freie Universität Berlin

Harald Nitsch
Albert-Ludwigs-Universität Freiburg

Michel Peytrignet
Schweizerische Nationalbank

Hans Eggert Reimers
Hochschule Wismar

Antti Ripatti
Bank of Finland

Michael Scharnagl
Deutsche Bundesbank

Franz Seitz
Fachhochschule Amberg/Weiden

Timo Teräsvirta
Stockholm School of Economics

Rolf Tschernig
SFB 373, Humboldt-Universität Berlin

Juan-Luis Vega
European Monetary Institute

Katrin Wesche
Universität Bonn

Carlo C.A. Winder
De Nederlandsche Bank

Jürgen Wolters
Freie Universität Berlin

Gören Zettergren
Sveriges Riksbank